T0210698

Bayesian Analysis in Natural Language Processing

Second Edition

Synthesis Lectures on Human Language Technologies

Editor
Graeme Hirst, *University of Toronto*

Synthesis Lectures on Human Language Technologies is edited by Graeme Hirst of the University of Toronto. The series consists of 50- to 150-page monographs on topics relating to natural language processing, computational linguistics, information retrieval, and spoken language understanding. Emphasis is on important new techniques, on new applications, and on topics that combine two or more HLT subfields.

Domain-Sensitive Temporal Tagging
Jannik Strötgen and Michael Gertz
2016

Linked Lexical Knowledge Bases: Foundations and Applications
Iryna Gurevych, Judith Eckle-Kohler, and Michael Matuschek
2016

Bayesian Analysis in Natural Language Processing
Shay Cohen
2016

Metaphor: A Computational Perspective
Tony Veale, Ekaterina Shutova, and Beata Beigman Klebanov
2016

Grammatical Inference for Computational Linguistics
Jeffrey Heinz, Colin de la Higuera, and Menno van Zaanen
2015

Automatic Detection of Verbal Deception
Eileen Fitzpatrick, Joan Bachenko, and Tommaso Fornaciari
2015

Natural Language Processing for Social Media
Atefeh Farzindar and Diana Inkpen
2015

Semantic Similarity from Natural Language and Ontology Analysis
Sébastien Harispe, Sylvie Ranwez, Stefan Janaqi, and Jacky Montmain
2015

Learning to Rank for Information Retrieval and Natural Language Processing, Second Edition
Hang Li
2014

Ontology-Based Interpretation of Natural Language
Philipp Cimiano, Christina Unger, and John McCrae
2014

Automated Grammatical Error Detection for Language Learners, Second Edition
Claudia Leacock, Martin Chodorow, Michael Gamon, and Joel Tetreault
2014

Bayesian Analysis in Natural Language Processing, Second Edition
Shay Cohen

ISBN: 978-3-031-01042-2 paperback
ISBN: 978-3-031-02170-1 ebook
ISBN: 978-1-68173-529-0 epub
ISBN: 978-3-031-00181-9 hardcover

DOI 10.1007/978-3-031-02170-1

A Publication in the Springer series
SYNTHESIS LECTURES ON ADVANCES IN AUTOMOTIVE TECHNOLOGY

Lecture #41
Series Editor: Graeme Hirst, *University of Toronto*
Series ISSN
Print 1947-4040   Electronic 1947-4059

ABSTRACT

Natural language processing (NLP) went through a profound transformation in the mid-1980s when it shifted to make heavy use of corpora and data-driven techniques to analyze language. Since then, the use of statistical techniques in NLP has evolved in several ways. One such example of evolution took place in the late 1990s or early 2000s, when full-fledged Bayesian machinery was introduced to NLP. This Bayesian approach to NLP has come to accommodate various shortcomings in the frequentist approach and to enrich it, especially in the unsupervised setting, where statistical learning is done without target prediction examples.

In this book, we cover the methods and algorithms that are needed to fluently read Bayesian learning papers in NLP and to do research in the area. These methods and algorithms are partially borrowed from both machine learning and statistics and are partially developed "in-house" in NLP. We cover inference techniques such as Markov chain Monte Carlo sampling and variational inference, Bayesian estimation, and nonparametric modeling. In response to rapid changes in the field, this second edition of the book includes a new chapter on representation learning and neural networks in the Bayesian context. We also cover fundamental concepts in Bayesian statistics such as prior distributions, conjugacy, and generative modeling. Finally, we review some of the fundamental modeling techniques in NLP, such as grammar modeling, neural networks and representation learning, and their use with Bayesian analysis.

KEYWORDS

natural language processing, computational linguistics, Bayesian statistics, Bayesian NLP, statistical learning, inference in NLP, grammar modeling in NLP, neural networks, representation learning

Bayesian Analysis
in Natural Language Processin

Second Edition

Shay Cohen
University of Edinburgh

SYNTHESIS LECTURES ON HUMAN LANGUAGE TECHNOLOGIES

ABSTRACT

Natural language processing (NLP) went through a profound transformation in the mid-1980s when it shifted to make heavy use of corpora and data-driven techniques to analyze language. Since then, the use of statistical techniques in NLP has evolved in several ways. One such example of evolution took place in the late 1990s or early 2000s, when full-fledged Bayesian machinery was introduced to NLP. This Bayesian approach to NLP has come to accommodate various shortcomings in the frequentist approach and to enrich it, especially in the unsupervised setting, where statistical learning is done without target prediction examples.

In this book, we cover the methods and algorithms that are needed to fluently read Bayesian learning papers in NLP and to do research in the area. These methods and algorithms are partially borrowed from both machine learning and statistics and are partially developed "in-house" in NLP. We cover inference techniques such as Markov chain Monte Carlo sampling and variational inference, Bayesian estimation, and nonparametric modeling. In response to rapid changes in the field, this second edition of the book includes a new chapter on representation learning and neural networks in the Bayesian context. We also cover fundamental concepts in Bayesian statistics such as prior distributions, conjugacy, and generative modeling. Finally, we review some of the fundamental modeling techniques in NLP, such as grammar modeling, neural networks and representation learning, and their use with Bayesian analysis.

KEYWORDS

natural language processing, computational linguistics, Bayesian statistics, Bayesian NLP, statistical learning, inference in NLP, grammar modeling in NLP, neural networks, representation learning

Bayesian Analysis
in Natural Language Processing
Second Edition

Shay Cohen
University of Edinburgh

SYNTHESIS LECTURES ON HUMAN LANGUAGE TECHNOLOGIES #41

Dedicated to Mia

Contents

List of Figures

List of Algorithms

List of Generative Stories

Preface (First Edition)

When writing about a topic that intersects two areas (in this case, Bayesian Statistics and Natural Language Processing), the focus and the perspective need to be considered. I took a rather practical one in writing this book, aiming to write it for those in the same position as myself during my graduate studies. At that time, I already had a reasonable grasp of the problems in natural language processing and knowledge of the basic principles in machine learning. I wanted to learn more about Bayesian statistics—in a rather abstract way—particularly the parts that are most relevant to NLP. Thus, this book is written from that perspective, providing abstract information about the key techniques, terminology and models that a computational linguist would need in order to apply the Bayesian approach to his or her work.

Most chapters in this book, therefore, are rather general and have relevance to other uses of Bayesian statistics. The last chapter in this book, though, presents some specific NLP applications for grammar models that are mostly (but not exclusively) used in NLP.

Ideally, this book should be read by a person who already has some idea about statistical modeling in NLP, and wants to gain more depth about the specific application of Bayesian techniques to NLP. The motivation for this decision to focus more on the mathematical aspects of Bayesian NLP is simple. Most computational linguists get exposed quite early in their graduate career or otherwise to the basic core terminology in NLP, the linguistic structures it predicts and perhaps some of the linguistic motivation behind them. Ideas from Bayesian statistics and other statistical tools are often "picked up" on the way. As such, there are sometimes misconceptions and a missing global picture. This book tries to provide some of these missing details to the reader.

There are several approaches to doing statistics, two of which are the frequentist approach and the Bayesian approach. The frequentist approach is also sometimes referred to as "classic statistics." One of the things that motivated me to learn more about Bayesian statistics is the rich and colorful history it has. To this day, the famous frequentist-Bayesian divide still exists. This kind of divide regarding the philosophy that statistical analysis should follow is even more persistently and more ardently argued about than theories of grammar were in the famous "linguistics war" between generative semanticians and generative grammarians. It does not end there—even within the Bayesian camp there are those who support a subjective interpretation of probability and those who support an objective one.

Although I was captivated by the mathematical elegance of Bayesian statistics when I was first exposed to the core ideas (in principle, Bayesian statistics relies on one basic principle of applying Bayes' rule to invert the relationship between data and parameters), I take a pragmatic approach and do not try to present Bayesian statistics as the ultimate theory for doing statistical

NLP. I also do not provide the philosophical arguments that support Bayesian statistics in this monograph. Instead, I provide the technical mechanisms behind Bayesian statistics, and advise the reader to determine whether the techniques work well for him or her in the problems they work on. Here and there, I also describe some connections that Bayesian statistics have to the frequentist approach, and other points of confluence. If the reader is interested in learning more about the philosophy behind Bayesian statistics, I suggest reading Jaynes (2003) and also looking at Barnett (1999). To better understand the history and the people behind Bayesian statistics, I suggest reading the book by McGrayne (2011). This book consists of eight chapters as following:

Chapter 1 is a refresher about probability and statistics as they relate to Bayesian NLP. We cover basic concepts such as random variables, independence between random variables, conditional independence, and random variable expectations; we also briefly discuss Bayesian statistics and how it differs from frequentist statistics. Most of this chapter can probably be skipped if one already has some basic background in computer science or statistics.

Chapter 2 introduces Bayesian analysis in NLP with two examples (the latent Dirichlet allocation model and Bayesian text regression), and also provides a high-level overview of the topic.

Chapter 3 covers an important component in Bayesian statistical modeling—the prior. We discuss the priors that are most commonly used in Bayesian NLP, such as the Dirichlet distribution, non-informative priors, the normal distribution and others.

Chapter 4 covers ideas that bring together frequentist statistics and Bayesian statistics through the summarization of the posterior distribution. It details approaches to calculate a point estimate for a set of parameters while maintaining a Bayesian mindset.

Chapter 5 covers one of the main inference approaches in Bayesian statistics: Markov chain Monte Carlo. It details the most common sampling algorithms used in Bayesian NLP, such as Gibbs sampling and Metropolis-Hastings sampling.

Chapter 6 covers another important inference approach in Bayesian NLP, variational inference. It describes mean-field variational inference and the variational expectation-maximization algorithm.

Chapter 7 covers an important modeling technique in Bayesian NLP, nonparametric modeling. We discuss nonparametric models such as the Dirichlet process and the Pitman-Yor process.

Chapter 8 covers basic grammar models in NLP (such as probabilistic context-free grammars and synchronous grammars), and the way to frame them in a Bayesian context (using models such as adaptor grammars, hierarchical Dirichlet process PCFGs and others).

In addition, the book includes two appendices that provide background information that offers additional context for reading this book. Each chapter is accompanied by at least five exercises. This book (perhaps with the exercises) could be used as teaching material. Specifically, it could be used to teach a number of lectures about Bayesian analysis in NLP. If a significant amount of time is devoted to Bayesian NLP in class (say, four lectures), I would suggest devoting one lecture to chapter 3, one lecture to chapter 4, one lecture to chapters 5 and 6 together, and one lecture to chapter 7. Topics from chapter 8 (such as adaptor grammars or Bayesian PCFGs) can be injected into the various lectures as examples.

Acknowledgments (First Edition)

I am indebted to all the people who helped me to write this book. First, I would like to especially thank Lea Frermann, Trevor Cohn, and Jacob Eisenstein, who carefully read a draft of this book, and left detailed feedback. I would also like to thank all other people who gave feedback in one form or another: Omri Abend, Apoorv Agarwal, Anahita Bhiwandiwalla, Jordan Boyd-Graber, Daniel Gildea, Sharon Goldwater, Mark Johnson, Mirella Lapata, Shalom Lappin, Adam Lopez, Brendan O'Connor, Mohammad Sadegh Rasooli, Siva Reddy, Stefan Riezler, Giorgio Satta, Stuart Shieber, Mark Steedman, Karl Stratos, Swabha Swayamdipta, Bonnie Webber and Dani Yogatama. Thanks also to Sharon Rosenfeld, who proofread this book to help make it more readable. Thanks also to Samantha Draper, Graeme Hirst, Michael Morgan and CL Tondo for helping with the publication of this book.

I would also like to thank all of the great students who attended my class at the Department of Computer Science in Columbia University in Spring 2013 ("Bayesian analysis in NLP") and indirectly helped me better understand what is the level of coverage needed from this book for young researchers making their first steps in the area of Bayesian NLP (students such as Jessica Forde, Daniel Perlmutter, and others whom I have already mentioned). Thanks also go to my collaborators on projects in the area of Bayesian NLP, who helped me shape my understanding of it: David Blei, Jordan Boyd-Graber, Kevin Gimpel, and Ke Zhai.

I want to also thank my mentors throughout all the years, and especially my advisor, Noah Smith, with whom I first studied Bayesian NLP, Michael Collins, my post-doc advisor, who supported me in spending time writing this book during my post-doctoral fellowship and in teaching the Bayesian NLP class at Columbia, and Mark Johnson, whose work, as well as our conversations and email exchanges, influenced me in writing this book.

Also, thanks to Sylvia Cohen, my spouse, who has always been there for me during the writing of this book. Similar thanks to Sylvia's family, who always made me feel at home in Pittsburgh, while I was studying topics such as Bayesian analysis. Finally, I would like to thank my parents and siblings—whose prior beliefs in me never changed, no matter what the evidence was.

Shay Cohen
Edinburgh
May 2016

Preface (Second Edition)

I did not expect to release a second edition for this book so quickly, but the last few years of fast-paced and exciting developments in the world of Natural Language Processing (NLP) have called for various updates, leading to this second edition.

The main addition to this book is Chapter 9, which focuses on representation learning and neural networks in NLP, particularly in a Bayesian context. This chapter was written based on the observation that in the past five years or so, NLP literature has been dominated by the use of neural networks; and as such, I believe the fundamentals needed to be addressed in this book. Adapting the content to the Bayesian "mission" of this book (coupled with the NLP context) was not always easy, and I will let the reader be the judge of whether I have accomplished my mission.

In addition to introducing this new chapter in this edition, several typographical errors have been fixed, and some additional content was integrated into various chapters.

There are several people who have helped with this edition. I want to thank Trevor Cohn, Marco Damonte, Jacob Eisenstein, Lea Frermann, Annie Louis, Chunchuan Lyu, Nikos Papasarantopoulos, Shashi Narayan, Mark Steedman, Rico Sennrich, and Ivan Titov for their help and comments. I also want to thank my students and postdocs who have taught me more than I have taught them in some areas of the new material in this book.

Shay Cohen
Edinburgh
February 2019

CHAPTER 1

Preliminaries

This chapter is mainly intended to be used as a refresher on basic concepts in Probability and Statistics required for the full comprehension of this book. Occasionally, it also provides notation that will be used in subsequent chapters in this book.

Keeping this in mind, this chapter is written somewhat differently than typical introductions to basic concepts in Probability and Statistics. For example, this chapter defines concepts directly for random variables, such as conditional distributions, independence and conditional independence, the chain rule and Bayes' rule rather than giving preliminary definitions for these constructs for events in a sample space. For a deeper introductory investigation of probability theory, see Bertsekas and Tsitsiklis (2002).

Sections 1.1–1.2 (probability measures and random variables) are given for completeness in a rather formal way. If the reader is familiar with these basic notions and their constructions, (s)he can skip to Section 1.3 where mechanisms essential to Bayesian learning, such as the chain rule, are introduced.

1.1   PROBABILITY MEASURES

At the core of probabilistic theory (and probabilistic modeling) lies the idea of a "sample space." The sample space is a set Ω that consists of all possible elements over which we construct a probability distribution. In this book, the sample space most often consists of objects relating to language, such as words, phrase-structure trees, sentences, documents or sequences. As we see later, in the Bayesian setting, the sample space is defined to be a Cartesian product between a set of such objects and a set of model parameters (Section 1.5.1).

Once a sample space is determined, we can define a *probability measure* for that sample space. A probability measure p is a function which attaches a real number to *events*—subsets of the sample space.

A probability measure has to satisfy three axiomatic properties:

- It has to be a non-negative function such that $p(A) \geq 0$ for any event A.

- For any countable disjoint sequence of events $A_i \subseteq \Omega, i \in \{1, \ldots\}$, if $A_i \cap A_j = \emptyset$ for $i \neq j$, it should hold that $p(\bigcup_i A_i) = \sum_i p(A_i)$. This means that the sum of probabilities of disjoint events should equal the probability of the union of the events.

- The probability of Ω is 1: $p(\Omega) = 1$.

There are a few consequences from these three axiomatic properties. The first is that $p(\emptyset) = 0$ (to see this, consider that $p(\Omega) + p(\emptyset) = p(\Omega \cup \emptyset) = p(\Omega) = 1$). The second is that $p(A \cup B) = p(A) + p(B) - p(A \cap B)$ for any two events A and B (to see this, consider that $p(A \cup B) = p(A) + p(B \setminus (A \cap B))$ and that $p(B) = p(B \setminus (A \cap B)) + p(A \cap B)$). And finally, the complement of an event A, $\Omega \setminus A$ is such that $p(\Omega \setminus A) = 1 - p(A)$ (to see this, consider that $1 = p(\Omega) = p((\Omega \setminus A) \cup A) = p(\Omega \setminus A) + p(A)$ for any event A).

In the general case, not *every* subset of the sample space should be considered an event. From a measure-theoretic point of view for probability theory, an event must be a "measurable set." The collection of measurable sets of a given sample space needs to satisfy some axiomatic properties.[1] A discussion of measure theory is beyond the scope of this book, but see Ash and Doléans-Dade (2000) for a thorough investigation of this topic.

For our discrete sample spaces, consisting of linguistic structures or other language-related discrete objects, this distinction of measurable sets from arbitrary subsets of the sample space is not crucial. We will consider all subsets of the sample space to be measurable, which means they could be used as events. For continuous spaces, we will be using well-known probability measures that rely on *Lebesgue's* measure. This means that the sample space will be a subset of a Euclidean space, and the set of events will be the subsets of this space that can be integrated over using Lebesgue's integration.

1.2   RANDOM VARIABLES

In their most basic form, random variables are functions that map each $w \in \Omega$ to a real value. They are often denoted by capital letters such as X and Z. Once such a function is defined, under some regularity conditions, it induces a probability measure over the real numbers. More specifically, for any $A \subseteq \mathbb{R}$ such that the pre-image, $X^{-1}(A)$, defined as, $\{\omega \in \Omega | X(\omega) \in A\}$, is an event, its probability is:

$$p_X(A) = p(X \in A) = p\left(X^{-1}(A)\right),$$

where p_X is the probability measure induced by the random variable X and p is a probability measure originally defined for Ω. The sample space for p_X is $\mathbb{R}$. The set of events for this sample space includes all $A \subseteq \mathbb{R}$ such that $X^{-1}(A)$ is an event in the original sample space Ω of p.

It is common to define a statistical model directly in terms of random variables, instead of explicitly defining a sample space and its corresponding real-value functions. In this case, random variables do not have to be interpreted as real-value functions and the sample space is understood to be a range of the random variable function. For example, if one wants to define a probability distribution over a language vocabulary, then one can define a random variable $X(\omega) = \omega$ with ω ranging over words in the vocabulary. Following this, the probability of a word in the vocabulary is denoted by $p(X \in \{\omega\}) = p(X = \omega)$.

[1]These axioms are: (1) Ω needs to be a measurable set; (2) The complement of a measurable set is a measurable set in the collection; (3) Any union of measurable sets is also measurable.

Random variables can also be multivariate. In that case, they would map elements of the sample space to a subset of $\mathbb{R}^d$ for some fixed d (or a tuple in some other space).[2]

1.2.1   CONTINUOUS AND DISCRETE RANDOM VARIABLES

This book uses the two most common kinds of random variables available in statistics: continuous and discrete. Continuous random variables take values in a continuous space, usually a subspace of $\mathbb{R}^d$ for $d \geq 1$. Discrete random variables, on the other hand, take values from a discrete, possibly countable set. In this book, discrete variables are usually denoted using capital letters such as X, Y and Z, while continuous variables are denoted using greek letters, such as θ and μ.

The continuous variables in this book are mostly used to define a prior over the parameters of a discrete distribution, as is usually done in the Bayesian setting. See Section 1.5.2 for a discussion of continuous variables. The discrete variables, on the other hand, are used to model structures that will be predicted (such as parse trees, part-of-speech tags, alignments, clusters) or structures which are observed (such as a sentence, a string over some language vocabulary or other such sequences).

The discrete variables discussed in this book are assumed to have an underlying *probability mass function* (PMF)—i.e., a function that attaches a weight to each element in the sample space, $p(x)$. This probability mass function induces the probability measure $p(X \in A)$, which satisfies:

$$p(X \in A) = \sum_{x \in A} p(x),$$

where A is a subset of the possible values X can take. Note that this equation is the result of the axiom of probability measures, where the probability of an event equals the sum of probabilities of disjoint events that precisely cover that event (singletons, in our case).

The most common discrete distribution we will be making use of is the multinomial distribution, which serves as a building block for many NLP models (see Chapter 3 and also Section B.1). With the multinomial space, Ω is a finite set of events, for example, a finite vocabulary of words. The PMF attaches a probability to each word in the vocabulary.

The continuous variables discussed in this book, on the other hand, are assumed to have a *probability density function* (PDF). Similarly to a PMF, this is a function that attaches a weight to each element in the sample space, $p(\theta)$. The PDF is assumed to be integrable over the sample space Ω. (Here integration refers to Lebesgue integration.) This probability density function induces a probability measure $p(\theta \in A)$, which is defined as:

$$p(\theta \in A) = \int_{\theta \in A} p(\theta)d\theta.$$

---

[2]The more abstract measure-theoretic definition of a random variable is a function from a sample space (with a given probability measure) to a measurable space E such that the preimage of this function, for any measurable set in E, is also measurable in the probability space. In most NLP applications, it is sufficient to treat random variables as real functions or functions which induce probability measures as described in this section.

The parallelism between PMFs and PDFs is not incidental. Both of these concepts can be captured using a unified mathematical framework based on measure theory. As mentioned earlier, this is beyond the scope of this book.

For notation, we use $p(X = x)$, with an explicit equal sign, to denote the PMF value of a discrete variable X. When the random variable discussed is obvious from context, we will just use notation such as $p(x)$ to denote $p(X = x)$. We denote the PMF itself (as a function) by $p(X)$ (without grounding X in a certain element in the sample space). We use $p(\theta)$ to denote both a specific PDF value of the random variable θ and also the PDF itself (as a function).

With real-valued random variables, there is a special distribution function called the *cumulative distribution function* (CDF). For a real-valued random variable θ, the CDF is a function $F: \mathbb{R} \to [0, 1]$ such that $F(y) = p(\theta \le y)$. CDF is also generalized to the multivariate case, where for a θ that represents a random variable with a range in $\mathbb{R}^d$, the CDF $F: \mathbb{R}^d \to [0, 1]$ is such that $F(y) = p(\theta_1 \le y_1, \ldots, \theta_d \le y_d)$. CDFs have a central role in statistical analysis, but are used less frequently in Bayesian NLP.

1.2.2   JOINT DISTRIBUTION OVER MULTIPLE RANDOM VARIABLES

It is possible to define several random variables on the same sample space. For example, for a discrete sample space, such as a set of words, we can define two random variables X and Y that take integer values—one could measure word length and the other could measure the count of vowels in a word. Given two such random variables, the joint distribution $P(X, Y)$ is a function that maps pairs of events (A, B) as follows:

$$p(X \in A, Y \in B) = p\left(X^{-1}(A) \cap Y^{-1}(B)\right).$$

It is often the case that we take several sets $\{\Omega_1, \ldots, \Omega_m\}$ and combine them into a single sample space $\Omega = \Omega_1 \times \ldots \times \Omega_m$. Each of the Ω_i is associated with a random variable. Based on this, a joint probability distribution can be defined for all of these random variables together. For example, consider $\Omega = V \times P$ where V is a vocabulary of words and P is a part-of-speech tag. This sample space enables us to define probabilities $p(x, y)$ where X denotes a word associated with a part of speech Y. In this case, $x \in V$ and $y \in P$.

With any joint distribution, we can *marginalize* some of the random variables to get a distribution which is defined over a subset of the original random variables (so it could still be a joint distribution, only over a subset of the random variables). Marginalization is done using integration (for continuous variables) or summing (for discrete random variables). This operation of summation or integration eliminates the random variable from the joint distribution. The result is a joint distribution over the non-marginalized random variables.

For the simple part-of-speech example above, we could either get the marginal $p(x) = \sum_{y \in P} p(x, y)$ or $p(y) = \sum_{x \in V} p(x, y)$. The marginals $p(X)$ and $p(Y)$ do not uniquely determine the joint distribution value $p(X, Y)$. Only the reverse is true. However, whenever X and Y

are *independent* then the joint distribution can be determined using the marginals. More about this in Section 1.3.2.

1.3 CONDITIONAL DISTRIBUTIONS

Joint probability distributions provide an answer to questions about the probability of several random variables to obtain specific values. Conditional distributions provide an answer to a different, but related question. They help to determine the values that a random variable can obtain, when other variables in the joint distribution are restricted to specific values (or when they are "clamped").

Conditional distributions are derivable from joint distributions over the same set of random variables. Consider a pair of random variables X and Y (either continuous or discrete). If A is an event from the sample space of X and y is a value in the sample space of Y, then:

$$p(X \in A | Y = y) = \frac{p(X \in A, Y = y)}{p(Y = y)}, \tag{1.1}$$

is to be interpreted as a conditional distribution that determines the probability of $X \in A$ conditioned on Y obtaining the value y. The bar denotes that we are clamping Y to the value y and identifying the distribution induced on X in the restricted sample space. Informally, the conditional distribution takes the part of the sample space where $Y = y$ and re-normalizes the joint distribution such that the result is a probability distribution defined only over that part of the sample space.

When we consider the joint distribution in Equation 1.1 to be a function that maps events to probabilities in the space of X, with y being fixed, we note that the value of $p(Y = y)$ is actually a normalization constant that can be determined from the numerator $p(X \in A, Y = y)$. For example, if X is discrete when using a PMF, then:

$$p(Y = y) = \sum_x p(X = x, Y = y).$$

Since $p(Y = y)$ is a constant with respect to the values that X takes, we will often use the notation:

$$p(X \in A | Y = y) \propto p(X \in A, Y = y),$$

to denote that the conditional distribution over X given Y is *proportional* to the joint distribution, and that normalization of this joint distribution is required in order to get the conditional distribution.

In their most general form, conditional distributions (Equation 1.1) can include more than a single random variable on both sides of the bar. The two sets of random variables for each side of the bar also do not have to be disjoint. In addition, we do not have to clamp the conditioned random variables to a single value—they can be clamped to any event. All of this leads to the following general form of conditional distributions. Let $X_1, \ldots, X_n$ be a set of random variables. Let $I = \{a_1, \ldots, a_m\}$ $J = \{b_1, \ldots, b_\ell\}$ be subsets of $\{1, \ldots, n\}$. In addition, let A_i for $i \in I$ be an event for the sample space of X_{a_i} and B_j for $j \in J$ be an event for the sample space of X_{b_j}. Based on this, we can define the following conditional distribution:

$$p\left(X_{a_1} \in A_1, \ldots, X_{a_m} \in A_m | X_{b_1} \in B_1, \ldots, X_{b_\ell} \in B_\ell\right) = \frac{p\left(X_{a_1} \in A_1, \ldots, X_{a_m} \in A_m, X_{b_1} \in B_1, \ldots, X_{b_\ell} \in B_\ell\right)}{p\left(X_{b_1} \in B_1, \ldots, X_{b_\ell} \in B_\ell\right)}.$$

The Chain Rule   The "chain rule" is a direct result of the definition of conditional probability distributions. It permits us to express a joint distribution in terms of a sequence of multiplications of conditional distributions. The simplest version of the chain rule states that for any two random variables X and Y, it holds that $p(X, Y) = p(X)p(Y|X)$ (assuming $p(Y|X)$ is always defined). In the more general case, it states that we can decompose the joint distribution over a sequence of random variables $X^{(1)}, \ldots, X^{(n)}$ to be:

$$p\left(X^{(1)}, \ldots, X^{(n)}\right) = p\left(X^{(1)}\right) \prod_{i=2}^{n} p\left(X^{(i)} | X^{(1)}, \ldots, X^{(i-1)}\right).$$

With the chain rule, we can also treat a subset of random variables as a single unit, so for example, it is true that:

$$p\left(X^{(1)}, X^{(2)}, X^{(3)}\right) = p\left(X^{(1)}\right) p\left(X^{(2)}, X^{(3)} | X^{(1)}\right),$$

or alternatively:

$$p\left(X^{(1)}, X^{(2)}, X^{(3)}\right) = p\left(X^{(1)}, X^{(2)}\right) p\left(X^{(3)} | X^{(1)}, X^{(2)}\right),$$

for any three random variables $X^{(1)}, X^{(2)}, X^{(3)}$.

1.3.1   BAYES' RULE

Bayes' rule is a basic result in probability that describes a relationship between two conditional distributions $p(X|Y)$ and $p(Y|X)$ for a pair of random variables (these random variables can also be continuous). More specifically, Bayes' rule states that for any such pair of random variables, the following identity holds:

$$p(Y = y | X = x) = \frac{p(X = x | Y = y)p(Y = y)}{p(X = x)}. \tag{1.2}$$

This result also generally holds true for any two events A and B with the conditional probability $p(X \in A | Y \in B)$.

The main advantage that Bayes' rule offers is *inversion* of the conditional relationship between two random variables—therefore, if one variable is known, then the other can be calculated as well, assuming the marginal distributions $p(X = x)$ and $p(Y = y)$ are also known.

Bayes' rule can be proven in several ways. One way to derive it is simply by using the chain rule twice. More specifically, we know that the joint distribution values can be rewritten as follows, using the chain rule, either first separating X or first separating Y:

$$
\begin{aligned}
p(X = x, Y = y) \\
= p(X = x)p(Y = y|X = x) \\
= p(Y = y)p(X = x|Y = y).
\end{aligned}
$$

Taking the last equality above, $p(X = x)p(Y = y|X = x) = p(Y = y)p(X = x|Y = y)$, and dividing both sides by $p(X = x)$ results in Bayes' rule as described in Equation 1.2.

Bayes' rule is the main pillar in Bayesian statistics for reasoning and learning from data. Bayes' rule can *invert* the relationship between "observations" (the data) and the random variables we are interested in predicting. This makes it possible to infer target predictions from such observations. A more detailed description of these ideas is provided in Section 1.5, where statistical modeling is discussed.

1.3.2 INDEPENDENT AND CONDITIONALLY INDEPENDENT RANDOM VARIABLES

A pair of random variables (X, Y) is said to be independent if for any A and B,

$$
p(X \in A|Y \in B) = p(X \in A),
$$

or alternatively $p(Y \in B|X \in A) = p(Y \in B)$ (these two definitions are correct and equivalent under very mild conditions that prevent ill-formed conditioning on an event that has zero probability).

Using the chain rule, it can also be shown that the above two definitions are equivalent to the requirement that $p(X \in A, Y \in B) = p(X \in A)p(Y \in B)$ for all A and B.

Independence between random variables implies that the random variables do not provide information about each other. This means that knowing the value of X does not help us infer anything about the value of Y—in other words, it does not change the probability of Y. (Or vice-versa—Y does not tell us anything about X.) While independence is an important concept in probability and statistics, in this book we will more frequently make use of a more refined notion of independence, called "conditional independence"—which is a generalization of the notion of independence described in the beginning of this section. A pair of random variables (X, Y) is conditionally independent given a third random variable Z, if for any A, B and z, it holds that $p(X \in A|Y \in B, Z = z) = p(X \in A|Z = z)$.

Conditional independence between two random variables (given a third one) implies that the two variables are not informative about each other, if the value of the third one is known.[3]

Conditional independence (and independence) can be generalized to multiple random variables as well. We say that a set of random variables $X_1, \ldots, X_n$, are mutually conditionally independent given another set of random variables $Z_1, \ldots, Z_m$ if the following applies for any $A_1, \ldots, A_n$ and $z_1, \ldots, z_m$:

$$p(X_1 \in A_1, \ldots, X_n \in A_n | Z_1 = z_1, \ldots, Z_m = z_m) =$$
$$\prod_{i=1}^{n} p(X_i \in A_i | Z_1 = z_1, \ldots, Z_m = z_m).$$

This type of independence is weaker than pairwise independence for a set of random variables, in which only pairs of random variables are required to be independent. (Also see exercises.)

1.3.3   EXCHANGEABLE RANDOM VARIABLES

Another type of relationship that can be present between random variables is that of *exchangeability*. A sequence of random variables $X_1, X_2, \ldots$ over Ω is said to be exchangeable, if for any finite subset, permuting the random variables in this finite subset, does not change their joint distribution. More formally, for any $S = \{a_1, \ldots, a_m\}$ where $a_i \geq 1$ is an integer, and for any permutation π on $\{1, \ldots, m\}$, it holds that:[4]

$$p(x_{a_1}, \ldots, x_{a_m}) = p(x_{a_{\pi(1)}}, \ldots, x_{a_{\pi(m)}}).$$

Due to a theorem by de Finetti (Finetti, 1980), exchangeability can be thought of as meaning "conditionally independent and identically distributed" in the following sense. De Finetti showed that if a sequence of random variables $X_1, X_2, \ldots$ is exchangeable, then under some regularity conditions, there exists a sample space Θ and a distribution over Θ, $p(\theta)$, such that:

$$p(X_{a_1}, \ldots, X_{a_m}) = \int_{\theta} \prod_{i=1}^{m} p(X_{a_i} | \theta) p(\theta) d\theta,$$

for any set of m integers, $\{a_1, \ldots, a_m\}$. The interpretation of this is that exchangeable random variables can be represented as a (potentially infinite) mixture distribution. This theorem is also called the "representation theorem."

The frequentist approach assumes the existence of a fixed set of parameters from which the data were generated, while the Bayesian approach assumes that there is some prior distribution over the set of parameters that generated the data. (This will become clearer as the book progresses.) De Finetti's theorem provides another connection between the Bayesian approach and

---

[3]To show that conditional independence is a generalized notion of independence, consider a Z that is a constant value.
[4]A permutation on $S = \{1, \ldots, n\}$ is a bijection $\pi \colon S \to S$.

the frequentist one. The standard "independent and identically distributed" (i.i.d.) assumption in the frequentist setup can be asserted as a setup of exchangeability where $p(\theta)$ is a point-mass distribution over the unknown (but single) parameter from which the data are sampled. This leads to the observations being unconditionally independent and identically distributed. In the Bayesian setup, however, the observations are correlated, because $p(\theta)$ is not a point-mass distribution. The prior distribution plays the role of $p(\theta)$. For a detailed discussion of this similarity, see O'Neill (2009).

The exchangeability assumption, when used in the frequentist setup, is weaker than the i.i.d. assumption, and fixes an important conceptual flaw (in the eye of Bayesians) in the i.i.d. assumption. In the i.i.d. setup the observed random variables are independent of each other, and as such, do not provide information about each other when the parameters are fixed. The probability of the nth observation (X_n), conditioned on the first $n - 1$ observations, is identical to the marginal distribution over the nth observation, no matter what the first $n - 1$ observations were. The exchangeability assumption, on the other hand, introduces correlation between the different observations, and as such, the distribution $p(X_n \mid X_1, \ldots, X_{n-1})$ will not be just $p(X_n)$.

Exchangeability appears in several contexts in Bayesian NLP. For example, in the LDA model (Chapter 2), the words in each document are exchangeable, meaning that they are conditionally independent given the topic distribution. The Chinese restaurant process (Chapter 7) is also an exchangeable model, which makes it possible to derive its posterior distribution.

1.4   EXPECTATIONS OF RANDOM VARIABLES

If we consider again the naïve definition of random variables, as functions that map the sample space to real values, then it is also useful to consider various ways in which we can summarize these random variables. One way to get a summary of a random variable is by computing its *expectation*, which is its weighted mean value according to the underlying probability model.

It is easiest to first consider the expectation of a continuous random variable with a density function. Say $p(\theta)$ defines a distribution over the random variable θ, then the expectation of θ, denoted $E[\theta]$ would be defined as:

$$E[\theta] = \int_\theta p(\theta)\theta d\theta.$$

For the discrete random variables that we consider in this book, we usually consider expectations of *functions* over these random variables. As mentioned in Section 1.2, discrete random variable values often range over a set which is not numeric. In these cases, there is no "mean value" for the values that these random variables accept. Instead, we will compute the mean value of a real-function of these random variables.

With f being such a function, the expectation $E[f(X)]$ is defined as:

$$E[f(X)] = \sum_x p(x)f(x).$$

For the linguistic structures that are used in this book, we will often use a function f that indicates whether a certain property holds for the structure. For example, if the sample space of X is a set of sentences, $f(x)$ can be an indicator function that states whether the word "spring" appears in the sentence x or not; $f(x) = 1$ if the word "spring" appears in x and 0, otherwise. In that case, $f(X)$ itself can be thought of as a *Bernoulli* random variable, i.e., a binary random variable that has a certain probability θ to be 1, and probability $1 - \theta$ to be 0. The expectation $E[f(X)]$ gives the probability that this random variable is 1. Alternatively, $f(x)$ can *count* how many times the word "spring" appears in the sentence x. In that case, it can be viewed as a sum of Bernoulli variables, each indicating whether a certain word in the sentence x is "spring" or not.

Expectations are linear operators. This means that if θ_1 and θ_2 are two random variables and a, b and c are real values, then

$$E[a\theta_1 + b\theta_2 + c] = a E[\theta_1] + b E[\theta_2] + c. \tag{1.3}$$

Equation 1.3 holds even if the random variables are not independent. Expectations are linear for both continuous and discrete random variables, even when such random variables are mixed together in the linear expression.

As with conditional distributions, one can define conditional expectation. For example $E[f(X)|Y = y]$ would be the expectation of $f(X)$ under the conditional distribution $p(X|Y = y)$. The function $g(y) = E[f(X)|Y = y]$ can be thought of as a random variable. In that case, it can be shown that $E[g(Y)] = E[E[f(X)|Y]] = E[f(X)]$. (This is a direct result of Fubini's theorem (Ash and Doléans-Dade, 2000). This theorem roughly states that under some mild conditions, any order of integration or summation over several random variables gives the same result.)

It is common practice to denote by subscript the underlying distribution which is used to compute the expectation, when it cannot be uniquely determined from context. For example, $E_q[f(X)]$ denotes the expectation of $f(X)$ with respect to a distribution q, i.e.:

$$E_q[f(X)] = \sum_x q(x) f(x).$$

There are several types of expectations for real-value random variables which are deemed important in various applications or when we are interested in summarizing the random variable. One such type of expectation is "moments": the n-th order moment of a random variable X around point c is defined to be $E[(X - c)^n]$. With $n = 1$ and $c = 0$, we get the *mean* of the random variable. With $c = E[X]$ and $n = 2$, we get the *variance* of the random variable, which also equals $E[X^2] - (E[X]^2)$.

The idea of moments can be generalized to several random variables. The most commonly used generalization is covariance. The covariance between two random variables X and Y is

$E[XY] - E[X]E[Y]$. Note that if $Y = X$, then the covariance is reduced to the variance of X. If two random variables are independent, then their covariance is 0. The opposite is not necessarily true—two random variables can be dependent, while covariance is still 0. In that case, the random variables are only uncorrelated, but not independent.

A handful of moments sometimes uniquely define a probability distribution. For example, a coin toss distribution (i.e., a Bernoulli distribution) is uniquely defined by the first moment, which gives the probability of the coin toss giving the outcome 1. A Gaussian distribution is uniquely defined by its first and second order moments (or mean and variance).

1.5   MODELS

The major goal of statistical modeling is to analyze data in order to make predictions, or to help understand the properties of a process in "nature" that exhibits randomness, through its modeling in mathematical terms. One way to define a statistical model is to represent it as a family of probability distribution functions over a set of random variables. Statistical models can also be described in terms of indices for probability distributions. In that case, a statistical model $\mathcal{M}$ is a set, such that each member of the set identifies a specific probability distribution.

For example, let $\mathcal{I}$ denote the segment $[0, 1]$ to define probability distributions over a random variable X that takes the values 0 or 1 (a Bernoulli variable, or a "coin flip" variable). Each $\theta \in \mathcal{I}$ is a number between 0 and 1. The distribution associated with that θ will be denoted by $p(X|\theta)$, such that: $p(X = 0|\theta) = \theta$ and $p(X = 1|\theta) = 1 - \theta$. This set of distributions, $\mathcal{M}$, is an example of a *parametric model*, as described below in Section 1.5.1.

The term "model" often refers, especially in colloquial discussions, to either a specific $p \in \mathcal{M}$ (such as "the estimated model"—i.e., a specific member of the model family that is identified through data), a non-specific $p \in \mathcal{M}$ or the set of all distributions in $\mathcal{M}$. We follow this norm in the book, and use the word "model" in all of these cases, where it is clear from context what the word refers to.

Models are often composed of well-studied distributions, such as the Gaussian distribution, Bernoulli distribution or the multinomial distribution. This means that there is a way to write the joint distribution as a product of conditional distributions, such that these conditional distributions are well-known distributions. This is especially true with generative models (Section 1.5.3). We assume some basic familiarity with the important distributions that are used in NLP, and also give in Appendix B a catalog of the especially common ones.

1.5.1   PARAMETRIC VS. NONPARAMETRIC MODELS

Parametric models are models such that the model family $\mathcal{M}$ indexes a set of distributions, all having identical structure. For example, the statistical model $\mathcal{M}$ is said to be parametric if every member of $\mathcal{M}$, a probability distribution $p \in \mathcal{M}$, is indexed by a finite set of parameters θ in some space Θ. Most often, Θ is a subset of $\mathbb{R}^d$ for some fixed d. This example is the main representative of parametric models that appear in this book or in NLP in general.

Parametric models stand in contrast to nonparametric models, where each distribution in the model family might have a different structure. The most common nonparametric models used in Bayesian NLP are such that the model size grows with the number of datapoints we use to carry out inference. They are a good fit for natural language data, because as more language data are observed, we expect them to cover a larger set of phenomena in language, whether syntactic, morphological or lexical, and as such, we need a larger model to account for these phenomena. Bayesian nonparametric models for NLP are covered in Chapter 7.

An important concept in statistical modeling is that of the *likelihood function*. The likelihood function is a function of the parameters, which gives the total probability of the observed data (see also Section 1.6). For example, if we observe n coin tosses, $x^{(1)}, \ldots, x^{(n)}$, each being 0 or 1, and our model family is the set of Bernoulli distributions parametrized by θ, the likelihood function is:

$$L\left(\theta | x^{(1)}, \ldots, x^{(n)}\right) = \prod_{i=1}^{n} p\left(x^{(i)} | \theta\right) = \prod_{i=1}^{n} \theta^{x^{(i)}}(1-\theta)^{1-x^{(i)}} = \theta^{\sum_{i=1}^{n} x^{(i)}}(1-\theta)^{n - \sum_{i=1}^{n} x^{(i)}}.$$

The *log-likelihood* is just the logarithm of the likelihood. In the above example it is $\log L\left(\theta | x^{(1)}, \ldots, x^{(n)}\right) = \left(\sum_{i=1}^{n} x^{(i)}\right) \log \theta + \left(n - \sum_{i=1}^{n} x^{(i)}\right) \log(1-\theta)$.

1.5.2   INFERENCE WITH MODELS

As mentioned earlier, one of the goals of statistical modeling is to use models to make predictions. This is especially true in NLP. Before the introduction of heavy Bayesian machinery, the *frequentist* statistical paradigm was used almost exclusively in NLP. While there are deep philosophical roots behind the difference between the Bayesian paradigm and the frequentist paradigm (Section 1.7), all this means from a practical point of view in NLP is that models were mostly *estimated*. This means that, with the help of "training" data, a single member of a model family is identified. Once such estimation is complete, we can proceed to *decode* unseen instances, i.e., make predictions, based on the estimated model.

The estimation step is often done by optimizing some statistically motivated objective function that measures the fit of an arbitrary model in the model family to the training data. (One such objective function is the log-likelihood objective function; see Section 4.2.1 for more information.) The frequentist paradigm justifies itself by having developed a mathematical framework which discusses what happens to our estimation process as the amount of data becomes larger. Its focus is on showing that when a sufficient amount of data is available, the estimated model will be close to the "truth," or at the very least, our estimated model will be an "optimal choice" according to one criterion or another. (An example for such a criterion is the maximum likelihood criterion.)

For example, statistical consistency is one notion developed in such a framework. It can be shown that, with the optimization of the log-likelihood objective function, under some regularity conditions, and under the assumption that data is generated from one of the model family members (the "true" model), the estimated model will become closer to that true model as we include more data in the estimation.[5]

Bayesian inference stands in stark contrast to this frequentist paraidgm of estimation, and conceptually suggests a clean and elegant way of doing statistical inference. Assume that $\mathcal{M}$ indexes a set of distributions over a random variable X. Each $\theta \in \mathcal{M}$ identifies a probability distribution from the model family, $p(X|\theta)$. At its core, the technical idea behind Bayesian inference is simple and is done using the following three steps:

- Define (using prior knowledge or some other means) some probability distribution over the elements in $\mathcal{M}$. This means that we define a probability distribution $p(\theta)$ that tells *a priori* how likely it is to choose a certain model to generate data we based our predictions on.

- Define a joint distribution which uses this prior, over the sample space $\Omega' = \mathcal{M} \times \Omega$, where Ω is the sample space of X. The joint distribution is:

$$p(\theta, X) = p(\theta)p(X|\theta).$$

- Given observed data x (a realization of the random variable X) use Bayes' rule to obtain a probability distribution over $\mathcal{M}$, the *posterior distribution*:

$$p(\theta|x) = \frac{p(\theta)p(x|\theta)}{\int_{\theta'} p(\theta')p(x|\theta')d\theta'}. \tag{1.4}$$

Note that all quantities on the right-hand side are known (because x is grounded in a specific value), and therefore, from a mathematical point of view, the posterior $p(\theta|x)$ can be fully identified.

In the above steps, our goal was to infer a *distribution* over the set of parameters, which essentially integrates information from the prior (this information tells us how *a priori* likely each parameter is) with the information we get about the parameters through the observed data. Instead of identifying a single distribution in $\mathcal{M}$ (as we would do in the frequentist setting), we now have a distribution over $\mathcal{M}$. There are many variants to this idea of inference in the Bayesian setting, and a major goal of this book is to cover a significant part of these variants—those which are necessary for understanding Bayesian NLP papers. In addition, the steps above

---

[5]The regularity conditions require the model to be identifiable; the parameter space to be compact; the continuity of the log-likelihood; and a bound on the log-likelihood function with respect to the data with an integrable function that does not depend on the parameters. See Casella and Berger (2002) for more details.

just give a mathematical formulation for Bayesian inference. In practice, much care is needed when applying Bayes' rule in Equation 1.4. Chapter 2 goes into more detail on how Bayesian inference is done for a simple model, and the rest of the book focuses on the harder cases where more care is required.

1.5.3   GENERATIVE MODELS

Generative models are statistical models that describe a joint distribution over three types of random variables:

- The "observed" random variables (often the "input space"), which are the random variables we have data for.

- The "latent" random variables, which are the random variables that play a role in the statistical model, for example, to reduce the dimension of the observed data, but which are never observed (in the Bayesian setting, these are usually, at the very least, the parameters of the model).

- The "predicted" random variables, which are the random variables that represent the target predictions.

This categorization for the random variables in the joint distribution is not mutually exclusive (though observed random variables are never latent). For example, the predicted random variables can be also latent, such as in the unsupervised setting (see Section 1.6).

An example of this categorization can be demonstrated in a sequence model for part-of-speech (POS) tagging, where the goal is to make predictions based only on a fixed set of sentences in a given language. The observed data are the sentences in that language, while the predicted structures are the part-of-speech tags—which, in this case, are also latent. In the Bayesian setting, the parameters of the model could be considered latent variables as well. If we try to learn a POS tagging model from examples of sentences with their corresponding correct POS tags (to generalize to unseen sentences), then the observed data are the sentences with their correct POS tags, and the parameters are considered as the latent variables. For a discussion about latent variables, see Section 1.5.3.

Generative models are often contrasted with *discriminative models*, in which the underlying statistical model does not define a probability distribution over the input space. Instead, the model is conditional, and we model the probability of a predicted structure *given* an element in the input space.[6]

The joint distributions that generative models describe often entail independence assumptions between the various random variables in the distribution. This means that the chain rule

---

[6] Any generative model can be transformed into a discriminative model by conditioning on a specific input instance. The reverse transformation from a discriminative model to a generative model is not possible without introducing an underspecified factor, a probability distribution over the input space.

Constants: K, number of mixture components; n, number of examples
Parameters: $\theta \in \mathbb{R}^K$, $\theta_i \geq 0$, $\sum_{i=1}^{K} \theta_i = 1$; $\mu_i \in \mathbb{R}^d$, $\Sigma_i \in \mathbb{R}^{d \times d}$, $i \in \{1, \ldots, K\}$
Latent variables: Z_j for $j \in \{1, \ldots, n\}$
Observed variables: X_j for $j \in \{1, \ldots, n\}$

- For $j \in \{1, \ldots, n\}$

  - Generate $z_j \in \{1, \ldots, K\}$ from Multinomial(θ)
  - Generate x_j from Normal(μ_{z_j}, Σ_{z_j})

Generative Story 1.1: The generative story for a Gaussian mixture model.

can be applied to the joint distribution, with a certain ordering over the random variables, so that the joint distribution is written in a more compact way as a product of factors—each describing a conditional distribution of a random variable or a set of random variables given a small, local set of random variables.

It is often the case that describing a joint distribution based only on the form of its factors can be confusing, or not sufficiently detailed. Representations such as graphical models (see Section 1.5.4) can be even more restrictive and less revealing, since they mostly describe the independence assumptions that exist in the model.

In these cases, this book uses a verbal *generative story* description, as a set of bullet points that procedurally describe how each of the variables is generated in the model. For example, generative story 1.1 describes a mixture of Gaussian models.

Behind lines 1 and 3 lurk simple statistical models with well-known distributions. The first line assumes a probability distribution $p(Z_j | \theta)$. The second assumes a Gaussian probability distribution $p(X_j | \mu_{z_j}, \Sigma_{z_j})$. Combined together, and taking into account the loop in lines 1–3, they yield a joint probability distribution:

$$p(X_1, \ldots, X_n, Z_1, \ldots, Z_n | \theta, \mu_1, \ldots, \mu_K, \Sigma_1, \ldots, \Sigma_K) = \prod_{j=1}^{n} p(X_j, Z_j | \theta, \mu_1, \ldots, \mu_K, \Sigma_1, \ldots, \Sigma_K).$$

In this book, generative story boxes are included with some information about the variables, constants and parameters that exist in the model. This can be thought of as the *signature* of the generative story. This signature often also tells, as in the above case, which variables are assumed to be observed in the data, and which are assumed to be latent. Clearly, this is not a property of the joint distribution itself, but rather depends on the context and the use of this joint distribution as a statistical model.

As mentioned above, generative stories identify a joint distribution over the parameters in the model, where this joint distribution is a product of several factors. This is related to the chain rule (Section 1.3). The generative story picks an ordering for the random variables, and the chain rule is applied using that order to yield the joint distribution. Each factor can theoretically condition on all possible random variables that were generated before, but the independence assumptions in the model make some of these variables unnecessary to condition on.

Latent Variables in Generative Models

Latent variables are random variables in the model which are assumed to be unobserved when doing inference from data (see also Section 1.5.3). As such, latent variables can generally refer to three distinct types of random variables:

- Random variables that augment, refine or link (as a cause) between observed random variables and the target predictions (this is especially true when the target predictions are observed during learning, in the supervised setting. See Section 1.6).

- Random variables that represent the target predictions, because these are not observed during learning (in the unsupervised setting, for example).

- In the Bayesian setting, random variables that represent the parameters of the generative model.

1.5.4   INDEPENDENCE ASSUMPTIONS IN MODELS

How do we actually construct a generative model given a phenomeon we want to model? We first have to decide which random variables compose the model. Clearly, the observed data need to be associated with a random variable, and so do the predicted values. We can add latent variables as we wish, if we believe there are hidden factors that link between the observed and predicted values.

Often, the next step is deciding exactly how these random variables relate to each other with respect to their *conditional independence*. At this point, we are not yet assigning distributions to the various random variables, but just hypothesizing about the information flow between them. These independence assumptions need to balance various trade-offs. On one hand, the weaker they are (i.e., the more dependence there is), the more expressive the model family is— in other words, the model family includes more distributions. On the other hand, if they are too expressive, we might run into problems such as overfitting with small amounts of data, or technical problems such as computationally expensive inference.

Looking at various models in NLP, we see that the independence assumptions we make are rather strong—it is usually the case that a given random variable depends on a small number of other random variables. In that sense, the model has "local factors" in its joint distribution.

For example, context-free grammars (see Chapter 8) make the independence assumption that any future rewrites of a partial derivation depend only on the current foot nonterminal of that partial derivation. Similarly, hidden Markov models (HMMs) make the assumption that "future observations" and "past observations" are conditionally independent given the identity of the state that links them together. This strong assumption is often mitigated by using a higher order HMM (with the transition to the next state depending on the last *two*, or more, previous states, and not just the last one).

Once the independence assumptions in the model are determined (either by writing the joint distribution with its factors, or perhaps through a graphical representation with a Bayesian network), we can proceed to describe an exact distribution for each factor, i.e., a conditional distribution in the joint distribution. This is where well-known distributions are typically used, such as Gaussians, multinomials or featurized log-linear models. The parameters of these conditional distributions depend on all of the random variables that are being conditioned on. For example, in generative story 1.1, the distribution function for x_j depends on the values previously drawn for z_j.

1.5.5   DIRECTED GRAPHICAL MODELS

As mentioned above, detailing the full generative story or joint distribution is necessary to fully comprehend the inner workings of a given statistical model. However, in cases where we are just interested in describing the independence assumptions that exist in the model, graphical representations can help to elucidate these assumptions.

Given that Bayesian models are often generative, the most important type of graphical representation for them is "directed graphical models" (or "Bayesian networks"). See Murphy (2012) for an introduction to other types of graphical models (GMs), such as undirected graphical models. In a Bayesian network, each random variable in the joint distribution is represented as a vertex in a graph. There are incoming edges to each vertex X from all random variables that X conditions on, when writing down the joint distribution and inspecting the factor that describes the distribution over X.

The basic type of independence assumption a Bayesian network describes is the following. A random variable X is conditionally independent of all its ancestors when conditioned on its immediate parents. This type of property leads to an extensive calculus and a set of graph-theoretic decision rules that can assist in determining whether one set of random variables in the model is independent of another set when conditioned on a third set (i.e., the random variables in the third set are assumed to be observed for that conditional independence test). The calculus includes a few logical relations, including symmetry: if X and Y are conditionally independent given Z, then Y and X are conditionally independent given Z; decomposition: if X and $Y \cup W$ are conditionally independent given Z, then X and Y are conditionally independent given Z; contraction: if X and Y are conditionally independent given Z, and X and Y are conditionally independent given $Y \cup Z$, then X is conditionally independent of $W \cup Y$ given Z; weak union:

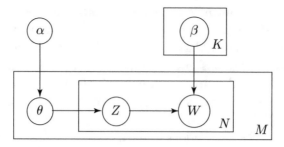

Figure 1.1: Graphical model for the latent Dirichlet allocation model. Number of topics denoted by K, number of documents denoted by M and number of words per document denoted by N.[7]

if X and $Y \cup Z$ are conditionally independent given W, then X and Y are conditionally independent given $Z \cup W$. Here, X, Y, Z and W are subsets of random variables in a probability distribution. See Pearl (1988) for more information.

Bayesian networks also include a graphical mechanism to describe a variable or unfixed number of random variables, using so-called "plate notation." With plate notation, a set of random variables is placed inside plates. A plate represents a set of random variables with some count. For example, a plate could be used to describe a set of words in a document. Figure 1.1 provides an example of a use of the graphical plate language. Random variables, denoted by circles, are the basic building blocks in this graphical language; the plates are composed of such random variables (or other plates) and denote a "larger object." For example, the random variable W stands for a word in a document, and the random variable Z is a topic variable associated with that word. As such, the plate as a whole denotes a document, which is indeed a larger object composed from N random variables from the type of Z and W.

In this notation, edges determine the conditional independence assumptions in the model. The joint distribution over all random variables can be read by topologically sorting the elements in the graphical representation, and then multiplying factors, starting at the root, such that each random variable (or a group of random variables in a plate) conditions on its parents, determined by the edges in the graph. For example, the graphical model in Figure 1.1 describes the following joint distribution:

$$\prod_{j=1}^{M} p\left(W_1^{(j)}, \ldots, W_n^{(j)}, Z_1^{(j)}, \ldots, Z_N^{(j)}, \theta^{(j)} | \beta_1, \ldots, \beta_K, \alpha\right)$$

$$= \prod_{j=1}^{M} \left(p(\theta^{(j)} | \alpha) \prod_{i=1}^{n} p\left(Z_i^{(j)} | \theta\right) p\left(W_i^{(j)} | Z_i^{(j)}, \theta^{(j)}, \beta_1, \ldots, \beta_K\right)\right). \qquad (1.5)$$

[7]Adapted from a drawing by Luis Pedro.

This joint distribution describes the latent Dirichlet allocation model (a model for generating M documents, with each document having N words), described more in detail in Chapter 2. Plates can also be nested (with several indices indexing random variables) or intersected.

Perhaps with somewhat of an abuse of notation, graphical models often also include vertices for the parameters of the model, even when they are not random variables (in a frequentist setting) or hyperparameters (in the Bayesian setting; see Chapter 3). Such nodes in the graphical model will never have incoming edges, only outgoing edges. The plate for the vector $\beta_1, \ldots, \beta_K$ in Figure 1.1 is an example of this. The same goes for the α node in the same figure. (A similar abuse of notation is often done when writing down distributions. For example, we would write $p(\theta|\alpha)$, *conditioning* on α, even though α is not a random variable, but a fixed hyperparameter value.)

This book makes little use of graphical models in describing statistical models, and the reader is instead referred to a machine learning book (e.g., Koller and Friedman, 2009), for more information about graphical models. Graphical modeling is a rich area of research, but goes beyond the scope of this book. Given the mechanism we have introduced to describe generative stories in the previous section, there is also little use of it in the material covered in this book.

1.6   LEARNING FROM DATA SCENARIOS

We are now equipped with the basic concepts from probability theory and from statistics so that we can learn from data. We can now create a statistical model, where the data we have is mapped to "observed" random variables. The question remains: how is our data represented? In NLP, researchers usually rely on fixed datasets from annotated or unannotated corpora. Each item in a fixed corpus is assumed to be drawn from some distribution. The data can be annotated (labeled) or unannotated (unlabeled). Learning can be supervised, semi-supervised or unsupervised. The various scenarios and prediction goals for each are described in Table 1.1.

An important concept common to all of these learning settings is that of marginal likelihood. The marginal likelihood is a quantity that denotes the likelihood of the observed data according to the model. In the Bayesian setting, marginalization is done over the parameters (taking into account the prior) and the latent variables.

Here are some learning cases along with their marginal likelihood.

- We are interested in doing unsupervised part-of-speech tagging. Therefore, the observed data points are $x^{(1)}, \ldots, x^{(n)}$, which are sentences. In addition, there is a distribution over POS sequences. Each $x^{(i)}$ is associated with a random variable $Z^{(i)}$ that denotes this POS sequence. The likelihood of a pair (X, Z) is determined by $p(X, Z|\theta) = p(Z|\theta)p(X|Z, \theta)$—i.e., in the generative story we first generate the POS tag sequence, and then the sentence. There is a prior over θ. Therefore, the final likelihood is:

Table 1.1: Common procedures for learning from data. Observed data comes from the X random variable distribution, target predictions from the Z random variable distribution (indexed as appropriately for different instances).

Learning Setting	Learning Input Data	Learning Output
Supervised (inductive)	$(x^{(1)}, z^{(1)}), \dots, (x^{(n)}, z^{(n)})$	Mechanism to predict z values on arbitrary input instances
Supervised (transductive)	$(x_0^{(1)}, z^{(1)}), \dots, (x_0^{(n)}, z_n)$ and $x_1^{(1)}, \dots, x_1^{(m)}$	Predictions of z values on $x_1^{(i)}, i \in \{1, \dots, m\}$
Semi-supervised	$(x_0^{(1)}, z_1), \dots, (x_0^{(n)}, z_n)$ and $x_1^{(1)}, \dots, x_1^{(m)}$	Mechanism to predict z values on arbitrary input instances
Unsupervised (instance-general)	$x^{(1)}, \dots, x^{(n)}$	Mechanism to predict z values on arbitrary input instances
Unsupervised (instance-specific)	$x^{(1)}, \dots, x^{(n)}$	Predictions of z on $x^{(1)}, \dots, x^{(n)}$

$$\mathcal{L}\left(x^{(1)}, \dots, x^{(n)}\right) = \int_\theta \left(\prod_{i=1}^n \sum_{z^{(i)}} p\left(z^{(i)}|\theta\right) p\left(x^{(i)}|z^{(i)}, \theta\right) \right) p(\theta)d\theta.$$

- We are interested in doing transductive[8] supervised part-of-speech tagging. Therefore, the observed data points are $\left(x^{(1)}, z^{(1)}\right), \dots, \left(x^{(n)}, z^{(n)}\right)$ (labeled data) and $x'^{(1)}, \dots, x'^{(m)}$ (sentences for which predictions are needed). The distributions over the X and Z variables are the same as in the previous case. Same, as well, for the prior. The marginal likelihood

[8]The scenario in transductive learning is such that training data in the form of inputs and outputs are available. In addition, the inputs for which we are interested in making predictions are also available during training.

is (where $Z'^{(i)}$ are the predicted sequences for $X'^{(i)}$):

$$
\mathcal{L}\left(x^{(1)}, \ldots, x^{(n)}, z^{(1)}, \ldots, z^{(n)}, x'^{(1)}, \ldots, x'^{(m)}\right)
$$
$$
= \int_{\theta} \left(\prod_{i=1}^{n} p\left(z^{(i)}|\theta\right) p\left(x^{(i)}|z^{(i)}, \theta\right) p(\theta) \right)
$$
$$
\times \left(\prod_{i=1}^{m} \sum_{z'^{(i)}} p\left(z'^{(i)}|\theta\right) p\left(x'^{(i)}|z'^{(i)}, \theta\right) \right) p(\theta)d\theta.
$$

- We are interested in doing inductive supervised part-of-speech tagging. Therefore, the observed data points are $(x^{(1)}, z^{(1)}), \ldots, (x^{(n)}, z^{(n)})$. The distributions over the X and Z variables is the same as in the previous case. Same, again, for the prior. The marginal likelihood is:

$$
\mathcal{L}\left(x^{(1)}, \ldots, x^{(n)}, z^{(1)}, \ldots, z^{(n)}\right) = \int_{\theta} \left(\prod_{i=1}^{n} p\left(z^{(i)}|\theta\right) p\left(x^{(i)}|z^{(i)}, \theta\right) \right) p(\theta)d\theta.
$$

Note that here, the marginal likelihood is not used to predict any value directly. But if the prior, for example, is parametrized as $p(\theta|\alpha)$, this marginal likelihood could be maximized with respect to α. See Chapter 4.

- We are interested in doing inductive supervised part-of-speech tagging, where the statistical model for the POS sequences assumes an additional latent variable for each sequence. Therefore, the likelihood is defined over X, Z and H, the latent variable. For example, H could be a *refinement* of the POS labels—adding an additional latent category that describes types of coarse POS tags such as nouns, verbs and prepositions. The observed data points are $(x^{(1)}, z^{(1)}), \ldots, (x^{(n)}, z^{(n)})$. The marginal likelihood is:

$$
\mathcal{L}\left(x^{(1)}, \ldots, x^{(n)}, z^{(1)}, \ldots, z^{(n)}\right)
$$
$$
= \int_{\theta} \left(\prod_{i=1}^{n} \sum_{h^{(i)}} p\left(h^{(i)}, z^{(i)}|\theta\right) p\left(x^{(i)}|h^{(i)}, z^{(i)}, \theta\right) \right) p(\theta)d\theta.
$$

The concept of likelihood is further explored in this book in various contexts, most prominently in Chapters 4 and 6.

Log-likelihood and marginal log-likelihood can also be used as an "intrinsic" measure of evaluation for a given model. This evaluation is done by holding out part of the observed data, and then evaluating the marginal log-likelihood on this held-out dataset. The higher this log-likelihood is for a given model, the better "fit" it has to the data.

The reason for doing this kind of evaluation on a *held-out* dataset is to ensure that the generalization power of the model is the parameter being tested. Otherwise, if we were to evaluate the log-likelihood on the observed data during *learning and initial inference*, we could always create a dummy, not-so-useful model that would give higher log-likelihood than any other model. This dummy model would be created by defining a probability distribution (unconstrained to a specific model family) which assigns probability $1/n$ to each instance in the observed data. Such distribution, however, would not generalize well for complex sample spaces. Still, evaluation of marginal log-likelihood on the training data could be used for other purposes, such as hyperparameter tuning.

1.7 BAYESIAN AND FREQUENTIST PHILOSOPHY (TIP OF THE ICEBERG)

The main difference between the Bayesian approach and the frequentist approach is the interpretation of the concept of "probability." The frequentist view, as its name implies, views probability (of an event) as a number that denotes its "relative frequency" in a large number of repeated identical experiments. The Bayesian view, on the other hand, views probability as a number that denotes our state of knowledge about the event. Within the supporters of Bayesian statistics, there are two camps. Those who view Bayesian probability as an objective, rational measure of the state of knowledge (objectivists), and those who view it as as indication of personal belief (subjectivists). This means that objectivists advocate a rather uniform inference from data between modelers who share the same knowledge about the problem, while subjectivists advocate that this inference may differ and highly depend on personal beliefs.

Both subjectivists and objectivists perform inference by applying Bayes' rule, and inverting the relationship between the data and the hypotheses or the model. Objectivists, however, want to minimize the influence that a person has on the inference process, so that the final conclusions are determined, as much as possible, based on the data. The attempt to minimize this influence is sometimes done by introducing "reference" or non-informative priors, such as Jeffreys prior (Section 3.3.2).

In science, the frequentist approach is associated with the hypothetico-deductive approach. This means that a hypothesis is formed, tested and finally accepted or rejected. The frequentist approach is based on the idea of falsification of a theory, and is conducted through statistical tests, hypothesis testing and other methods which support this idea. The Bayesian approach, on the other hand, is more typically associated with inductive inference. Data is collected, and then we make an update to our beliefs about the theory at hand. Some might argue that the Bayesian approach can also be thought of as hypothetico-deductive (see for example Gelman and Shalizi (2013)). For a discussion of the Bayesian and frequentist philosophy, see Jaynes (2003).

1.8 SUMMARY

In this chapter we described the fundamental concepts for Probability and Statistics required for understanding this book. Some of the concepts we described include:

- Probability measures, probability distributions and sample spaces.

- Random variables (which are functions over the sample space).

- Joint probability distributions (which define a probability distribution over several random variables) and conditional probability distributions (which define a probability distribution over a set of random variables, while permitting clamping for the values of others).

- Independence between random variables (which implies that two sets of random variables are not informative about one another) and conditional independence between random variables (which implies that two sets of random variables are not informative about one another assuming we know the value of a third set of random variables).

- Bayes' rule and the chain rule.

- Expectations (which compute the mean of a function, weighted against a probability distribution).

- Models (which are sets of probability distributions).

- Estimation (identifying a specific member of a model family based on data; most commonly used in the frequentist setting).

- Bayesian statistical inference (which requires the use of Bayes' rule to compute a probability distribution, the posterior, over the parameter space, given observed data).

1.9   EXERCISES

1.1. Let p be a probability measure over Ω and A, B and C three events (subsets of Ω). Using the axioms of probability measures, prove that

$$p(A \cup B \cup C)$$
$$= p(A) + p(B) + p(C) - p(A \cap B) - p(A \cap C) - p(B \cap C) + p(A \cap B \cap C).$$

(This formula can be generalized to an arbitrary number of events, based on the inclusion-exclusion principle.)

1.2. Let Ω be the set of natural numbers. Can you define a probability measure p over Ω such that $p(x) = p(y)$ for any $x, y \in \Omega$? If not, show that such measure does not exist.

1.3. Describe the distribution of two random variables X and Y, such that X and Y are uncorrelated but not independent.

1.4. For a given n, describe n random variables such that any subset of them is independent, but all n random variables together are not.

1.5. Consider the graphical model in Figure 1.1 and its joint distribution in Equation 1.5. Fix $j \in \{1, \ldots, N\}$. Using the definition of conditional independence, show that $W_i^{(j)}$ is conditionally independent of $W_k^{(j)}$ for $k \neq i$ given $Z_i^{(j)}$. In addition, show that $Z_i^{(j)}$ is conditionally independent of $Z_\ell^{(k)}$ for $k \neq j$ and any ℓ, given $\theta^{(j)}$. Is $Z_i^{(j)}$ conditionally independent of $Z_\ell^{(j)}$ given $\theta^{(j)}$ for $\ell \neq i$?

CHAPTER 2

Introduction

Broadly interpreted, Natural Language Processing (NLP) refers to the area in Computer Science that develops tools for processing human languages using a computer. As such, it borrows ideas from Artificial Intelligence, Linguistics, Machine Learning, Formal Language Theory and Statistics. In NLP, natural language is usually represented as written text (as opposed to speech signals, which are more common in the area of Speech Processing).

There is another side to the exploration of natural language using computational means—through the field of Computational Linguistics. The goal of exploring language from this angle is slightly different than that of NLP, as the goal is to use computational means to scientifically understand language, its evolution, acquisition process, history and influence on society. A computational linguist will sometimes find herself trying to answer questions that linguists are attempting to answer, only using automated methods and computational modeling. To a large extent, the study of language can be treated from a computational perspective, since it involves the manipulation of symbols, such as words or characters, similarly to the ways other computational processes work.

Computational Linguistics and NLP overlap to a large extent, especially in regards to the techniques they use to learn and perform inference with data. This is also true with Bayesian methods in these areas. Consequently, we will refer mostly to NLP in this book, though most of the technical descriptions in this book are also relevant to topics explored in Computational Linguistics.

Many of the efforts in modern Natural Language Processing address written text at the sentential level. Machine translation, syntactic parsing (the process of associating a natural language sentence with a grammatical structure), morphological analysis (the process of analyzing the structure of a word and often decompose it into its basic units such as morphemes) and semantic parsing (the process of associating a natural language sentence with a meaning-representation structure) all analyze sentences to return a linguistic structure. Such predicted structures can be used further in a larger natural language application. This book has a similar focus. Most of the Bayesian statistical models and applications we discuss are developed at the sentential level. Still, we will keep the statistical models used more abstract, and will not necessarily commit to defining distributions over sentences or even natural language elements.

Indeed, to give a more diverse view for the reader, this introductory chapter actually discusses a simple model over whole documents, called the "latent Dirichlet allocation" (LDA) model. Not only is this model not defined at the sentential level, it originally was not framed in a Bayesian context. Yet there is a strong motivation behind choosing the LDA model in this introductory chapter. From a technical point of view, the LDA model is simple, but demonstrates most of the fundamental points that repeatedly appear in Bayesian statistical modeling in NLP. We also discuss the version of LDA used now, which is Bayesian.

Before we begin our journey, it is a good idea to include some historical context about the development of Bayesian statistics in NLP and introduce some motivation behind its use. This is the topic of the next section, followed by a section about the LDA model.

2.1 OVERVIEW: WHERE BAYESIAN STATISTICS AND NLP MEET

Bayesian statistics had been an active area of research in statistics for some time before it was introduced to NLP. It has a rich and colorful history that dates back to the 1700s, with seminal ideas introduced by luminaries such as Thomas Bayes and Pierre-Simon Laplace.

NLP, on the other hand, has a shorter history. It dates back perhaps as early as the 1950s, but statistical techniques for NLP in its current form were introduced much later, in the mid 1980s.[1] Early work on statistical analysis of language enabled rich Bayesian NLP literature to emerge a few decades later. In the early days of statistical NLP, most of the data-driven techniques used the frequentist approach, and were based on parameter estimation driven by objective functions such as the log-likelihood, or otherwise some information-theoretic criteria. This seemed to have laid the groundwork for the subtle introduction of Bayesian statistics in the form of Bayesian point estimation (Chapter 4).

Indeed, the earliest use of the Bayesian approach in NLP did not exploit the Bayesian approach to its fullest extent, but rather did so only superficially. This approach was mostly based on maximum *a posteriori* estimation (see Section 4.2.1), in which a Bayesian prior was used as a penalty term added to the log-likelihood in order to bias a point estimate so that it had better predictive power on unseen data. In these cases, the Bayesian approach was more of an additional *interpretation* to an existing frequentist method. Bayesian techniques in NLP were also often referred to at that point, or were implicitly considered to be, smoothing techniques. For example, additive smoothing was heavily used in these early days (see Section 4.2.1).

The more intensive use of Bayesian techniques and Bayesian machinery in NLP started later, around the mid 2000s, in tandem with the increasing popularity of Bayesian methods in the machine learning community. At first, the literature focused on describing how to approach well-known problems in NLP, such as part-of-speech tagging and context-free parsing using the "fully Bayesian approach." At that point, generic models such as hidden Markov models (HMMs) and probabilistic context-free grammars (PCFGs) were mostly used (Goldwater and Griffiths, 2007, Johnson et al., 2007a). Later on, Bayesian models emerged for very specific NLP problems, including Bayesian models for segmentation problems at various lev-

---

[1]The idea of statistical analysis of language had been explored before that by people such as Warren Weaver, Claude Shannon, Victor Yngve, and others, but not in the way and level it has been done in modern NLP.

els of text (Eisenstein and Barzilay, 2008); morphological analysis (Dreyer and Eisner, 2011, Johnson et al., 2007b); multilingual learning (Snyder and Barzilay, 2008, Snyder et al., 2008); machine translation (Blunsom and Cohn, 2010a); syntactic parsing, both supervised (Shindo et al., 2012) and unsupervised (Blunsom and Cohn, 2010b); discourse problems such as entity or event coreference resolution (Bejan et al., 2009, Haghighi and Klein, 2007) and document-level discourse (Chen et al., 2009); and even linguistic discovery (Daume III, 2009, Daume III and Campbell, 2007, Lin et al., 2009).

As mentioned earlier, the focus of this book is models that are developed at the sentential level; these models are the principal part of what we refer to as "Bayesian NLP" in this book. The predictions are usually made with respect to some linguistic structure. However, there has been a significant amount of work done on other kinds of text processing that has developed Bayesian models and machinery. Most notably, the topic modeling community has been making heavy use of Bayesian statistics since the introduction of the latent Dirichlet allocation model (Blei et al., 2003).

Most of the recent efforts to use Bayesian statistics with NLP have focused on the unsupervised learning setting, in which only example inputs are available to the learner, without any examples for the predicted structures. More generally, most models have been developed for use with latent variables. (Unsupervised learning is a specific case of latent variable learning, in which the whole predicted structure is missing during learning or inference.) In the partially supervised setting these latent variables are just used as auxiliary variables to improve model expressivity. "Partially supervised" refers to the case in which annotated data of the same type one wants to predict are available during inference or training, but the model includes additional random variables which are unobserved. Machine translation can be framed in such a setting, with the target and source language sentences available during learning, but not alignment or other structures that link them. A milder version of such latent-variable learning is that of learning PCFGs with latent heads—a full parse tree is given during training, but the states that refine the syntactic categories in the tree are not given (see Chapter 8).

From a technical point of view, there is no reason to abstain from using Bayesian statistics in the supervised learning setting. In fact, most introductory text about Bayesian statistics usually assume complete data are available. Still, in NLP, the use of Bayesian statistics organically developed for scenarios with missing data and latent variables (such as unsupervised learning), likely for the following reasons.

- **Discriminative models generally do better than generative models in the supervised setting.** In the supervised case with complete data available, discriminative models—in which the input to the prediction algorithm is not statistically modeled—usually lead to better performance for a variety of natural language problems. Most frequently, the discriminative setting is used with conditional MaxEnt models (Berger et al., 1996) that have a log-linear form—i.e., the distributions for these models are normalized (to form a probability), exponentiated linear functions of various features extracted from the objects the distributions are defined over. The Bayesian approach in NLP, on the other hand, is inherently generative. The joint distribution is defined over the parameters, over the predicted structure *and* over the inputs as well. However, this comes with a modeling cost. Generative models usually require stating more explicitly what are the independence assumptions that are being made in the model. All interactions between the various components in the model are specified as a graphical model or as a generative story (Section 1.5.3). In the discriminative setting, arbitrary overlapping features are often used.[2]

• **Priors play a much more important role in the unsupervised setting than in the supervised setting.** In the supervised setting, even when the generative case is considered, the log-likeliood function gives a strong signal for the identification of the underlying parameters of the model. In the unsupervised setting, on the other hand, priors (especially those that are structured and incorporate prior knowledge about the domain of the problem) have larger effects on the estimation problem.

• **The parameters of the model in the Bayesian setting already introduce latent variables.** Since the parameters of the model in Bayesian NLP are a random variable that is never observed, it comes more naturally to add other latent variables to the model and perform inference over them as well. This is especially true because of the advanced inference techniques that have been developed in the Bayesian setting with latent variables.

Much of the technical Bayesian machinery developed for NLP relies strongly on recent developments in Statistics and Machine Learning. For example, variational Bayesian inference became popular in the NLP community after it had already been discovered and used in the Statistics and Machine Learning community for some time. The machinery developed in NLP is more specific to scenarios that arise with language, but still includes general machinery for important structured models that can be used outside of NLP.

Bayesian statistics in general has several advantages over the more classic frequentist approach to statistics. First and foremost, the theory behind it is simple. Bayesian statistics provides a principle to combine data with existing information (or prior beliefs) all through a simple application of Bayes' rule. The uncertainty about the choice of model or parameters is all handled through distributions, more specifically, the posterior distribution. Mathematically speaking, the theory is therefore very elegant. Unlike the case with frequentist statistics, Bayesian statistics has a unified approach to handling data both when large and small amounts of data are available.

---

[2]Here, "overlapping features" refers to features that are not easy to describe in a clean generative story—because they contain overlapping information, and therefore together "generate" various parts of the structure or the data multiple times. In principle, there is no issue with specifying generative models with overlapping features or models with complex interaction such as log-linear models that define distribution both over the input and output spaces. However, such generative models are often intractable to work with, because of the normalization constant which requires summing an exponential function both over the input space and the output space. Therefore, general log-linear models are left to the discriminative setting, in which the normalization constant is only required to be computed by summing over the output space for a given point in the input space.

Computationally, we may treat each case differently (because of limited computational power), but the basic principle remains the same.

One of the greatest advantages of using Bayesian statistics in NLP is the ability to introduce a prior distribution that can bias inference to better solutions. For example, it has been shown in various circumstances that different prior distributions can model various properties of natural language, such as the sparsity of word occurrence (i.e., most words in a dictionary occur very few times or not at all in a given corpus), the correlation between refined syntactic categories and the exponential decay of sentence length frequency. However, as is described below and in Chapter 3, the current state of the art in Bayesian NLP does not exploit this degree of freedom to its fullest extent. In addition, nonparametric methods in Bayesian statistics give a principled way to identify appropriate model complexity supported by the data available.

Bayesian statistics also serves as a basis for modeling cognition, and there is some overlap between research in Cognitive Science and NLP, most notably through the proxy of language acquisition research (Doyle and Levy, 2013, Elsner et al., 2013, Frank et al., 2013, 2014, Fullwood and O'Donnell, 2013, Pajak et al., 2013). For example, Bayesian nonparametric models for word segmentation were introduced to the NLP community (Börschinger and Johnson, 2014, Johnson, 2008, Johnson et al., 2010, 2014, Synnaeve et al., 2014) and were also used as models for exploring language acquisition in infants (Goldwater et al., 2006, 2009). For reviews of the use of the Bayesian framework in Cognitive Science see, for example, Griffiths et al. (2008, 2010), Perfors et al. (2011), Tenenbaum et al. (2011).

Bayesian NLP has been flourishing, and its future continues to hold promise. The rich domain of natural language offers a great opportunity to exploit the basic Bayesian principle of encoding into the model prior beliefs about the domain and parameters. Much knowledge about language has been gathered in the linguistics and NLP communities, and using it in a Bayesian context could potentially improve our understanding of natural language and its processing using computers. Still, the exploitation of this knowledge through Bayesian principles in the natural language community has been somewhat limited, and presents a great opportunity to develop this area in that direction. In addition, many problems in machine learning are now approached with a Bayesian perspective in mind; some of this knowledge is being transferred to NLP, with statistical models and inference algorithms being tailored and adapted to its specific problems.

There are various promising directions for Bayesian NLP such as understanding better the nature of prior linguistic knowledge about language that we have, and incorporating it into prior distributions in Bayesian models; using advanced Bayesian inference techniques to scale the use of Bayesian inference in NLP and make it more efficient; and expanding the use of advanced Bayesian nonparametric models (see Section 7.5) to NLP.

2.2   FIRST EXAMPLE: THE LATENT DIRICHLET ALLOCATION MODEL

We begin the technical discussion with an example model for topic modeling: the latent Dirichlet allocation (LDA) model. It demonstrates several technical points that are useful to know when approaching a problem in NLP with Bayesian analysis in mind. The original LDA paper by Blei et al. (2003) also greatly popularized variational inference techniques in Machine Learning and Bayesian NLP, to which Chapter 6 is devoted.

LDA elegantly extends the simplest computational representation for documents—the bag-of-words representation. With the bag-of-words representation, we treat a document as a multiset of words (or potentially as a set as well). This means that we dispose of the order of the words in the document and focus on just their isolated appearance in the text. The words are assumed to originate in a fixed vocabulary that includes all words in all documents (see Zhai and Boyd-Graber (2013) on how to avoid this assumption).

The bag-of-words representation is related to the "unigram language model," which also models sentences by ignoring the order of the words in these sentences.

As mentioned above, with the bag-of-words model, documents can be mathematically represented as multisets. For example, assume there is a set V of words (the vocabulary) with a special symbol $\diamond$, and a text such as[3]:

> Goldman Sachs said Thursday it has adopted all 39 initiatives it proposed to strengthen its business practices in the wake of the 2008 financial crisis, a step designed to help both employees and clients move past one of most challenging chapters in the company's history. $\diamond$

The symbol $\diamond$ terminates the text. All other words in the document must be members of $V \setminus \{\diamond\}$. The mathematical object that describes this document, d, is the multiset $\{w : c\}$, where the notation $w : c$ is used to denote that the word w appears in the document c times. For example, for the above document, *business* : 1 belongs to its corresponding multiset, and so does *both* : 1. A bag of words can have even more extreme representation, in which counts are ignored, and $c = 1$ is used for all words. From a practical perspective, the documents are often preprocessed, so that, for example, function words or extremely common words are removed.

To define a probabilistic model over these multisets, we first assume a probability distribution over V, $p(W|\beta)$. This means that β is a set of parameters for a multinomial distribution such that $p(w|\beta) = \beta_w$. This vocabulary distribution induces a distribution over documents, denoted by the random variable D (a random multiset), as follows:

$$p(D = d|\beta) = \prod_{(w:c)\in d} p(w|\beta)^c = \prod_{(w:c)\in d} (\beta_w)^c. \tag{2.1}$$

---

[3]The text is taken from *The Wall Street Journal Risk and Compliance Journal* and was written by Justin Baer (May 23, 2013).

This bag-of-words model appears in many applications in NLP, but is usually too weak to be used on its own for the purpose of modeling language or documents. The model makes an extreme *independence assumption*—the occurrence of all words in the document are independent of each other. Clearly this assumption is not satisfied by text because there are words that tend to co-occur. A document about soccer will tend to use the word "goal" in tandem with "player" and "ball," while a document about U.S. politics will tend to use words such as "presidential," "senator" and "bill." This means that the appearance of the word "presidential" in a document gives us a lot of information about what other words may appear in the document, and therefore the independence assumption that bag-of-words models make fails. In fact, this extreme independence assumption does not even capture the most intuitive notion of word repetition in a document—actual content words—especially words denoting entities, which are more likely to appear later in a document if they already appeared earlier in the document.

There is no single remedy to this strict independence assumption that the bag-of-words model makes. The rich literature of document modeling is not the focus of this book, but many of the current models for document modeling are subject to the following principle, devised in the late 1990s. A set of "topics" is defined. Each word is associated with a topic, and this association can be made probabilistic or crisp. It is also not mutually exclusive—words can belong to various topics with different degrees of association. In an inference step, given a set of documents, each document is associated with a set of topics, which are being learned from the data. Given that the topics are learned automatically, they are not labeled by the model (though they could be in a post-processing step after inference with the topic model), but the hope is to discover topics such as "soccer" (to which the word "goal" would have strong association, for example) or "politics." Topics are discovered by assembling a collection of words for each topic, with a corresponding likelihood for being associated with that topic.

This area of topic modeling has flourished in the recent decade with the introduction of the latent Dirichlet allocation model (Blei et al., 2003). The idea behind the latent Dirichlet allocation model is extremely intuitive and appealing, and it builds on previous work for modeling documents, such as the work by Hofmann (1999b). There are K topics in the model. Each topic $z \in \{1, \ldots, K\}$ is associated with a conditional probability distribution over V, $p(w \mid z) = \beta_{z,w}$. ($\beta_z$ is the multinomial distribution over V for topic z). LDA then draws a document d in three phases (conditioned on a fixed number of words to be sampled for the document, denoted by N) using generative story 2.1.[4]

LDA weakens the independence assumption made by the bag-of-words model in Equation 2.1: the words are not completely independent of each other, but are independent of each other given their *topic*. First, a distribution over topics (for the entire document) is generated.

---

[4]To make the LDA model description complete, there is a need to draw the number of words N in the document, so the LDA model can generate documents of variable length. In Blei's et al. paper, the number of words in the document is drawn from a Poission distribution with some rate λ. It is common to omit this in LDA's description, since the document is assumed to be observed, and as a result, the number of words is known during inference. Therefore, it is not necessary to model N probabilistically.

Constants: K, N integers
Parameters: β
Latent variables: θ, z_i for $i \in \{1, \ldots, N\}$
Observed variables: $w_1, \ldots, w_N$ (d)

- -

- Draw a multinomial distribution θ over $\{1, \ldots, K\}$. ($\theta \in \mathbb{R}^K$, $\theta_i \geq 0$ for $i \in \{1, \ldots, K\}$, $\sum_{i=1}^{K} \theta_i = 1$).

- Draw a topic $z_i \sim \text{Multinomial}(\theta)$ for $i \in \{1, \ldots, N\}$ ($z_i \in \{1, \ldots, K\}$).

- Draw a word $w_i \sim \text{Multinomial}(\beta_{z_i})$ for $i \in \{1, \ldots, N\}$ ($w_i \in V$).

- The document d consists of the multiset generated from $w_1, \ldots, w_N$:

$$d = \{w : c \mid w \in V, c = \sum_{j=1}^{N} I(w_j = w)\},$$

where $I(\gamma)$ is 1 if proposition γ is true and 0 otherwise.

Generative Story 2.1: The generative story for the latent Dirichlet allocation model. Figure 1.1 gives a graphical model description for the LDA. The generative model here assumes $M = 1$ when compared to the graphical model in Figure 1.1 (i.e., the model here generates a single document). An outer loop is required to generate multiple documents. The distribution over θ is not specified in the above, but with LDA it is drawn from the Dirichlet distribution.

Second, a list of topics for each word in the document is generated. Third, each word is generated according to a multinomial distribution associated with the topic of that word index.

Consider line 1 in the description of the LDA generative model (generative story 2.1). The distribution from which θ is drawn is not specified. In order to complete the description of the LDA, we need to choose a "distribution over multinomial distributions" such that we can draw from it a topic distribution. Each instance θ is a multinomial distribution with $\theta_z \geq 0$ and $\sum_{z=1}^{K} \theta_z = 1$. Therefore, we need to find a distribution over the set

$$\left\{ \theta \mid \forall z \, \theta_z \geq 0 \ , \sum_{z=1}^{K} \theta_z = 1 \right\}.$$

LDA uses the *Dirichlet* distribution for defining a distribution over this probability simplex.[5] This means that the distribution over θ is defined as follows:

$$p(\theta_1, \ldots, \theta_K | \alpha_1, \ldots, \alpha_K) = C(\alpha) \prod_{k=1}^{K} \theta_k^{\alpha_k - 1}, \tag{2.2}$$

where the function $C(\alpha)$ is defined in Section 2.2.1 (Equation 2.3, see also Appendix B), and serves as the normalization constant of the Dirichlet distribution.

The Dirichlet distribution depends on K *hyperparameters*, $\alpha_1, \ldots, \alpha_K$, which can be denoted using a vector $\alpha \in \mathbb{R}^K$. It is notationally convenient to denote the Dirichlet distribution then by $p(\theta_1, \ldots, \theta_K \mid \alpha)$ to make this dependence explicit. This does not imply that α itself is a random variable or event that we condition on, but instead is a set of parameters that determines the behavior of the specific instance of the Dirichlet distribution (see note about this notation in Section 1.5.5).

The reason for preferring the Dirichlet distribution is detailed in Chapter 3, when the notion of conjugacy is introduced. For now, it is sufficient to say that the choice of the Dirichlet distribution is natural because it makes *inference* with LDA much easier—drawing a multinomial from a Dirichlet distribution and then subsequently drawing a topic from this multinomial is mathematically and computationally convenient. The Dirichlet distribution has other desirable properties which are a good fit for modeling language, such as encouraging sparse multinomial distributions with a specific choice of hyperparameters (see Section 3.2.1).

Natural language processing models are often constructed using multinomial distributions as the basic building blocks for the generated structure. This includes parse trees, alignments, dependency trees and others. These multinomial distributions compose the *parameters* of the model. For example, the parameters of a probabilistic context-free grammar (see Chapter 8) are a set of multinomial distributions for generating the right-hand side of a rule conditioned on the left-hand side.

One of the core technical ideas in the Bayesian approach is that the parameters are considered to be random variables as well, and therefore the generative process draws values for these model parameters. It is not surprising, therefore, that the combination of convenience in inference with Dirichlet-multinomial models and the prevalence of multinomial distributions in generative NLP models yields a common and focused use of the Dirichlet distribution in Bayesian NLP.

There is one subtle dissimilarity between the way the Dirichlet distribution is used in Bayesian NLP and the way it was originally defined in the LDA. The topic distribution θ in LDA does not represent the *parameters* of the LDA model. The only parameters in LDA are the topic multinomials β_k for $k \in \{1, \ldots, K\}$. The topic distribution θ is an integral part of

---

[5]A K-dimensional simplex is a K-dimensional polytope, i.e., the convex hull of $K + 1$ vertices. The vertices that define a *probability simplex* are the basis vectors e_i for $i \in \{1, \ldots, K\}$ where $e_i \in \mathbb{R}^k$ is a vector such that it is 0 everywhere. but is 1 in the ith coordinate.

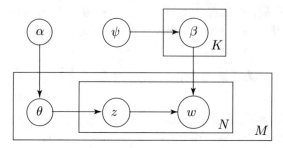

Figure 2.1: The fully Bayesian version of the latent Dirichlet allocation model. A prior over β is added (and β now are random variables). Most commonly, this prior is a (symmetric) Dirichlet distribution with hyperparameter ψ.

the model, and is drawn separately for each document. To turn LDA into a Bayesian model, one should draw β from a Dirichlet distribution (or another distribution). This is indeed now a common practice with LDA (Steyvers and Griffiths, 2007). A graphical model for this fully Bayesian LDA model is given in Figure 2.1.

Since the Dirichlet distribution is so central to Bayesian NLP, the next section is dedicated to an exploration of its basic properties. We will also re-visit the Dirichlet distribution in Chapter 3.

2.2.1 THE DIRICHLET DISTRIBUTION

The Dirichlet distribution is a multivariate distribution over the probability simplex of a fixed dimension. This means it defines a distribution over K continuous random variables, $0 \le \theta_k \le 1$ for $k \in \{1, \ldots, K\}$ such that:

$$\sum_{k=1}^{K} \theta_k = 1.$$

Its probability density depends on K positive real values, $\alpha_1, \ldots, \alpha_K$. The PDF appears in Equation 2.2 where $C(\alpha)$ is a normalization constant defined as:

$$C(\alpha) = \frac{\Gamma(\sum_{k=1}^{K} \alpha_k)}{\Gamma(\alpha_1) \ldots \Gamma(\alpha_K)}, \tag{2.3}$$

with $\Gamma(x)$ being the Gamma function for $x \ge 0$ (see also Appendix B)—a generalization of the factorial function such that whenever x is natural number it holds that $\Gamma(x) = (x - 1)!$.

Vectors in the "probability simplex," as the name implies, can be treated as probability distributions over a finite set of size K. This happens above, with LDA, where θ is treated as a probability distribution over the K topics (each topic is associated with one of the K dimensions of the probability simplex), and used to draw topics for each word in the document.

Naturally, the first and second moments of the Dirichlet distribution depend on α. When denoting $\alpha^* = \sum_{k=1}^{K} \alpha_k$, it holds that:

$$E[\theta_k] = \frac{\alpha_k}{\alpha^*},$$
$$\text{var}(\theta_k) = \frac{\alpha_k(\alpha^* - \alpha_k)}{(\alpha^*)^2(\alpha^* + 1)},$$
$$\text{Cov}(\theta_j, \theta_k) = -\frac{\alpha_j \alpha_k}{(\alpha^*)^2(\alpha^* + 1)}.$$

The mode[6] of the Dirichlet distribution (when $\alpha_k > 1$ for all k) is

$$\text{mode}(\theta_k) = \frac{\alpha_k - 1}{\alpha^* - K}.$$

The mode is not defined if any $\alpha_k < 1$, since in that case, the density of the Dirichlet distribution is potentially unbounded.

The Beta Distribution   In the special case where $K = 2$, the Dirichlet distribution is also called the Beta distribution, and has the following density:

$$p(\theta_1, \theta_2 \mid \alpha_1, \alpha_2) = \frac{\Gamma(\alpha_1 + \alpha_2)}{\Gamma(\alpha_1)\Gamma(\alpha_2)} \theta_1^{\alpha_1 - 1} \theta_2^{\alpha_2 - 1}.$$

Since $\theta_1 + \theta_2 = 1$, the Beta distribution can be described as a univariate distribution over $\theta' \in [0, 1]$:

$$p(\theta' \mid \alpha_1, \alpha_2) = \frac{\Gamma(\alpha_1 + \alpha_2)}{\Gamma(\alpha_1)\Gamma(\alpha_2)} (\theta')^{\alpha_1 - 1} (1 - \theta')^{\alpha_2 - 1}. \tag{2.4}$$

Symmetric Dirichlet   It is often the case that instead of using K different parameters, the Dirichlet distribution is used with α such that $\alpha_1 = \alpha_2 = \ldots = \alpha_K = \alpha' \in \mathbb{R}^+$. In this case, the Dirichlet distribution is also called a symmetric Dirichlet distribution. The α' hyperparameter is called the *concentration hyperparameter*.

The reason for collapsing $\alpha_1, \ldots, \alpha_K$ into a single parameter is two-fold: (i) this considerably simplifies the distribution, and makes it easier to tackle learning, and (ii) *a priori*, if latent variables exist in the model, and they are drawn from a multinomial (which is drawn from a Dirichlet distribution), it is often the case that the role of various events in the multinomial are interchangeable. This is the case, for example, with the LDA model. Since only the text is observed in the data (without either the topic distribution or the topics associated with each word), the role of the K topics can be permuted. If $\alpha_1, \ldots, \alpha_K$ are not estimated by the learning algorithm, but instead clamped at a certain value, it makes sense to keep the role of α_k symmetric by using a symmetric Dirichlet.

---

[6]The mode of a probability distribution is the most likely value according to that distribution. It is the value(s) at which the PMF or PDF obtain their maximal value.

Parameters: θ
Latent variables: Z (and also θ)
Observed variables: X

- -

- Draw a set of parameters θ from $p(\theta)$.

- Draw a latent structure z from $p(z|\theta)$.

- Draw the observed data x from $p(x|z, \theta)$.

Generative Story 2.2: The generative story for a Bayesian model.

Figure 2.2 plots the density in Equation 2.4 when $\alpha_1 = \alpha_2 = \alpha' \in \mathbb{R}$ for several values of α', and demonstrates the choice of the name "concentration parameter" for α'. The closer α' is to 0, the more sparse the distribution is, with most of the mass concentrated on near-zero probability. The larger α' is, the more *concentrated* the distribution around its mean value. Since the figure describes a symmetric Beta distribution, the mean value is 0.5 for all values of α'. When $\alpha' = 1$, the distribution is uniform.

The fact that small values for α' make the Dirichlet distribution sparse is frequently exploited in the NLP Bayesian literature. This point is discussed at greater length in Section 3.2.1. It is also demonstrated in Figure 2.3.

2.2.2   INFERENCE

As was briefly mentioned earlier, in topic modeling the topics are considered to be latent. While datasets exist in which documents are associated with various human-annotated topics, the vast majority of document collections do not have such an annotation—certainly not in the style of the LDA model, where each word has some degree of association with each topic. In fact, asking an annotator to annotate topics the way they are defined in an LDA-style topic model is probably an ill-defined task because these topics are often not crisp or fully interpretable in their word association (see Chang et al. (2009) for a study on human interpretation of topic models; also see Mimno et al. (2011) and Newman et al. (2010) for automatic topic coherence evaluation). For LDA, this means that the distribution over topics, θ, and the topic identity for each word are *latent variables*—they are never observed in the data, which are just pure text.

This is typical in Bayesian NLP as well. Usually, there is a random variable X (a document or a sentence, for example) which is associated with a predicted structure, denoted by a random variable Z. The generation of X and Z is governed by some distribution parametrized by θ. The parameters θ themselves are a random variable that is governed, for example, by the Dirichlet

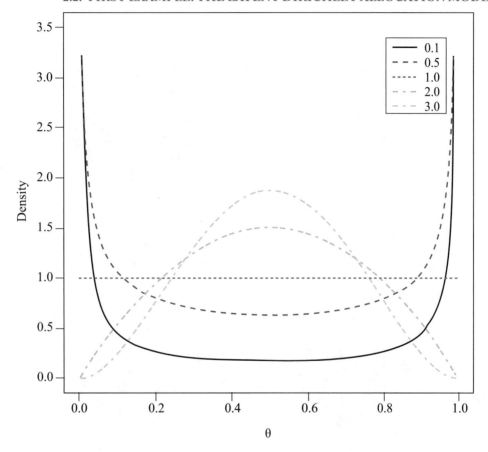

Figure 2.2: The Beta distribution density function when $\alpha_1 = \alpha_2 = \alpha'$ for $\alpha' \in \{0.1, 0.5, 1, 2, 3\}$.

distribution, or more generally by a distribution $p(\theta)$. This distribution is also called *the prior distribution*. Generative story 2.2 describes this process.

There is a striking similarity to the LDA generative process, where the topic distribution plays the role of the set of parameters, the topic assignments play the role of the latent structure, and the words in the document play the role of the observed data.

The generative process above dictates the following *joint* probability distribution $p(X, Z, \theta)$:

$$p(x, z, \theta) = p(\theta)p(z \mid \theta)p(x \mid \theta, z).$$

The goal of Bayesian inference is naturally to either infer the latent structure z (or a distribution over it), or infer the parameters θ (or a distribution over them). More generally, the goal of Bayesian inference is to obtain the *posterior distribution* over the non-observed random

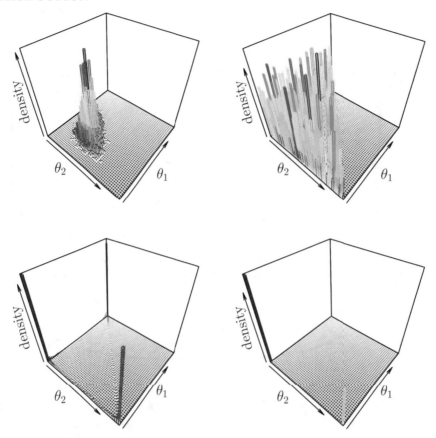

Figure 2.3: A plot of sampled data from the symmetric Dirichlet distribution with $K = 3$, with various α. Top-left: $\alpha = 10$, top-right: $\alpha = 1$, bottom-left: $\alpha = 0.1$, bottom-right: $\alpha = 0.01$. The plot demonstrates that for $\alpha < 1$, the Dirichlet distribution is centered on points in the probability simplex which are sparse. For the value $\alpha = 1$, the probability distribution should be uniform.

variables in the model, given the observed data x. For the general Bayesian model above, the posterior is $p(Z, \theta | x)$.

Note that the predictions are managed through distributions (such as the posterior) and not through fixed values. Bayesian inference, at its basic level, does not commit to a single z or θ. (However, it is often the case that we are interested in a point estimate for the parameters, see Chapter 4, and even more often—a fixed value for the predicted structure.)

To identify this posterior, Bayesian statistics exploits the treatment of θ as a random variable through a basic application of Bayes' rule. More specifically, the posterior is identified as:

$$p(z, \theta \mid x) = \frac{p(\theta)p(z \mid \theta)p(x \mid z, \theta)}{p(x)}. \tag{2.5}$$

The quantity $p(x)$ acts as a *marginalization constant* that ensures that the probability in Equation 2.5 integrates (and sums) to one. Therefore, assuming θ is continuous, as is usually the case, the following holds:

$$p(x) = \int_{\theta} p(\theta) \left(\sum_{z} p(z \mid \theta)p(x \mid z, \theta) \right) d\theta. \tag{2.6}$$

Mathematically, Bayesian inference is easy and elegant. It requires inverting the conditional distributions of $p(x, z, \theta)$ using Bayes' rule so that the posterior is computed. All of the quantities in Equation 2.5 are theoretically known. There is only the need to rely on the simplest, most basic results from probability theory.

Still, Bayesian inference is not always trivial to implement or to computationally execute. The main challenge is computing the marginalization constant (Equation 2.6), which is required to make the predictions. The marginalization constant requires summing over a discrete (possibly infinite) set and integrating over a continuous set. This is often intractable, but prior conjugacy can alleviate this problem (Chapter 3). Even when only one of these marginalizations is required (such as the case with variational inference, see Chapter 6), inference can still be complex.

This intractability is often overcome by using approximate inference methods, such as *Markov chain Monte Carlo* methods or *variational inference*. These are discussed in Chapters 5 and 6, respectively.

2.2.3   SUMMARY

The core ideas in LDA modeling and inference have striking similarities to some of the principles used in Bayesian NLP. Most notably, the use of the Dirichlet distribution to define multinomial distributions is common in both.

LDA requires inferring a posterior over topic assignments for each word in each document and the distribution over topics for each document. These are the two latent variables in the LDA model. Analogously, in Bayesian NLP, we often require inferring a latent structure (such as a parse tree or a sequence) and the parameters of the model.

Inference of the kind described in this chapter, with LDA, with Bayesian models and more generally, with generative models, can be thought of as the reverse-engineering of a generative device, that is the underlying model. The model is a device that continuously generates samples of data, of which we see only a subset of the final output that is generated by this device. In the case of LDA, the device generates raw text as output. Inference works backward, trying to identify the missing values (topic distributions and the topic themselves) that were used to generate this text.

2.3   SECOND EXAMPLE: BAYESIAN TEXT REGRESSION

Even though Bayesian NLP has focused mostly on unsupervised learning, Bayesian inference in general is not limited to learning from incomplete data. It is also often used for prediction problems such as classification and regression where the training examples include both the inputs and the outputs of the model.

In this section, we demonstrate Bayesian learning in the case of text regression, predicting a continuous value based on a body of text. We will continue to use the notation from Section 2.2 and denote a document by d, as a set of words and word count pairs. In addition, we will assume some continuous value that needs to be predicted, denoted by the random variable Y. To ground the example, D can be a movie review, and Y can be a predicted average number of stars the movie received by critics or its revenue (Joshi et al., 2010). The prediction problem is therefore to predict the number of stars a movie receives from the movie review text.

One possible way to frame this prediction problem is as a Bayesian linear regression problem. This means we assume that we receive as input for the inference algorithm a set of examples $\left(d^{(i)}, y^{(i)}\right)$ for $i \in \{1, \ldots, n\}$. We assume a function $f(d)$ that maps a document to a vector in $\mathbb{R}^K$. This is the feature function that summarizes the information in the document as a vector, and on which the final predictions are based. For example, K could be the size of the vocabulary that the documents span, and $[f(d)]_j$ could be the count of the jth word in the vocabulary in document d.

A linear regression model typically assumes that there is a stochastic relationship between Y and d:

$$Y = \theta \cdot f(d) + \epsilon,$$

where $\theta \in \mathbb{R}^K$ is a set of parameters for the linear regression model and ϵ is a noise term (with zero mean), most often framed as a Gaussian variable with variance σ^2. For the sake of simplicity, we assume for now that σ^2 is known, and we need not make any inference about it. As a result, the learning problem becomes an inference problem about θ.

As mentioned above, ϵ is assumed to be a Gaussian variable under the model, and as such Y itself is a Gaussian with mean value $\theta \cdot f(d)$ for any fixed θ and document d. The variance of Y is σ^2.

In Bayesian linear regression, we assume a prior on θ, a distribution $p(\theta|\alpha)$. Consequently, the joint distribution over θ and $Y^{(i)}$ is:

$$p\left(\theta, Y^{(1)} = y^{(1)}, \ldots, Y^{(n)} = y^{(n)} \mid d^{(1)}, \ldots, d^{(n)}, \alpha\right) = p\left(\theta \mid \alpha\right) \prod_{i=1}^{n} p\left(Y^{(i)} = y^{(i)} \mid \theta, d^{(i)}\right).$$

In this case, Bayesian inference will use Bayes' rule to find a probability distribution over θ conditioned on the data, $y^{(i)}$ and $d^{(i)}$ for $i \in \{1, \ldots, n\}$. It can be shown that if we choose a conjugate prior to the likelihood over $Y^{(i)}$, which in this case is also a normal distribution, then the distribution $p\left(\theta \mid y^{(1)}, \ldots, y^{(n)}, d^{(1)}, \ldots, d^{(n)}\right)$ is also a normal distribution.

This conjugacy between the normal distribution and itself is demonstrated in more detail in Chapter 3. Also see exercise 6 in this chapter. There are two natural extensions to the scenario described above. One in which $Y^{(i)}$ are multivariate, i.e., $y^{(i)} \in \mathbb{R}^M$. In that case, θ is a matrix in $\mathbb{R}^{M \times K}$. The other extension is one in which the variance σ^2 (or the covariance matrix controlling the likelihood and the prior, in the multivariate case) is unknown. Full derivations of Bayesian linear regression for these two cases are given by Minka (2000).

2.4   CONCLUSION AND SUMMARY

Earlier use of Bayesian statistics in NLP mostly relied on Bayesian point estimation. See Chapter 4 for a survey of techniques to obtain a point estimate in the Bayesian setting. Modern use of Bayesian statistics in NLP makes use of both the theoretical and technical machinery that is available and has been recently developed in the statistics and machine learning communities. Bayesian machinery specifically tailored for NLP models, such as PCFGs or HMMs, is also sometimes described. See Chapter 8.

Beyond NLP, from a practical point of view, both the classic frequentist methods and the Bayesian methods have advantages and disadvantages. Bayesian inference gives a natural and principled way of combining prior beliefs with data, through Bayes' rule. Inference means inferring a posterior distribution, which in turn can be used as a prior when new data is available; it also provides interpretable results (for example, with Bayesian confidence intervals). Conceptually, the Bayesian approach also provides inference that depends on the data and is exact. However, sometimes it is computationally intractable to perform this kind of inference, and approximation methods must be used. The Bayesian approach also relies on a selection of a prior distribution, but does not instruct on exactly how it should be chosen. For a thorough discussion of the advantages and disadvantages in Bayesian analysis, see, for example Berger (1985).

2.5   EXERCISES

2.1. Consider the generative story below.

Can the posterior $p\left(Z^{(1)}, \ldots, Z^{(n)}, \theta | x^{(1)}, \ldots, x^{(n-1)}\right)$ be analytically identified? If so, write down its expression.

Constants: n integer
Hyperparameters: $\alpha > 0$
Latent variables: $Z^{(1)}, \ldots, Z^{(n)}$
Observed variables: $X^{(1)}, \ldots, X^{(n)}$

- -

- Draw a multinomial θ of size two from a symmetric Beta distribution with hyperparameter $\alpha > 0$.

- Draw $z^{(1)}, \ldots, z^{(n)}$ from the multinomial θ where $z^{(i)} \in \{0, 1\}$.

- Set $n - 1$ binary random variables $x^{(1)}, \ldots, x^{(n-1)}$ such that $x^{(i)} = z^{(i)} z^{(i+1)}$.

2.2. Consider the graphical model for Bayesian LDA (Figure 2.1). Write down an expression for the joint distribution over the *observed* variables (the words in the document). (Use the Dirichlet distribution for the topic distributions.)

2.3. Alice has a biased coin that lands more often on "tails" than "heads." She is interested in placing a symmetric Beta prior over this coin with hyperparameter α. A draw θ from this Beta distribution will denote the probability of tails. ($1 - \theta$ is the probability of heads.) What range of values for α complies with Alice's knowledge of the coin's unfairness?

2.4. As mentioned in this chapter, choosing a hyperparameter $\alpha < 1$ with the symmetric Dirichlet encourages sparse draws from the Dirichlet. What are some properties of natural language that you believe are useful to mathematically model using such sparse prior distribution?

2.5. The LDA model assumes independence between the topics being drawn for each word in the document. Can you describe the generative story and the joint probability distribution for a model that assumes a bigram-like distribution of topics? This means that each topic $Z^{(i)}$ depends on $Z^{(i-1)}$. In what scenarios is this model more sensible for document modeling? Why?

2.6. Complete the details of the example in Section 2.3. More specifically, find the posterior over θ given $y^{(i)}$ and $d^{(i)}$ for $i \in \{1, \ldots, n\}$, assuming the prior over $p(\theta \mid \mu, \lambda^2)$ is a normal distribution with mean μ and variance λ^2.

CHAPTER 3

Priors

Priors are a basic component in Bayesian modeling. The concept of priors and some of their mechanics must be introduced quite early in order to introduce the machinery used in Bayesian NLP. At their core, priors are distributions over a set of hypotheses, or when dealing with parametric model families, over a set of parameters. In essence, the prior distribution represents the prior beliefs that the modeler has about the identity of the parameters from which data is generated, *before* observing any data.

One of the criticisms of Bayesian statistics is that it lacks objectivity in the sense that different prior families will lead to different inference based on the available data, especially when only small amounts of data are available. There are circumstances in which such a view is justified (for example, the Food and Drug Administration held this criticism against the Bayesian approach for some time (Feinberg, 2011); the FDA has since made use of Bayesian statistics in certain circumstances), but this lack of objectivity is less of a problem in solving engineering problems than in natural language processing. In NLP, the final "test" for the quality of a model (or decoder, to be more precise) that predicts a linguistic structure given some input such as a sentence, often uses an evaluation metric that is not directly encoded in the statistical model. The existence of a precise evaluation metric, coupled with the use of unseen data (in the supervised case; in the unsupervised case, either the unseen data or the data on which inference is performed can be used) to calculate this evaluation metric eliminates the concern of subjectivity.

In fact, the additional degree of freedom in Bayesian modeling, the prior distribution, can be a great advantage in NLP. The modeler can choose a prior that biases the inference and learning in such a way that the evaluation metric is maximized. This is not necessarily done directly as a mathematical optimization problem, but through experimentation.

This point has been exploited consistently in the Bayesian NLP literature, where priors are chosen because they exhibit certain useful properties that are found in natural language. In the right setting, the Dirichlet distribution is often shown to lead to sparse solutions (see Chapter 2). The logistic normal distribution, on the other hand, can capture relationships between the various parameters of a multinomial distribution. Other hand-crafted priors have also been used, mirroring a specific property of language.

This chapter covers the main types of priors that are used in Bayesian NLP. As such, it discusses conjugate priors at length (Section 3.1) and specifically focuses on the Dirichlet distribution (Section 3.2.1). The discussion of the Dirichlet distribution is done in the context of priors over multinomials (Section 3.2), as the multinomial distribution is the main modeling workhorse in Bayesian NLP.

3.1   CONJUGATE PRIORS

Basic inference in the Bayesian setting requires computation of the posterior distribution (Chapter 2)—the distribution over the model parameters which is obtained by integrating the information from the prior distribution together with the observed data. Without exercising caution, and putting restrictions on the prior distribution or the likelihood function, this inference can be intractable. When performing inference with incomplete data (with latent variables), this issue becomes even more severe. In this case, the posterior distribution is defined over both of the parameters and the latent variables.

Conjugate priors eliminate this potential intractability when no latent variables exist, and also help to a large extent when latent variables do exist in the model. A prior family is conjugate to a likelihood if the posterior, obtained as a calculation of

$$posterior = \frac{prior \times likelihood}{evidence},$$

is also a member of the prior family.

We now describe this idea in more detail. We begin by describing the use of conjugate priors in the case of having empirical observations for all random variables in the model (i.e., without having any latent variables). Let $p(\theta \mid \alpha)$ be some prior with *hyperparameters* α. The hyperparameters by themselves are parameters—only instead of parametrizing the likelihood function, they parametrize the prior. They can be fixed and known, or be inferred. We assume the hyperparameters are taken from a set of hyperparameters A. In addition, let $p(X \mid \theta)$ be a distribution function for the likelihood of the observed data. We observe an instance of the random variable $X = x$. Posterior inference here means we need to identify the distribution $p(\theta|x)$. We say that the prior family $p(\theta|\alpha)$ is a *a conjugate prior* with respect to the likelihood $p(X \mid \theta)$ if the following holds for the posterior:

$$p(\theta \mid x, \alpha) = p(\theta \mid \alpha'),$$

for some $\alpha' = \alpha'(x, \alpha) \in A$. Note that α' is a function of the observation x and α, the hyperparameter with which we begin the inference. (This means that in order to compute the posterior, we need to be able to compute the function $\alpha'(x, \alpha)$.)

The mathematical definition of conjugate priors does not immediately shed light on why they make Bayesian inference more tractable. In fact, according to the deinfition above, the use of a conjugate prior does not *guarantee* computational tractability. Conjugate priors are useful when the function $\alpha'(x, \alpha)$ can be efficiently computed, and indeed this is often the case when conjugate priors are used in practice.

When $\alpha'(x, \alpha)$ can be efficiently computed, inference with the Bayesian approach is considerably simplified. As mentioned above, to compute the posterior over the parameters, all we need to do is compute $\alpha'(x, \alpha)$, and this introduces a new set of hyperparameters that define the posterior.

The following example demonstrates this idea about conjugate priors for normal variables. In this example, contrary to our persistent treatment of the variable X as a discrete variable up to this point, X is set to be a continuous variable. This is done to demonstrate the idea of conjugacy with a relatively simple, well-known example—the conjugacy of the normal distribution to itself (with respect to the mean value parameters).

Example 3.1

Let X be drawn from a normal distribution with expected value θ and *fixed* known variance σ^2 (it is neither a parameter nor hyperparameter), i.e., the density of X for a point x is:

$$p(x \mid \theta) = \frac{1}{\sigma\sqrt{2\pi}} \exp\left(-\frac{1}{2}\left(\frac{x-\theta}{\sigma}\right)^2\right).$$

In addition, θ is drawn from a prior family that is also Gaussian, controlled by the hyperparameter set $A = \mathbb{R} \times \mathbb{R}^+$ where every $\alpha \in A$ is a pair (μ, λ^2). The value of μ denotes the expected value of the prior and the value of λ^2 denotes the variance. Assume we begin inference with a prior such that $\mu \in \mathbb{R}$ and $\lambda^2 = \sigma^2$—i.e., we assume the variance of the prior is identical to the variance in the likelihood. (This is assumed for the simplicity of the posterior derivation, but it is not necessary to follow this assumption to get a similar derivation when the variances are not identical.) The prior, therefore, is:

$$p(\theta \mid \alpha) = \frac{1}{\sigma\sqrt{2\pi}} \exp\left(-\frac{1}{2}\left(\frac{\theta-\mu}{\sigma}\right)^2\right).$$

Assume a single observation x is observed, based on which the likelihood function is formed. The quantity of interest is the posterior distribution $p(\theta|x, \alpha)$. Bayesian inference dictates that it has the following form:

$$p(\theta|x, \alpha) = \frac{p(\theta \mid \alpha)p(x|\theta)}{\int_\theta p(\theta \mid \alpha)p(x|\theta)d\theta}. \tag{3.1}$$

The numerator equals:

$$p(\theta \mid \alpha)p(x|\theta) = \left(\frac{1}{\sigma\sqrt{2\pi}}\exp\left(-\frac{1}{2}\left(\frac{x-\theta}{\sigma}\right)^2\right)\right) \times \left(\frac{1}{\sigma\sqrt{2\pi}}\exp\left(-\frac{1}{2}\left(\frac{\theta-\mu}{\sigma}\right)^2\right)\right)$$

$$= \frac{1}{2\pi\sigma^2}\exp\left(-\frac{1}{2}\left(\frac{(x-\theta)^2+(\theta-\mu)^2}{\sigma^2}\right)\right). \tag{3.2}$$

Algebraic manipulation shows that:

$$(x-\theta)^2 + (\theta-\mu)^2 = \frac{\left(\theta-\frac{x+\mu}{2}\right)^2 + \frac{1}{2}(x-\mu)^2}{1/2}.$$

The term $\frac{1}{2}(x-\mu)^2$ does not depend on θ, and therefore it will cancel from both the numerator and the denominator. It can be taken out of the integral in the denominator. (We therefore do not include it in the equation below.) Then, Equation 3.1 can be rewritten as:

$$p(\theta|x,\alpha) = \frac{p(\theta \mid \alpha)p(x|\theta)}{\int_\theta p(\theta \mid \alpha)p(x|\theta)d\theta} = \frac{\exp\left(-\frac{\left(\theta-\frac{x+\mu}{2}\right)^2}{\sigma^2/2}\right)}{C(x,\alpha)}. \tag{3.3}$$

The term in the denominator,

$$C(x,\alpha) = \int_\theta \exp\left(-\frac{\left(\theta-\frac{x+\mu}{2}\right)^2}{\sigma^2/2}\right)d\theta,$$

is a normalization constant that ensures that $p(\theta|x,\alpha)$ integrates to 1 over θ. Since the numerator of Equation 3.3 has the form of a normal distribution with mean value $\frac{x+\mu}{2}$ and variance $\sigma^2/2$, this means that Equation 3.3 is actually the density of a normal distribution such that $\alpha'(x,\alpha) = \left(\frac{x+\mu}{2}, \frac{\sigma}{\sqrt{2}}\right)$, where μ and σ^2 are defined by α. See Appendix A for further detail. The normalization constant can easily be derived from the density of the normal distribution with these specific hyperparameters.

The conclusion from this example is that the family of prior distributions $\{p(\theta|\alpha)|\alpha = (\mu, \sigma^2) \in \mathbb{R} \times (0, \infty)\}$ is conjugate to the normally distributed likelihood with a fixed variance (i.e., the likelihood is parametrized only by the mean value of the normal distribution).

In a general case, with $\alpha = (\mu, \sigma_0)$ (i.e., $\theta \sim \text{Normal}(\mu, \sigma_0^2)$ and n observations being identically distributed (and independent given θ) with $X^{(i)} \sim \text{Normal}(\theta, \sigma^2)$), it holds that:

$$\alpha'\left(x^{(1)}, \ldots, x^{(n)}, \alpha\right) = \left(\frac{\mu + \sum_{i=1}^{n} x^{(i)}}{n+1}, \sqrt{(1/\sigma_0^2 + n/\sigma^2)^{-1}}\right), \tag{3.4}$$

i.e., the posterior distribution is a normal distribution with a mean and a variance as specified in Equation 3.4. Note that full knowledge of the likelihood variance is assumed both in the example and in the extension above. This means that the prior is defined only over θ and not σ. When the variances are not known (or more generally, when the covariance matrices of a multivariate normal variable are not known) and are actually drawn from a prior as well, more care is required in defining a conjugate prior for the variance (more specifically, the *Inverse-Wishart* distribution would be the conjugate prior in this case defined over the covariance matrix space).

Example 3.1 and Equation 3.4 demonstrate a recurring point with conjugate priors and their corresponding posteriors. In many cases, the hyperparameters α take the role of "pseudo-observations" in the function $\alpha'(x, \alpha)$. As described in Equation 3.4, μ is added to the sum of the rest of the observations and then averaged together with them. Hence, this hyperparameter functions as an additional observation with value μ which is taken into account in the posterior.

To avoid confusion, it is worth noting that both the prior and the likelihood were normal in this example of conjugacy, but usually conjugate prior and likelihood are not members of the same family of distributions. With Gaussian likelihood, the conjugate prior is also Gaussian (with respect to the mean parameter) because of the specific algebraic properties of the normal density function.

3.1.1 CONJUGATE PRIORS AND NORMALIZATION CONSTANTS

Consider posterior inference in Equation 3.1. The key required calculation was computing the normalization constant $\int_\theta p(\theta|\alpha)p(x|\theta)d\theta$ in order to fully identify the posterior distribution.[1] This normalization constant is also equal to $p(x|\alpha)$, since it is just a marginalization of θ from the joint distribution $p(\theta, x|\alpha)$.

Therefore, the key step required in computing the posterior is calculating $p(x|\alpha)$, also called "the evidence." The posterior can be then readily evaluated at each point θ by dividing the product of the prior and the likelihood by the evidence.

The use of conjugate prior in Example 3.1 eliminated the need to *explicitly* calculate this normalization constant, but instead we were able to calculate it more indirectly. Identifying that

---

[1]As we see in later Chapters 5 and 6, we can avoid calculating this marginalization constant by using approximate inference such as MCMC sampling and variational inference.

Equation 3.2 has the algebraic form (up to a constant) of the normal distribution immediately dictates that the posterior is a normal variable with the appropriate $\alpha'(x, \alpha)$. Therefore, explicitly computing the evidence $p(x|\alpha)$ is unnecessary, because the posterior was identified as a (normal) distribution, for which its density is fully known in an analytic form.

If we are interested in computing $p(x|\alpha)$, we can base our calculation on the well-known density of the normal distribution. Equation 3.1 implies that for any choice of θ, it holds that

$$p(x|\alpha) = \int_\theta p(\theta|\alpha)p(x|\theta)d\theta = \frac{p(\theta|\alpha)p(x|\theta)}{p(\theta|x, \alpha)}. \tag{3.5}$$

This is a direct result of applying the chain rule in both directions:

$$p(x, \theta|\alpha) = p(x|\alpha)p(\theta|\alpha, x) = p(\theta|\alpha)p(x|\theta, \alpha).$$

Note that even though the right-hand side of Equation 3.5 seems to be dependent on θ, if we were to algebraically manipulate the right-hand side, all terms that include θ will cancel, because the left-hand side does not introduce any dependence on θ. The right-hand side, as mentioned, is true for *any* choice of θ. In the case of the normal distribution from Example 3.1, all three distributions in Equation 3.5 are normal distributions, for which we can calculate the density using its formula. (It is important to note that the calculation of the normalization constant of the normal distribution, either in univariate or multivariate form, is also known and can be easily computed.)

This kind of algebraic relationship exists for most conjugate priors with well-known densities. The algebraic convenience that often occurs with conjugate priors can lead to somewhat inaccurate definitions of conjugate priors, the most common one being that "conjugate priors are priors which lead to a closed-form solution for the posterior." Even though this is true in many cases, the strict definition of conjugate priors is that the posterior that is obtained from a given prior in the prior family and a given likelihood function belongs to the same prior family. As such, conjugacy is always determined in the context of a likelihood function and a family of priors.

3.1.2   THE USE OF CONJUGATE PRIORS WITH LATENT VARIABLE MODELS

Earlier in this section, it was demonstrated that conjugate priors make Bayesian inference tractable when complete data is available. Example 3.1 demonstrated this by showing how the posterior distribution can easily be identified when assuming a conjugate prior. Explicit computation of the evidence normalization constant with conjugate priors is often unnecessary, because the product of the likelihood together with the prior lead to an algebraic form of a well-known distribution.

As mentioned earlier, the calculation of the posterior normalization constant is the main obstacle in performing posterior inference. If this is the case, we can ask: do conjugate priors help in the case of latent variables being present in the model? With latent variables, the normalization constant is more complex, because it involves the marginalization of both the parameters and the latent variables. Assume a full distribution over the parameters θ, latent variables z and observed variables x (both being discrete), which factorize as follows:

$$p(\theta, z, x \mid \alpha) = p(\theta \mid \alpha)p(z \mid \theta)p(x \mid z, \theta).$$

The posterior over the latent variables and parameters has the form (see Section 2.2.2 for a more detailed example of such posterior):

$$p(\theta, z \mid x, \alpha) = \frac{p(\theta \mid \alpha)p(z \mid \theta)p(x \mid z, \theta)}{p(x \mid \alpha)},$$

and therefore, the normalization constant $p(x \mid \alpha)$ equals:

$$p(x \mid \alpha) = \sum_z \left(\int_\theta p(\theta)p(z \mid \theta)p(x \mid z, \theta)d\theta \right) = \sum_z D(z), \tag{3.6}$$

where $D(z)$ is defined to be the term inside the sum above. Equation 3.6 demonstrates that conjugate priors are useful even when the normalization constant requires summing over latent variables. If the prior family is conjugate to the distribution $p(X, Z \mid \theta)$, then the function $D(z)$ will be mathematically easy to compute for any z. However, it is *not* true that $\sum_z D(z)$ is always tractable, since the form of $D(z)$ can be quite complex.

On a related note, if the order of summation and integration is switched, then it holds that:

$$p(x \mid \alpha) = \int_\theta p(\theta) \left(\sum_z p(z \mid \theta)p(x \mid z, \theta) \right) d\theta = \int_\theta p(\theta)D'(\theta)d(\theta),$$

where $D'(\theta)$ is defined as the term that sums over z. Then, it is often the case that for every θ, $D'(\theta)$ can be computed using dynamic programming algorithms or other algorithms that sum over a discrete space (for example, if the latent variable space includes parse trees with an underlying PCFG grammar, then $D'(\theta)$ can be computed using a variant of the CKY algorithm, the inside algorithm. See Chapter 8 for further discussion.) Switching integration and summation does not make the problem of computing the marginalization constant $p(x|\alpha)$ tractable. The outside integral over the function $D'(\theta)$ is often still infeasible.

Still, the fact that a tractable solution for the *inner* term results from switching the integration and the sum is very useful for approximate inference, especially for variational inference. This is exactly where the conjugacy of the prior comes in handy even with an intractable posterior with latent variables. This is discussed further in Chapter 6.

3.1.3 MIXTURE OF CONJUGATE PRIORS

Mixture models are a simple way to extend a family of distributions into a more expressive family. If we have a set of distributions $p_1(X), \ldots, p_M(X)$, then a mixture model over this set of distributions is parametrized by an M dimensional probability vector $(\lambda_1, \ldots, \lambda_M)$ ($\lambda_i \geq 0$, $\sum_i \lambda_i = 1$) and defines distributions over X such that:

$$p(X|\lambda) = \sum_{i=1}^{M} \lambda_i \, p_i(X).$$

Section 1.5.3 gives an example of a mixture-of-Gaussians model. The idea of mixture models can also be used for prior families. Let $p(\theta \mid \alpha)$ be a prior from a prior family with $\alpha \in A$. Then, it is possible to define a prior of the form:

$$p\left(\theta \mid \alpha^1, \ldots, \alpha^M, \lambda_1, \ldots, \lambda_M\right) = \sum_{i=1}^{M} \lambda_i \, p\left(\theta \mid \alpha^i\right),$$

where $\lambda_i \geq 0$ and $\sum_{i=1}^{M} \lambda_i = 1$ (i.e., λ is a point in the $M - 1$ dimensional probability simplex). This new prior family, which is hyperparametrized by $\alpha^i \in A$ and λ_i for $i \in \{1, \ldots M\}$ will actually be conjugate to a likelihood $p(x \mid \theta)$ *if* the original prior family $p(\theta \mid \alpha)$ for $\alpha \in A$ is also conjugate to this likelihood.

To see this, consider that when using a mixture prior, the posterior has the form:

$$p\left(\theta \mid x, \alpha^1, \ldots, \alpha^M, \lambda\right) = \frac{p(x \mid \theta)p(\theta \mid \alpha^1, \ldots, \alpha^M, \lambda)}{\int_\theta p(x \mid \theta)p(\theta \mid \alpha^1, \ldots, \alpha^M, \lambda)d\theta}$$
$$= \frac{\sum_{i=1}^{M} \lambda_i \, p(x \mid \theta)p(\theta \mid \alpha^i)}{\sum_{i=1}^{M} \lambda_i \, Z_i},$$

where

$$Z_i = \int_\theta p\left(x \mid \theta\right) p\left(\theta \mid \alpha^i\right) d\theta.$$

Therefore, it holds that:

$$p\left(\theta \mid x, \alpha^1, \ldots, \alpha^M, \lambda\right) = \frac{\sum_{i=1}^{M} (\lambda_i \, Z_i)p(\theta \mid x, \alpha^i)}{\sum_{i=1}^{M} \lambda_i \, Z_i},$$

because $p(x|\theta)p(\theta|\alpha^i) = Z_i\, p(\theta|x, \alpha^i)$. Because of conjugacy, each $p(\theta|x, \alpha^i)$ is equal to $p(\theta|\beta^i)$ for some $\beta^i \in A$ ($i \in \{1, \ldots, M\}$). The hyperparameters β^i are the updated hyperparameters following posterior inference. Therefore, it holds:

$$p\left(\theta \mid x, \alpha^1, \ldots, \alpha^M, \lambda\right) = \sum_{i=1}^{M} \lambda_i'\, p(\theta \mid \beta^i),$$

for $\lambda_i' = \lambda_i Z_i / \left(\sum_{i=1}^{M} \lambda_i Z_i\right)$.

When the prior family parametrized by α is K-dimensional Dirichlet (see Section 2.2.1 and Equation 2.2), then:

$$Z_i = \frac{\prod_{j=1}^{K} \Gamma\left(\alpha_j^i + x_j\right)}{\Gamma\left(\sum_{j=1}^{K} \alpha_j^i + x_j\right)}.$$

We conclude this section about mixtures of conjugate priors with an example of using such a mixture prior for text analysis. Yamamoto and Sadamitsu (2005) define a topic model, where a mixture of Dirichlet distributions is defined as the prior distribution over the vocabulary. Each draw from this mixture provides a multinomial distribution over the vocabulary. Following that draw, the words in the document are drawn independently in the generative process.

Yamamoto and Sadamitsu describe the mixture components of their Dirichlet mixture distribution as corresponding to topics. In this sense, there is a large distinction between their model and LDA, which samples a topic *distribution* for *each* document separately. When measuring performance on a held-out dataset using perplexity (see Appendix A and Section 1.6), their model consistently scored better than LDA on a set of 100,000 newspaper articles in Japanese. Their model performance was also saturated for 20 topics, while the perplexity of the LDA continued to decrease for a much larger number of topics. This perhaps points to a better fit—their model uses fewer topics (and therefore is simpler), but still has lower perplexity than LDA.

3.1.4   RENORMALIZED CONJUGATE DISTRIBUTIONS

In the previous section, we saw that one could derive a more expressive prior family by using a basic prior distribution in a mixture model. Renormalizing a conjugate prior is another way to change the properties of a prior family while still retaining conjugacy.

Let us assume that a prior $p(\theta|\alpha)$ is defined over some parameter space Θ. It is sometimes the case that we want to further constrain Θ into a smaller subspace, and define $p(\theta|\alpha)$ such that its support is some $\Theta_0 \subset \Theta$. One way to do so would be to define the following distribution p' over Θ_0:

$$p'(\theta|\alpha) = \frac{p(\theta|\alpha)}{\int_{\theta' \in \Theta_0} p(\theta'|\alpha)d\theta'}. \tag{3.7}$$

This new distribution retains the same ratio between probabilities of elements in Θ_0 as p, but essentially allocates probability 0 to any element in $\Theta \setminus \Theta_0$.

It can be shown that if p is a conjugate family to some likelihood, then p' is conjugate to the same likelihood as well. This example actually demonstrates that conjugacy, in its pure form does not necessitate tractability by using the conjugate prior together with the corresponding likelihood. More specifically, the integral over Θ_0 in the denominator of Equation 3.7 can often be difficult to compute, and approximate inference is required.

The renormalization of conjugate distributions arises when considering probabilistic context-free grammars with Dirichlet priors on the parameters. In this case, in order for the prior to allocate zero probability to parameters that define *non-tight* PCFGs, certain multinomial distributions need to be removed from the prior. Here, tightness refers to a desirable property of a PCFG so that the total measure of all finite parse trees generated by the underlying context-free grammar is 1. For a thorough discussion of this issue, see Cohen and Johnson (2013).

3.1.5 DISCUSSION: TO BE OR NOT TO BE CONJUGATE?

It is worth noting that the development of conjugate priors came with the intention of defining priors that are not just analytically tractable (i.e., the posterior belongs to the prior family), but are also (i) rich enough to express the modeler's prior information and beliefs, and (ii) interpretable, so that the modeler can understand what prior information is being injected into the posterior when choosing a certain member of the prior family (Raiffa and Schlaifer, 1961). However, the requirement for analytic tractability confines the set of possible priors for most likelihood functions. Once the requirement of analytical tractability is met, it is difficult to verify that richness and interpretability are met as well. In fact, one of the criticisms of Bayesian statistics is that in many cases Bayesians rely on computationally convenient priors, and are therefore able to tackle only the most simple examples with respect to richness and interpretability (Carlin and Louis, 2000).

In NLP, the need for computationally convenient priors is especially important. NLP mainly predicts combinatorial structures such as trees and sequences, for which inference is computationally expensive, and it is prohibitive to use priors that do not offer computational tractability. For this reason, for example, the Dirichlet distribution is often used in Bayesian NLP; the Dirichlet distribution is conjugate to the multinomial likelihood and the multinomial family and, in turn, serves as the most fundamental building block of generative models over sequences, trees, and other structures that arise in NLP. Section 3.2 discusses this at length.

Still, one can argue that with the advent of new hardware and state-of-the-art approximation algorithms, it is possible to tackle problems in NLP with priors that are not necessarily computationally convenient. MCMC sampling (Chapter 5) and variational inference (Chapter 6) can be used in these cases.

It is also important to note that conjugacy of the prior to the likelihood does not *guarantee* tractability of inference with the model. The function $\alpha'(x, \alpha)$ needs to be efficiently computable in order for conjugacy to be useful. To demonstrate this point, consider a parameter space Θ. The set of *all* distributions defined over Θ, denoted by $\mathcal{P}$, is actually a conjugate prior family to *any* distribution of the form $p(X \mid \theta)$ simply because it holds trivially that $p(\theta \mid X) \in \mathcal{P}$. Clearly, the conjugate prior family $\mathcal{P}$ is intractable because $\alpha'(x, \alpha)$ cannot be computed efficiently.

At the other extreme, a prior family that includes a single prior distribution that places all of the probability mass on a single point in the parameter space would also be a conjugate prior (to any model using this parameter space). The posterior can be trivially computed in this case (it is the distribution that is the single member in the prior family, because the support of the posterior over the parameters is always subsumed by the support of the prior), but conjugacy in this case is not useful, simply because the prior family is not sufficiently rich.

3.1.6 SUMMARY

Conjugate priors are defined in the context of a prior *family* and a distribution for the variables in the model over the observations and latent variables. In many cases, conjugate priors ensure the tractability of the computation of the normalization constant of the posterior. For example, conjugate priors often lead to closed-form analytic solutions for the posterior given a set of observations (and values for the latent variables, if they exist in the model).

Conjugate priors are often argued to be too simplistic, but they are very helpful in NLP because of the computational complexity of NLP models. Alternatives to conjugate priors are often less efficient, but with the advent of new hardware and approximation algorithms, these alternatives have become more viable.

3.2 PRIORS OVER MULTINOMIAL AND CATEGORICAL DISTRIBUTIONS

The nature of structures that are predicted in natural language processing is an excellent fit for modeling using the categorical distribution. The categorical distribution is a generalization of the Bernoulli distribution, which specifies how K outcomes (such as topics in a document or on the right-hand sides of context-free rules headed by a non-terminal) are distributed. The categorical distribution is specified by a parameter vector $\theta \in \mathbb{R}^K$, where θ satisfies the following two properties:

$$\forall k \in \{1, \ldots, K\} \; \theta_k \geq 0, \tag{3.8}$$

$$\sum_{k=1}^{K} \theta_k = 1. \tag{3.9}$$

The space of allowed parameters for the categorical distribution over K outcomes,

$$\Theta = \left\{ \theta \in \mathbb{R}^K \,|\, \theta \; satisfies \; Equations \; 3.8\text{–}3.9 \right\},$$

is also called "the probability simplex of dimension $K - 1$"—there is one fewer degree of freedom because of the requirement for all probabilities to sum to 1. The set Θ defines a simplex, i.e., geometrically it is a $K - 1$ dimensional polytope, which is the convex hull of K vertices; the vertices are the points such that all probability mass is placed on a single event. All other probability distributions can be viewed as a combination of these vertices. Each point in this simplex defines a categorical distribution.

If $X \sim \text{Categorical}(\theta)$, then the probability distribution over X is defined as[2]:

$$p(X = i | \theta) = \theta_i,$$

where $i \in \{1, \ldots, K\}$. While the categorical distribution generalizes the Bernoulli distribution, the multinomial distribution is actually a generalization of the *binomial distribution* and describes a distribution for a random variable $X \in \mathbb{N}^K$ such that $\sum_{i=1}^{K} X_i = n$ for some fixed n, a natural number, which is a parameter of the multinomial distribution. The parameter n plays a similar role to the "experiments count" parameter in the binomial distribution. Then, given $\theta \in \Theta$ and n as described above, the multinomial distribution is defined as:

$$p(X_1 = i_1, \ldots, X_K = i_K) = \frac{n!}{\prod_{j=1}^{K} i_j!} \prod_{j=1}^{K} \theta_j^{i_j},$$

where $\sum_{j=1}^{K} i_j = n$.

Even though the categorical distribution and the multinomial distribution differ, there is a strong relationship between them. More specifically, if X distributes according to a categorical distribution with parameters θ, then the random variable $Y \in \{0, 1\}^K$ defined as:

$$Y_i = I(X = i), \tag{3.10}$$

---

[2]The Bayesian NLP literature often refers to categorical distributions as "multinomial distributions," but this is actually a misnomer (a misnomer that is nonetheless used in this book, in order to be consistent with the literature).

is distributed according to the multinomial distribution with parameters θ and $n = 1$. It is often the case that it is mathematically convenient to represent the categorical distribution as a multinomial distribution of the above form, using binary indicators. In this case, the probability function $p(Y|\theta)$ can be written as $\prod_{i=1}^{K} \theta_i^{y_i}$.

There have been various generalizations and extensions to the Dirichlet distribution. One such example is the generalized Dirichlet distribution, which provides a richer covariance structure compared to the Dirichlet distribution (see also Section 3.2.2 about the covariance structure of the Dirichlet distribution). Another example is the Dirichlet-tree distribution (Minka, 1999) which gives a prior over distributions that generate leaf nodes in a tree-like stochastic process.

In the rest of this section, the categorical distribution will be referred to as a multinomial distribution to be consistent with the NLP literature. This is not a major issue, since most of the discussion points in this section are valid for both distributions.

3.2.1   THE DIRICHLET DISTRIBUTION RE-VISITED

The Dirichlet distribution is ubiquitous in Bayesian NLP, because it is the simplest conjugate distribution to the categorical (and multinomial) distribution. Its definition and an example of its use with the latent Dirichlet allocation model for topic modeling are given in Section 2.2. For completeness, we repeat Equation 2.2 below, and reiterate that the Dirichlet distribution is parametrized by a vector $\alpha \in \mathbb{R}^K$ such that:

$$p(\theta_1, \ldots, \theta_K | \alpha_1, \ldots, \alpha_K) = C(\alpha) \prod_{k=1}^{K} \theta_k^{\alpha_k - 1},$$

where $(\theta_1, \ldots, \theta_K)$ is a vector such that $\theta_i \geq 0$ and $\sum_{i=1}^{K} \theta_i = 1$.

Here, we continue to provide a more complete description of the Dirichlet distribution and its properties.

Conjugacy of the Dirichlet Distribution

The conjugacy of the Dirichlet distribution to the categorical distribution is a direct result of "algebraic similarity" between the density of the Dirichlet distribution and the multinomial probability distribution.

Example 3.2   Let $\theta \sim \text{Dirichlet}(\alpha)$ with $\alpha = (\alpha_1, \ldots, \alpha_K) \in \mathbb{R}^K$. Let X be a binary random vector of length K that defines a multinomial distribution as described in Equation 3.10. The parameter vector of this categorical distribution is θ. Assume that x, a sample of X, is observed. Then:

$$p(\theta \mid x, \alpha) \propto p(\theta|\alpha)p(x \mid \theta) \propto \left(\prod_{i=1}^{K} \theta_i^{\alpha_i - 1} \right) \times \left(\prod_{i=1}^{K} \theta_i^{x_i} \right) = \prod_{i=1}^{K} \theta_i^{\alpha_i + x_i - 1}. \qquad (3.11)$$

Note the use of $\propto$ (i.e., "proportional to") instead of "equal to." Two normalization constants in Equation 3.11 were omitted to simplify the identification of the posterior. The first constant is $p(x \mid \alpha)$, the marginalization constant. The second constant is the normalization constant of the Dirichlet distribution (Equation 2.3). The reason we can omit them is that these constants do not change with θ, and the distribution we are interested in is defined over θ.

Equation 3.11 has the algebraic form (without the normalization constant) of a Dirichlet distribution with $\alpha'(x, \alpha) = \alpha + x$. This means that the posterior distributes according to a Dirichlet distribution with hyperparameters $\alpha + x$.

Example 3.2 demonstrates again the principle of hyperparameters acting as pseudo-observations. The initial hyperparameters α are added to the observations to derive the posterior, as if outcome i was observed α_i times (though, note that α_i does not need to be integral).

In the general case of observing $x^{(1)}, \ldots, x^{(n)}$ from a categorical distribution (where each sample is independent of the other given θ), the resulting posterior has hyperparameters $\alpha + \sum_{i=1} x^{(i)}$, where each $x^{(i)}$ is a binary vector of length K.

The Dirichlet Distribution and Sparsity

A symmetric Dirichlet distribution (Section 2.2.1) is hyperparametrized by $\alpha > 0$. It is a specific case of the Dirichlet distribution in which the hyperparameter vector of the general Dirichlet distribution contains only identical values to α. When the hyperparameter of a symmetric Dirichlet distribution $\alpha \in \mathbb{R}$ is chosen such that $\alpha < 1$, any point $x \in \mathbb{R}^K$ drawn from the respective Dirichlet will have most of its coordinates close to 0, and only a few will have a value significantly larger than zero.

The intuition behind this property of the symmetric Dirichlet distribution can be understood when inspecting the main term in the density of the Dirichlet distribution: $\prod_{i=1}^{K} \theta_i^{\alpha-1}$. When $\alpha < 1$, this product becomes $\dfrac{1}{\prod_{i=1}^{K} \theta_i^{\beta}}$ for $0 < \beta = \alpha - 1$. Clearly, this product becomes very large if one of the θ_i is close to 0. If many of the θ_i are close to 0, this effect is multiplied, which makes the product even larger. It is therefore true that most of the density for the symmetric Dirichlet with $\alpha < 1$ is concentrated around points in the probability simplex where the majority of the θ_i are close to 0.

This property of the symmetric Dirichlet has been exploited consistently in the Bayesian NLP literature. For example, Goldwater and Griffiths (2007) defined a Bayesian part-of-speech tagging with hidden Markov models (Chapter 8), in which they used a Dirichlet prior as a prior over the set of multinomials for the transition probabilities and emission probabilities in the trigram hidden Markov model.

For the first set of experiments, Goldwater and Griffiths used a fixed sparse hyperparameter for all transition probabilities and a fixed, different hyperparameter for all emission probabilities. Their findings show that choosing a small value for the transition hyperparameter (0.03) together with a choice of hyperparameter 1 for the emission probabilities achieves the best prediction accuracy of the part-of-speech tags. This means that the optimal transition multinomials are similarly likely to be very sparse. This is not surprising, since only a small number of part-of-speech tags can appear in a certain context. However, the emission hyperparameter 1 means that the Dirichlet distribution is simply a uniform distribution. The authors argued that the reason a sparse prior was not very useful for the emission probabilities is that all emission probabilities shared the same hyperparameter.

Indeed, when they improved their model, and inferred a different hyperparameter for each emission distribution (hyperparameter inference is discussed in Chapters 5 and 6), the results improved. In addition, the inferred hyperparameters for the emission distributions were quite close to 0, implying a very sparse distribution for the set of emitted words for a given tag, as one would intuit.

Toutanova and Johnson (2008) also described a model for a Bayesian semi-supervised[3] part-of-speech tagging that uses the Dirichlet distribution to encourage sparsity in the parameter space. Unlike the model of Goldwater and Griffiths, their model is not based on hidden Markov models, but instead adapts the LDA model for the purpose of POS tagging. The model includes a multinomial component that generates tags conditioned on their words (as opposed to words conditioned on their tags, as in HMMs). This component was associated with a sparse Dirichlet prior, to capture the notion that most words are associated with very few tags, mainly a single part-of-speech tag. The hyperparameter α they used ranged between 0.2 to 0.5, depending on the size of the dictionary used.

They contrasted their model with an almost identical model that does *not* include a Bayesian prior on the components of $p(T \mid W)$ (where T denotes a random variable of tag sequences, and W denotes a random variable for word sequences, i.e., sentences), to determine whether the sparse Dirichlet prior helps to obtain better tagging accuracy. The non-Bayesian model is similar to the probabilistic latent semantic analysis model, PLSA (Hofmann, 1999a). They reported that this was indeed the case—the LDA-like model achieved an error reduction of up to 36% compared to PLSA.

In general, sparsity of a prior distribution can effectively support models for natural language. Most often, this property is a useful property for modeling language at the lexical level: whenever associating a word with a set of clusters (such as syntactic categories), the word is associated with a relatively small number of clusters. This property is a great fit for modeling with a sparse Dirichlet distribution, and has been exploited in the Bayesian NLP literature multiple times.

Gamma Representation of the Dirichlet

The Dirichlet distribution has a reductive representation to the Gamma distribution. This representation does not contribute directly to better modeling, but helps to demonstrate the limi-

---

[3]Toutanova and Johnson's study is considered here to be in the semi-supervised realm because they used a part-of-speech tagging dictionary for some of the words, i.e., they had a specification of the parts of speech that these words can be associated with. This approach was also taken in some of the experiments that Goldwater and Griffiths performed.

tations of the Dirichlet distribution, and suggest alternatives to it (such as the one described in the next section).

Let $\mu_i \sim \Gamma(\alpha_i, 1)$ be K i.i.d. random variables distributed according to the Gamma distribution with shape $\alpha_i > 0$ and scale 1 (see also Appendix B). Then, the definition of

$$\theta_i = \frac{\mu_i}{\sum_{i=1}^{K} \mu_i}, \tag{3.12}$$

for $i \in \{1, \ldots, K\}$ yields a random vector θ from the probability simplex of dimension $K - 1$, such that θ distributes according to the Dirichlet distribution with hyperparameters $\alpha = (\alpha_1, \ldots, \alpha_K)$.

The representation of the Dirichlet as *independent*, normalized, Gamma variables explains a limitation inherent to the Dirichlet distribution. There is no explicit parametrization of the rich structure of relationships between the coordinates of θ. For example, given $i \neq j$, the ratio θ_i / θ_j, when treated as a random variable, is independent of any other ratio θ_k / θ_ℓ calculated from two other coordinates, $k \neq \ell$. (This is evident from Equation 3.12: the ratio $\theta_i = \theta$ is $\mu_i = \mu_j$, where all μ_i for $i \in \{1, \ldots, K\}$ are independent.) Therefore, the Dirichlet distribution is not a good *modeling choice* when the θ parameters are better modeled even with a weak degree of dependence.

Natural language elements, however, have a large dependence between one another. For example, consider a Bayesian unigram language model (i.e., a language model that treats a sentence as a bag of words), where the model is parametrized through θ, which is a distribution over K words in a vocabulary. When estimated from data, these parameters exhibit great dependence, depending on the domain of the data. It is highly likely that an increase or decrease in the frequency of words that are semantically related to each other (where these changes are compared to a language model learned from another unrelated text) is simultaneous, comparing one data domain to another. A text about veterinary science will have a simultaneous increase in the probability of words such as "dog," "cat" and "fur" compared to a text about religion—though each word separately can have a unique probability, high or low. A prior distribution on this unigram model encapsulates our prior beliefs, varying across text domains, for example, about the parameters. Using the Dirichlet distribution is unsatisfactory, because it is unable to capture a dependency structure between the words in the vocabulary.

The next section explains how this independence property of the Dirichlet distribution can be partially remedied, through the use of a different distribution as a prior over the multinomial distribution.

Summary

The Dirichlet distribution is often used as a conjugate prior to the categorical and multinomial distributions. This conjugacy makes it extremely useful in Bayesian NLP, because the categorical distribution is ubiquitous in NLP modeling. The Dirichlet distribution has the advantage of potentially encouraging sparse solutions, when its hyperparameters are set properly. This property has been repeatedly exploited in the NLP literature, because distributions over linguistic elements such as part-of-speech tags or words typically tend to be sparse. The Dirichlet distribution also comes with limitations. For example, this distribution assumes a nearly independent structure between the coordinates of points in the probability simplex that are drawn from it.

3.2.2 THE LOGISTIC NORMAL DISTRIBUTION

The logistic normal distribution was suggested by Aitchison (1986) in order to overcome the limitations of the Dirichlet distribution with compositional data in the probability simplex. A random vector $\theta \in \mathbb{R}^K$ is distributed according to the (additive) logistic normal distribution with parameters $\alpha = (\eta, \Sigma)$ where $\eta = (\eta_1, \ldots, \eta_{K-1}) \in \mathbb{R}^{K-1}$ and $\Sigma \in \mathbb{R}^{(K-1)\times(K-1)}$ is a covariance matrix (i.e., it is positive-definite and symmetric) if:

$$\theta_i = \frac{\exp(\mu_i)}{1 + \sum_{j=1}^{K-1} \exp(\mu_j)} \quad \forall i \in \{1, \ldots, K-1\}, \tag{3.13}$$

$$\theta_K = \frac{1}{1 + \sum_{j=1}^{K-1} \exp(\mu_j)}, \tag{3.14}$$

for some $\mu \in \mathbb{R}^{K-1}$ random vector that distributes according to the multivariate normal distribution with mean value η and covariance matrix Σ.

Therefore, the logistic normal distribution, as its name implies, is a multivariate normal variable that has been transformed using the logistic transformation. The reason that this multivariate normal variable needs to be $K - 1$ dimensional instead of K dimensional is to eliminate a redundant degree of freedom: had the logistic normal distribution used a K dimensional multivariate normal variable, one of them could have been canceled by choosing one of the coordinates and subtracting them from all the others (the resulting subtracted vector would still be a multivariate normal variable).

An additional dependence structure that does not exist in the Dirichlet distribution appears in the logistic normal distribution because of the explicit dependence structure represented through the covariance matrix Σ. Therefore, in light of the discussion in Section 3.2.1, the logistic normal distribution is an alternative to the Dirichlet distribution. Unlike the Dirichlet distribution, the logistic normal distribution is not conjugate to the multinomial distribution.

Figure 3.1 provides a plot of the logistic normal distribution with various hyperparameters for $K = 3$ and $n = 5,000$ (i.e., the number of samples drawn is 5,000). With independence between the dimensions, and variance 1 for each dimension, the distribution is spread over the whole probability simplex. When the correlation is negative and close to -1, we see a more narrow spread. With large variance (and independence between the coordinates), the logistic normal behaves almost like a sparse distribution.

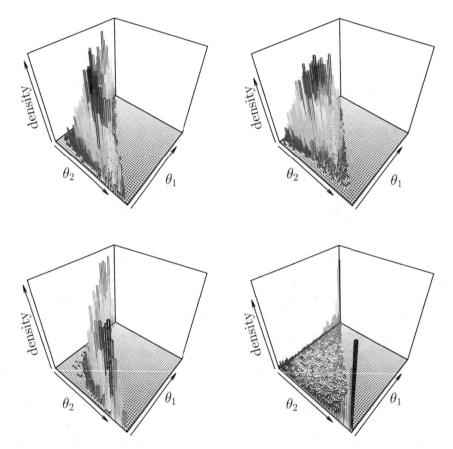

Figure 3.1: A plot of sampled data from the logistic normal distribution with $K = 3$, with various Σ. The hyperparameter μ is always $(0, 0)$. Top-left: $\Sigma = \begin{pmatrix} 1 & 0 \\ 0 & 1 \end{pmatrix}$, top-right: $\Sigma = \begin{pmatrix} 1 & 0.7 \\ 0.7 & 1 \end{pmatrix}$, bottom-left: $\Sigma = \begin{pmatrix} 1 & -0.7 \\ -0.7 & 1 \end{pmatrix}$, bottom-right: $\Sigma = \begin{pmatrix} 5 & 0 \\ 0 & 5 \end{pmatrix}$.

Properties of the Additive Logistic Normal Distribution

Using the Jacobian transformation method (see Appendix A), Aitchison (1986) shows that the density of the additive logistic normal distribution is:

$$p(\theta \mid \eta, \Sigma)$$

$$= \frac{1}{\sqrt{(2\pi)^K \det(\Sigma)}} \times \left(\prod_{i=1}^{K} \theta_i\right)^{-1}$$

$$\exp\left(-\frac{1}{2}(\log(\theta_{-K}/\theta_K) - \eta)^\top \Sigma^{-1} \log(\theta_{-K}/\theta_K) - \eta)\right),$$

where $\theta_{-K} = (\theta_1, \ldots, \theta_{K-1})$ and $\log(\theta_{-K}/\theta_K) \in \mathbb{R}^{K-1}$ with:

$$[\log(\theta_{-K}/\theta_K)]_i = \log(\theta_i/\theta_K) \quad \forall i \in \{1, \ldots, K-1\}.$$

This density is only defined on the probability simplex. Both the moments and the logarithmic moments of the logistic normal distribution are well-defined for all positive orders. These moments are $E[\prod_{i=1}^{K} \theta_i^{a_i}]$ and $E[\prod_{i=1}^{K} (\log \theta_i)^{a_i}]$ for $a_i > 0$. Unfortunately, even though these moments exist, there are no closed-form expressions for them.

Since the log-ratio between θ_i and θ_j is distributed according to the normal distribution, the following holds (Aitchison, 1986):

$$E[\log(\theta_i/\theta_j)] = \eta_i - \eta_j,$$
$$\text{Cov}(\log(\theta_i/\theta_j), \log(\theta_k/\theta_\ell)) = \sigma_{\ell k} + \sigma_{ji} - \sigma_{i\ell} - \sigma_{kj}.$$

In addition,

$$E[\theta_i/\theta_j] = \exp\left(\mu_i - \mu_j + \frac{1}{2}\left(\sigma_{ii} - 2\sigma_{ij} + \sigma_{jj}\right)\right).$$

Uses of the Logistic Normal Distribution

The use of the logistic normal (additive and multiplicative) distribution is not as common as the use of the Dirichlet distribution (in Bayesian NLP). The main reason for this is that inference with the logistic normal is cumbersome, even with approximate inference such as the MCMC method or variational inference (which are discussed in Chapters 6 and 5). More than being cumbersome, this type of inference is also computationally intensive. Still, this does not preclude the use of the logistic normal distribution in both the MCMC setting (Mimno et al., 2008) or the variational setting (Blei and Lafferty, 2006).

A recent example of a use of the (additive) logistic normal distribution for text analysis is the correlated topic model (CTM) of Blei and Lafferty (2006). Blei and Lafferty present a model that is identical to the LDA model (see Section 2.2), only a logistic normal distribution is used to draw topic distribution for each topic, instead of the Dirichlet distribution, as in the LDA model.

The authors' main motivation was to model correlation between topics. They assumed that given a large corpus of documents, the topics in the corpus are related to each other. For example, topics such as genetics and computational biology are both under the umbrella of biology, and when a document is about one, it is more likely to be about the other. On the other hand, astronomy is usually weakly related, if at all, to biology, and therefore we expect a correlation close to 0, or even negative, between topics under the umbrella of astronomy and biology.

The authors compared the LDA and CTM on articles from the journal *Science*. Their findings were that the CTM achieved a better fit (when measured using average held-out log-likelihood; see Section 1.6 for more detail) than LDA. In addition, CTM's probability peaked with $K = 90$ (i.e., 90 topics), while LDA's probability peaked with 30 topics. This implies that the CTM was able to make better use of available topics for the dataset used.

The additive logistic normal distribution was also used as a prior for structured problems, such as dependency grammar induction. Cohen et al. (2009) explore the use of the logistic normal distribution as a prior on the dependency model with valence (Klein and Manning, 2004), and demonstrate significant improvements in model estimation with this prior. Cohen et al. compared it with the use of the Dirichlet distribution and to not using a prior at all. The Dirichlet distribution behaved quite similarly to the case of not having a prior at all. The problem they modeled, as mentioned above, is that of dependency grammar induction, in which the prediction target is dependency trees (see Chapter 8) predicted from a sequence of part-of-speech tags.

This study was further developed by Cohen and Smith (2010b), with suggestions for extensions of the logistic normal distribution that go beyond the locality of a single multinomial. See the next section for further discussion.

The Partitioned Logistic Normal Distribution

The logistic normal distribution is a distribution over the probability simplex, which corresponds to a single multinomial. In NLP, the generative models used often consist of a family of multinomial distributions. In this case, the parameters θ consist of K subvectors, $\theta^1, \ldots, \theta^K$, where each θ^k is in an N_k-dimensional vector in the probability simplex. See Chapter 8 for a more detailed explanation.

In these cases, the natural choice of a prior over the whole set of multinomials would be:

$$p(\theta) = \prod_{k=1}^{K} p\left(\theta^k\right),$$

Constants: K, N_k for $k \in \{1, \ldots, K\}$ integers

Hyperprameters: $\eta \in \mathbb{R}^{(\sum_{k=1}^{K} N_k) - K}$ mean vector, Σ the corresponding covariance matrix

Target random variables: θ^k vectors in the probability simplex of dimension $N_k - 1$ for $k \in \{1, \ldots, K\}$

Auxiliary random variables: $\mu^k \in \mathbb{R}^{N_k - 1}$ for $k \in \{1, \ldots, K\}$

- -

- Generate a multivariate normal variable $\mu \in \mathbb{R}^{\sum_{i=1}^{K} N_k - K}$. The multivariate normal variable has mean η and covariance matrix Σ of size $(\sum_{i=1}^{K} N_k - K) \times (\sum_{i=1}^{K} N_k - K)$.

- Break μ into K subvectors, each of length $N_k - 1$.

- The random vector θ is set to:

$$\theta_i^k = \frac{\exp(\mu_i^k)}{\prod_{j=1}^{N_k - 1} \left(1 + \exp(\mu_j^k)\right)} \quad \forall i \in \{1, \ldots, N_k - 1\},$$

$$\theta_{N_k}^k = \frac{1}{\prod_{j=1}^{N_k - 1} \left(1 + \exp(\mu_j^k)\right)}.$$

Generative Story 3.1: The generative story for the partitioned logistic normal distribution.

where each distribution $p\left(\theta^k\right)$ can be, for example, a Dirichlet or a logistic normal. However, this decomposition does not introduce a covariance structure between events in different multinomials; there is a clear independence assumption in the prior between multinomials of different index k.

One way to overcome this issue is by using the *partitioned* logistic normal distribution (Aitchison, 1986). The partitioned logistic normal distribution is similar to the logistic normal distribution, only it is defined as a prior on a whole collection of multinomial distributions, such as $\theta^1, \ldots, \theta^K$. To generate such a collection of multinomials, the generative process is given in generative story 3.1.

The covariance matrix Σ now permits correlations between all components of the vector θ.

The partitioned logistic normal is related to the shared logistic normal distribution, introduced by Cohen and Smith (2009). Both incorporate a covariance structure that exists outside of multinomial boundaries, as defined by the natural factorization of a set of parameters into multinomials. The shared logistic normal encodes such covariance more implicitly, by averaging several Gaussian variables ("normal experts") that are then exponentiated and normalized. See also Cohen and Smith (2010b) for discussion.

The Multiplicative Logistic Normal Distribution

Another type of a logistic normal distribution is that of the *multiplicative* logistic normal. The definition of the multiplicative logistic normal distribution resembles that of the additive one. The difference is in Equations 3.13–3.14, which are substituted with:

$$\theta_i = \frac{\exp(\mu_i)}{\prod_{j=1}^{K-1} \left(1 + \exp(\mu_j)\right)} \quad \forall i \in \{1, \dots, K-1\},$$

$$\theta_K = \frac{1}{\prod_{j=1}^{K-1} \left(1 + \exp(\mu_j)\right)}.$$

The multiplicative logistic normal distribution is not often used in Bayesian NLP models, and is given here mostly for completeness.

The Logistic Normal Distribution vs. the Dirichlet Distribution

According to Aitchison (1986), the family of logistic normal distributions and the family of Dirichlet distributions are quite disparate, and it is hard to find a distribution in one family that approximates another distribution in the other family in a useful manner.

Aitchison points out that the value of the minimal KL divergence (Kullback–Leibler divergence, see Appendix A) between a Dirichlet distribution with hyperparameters $\alpha = (\alpha_1, \dots, \alpha_K)$ and the family of logistic normal distributions can be approximated as follows. Whenever α_i are relatively large values, then the minimal KL divergence is approximately $(1/12) \left(\sum_{i=1}^{K} \alpha_i^{-1} + 2/(\sum_{i=1}^{K} \alpha_i) \right)$.

Dirichlet distributions tend to logistic normality as α_i goes to infinity. More specifically, when θ is distributed from a Dirichlet distribution with hyperparameters α, as $\alpha \to \infty$, it holds that $p(\theta|\alpha)$ behaves very much like a logistic normal distribution with hyperparameters $\mu \in \mathbb{R}^{K-1}$ and $\Sigma \in \mathbb{R}^{K-1} \times \mathbb{R}^{K-1}$ such that:

$$
\begin{aligned}
\mu_i &= \psi(\alpha_i) - \psi(\alpha_K) & & i \in \{1, \dots, K-1\} \\
\Sigma_{ii} &= \psi'(\alpha_i) + \psi(\alpha_K) & & i \in \{1, \dots, K-1\} \\
\Sigma_{ij} &= \psi'(\alpha_K) & & i \neq j, i, j \in \{1, \dots, K-1\},
\end{aligned}
$$

where ψ is the digamma function and ψ' is its derivative (see Appendix B).

Summary
Despite its lack of conjugacy to the categorical distribution, the logistic normal distribution is a useful prior for the categorical distribution. While the Dirichlet exhibits an independence structure in the probability simplex, the logistic normal distribution exploits an explicit dependence structure originating in a multivariate normal distribution.

There are two variants of the logistic normal distribution: the additive and the multiplicative. Usually, if a distribution is referred to as being a logistic normal, but no additional reference is made to the type of logistic normal used, the additive is the one being referred to.

3.2.3   DISCUSSION

As Aitchison (1986) points out, several studies have been conducted in an attempt to generalize the Dirichlet distribution to a family that has more dependence structure in it (see Section 3.2.1), and that subsumes the family of Dirichlet distributions. Two such attempts are the scaled Dirichlet distribution and the Connor-Mosimann distribution.

The scaled Dirichlet distribution is parametrized by two vectors α and β, all positive, of the same length. Its density is then the following:

$$p(\theta|\alpha, \beta) = \frac{\Gamma(\sum_{i=1}^{d} \alpha_i)}{\prod_{i=1}^{d} \Gamma(\alpha_i)} \times \frac{\prod_{i=1}^{d} \beta_i^{\alpha_i} \theta_i^{\alpha_i - 1}}{\left(\sum_{i=1}^{d} \beta_i \theta_i\right)^{\sum_{i=1}^{d} \alpha_i}},$$

where $\Gamma(x)$ is the Gamma function. The Connor-Mosimann distribution, on the other hand, has the following density (it is also parametrized by $\alpha, \beta \in \mathbb{R}^d$ with all positive values):

$$p(\theta|\alpha, \beta) = \prod_{i=1}^{d} \frac{\theta_i^{\alpha_i - 1}}{B(\alpha_i, \beta_i)},$$

where $B(\alpha_i, \beta_i)$, is the Beta function, defined as:

$$B(\alpha_i, \beta_i) = \frac{\Gamma(\alpha_i)\Gamma(\beta_i)}{\Gamma(\alpha_i + \beta_i)}.$$

Both of these attempts only slightly improve the dependence structure of the Dirichlet distribution, and as Aitchison points out, the problem of finding a class of distributions that generalizes the Dirichlet distribution and enriches it with more dependence structure is still open.

3.2.4   SUMMARY

Multinomial distributions are an important building block in NLP models, especially when considering generative modeling techniques. Most linguistic structures in NLP can be described in terms of parts that originate in multinomial distributions. For example, each rule in a phrase-structure tree, with a probabilistic context-free grammar model, originates in a multinomial distribution that generates the right-hand sides of rules from a multinomial associated with the left-hand side nonterminal.

As such, there has been an extensive use of priors over multinomials in Bayesian NLP, most notably, with the Dirichlet distribution. The choice of the Dirichlet originates in its conjugacy to the multinomial distribution, which leads to tractability, but it can also be used to encourage the model to manifest properties such as sparsity.

The second multinomial prior family discussed in this section is the family of logistic normal distributions. Unlike the Dirichlet, the logistic normal family of distributions incorporates explicit covariance structure between the various parameters of the multinomial distribution. It has additive and multiplicative versions.

3.3   NON-INFORMATIVE PRIORS

The priors discussed up to this point are mostly *informative*. With informative priors, there is an attempt on the part of the modeler to capture a certain belief about the parameters in the prior, and incorporate it into the analysis. For example, with the Dirichlet prior, this belief can be about the sparsity of the parameter space. With the logistic normal distribution, on the other hand, this belief can be related to some parameter dependence structure in the parameter space.

It is sometimes the case that there is a preference for a *non-informative* prior—i.e., a prior that does not bias the analysis in any way. The need for such a type of prior emerges when there are no definite prior beliefs about the parameters.

Using non-informative priors may seem counter-intuitive: in NLP, one of the reasons for using the Bayesian approach is precisely to bias the predictions toward more plausible structures through the use of a well-informed prior. If there are no prior beliefs, why should one use the Bayesian approach to begin with?

The answer to that question is not straightforward. This question is the root of the debate between "subjectivists" and "objectivists"—those who view Bayesian probability as a degree of personal belief, and those who believe it should denote an objective rational measure of knowledge, and as such, should not be influenced by subjective prior choice. Non-informative priors fit better the view of objectivists. Some of the supporters of this view derive Bayesian statistics through a set of axioms (Cox, 1946, Jaynes, 2003), and believe that this view is better for scientific reasoning than the subjective view. See also Section 1.7.

The use of non-informative priors often leads to congruence with frequentist methodology, as discussed in Chapter 4. But still, using a non-informative prior permits inference that explores the space of parameters more effectively if the posterior over the parameters is integrated when making predictions about the structure.

This point is demonstrated by Goldwater and Griffiths (2007). When the authors compared their HMM models for part-of-speech tagging (one model is a fully Bayesian HMM model with a uniform prior over the parameters of the transition and the emission matrices, and the other is a vanilla HMM model that is estimated using maximum likelihood), they discovered that averaging their predictions uniformly over the space of parameters improved the prediction of part-of-speech tags.

Still, non-informative priors in Bayesian NLP are most often used as *hyperpriors*—that is, as hierarchical priors on top of the hyperparameters, and not the parameters of the model. This is discussed in Section 3.5.

3.3.1   UNIFORM AND IMPROPER PRIORS

One approach to choosing a non-informative prior $p(\theta)$ over the parameter space Θ follows intuition: choose a prior that assigns the same density to all $\theta \in \Theta$.

For example, whenever the set Θ is a subset of $\mathbb{R}^d$ and has a finite volume $v(\Theta)$ (according to Lebesgue measure), then the uniform prior over Θ is simply the constant distribution $p(\theta) = 1/v(\Theta)$. However, forcing a uniform distribution over a set Θ sometimes leads to *improper* priors. An improper prior $p(\theta)$ is a "prior" that violates the integrate-to-one requirement from $p(\theta)$:

$$\int_{\theta} p(\theta)d\theta = \infty.$$

For example, there is no uniform distribution on the real line $\mathbb{R}$ (or more generally, any unbounded set in $\mathbb{R}^d$ for $d \in \mathbb{N}$), simply because for any $c > 0$, the integral $\int_{-\infty}^{\infty} cd\theta$ diverges to infinity. As a consequence, any attempt to define a uniform prior on the real line will lead to an improper prior.

Even when the prior is improper, it is still technically (or algebraically) possible to use Bayes' rule to calculate the posterior,

$$p(\theta|x) = \frac{p(\theta)p(x \mid \theta)}{\int_{\theta} p(\theta)p(x \mid \theta)d\theta},$$

and get a proper posterior distribution—if the integral $\int_{\theta} p(\theta)p(x \mid \theta)d\theta$ converges. For this reason, improper priors are sometimes used by Bayesians, as long as the posterior is well-defined.

When using $p(\theta) = c$ for $c > 0$, i.e., a uniform (possibly improper) prior, there is an overlap between Bayesian statistics and maximum likelihood estimation, which is a purely frequentist method. This is discussed in Section 4.2.1.

When a flat uniform prior becomes an improper prior, it is possible to instead use a *vague* prior. Such a prior is not improper, but it is also not uniform. Instead, it has a large spread, such that its tail goes to 0 to avoid divergence of the prior when integrating over the parameter space. The tail is usually "heavy" in order to retain a distribution that is as close as possible to uniform.

3.3.2 JEFFREYS PRIOR

One criticism of non-informative priors, as described above, is that they are not invariant to re-parameterization. This means that if θ is transformed into a new representation for the parameters, using a one-to-one (perhaps even smooth) mapping, the resulting non-informative prior will have different properties, and will not remain a uniform prior, for example.

Intuitively, if a prior is not informative about the parameters, the prior should stay consistent under re-parametrization. This means that the probability mass assigned to a set of parameters should remain the same as the probability mass assigned to the set of these parameters after being re-parametrized. For this reason, statisticians have sought out sets of priors that could still be considered to be non-informative, but remain invariant to transformations of the parameters. One example of such a prior is Jeffreys prior (Jeffreys, 1961).

Jeffreys priors are defined based on the *Fisher information* in the parameters. In the case of multivariate parameter vector θ, coupled with a likelihood function $p(x|\theta)$, the Fisher information $i(\theta)$ is a function of the parameter values, which returns a matrix:

$$(i(\theta))_{ij} = -E\left[\left(\frac{\partial^2}{\partial\theta_i\theta_j}\log p(x|\theta)\right)\bigg|\theta\right].$$

When θ is univariate, then the Fisher information reduces to be the variance of the *score function*, which is the derivative of the log-likelihood function. Jeffreys (1961) proposed to define the following prior:

$$p(\theta) \propto \sqrt{\det(i(\theta))}.$$

Eisenstein et al. (2011) used a Jeffreys prior in their Sparse Additive Generative (SAGE) model on a parameter that serves as a variance value for a draw from the Gaussian distribution. Several draws from the Gaussian distribution, each with their own variance, are combined with a "background distribution" to produce a distribution over a set of words, representing a topic. Eisenstein et al. claim that the use of the normal-Jeffreys combination (compared to a normal-exponential combination they also tried) encourages sparsity, and also alleviates the need to choose a hyperparameter for the prior (the Jeffreys prior they use is not parametrized).

Still, the use of Jeffreys priors in current Bayesian NLP work is uncommon. It is more common to use uniform non-informative priors or vague priors using the Gamma distribution. However, the strong relationship between the Dirichlet and multinomial distributions appears again in the context of Jeffreys priors. The symmetric Dirichlet with hyperparameter $1/2$ (see Section 3.2.1) is the Jeffreys prior for the multinomial distribution.

In cases where a hierarchical prior is of interest (see Section 3.5), and the structure of the model is Dirichlet-multinomial, one could choose to use a Jeffreys prior for the Dirichlet distribution hyperparameters (Yang and Berger, 1998). If the Dirichlet distribution is parametrized by $\alpha_1, \ldots, \alpha_K > 0$, then Jeffreys prior for over α is $p(\alpha) \propto \sqrt{\det(i(\alpha_1, \ldots, \alpha_K))}$ where:

$$[i(\alpha_1, \ldots, \alpha_K)]_{ii} = \psi'(\alpha_i) - \psi'\left(\sum_{i=1}^{K} \alpha_i\right) \qquad i \in \{1, \ldots, K\}$$

$$[i(\alpha_1, \ldots, \alpha_K)]_{ij} = -\psi'\left(\sum_{i=1}^{K} \alpha_i\right) \qquad i \neq j; i, j \in \{1, \ldots, K\}.$$

3.3.3 DISCUSSION

There is no clear agreement in the statistics community on what it means for a prior to be non-informative. Some argue that uniform priors are non-informative because they assign an equal probability to all parameters in the parameter space. However, when they exist, uniform priors are not invariant to re-parametrization and therefore are not considered to be non-informative by many statisticians. Jeffreys priors, on the other hand, are invariant to re-parametrization, but they can have a preference bias for certain parts of the parameter space.

3.4 CONJUGACY AND EXPONENTIAL MODELS

The exponential family is an important family of models that is useful in statistics and is highly common in NLP as well. To begin, denote the parameter space of an exponential model by Θ, and the sample space by Ω. For defining a specific exponential model, we are required to define the following functions:

- $\eta: \Theta \to \mathbb{R}^d$ for some d

- $t: \Omega \to \mathbb{R}^d$ (t is also called "the sufficient statistics")

- $h: \Omega \to (\mathbb{R}^+ \cup \{0\})$ (also called "the base measure")

These functions define the following model:

$$p(x|\theta) = h(x) \exp(\eta(\theta) \cdot t(x) - A(\theta)),$$

where $A(\theta)$ is used as a normalization constant (and is also called "the log-partition function"), defined as:

$$A(\theta) = \log\left(\sum_x h(x) \exp(\eta(\theta) \cdot t(x))\right).$$

Many well-known distributions fall into this category of the exponential family. For example, the categorical distribution for a space Ω with d events, $\Omega = \{1, \ldots, d\}$, and parameters $\theta_1, \ldots, \theta_d$, can be represented as an exponential model with:

$$\eta_i(\theta) = \log(\theta_i), \tag{3.15}$$
$$t_i(x) = I(x = i), \tag{3.16}$$
$$h(x) = 1. \tag{3.17}$$

Many other distributions fall into that category, such as the Gaussian distribution, the Dirichlet distribution, the Gamma distribution and others.

An exponential model can be reparametrized, where the new set of parameters is $\eta(\Omega)$, and η is replaced with the identity function. In this case, we say that the exponential model is in natural form (with "natural parameters"). The rest of the discussion focuses on exponential models in natural form, such that:

$$p(x|\eta) = h(x) \exp(\eta \cdot t(x) - A(\eta)). \tag{3.18}$$

There is a strong relationship between the log-partition function and the mean of the sufficient statistics. More specifically, it can be shown that:

$$\frac{\partial A(\eta)}{\partial \eta_i} = E[t_i(X)].$$

This fact is used in NLP quite often when we are required to compute the gradient of a log-linear model to optimize its parameters. In the case of Ω being a combinatorial discrete space, such as a set of parse trees or labeled sequences, dynamic programming algorithms can be used to compute these expectations. See Chapter 8 for more detail.

Since we discuss the Bayesian setting, it is natural to inquire about what a conjugate prior is for an exponential model. A conjugate prior for the model in Equation 3.18 is also an exponential model of the following general form:

$$p(\eta|\xi_0, \xi) = f(\xi_0, \xi) \exp(\xi^\top \eta - \xi_0 A(\eta)),$$

where $\xi \in \mathbb{R}^d$, $\xi_0 \in \mathbb{R}$ and $f: \mathbb{R}^d \to (\mathbb{R}^+ \cup \{0\})$. This general result can be used to prove many of the conjugacy relationships between pairs of well-known distributions. (See the exercises at the end of this chapter.) There is also a strong relationship between exponential models in their natural form and log-linear models. More information about log-linear models is found in Section 4.2.1.

3.5 MULTIPLE PARAMETER DRAWS IN MODELS

Consider the basic Bayesian model, in which parameters are drawn from a prior $p(\theta)$ and then the data is drawn from a distribution $p(X|\theta)$. Here, the data is abstractly represented using

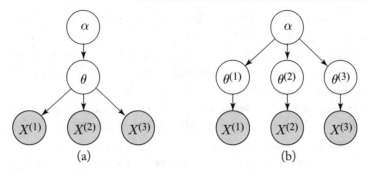

Figure 3.2: A graphical depiction of the two levels at which a prior can be placed for a model with three observations. (a) Parameters for all of the observations are being drawn once; (b) multiple parameters are re-drawn for each observation, in an empirical Bayes style. Shaded nodes are observed.

a random variable X, but it is often the case that the observed data is composed of multiple observations $x^{(1)}, \ldots, x^{(n)}$, all drawn from the distribution $p(X|\theta)$.

In this case, one way to write the joint distribution over the data and parameters is:

$$p\left(\theta, x^{(1)}, \ldots, x^{(n)}\right) = p(\theta) \prod_{i=1}^{n} p\left(x^{(i)}|\theta\right).$$

A more careful look into this equation reveals that there is an additional degree of freedom in the placement of the prior. Instead of drawing the parameters once for all data points, one could draw a set of parameters for *each* data point. In such a case, the joint distribution is:

$$p\left(\theta^{(1)}, \ldots, \theta^{(n)}, x^{(1)}, \ldots, x^{(n)}\right) = \prod_{i=1}^{n} p\left(\theta^{(i)}\right) p\left(x^{(i)}|\theta^{(i)}\right).$$

This type of model is also called a *compound sampling model*. With this approach to prior modeling, the distribution

$$p\left(\theta^{(1)}, \ldots, \theta^{(n)}\right) = \prod_{i=1}^{n} p\left(\theta^{(i)}\right) \tag{3.19}$$

can be considered to be a single prior over the joint set of parameters $(\theta^{(1)}, \ldots, \theta^{(n)})$. These two approaches are graphically depicted in Figure 3.2.

Conceptually, both approaches to prior placement have advantages and disadvantages when modeling natural language. Drawing the parameters for each observation permits more flexibility across the observations (or the predicted structures, in the case of latent variable models), allowing the model to capture variation across the corpus, that arises, for example, because of difference in authors or genres. Generating the parameter at the top level (only once) suggests that inference needs to be done in a smaller space: there is a need to find the posterior over a single set of parameters. This reduces the complexity of the model.

When parameters are drawn separately for each datum (i.e., we use the prior in Equation 3.19), it is often useful to assume some kind of dependencies between these parameters. We are also interested in inferring the hyperparameters, in order to infer dependencies between the parameters. There are two dominating approaches to conducting this type of inference. Both approaches assume that the prior $p(\theta)$ from which $\theta^{(i)}$ are drawn is controlled by hyperparameters, so that we have $p(\theta|\alpha)$ for some α.

The first approach is called empirical Bayes (Berger, 1985). Empirical Bayes here means that the hyperparameters are *estimated* as well, usually by using a maximum likelihood criterion. For more information about empirical Bayes, see Section 4.3.

The second approach is hierarchical Bayesian modeling. Hierarchical Bayesian models are models in which the hyperparameters (which parametrize the prior) themselves are associated with a (hyper)prior as well. A hierarchical Bayesian model would add an additional level of priors, usually parametric (parametrized by $\lambda \in \Lambda$), $p(\alpha \mid \lambda)$ such that the joint distribution is:

$$p\left(\alpha, \theta^{(1)}, \ldots, \theta^{(n)}, x^{(1)}, \ldots, x^{(n)}|\lambda\right) = p(\alpha \mid \lambda) \prod_{i=1}^{n} p\left(\theta^{(i)}|\alpha\right) p\left(x^{(i)}|\theta\right).$$

The choice of a second stage prior (or *hyperprior*) has a less noticeable effect than the choice of a first stage prior on the predictions the model makes. Therefore, vague priors and priors that are mathematically convenient are more common as priors over hyperparameters, even though they might not be the best fit for our beliefs about the model.

Unfortunately, many Bayesian NLP papers do not make it explicit in their model description whether parameters are drawn for each example or whether there is a single set of parameters for all observations and latent structures. This ambiguity mostly arises because typically, the generative process of a Bayesian NLP model is described for a single observation (or latent structure). The "loop" over all observations is not made explicit in the description of the model.

With hidden Markov models, for example (Chapter 8), with a single draw of the parameters for the HMM, there is an implicit treatment in many papers of the issue with multiple sequences as datapoints. One can assume that all sequences in the data are concatenated together into a single sequence, with a separator symbol between them. Then, we can proceed with inference for this single sequence. This leads to an equivalent scenario as having multiple sequences, where the probabilities for transitioning from the separator symbol to any other symbol are treated as initial probabilities.

As a general rule, readers of Bayesian NLP papers should usually assume that there is a single set of parameters drawn for all observations unless the paper is set in the empirical Bayesian setting or in a hierarchical Bayesian setting. This general rule is overridden by other clues about the placement of the prior, such as the derivation of the inference algorithm or other Bayesian baselines that the method in the paper is compared against.

This book tries to be as explicit as possible about the placement of the prior. The prior is abstractly defined at the top level, but the reader should consider that in many cases, θ actually represents multiple draws of parameters, with the prior defined in Equation 3.19.

Both hierarchical Bayesian modeling and empirical Bayes can be used in the case of a single parameter draw for all parameters. However, they are most often used in NLP in the context of multiple parameter draws, especially in the empirical Bayes setting.

3.6   STRUCTURAL PRIORS

A large body of work in Bayesian NLP focuses on cases in which the model *structure* is fixed. Model structure here is not rigorously defined, but it refers to the representation that makes the core underlying independence assumptions in the model. It can be, for example, a context-free grammar or a directed graphical model. For this structure to be functional in the context of data, it is associated with parameters for its various components. PCFGs, for example, associated each rule with a rule probability.

Since we usually assume the structure is fixed, the priors in Bayesian NLP are defined over the parameters of this structure. Setting a prior over the model structure is more complex. One implicit way to do it is to have the structure make very few independence assumptions, and incorporate many components that are potentially not used for a given fixed set of parameters (such as all possible right-hand sides for a context-free grammar). Then, choosing a sparse prior for this model (for example, a symmetric Dirichlet with a small concentration hyperparameter), will essentially lead to selecting a subset of these components from the model.

There are several more explicit examples of the use of structural priors in NLP. Eisner (2002), for example, defines a structural "transformational prior" over the right-hand sides of context-free rules. Eisner's goal was to introduce rules into the grammar that were never seen in the training data. The introduction of rules is done by introducing local edit operations to existing rules. The full set of rules is represented as a graph, where the nodes correspond to the rules, and edges correspond to possible transitions from one rule to another using a local edit operation (removing a nonterminal in the right-hand side, adding one or replacing it). The edges in this graph are weighted, and determine the probability of the rule in the final grammar.

Other cases for setting structural priors in a Bayesian setting include that of Stolcke and Omohundro (1994). Stolcke was interested in learning the structure of a grammar using a "Bayesian merging model." See Section 8.9 for more information.

3.7   CONCLUSION AND SUMMARY

The prior distribution is the basic mechanism in Bayesian statistics used to help manage uncertainty in the parameters. The prior distribution has to be chosen with two trade-offs in mind: the prior's expressivity and ability to capture properties in the parameter space, and its tractability for posterior inference.

Conjugate priors are one type of prior that focuses more on the second aspect of this trade-off. Since Bayesian NLP models are usually based on categorical distributions, the use of the Dirichlet distribution, which is a conjugate prior to the categorical distribution, is prevalent in Bayesian NLP.

The Dirichlet distribution has some limitations, and other priors over multinomials, such as the logistic normal distribution, can be used instead of the Dirichlet. Such priors are harder to tackle computationally, but this challenge can be overcome using approximate inference methods.

It is often the case in Bayesian NLP that hierarchical priors are used, and uncertainty about the hyperparameters is actually managed using another prior. This type of prior (also called hyperprior) is less susceptible to performance degradation as a result of an unsuitable choice of prior family. This is due to hyperprior's location in the hierarchy of the model, which is farther from the parameters than the direct prior over the parameters.

There are two approaches in Bayesian NLP for placing the prior. The first option is to put the prior at the top level, with parameters being drawn once for all observations. A second option is for parameters to be drawn separately for each of the observations (or latent structures). This approach is often associated with hierarchical priors and empirical Bayes estimation (see Section 4.3).

Priors are an important part of the mechanics behind Bayesian inference. More abstractly, they should be viewed as a way to model the prior beliefs of the modeler about the various hypotheses (or parameters, for parametric models).

An unexplored territory that could be of special interest to Bayesian NLP is that of *prior elicitation*. With prior elicitation, priors are constructed based on expert knowledge (in the language domain, such expert could be a linguist). In some areas of research, the expert would simply have to pick a hyperparameter setting for the prior family. In NLP, such prior elicitation can perhaps be used to incorporate linguistic information using a clear set of principles.

3.8   EXERCISES

3.1.   Following Section 3.1.4, show that if a distribution is conjugate to another, the relationship is maintained when the first distribution is renormalized to a subset of the parameter space.

3.2.   Verify that the multinomial or categorical distribution can be represented as an exponential model (i.e., show that Equations 3.15–3.17 are correct).

3.3.   Show that the Dirichlet distribution can be represented as an exponential model, and use Section 3.4 to show the Dirichlet-multinomial conjugacy.

3.4.   Alice designed a model that is parametrized by a single integer parameter, $p(X|\lambda)$ where $\lambda \in \mathbb{N}$. She is now interested in defining a prior $p(\lambda)$. Alice does not have much information about the parameter or prior knowledge about the problem, so she wants to define a uniform prior over $\mathbb{N}$ for λ. Show that any such prior is going to be improper.

3.5.   Alice, from the previous question, is not happy with her prior being improper. She learned more about the problem she is modeling, and now believes that λ should be centered around 0, and drop exponentially as $|\lambda|$ increases. Can you suggest a proper prior for λ? (It should be hyperparametrized by a single parameter α that decides on the rate of the exponential decay.)

CHAPTER 4

Bayesian Estimation

The main goal of Bayesian inference is to derive (from data) a posterior distribution over the latent variables in the model, most notably the parameters of the model. This posterior can be subsequently used to probabilistically infer the range of parameters (through Bayesian interval estimates, in which we make predictive statements such as "the parameter θ is in the interval $[0.5, 0.56]$ with probability 0.95"), compute the parameters' mean or mode, or compute other expectations over quantities of interest. All of these are ways to *summarize* the posterior, instead of retaining the posterior in its fullest form as a distribution, as described in the previous two chapters.

In the traditional use of Bayesian statistics, this posterior summarization is done in order to generate interpretable conclusions about the nature of the problem or data at hand. Differing from the traditional use of Bayesian statistics, natural language processing is not usually focused on summarizing the posterior for this kind of interpretation, but is instead focused on improving the predictive power of the model for unseen data points. Examples for such predictions are the syntactic tree of a sentence, the alignment of two sentences or the morphological segmentation of a word.[1]

The most basic way to summarize the posterior for the use of an NLP problem is to compute a point estimate from the posterior. This means that we identify a single point in the parameter space (and therefore, a distribution from the model family) to be used for further predictions. At first it may seem that such an approach misses the point behind Bayesian inference, which aims to manage uncertainty about the parameters of the model using full distributions; however, posterior summarization, such as the posterior mean, often integrates over many values of the parameters, and therefore, future predictions using this posterior summary rely heavily on the prior (the posterior takes into account the prior), especially when small amounts of data are available.

Posterior summarization is usually contrasted with the "fully Bayesian" approach, in which predictions use the full posterior for any prediction. An example of a fully Bayesian approach is the integration of the posterior over the parameters against the likelihood function to find the highest scoring structure, averaging over all possible parameters. To understand the difference between this fully Bayesian approach and identifying a point estimate, see Section 4.1. While

---

[1]There are cases in which the actual values of the parameters are of interest in NLP problems. The parameters can be used during the development phase, to determine which features in a model assist the most in improving its predictive power. The actual values can also be used to interpret the model and understand the patterns that it has learned. This information can be used iteratively to improve the expressive power of the model.

the Bayesian approach is more "correct" probabilistically, from a Bayesian point of view, it is often intractable to follow. On the other hand, posterior summarization, like frequentist point estimates, leads to lightweight models that can be easily used in future predictions.

This chapter includes a discussion of several ways in which the posterior can be summarized, and also relates some of these approaches to frequentist estimation. The chapter includes two main parts: the first part appears in Section 4.2, and details the core ways to summarize a posterior in Bayesian NLP; the second part appears in Section 4.3, and explains the empirical Bayes approach, in which point estimates are obtained for the *hyperparameters*, which can often be used as a substitute for a point estimate for the parameters themselves.

The techniques described in this chapter stand in contrast to the techniques described in Chapter 5 (sampling methods) and Chapter 6 (variational inference). The techniques in these latter chapters describe ways to fully identify the posterior, or at least identify a means to draw samples from it. While the techniques in these chapters are often used for fully-Bayesian inference, they can also be used to identify the posterior and then summarize it using the approaches described in this chapter.

4.1   LEARNING WITH LATENT VARIABLES: TWO VIEWS

In the unsupervised setting, in which only "input" examples are available (for the training process), without examples of the "output," one usually makes a distinction made between two approaches to learning.

In the first approach, inference is done on all of the observed data available. This includes the data on which we want our final predictions to be made. In the second approach, one adheres to the machine learning tradition of splitting the training data into a training set (and potentially a development set) and a test set; next, one estimates the model parameters using the training set, performs some fine tuning using the development set, and finally decodes unseen examples in the test set in order to evaluate the predictive power of the model.

There are examples of following both of these approaches in Bayesian NLP. Naturally, the first approach is appropriate only in an unsupervised setting, and not in a supervised case. It is therefore not surprising that the first approach is common in Bayesian NLP—as discussed in Chapter 2, Bayesian NLP focuses to a large degree on unsupervised learning from data.

The fully Bayesian approach can be used with a separate training and test set, but this separation is more common in Bayesian NLP when using Bayesian point estimation. The fully Bayesian approach usually requires computationally heavy approximate inference algorithms. This setting is not always a good fit for NLP, as NLP systems often require lightweight models with fast inference on unseen data points. This is especially true for NLP systems which are deployed for commercial or other large-scale use. In these circumstances, Bayesian point estimation can function as a balance between the Bayesian approach and the need for lightweight models.

As mentioned above, Bayesian point estimation is not the only option for combining Bayesian inference with the train-test traditional machine learning methodology. If the training set in an unsupervised problem includes the instances $x^{(1)}, \ldots, x^{(n)}$ and we are interested in decoding a new example x' with a structure z', we can infer the full posterior over the parameters using the training instances:

$$p\left(\theta | x^{(1)}, \ldots, x^{(n)}\right) = \sum_{z^{(1)}, \ldots, z^{(n)}} p\left(\theta, z^{(1)}, \ldots, z^{(n)} | x^{(1)}, \ldots, x^{(n)}\right),$$

and then proceed by decoding from the approximate posterior:

$$p\left(z' \mid x^{(1)}, \ldots, x^{(n)}, x'\right) \approx \int_{\theta} p\left(z' | \theta, x'\right) p\left(\theta | x^{(1)}, \ldots, x^{(n)}\right) d\theta. \tag{4.1}$$

This approximation is especially accurate when n is large. In order for the posterior to be exact, we would need to condition the parameter distribution on x' as well, i.e.:

$$p\left(z' \mid x^{(1)}, \ldots, x^{(n)}, x'\right) = \int_{\theta} p\left(z' \mid \theta, x'\right) p\left(\theta \mid x^{(1)}, \ldots, x^{(n)}, x'\right) d\theta. \tag{4.2}$$

But with a large n the effect of x' on the posterior is negligible, in which case Equation 4.1 describes a good approximation for the right hand-side of Equation 4.2. The derivation of Equation 4.2 is a direct result of the independence between input (and output) instances conditioned on the set of parameters θ.

Integrating the likelihood in this manner against the posterior is quite complex and computationally inefficient. For this reason, we often resort to approximation methods when inferring this posterior (such as sampling or variational inference), or alternatively, use Bayesian point estimation.

4.2 BAYESIAN POINT ESTIMATION

The focus of Bayesian point estimation is on summarizing the posterior over the parameters into a fixed set of parameters. This kind of estimation often has a strong relationship to frequentist approaches to estimation, such as maximum likelihood estimation or regularized maximum likelihood estimation. This relationship is most evident in the case of deriving a Bayesian estimate using Bayesian maximum a posterior (MAP) estimation, as described in the next section.

4.2.1 MAXIMUM A POSTERIORI ESTIMATION

This section begins by considering MAP estimation in the complete data setting (i.e., in the supervised setting). Let $p(\theta)$ be some prior for a model with likelihood $p(X|\theta)$. The generative process is such that θ is drawn from the prior, and then $x^{(1)}, \ldots, x^{(n)}$ are drawn independently (given θ) with probability $p(x^{(i)} \mid \theta)$. The random variables that correspond to these observations are $X^{(1)}, \ldots, X^{(n)}$. The MAP estimation chooses the point estimate θ^* which is the mode of the posterior:

$$\theta^* = \arg\max_{\theta} p\left(\theta \mid x^{(1)}, \ldots, x^{(n)}\right) = \arg\max_{\theta} \frac{p(\theta)p\left(x^{(1)}, \ldots, x^{(n)} \mid \theta\right)}{p\left(x^{(1)}, \ldots, x^{(n)}\right)}.$$

The motivation behind MAP estimation is simple and intuitive: choose the set of parameters that are most likely according to the posterior, which takes into account both the prior and the observed data. Note that $p\left(x^{(1)}, \ldots, x^{(n)}\right)$ does not depend on θ which is maximized over, and therefore:

$$\theta^* = \arg\max_{\theta} p(\theta)p\left(x^{(1)}, \ldots, x^{(n)} \mid \theta\right).$$

In addition, since $X^{(i)}$ for $i \in \{1, \ldots, n\}$ are independent given θ and since the log function is monotone, the MAP estimator corresponds to:

$$\theta^* = \arg\max_{\theta} \log p(\theta) + L(\theta), \tag{4.3}$$

where

$$L(\theta) = \sum_{i=1}^{n} \log p(x^{(i)} \mid \theta).$$

If $p(\theta)$ is constant (for example, when $p(\theta)$ denotes a uniform distribution over the probability simplex, a symmetric Dirichlet with hyperparameter 1), then Equation 4.3 recovers the maximum likelihood (ML) solution. The function $L(\theta)$ equals the log-likelihood function used with ML estimation. A uniform prior $p(\theta)$ is considered to be a non-informative prior, and is discussed more in Section 3.3.

More generally, the term $\log p(\theta)$ serves as a penalty term in the objective in Equation 4.3. This penalty term makes the objective smaller when θ is highly unlikely according to the prior.

Relationship to Minimum Description Length

Minimum Description Length (MDL) refers to an idea in machine learning that is based on the old principle of Occam's Razor. The MDL principle suggests that a hypothesis (or a set of parameters, in our case) should be chosen so that it encodes the observed data in the most succinct manner. This succinct representation should naturally encode the hypothesis itself.

MAP estimation exactly follows the framework of MDL for probabilistic encoding. If we negate log terms for the prior and the likelihood in Equation 4.3, the optimization problem turns from a maximization to a minimization problem. The term $-\log p(\theta)$ denotes the number of natbits it takes to encode the hypothesis according to a certain code. This code is optimal for encoding hypotheses (i.e., it minimizes the expected code length) that distribute according to $p(\theta)$.

Similarly, the log-likelihood term denotes the number of natbits it takes to encode the data, based on the hypothesis θ it conditions on, using a code that minimizes the expected number of natbits it takes to encode data distributed according to the likelihood for this θ.

These two natbit-quantified values together compose a measure for the number of natbits required to represent the hypothesis learned from the data. They combine our prior beliefs and our observations from data. We then minimize these values together following principles such as Occam's razor.

When $\log_2$ is used instead of the natural logarithm, the unit of measurement changes from natbits to bits. The choice of a base for the logarithm does not change the MAP solution.

The Dirichlet and Additive Smoothing

Sparse counts need to be carefully handled in language data. For example, it is well-known that distributions over words, or more generally, over n-grams, follow a Zipfian distribution; this means that there is a heavy tail of rare n-grams, and most of the probability mass is concentrated on a relatively small set of n-grams. Since the tail is quite heavy, and includes most of the word types in the language, it cannot be ignored. Yet, it is hard to estimate the probabilities of each element in this tail, because single elements from this tail do not occur often in corpora. Assigning non-zero probability only to n-grams that actually occur in the text that we use to estimate the probabilities can lead to zero probabilities for n-grams that appear in a held-out dataset. This can be quite detrimental to any model, as it makes the model brittle and not robust to noise. To demonstrate this, consider that if any model assigns zero probability to even a single unseen n-gram that occurs when testing the model, the log-likelihood of the whole data diverges to negative infinity.[2] More generally, the variance of naïve estimates for n-grams that occur infrequently is very large. We turn now to describe a connection between approaches to solve this sparsity issue and the Dirichlet distribution.

Consider the case in which θ is drawn from a symmetric Dirichlet, with hyperparameter $\alpha > 0$. In addition, $x^{(1)}, \ldots, x^{(n)}$ are drawn from the multinomial distribution θ (each $x^{(i)} \in \{0,1\}^K$ is such that $\sum_{j=1}^{K} x_j^{(i)} = 1$ for every i). In Section 3.2.1, we showed that the posterior $p(\theta \mid x^{(1)}, \ldots, x^{(n)}, \alpha)$ is also a Dirichlet, with hyperparameters $(\alpha, \alpha, \ldots, \alpha) + \sum_{i=1}^{n} x^{(i)}$.

The density of the Dirichlet distribution has a single maximum point when all hyperparameters are larger than 1. In this case, if θ^* is the posterior maximizer, then:

---

[2]For this reason, certain language modeling toolkits, such as the SRI language modeling toolkit (Stolcke, 2002), have the option to ignore unseen words when computing perplexity on unseen data.

$$\theta_j^* = \frac{(\alpha - 1) + \sum_{i=1}^{n} x_j^{(i)}}{K(\alpha - 1) + \sum_{j=1}^{K} \sum_{i=1}^{n} x_j^{(i)}}. \tag{4.4}$$

When $\alpha = 1$, the $\alpha - 1$ terms in the numerator and the denominator disappear, and we recover the maximum likelihood estimate—the estimate for θ^* is just composed of the relative frequency of each event. Indeed, when $\alpha = 1$, the prior $p(\theta|\alpha)$ with the Dirichlet is just a uniform non-informative prior, and therefore we recover the MLE (see previous section and Equation 4.3).

When $\alpha > 1$, the MAP estimation in Equation 4.4 with Dirichlet-multinomial corresponds to a *smoothed* maximum likelihood estimation. A pseudo-count, $\alpha - 1$, is added to each observation. This type of smoothing, also called additive smoothing, or Laplace-Lidstone smoothing, has been regularly used in data-driven NLP since its early days, because it helps to alleviate the problem of sparse counts in language data. (With $\alpha < 1$, there is a discounting effect, because $\alpha - 1 < 0$.)

Additive smoothing is especially compelling because it is easy to implement. The interpretation as a MAP solution has its added value, but it is not the origin of additive smoothing. Indeed, additive smoothing has been used for n-gram models in the NLP community since the late 80s, without necessarily referring to its Bayesian interpretation.

Chen and Goodman (1996) describe a thorough investigation of smoothing techniques for language modeling, and compare additive smoothing to other smoothing techniques. Their findings were that additive smoothing is far from being the optimal solution for an accurate estimation of n-gram models. Katz smoothing (Katz, 1987) and interpolation with lower order estimation of n-gram language models (Jelinek and Mercer, 1980) performed considerably better on a held-out data set (the reported performance measure is cross-entropy; see Appendix A). Not surprisingly, smoothing the counts by adding 1 to all of them (as has been argued to be a "morally correct" choice by Lidstone (1920) and Jeffreys (1961)) did not perform as well as smoothing by varying the pseudo-counts added to the n-gram counts.[3]

In spite of its lack of optimality, additive smoothing still remains a basic tool in NLP which is often tried out after vanilla maximum likelihood estimation. This is probably due to additive smoothing's efficiency and straightforward implementation as an extension of maximum likelihood estimation. However, it is often the case that in order to achieve state-of-the-art performance with maximum likelihood estimation, a more complex smoothing scheme is required, such as interpolation or incorporation of lower order models.

---

[3]Modern language models more often use smoothing techniques such as the one by Kneser and Ney (1995), for which a Bayesian interpretation was discovered relatively recently (under a nonparametric model). See Chapter 7.4.1.

MAP Estimation and Regularization

There is a strong connection between maximum *a posteriori* estimation with certain Bayesian priors and a frequentist type of regularization, in which an objective function, such as the log-likelihood, is augmented with a regularization term to avoid overfitting. We now describe this connection with log-linear models.

Log-linear models are a common type of model for supervised problems in NLP. In the generative case, a model is defined on pairs (x, z) where x is the input to the decoding problem and z is the structure to be predicted. The model form is the following:

$$p(X, Z | \theta) = \frac{\exp\left(\sum_{j=1}^{K} \theta_j f_j(X, Z)\right)}{A(\theta)},$$

where $f(x, z) = (f_1(x, z), \ldots, f_K(x, z))$ is a *feature vector* that extracts information about the pair (x, z) in order to decide on its probability according to the model.

Each function $f_i(x, z)$ maps (x, z) to $\mathbb{R}$, and is often just a binary function, taking values in $\{0, 1\}$ (to indicate the existence or absence of a sub-structure in x and z), or integrals, taking values in $\mathbb{N}$ (to count the number of times a certain sub-structure appears in x and z).

The function $A(\theta)$ is the partition function, defined in order to normalize the distribution:

$$A(\theta) = \sum_x A(\theta, x), \tag{4.5}$$

where

$$A(\theta, x) = \sum_z \exp\left(\sum_{j=1}^{K} \theta_j f_j(x, z)\right).$$

Alternatively, in a *discriminative* setting, only the predicted structures are modeled, and the log-linear model is defined as a conditional model:

$$p(Z | X, \theta) = \frac{\exp\left(\sum_{j=1}^{K} \theta_j f_j(X, Z)\right)}{A(\theta, X)}.$$

In this case, $A(\theta)$ in Equation 4.5 is not needed. This is important, because $A(\theta)$ is often intractable to compute because of the summation over all possible x, is not needed. On the other hand, the function $A(\theta, x)$ is often tractable to compute for a specific x, using algorithms such as dynamic programming algorithms (Chapter 8).

When $Z \in \{-1, 1\}$, log-linear models are framed as "logistic regression" (binary) classifiers. In that case, we define (note the lack of need for having a feature function that depends on the label because of the sum-to-1 constraint on the label probabilities):

$$p(Z|X, \theta) = \begin{cases} \dfrac{1}{1 + \exp\left(-\sum_{j=1}^{K} \theta_j f_j(X)\right)} & \textit{if} \quad Z = 1 \\[4mm] \dfrac{\exp\left(-\sum_{j=1}^{K} \theta_j f_j(X)\right)}{1 + \exp\left(-\sum_{j=1}^{K} \theta_j f_j(X)\right)} & \textit{if} \quad Z = -1. \end{cases}$$

Either way, both with generative and discriminative log-linear models or with logistic regression, the classical approach in NLP for estimating the parameters θ is to maximize a log-likelihood objective with respect to θ. In the generative case, the objective is:

$$\sum_{i=1}^{n} \log p\left(x^{(i)}, z^{(i)} \mid \theta\right),$$

and in the discriminative case it is[4]:

$$\sum_{i=1}^{n} \log p\left(z^{(i)} \mid x^{(i)}, \theta\right).$$

A naïve maximization of the likelihood often leads to overfitting the model to the training data. The parameter values are not constrained or penalized for being too large; therefore, the log-likelihood function tends to fit the parameters in such a way that even patterns in the data that are due to noise or do not represent a general case are taken into account. This makes the model not generalize as well to unseen data. With certain low-frequency features that are associated with a single output, the feature weights might even diverge to infinity.

Regularization is one solution to alleviate this problem. With L_2-regularization,[5] for example, the new objective function being optimized is (in the generative case):

$$\sum_{i=1}^{n} \log p\left(x^{(i)}, z^{(i)} \mid \theta\right) + R(\theta), \tag{4.6}$$

where

---

[4]Modern machine learning makes use of other discriminative learning algorithms for learning linear models similar to that, most notably max-margin algorithms and the perceptron algorithm.

[5]The L_2 norm of a vector $x \in \mathbb{R}^d$ is its Euclidean length: $\sqrt{\sum_{i=1}^{d} x_i^2}$.

$$R(\theta) = -\frac{1}{2\sigma^2} \left(\sum_{j=1}^{K} \theta_j^2 \right),$$

for some fixed $\sigma \in \mathbb{R}$. The regularized discriminative objective function is defined analogously, replacing the log-likelihood with the conditional log-likelihood.

The intuition behind this kind of regularization is simple. When the parameters become too large in the objective function (which happens when the objective function also fits the noise in the training data, leading to overfitting), the regularization term (in absolute value) becomes large and makes the entire objective much smaller. Therefore, depending on the value of σ, the regularization term $R(\theta)$ encourages solutions in which the features are closer to 0.

Even though this type of regularization is based on a frequentist approach to the problem of estimation, there is a connection between this regularization and Bayesian analysis. When exponentiating the regularization term and multiplying by a constant (which does not depend on θ), this regularization term becomes the value of the density function of the multivariate normal distribution, defined over θ, with zero mean and a diagonal covariance matrix with σ^2 on the diagonal.

This means that maximizing Equation 4.6 corresponds to maximizing:

$$\sum_{i=1}^{n} \log p \left(x^{(i)}, z^{(i)} \mid \theta \right) + \log p \left(\theta \mid \sigma^2 \right), \tag{4.7}$$

with $p \left(\theta | \sigma^2 \right)$ being a multivariate normal prior over the parameters θ. The mean value of this multivariate normal distribution is 0, and its covariance is $\sigma^2 I_{K \times K}$. Equation 4.7 has exactly the same structure as in Equation 4.3. Therefore, the L_2-regularization corresponds to a MAP estimation with a Gaussian prior over the parameters.

There are other alternatives to L_2 regularization. Consider, for example, the following prior on θ:

$$p(\theta \mid \lambda) = \prod_{j=1}^{K} p(\theta_j \mid \lambda)$$
$$p(\theta_j \mid \lambda) = \frac{1}{2\lambda} \exp \left(-\frac{|\theta_j|}{\lambda} \right). \tag{4.8}$$

The distribution over each θ_j in Equation 4.8 is also called the Laplace distribution (its mean is 0 and its variance is $2\lambda^2$; see Appendix B). The prior $p(\theta|\lambda)$ coupled with MAP estimation leads to a maximization problem of the form (ignoring constants):

$$\sum_{i=1}^{n} \log p \left(x^{(i)}, z^{(i)} \mid \theta \right) - \frac{1}{\lambda} \left(\sum_{j=1}^{K} |\theta_j| \right).$$

This type of regularization is also called L_1 regularization, and it is known to encourage sparse estimates for θ—i.e., θ in which many of the coordinates are exactly 0 (Bishop, 2006). The L_1 norm is actually used as a relaxation for a regularization term $\mathrm{Supp}(\theta)$ which is defined as:

$$\mathrm{Supp}(\theta) = |\{i \mid \theta_i \neq 0\}|.$$

Minimizing the support directly in conjunction with the log-likelihood is intractable, so relaxation such as L_1 is used.

MAP Estimation with Latent Variables

When latent variables are introduced to the estimation problem (such as in the case of unsupervised learning), MAP estimation can become much more cumbersome. Assume a joint distribution that factorizes as follows:

$$p \left(x^{(1)}, \ldots, x^{(n)}, z^{(1)}, \ldots, z^{(n)}, \theta \mid \alpha \right) = p(\theta | \alpha) \prod_{i=1}^{n} p \left(z^{(i)} \mid \theta, \alpha \right) p \left(x^{(i)} \mid z^{(i)}, \theta, \alpha \right).$$

The latent structures are denoted by the random variables $Z^{(i)}$, and the observations are denoted by the random variables $X^{(i)}$. The posterior has the form:

$$p \left(\theta, z^{(1)}, \ldots, z^{(n)} \mid x^{(1)}, \ldots, x^{(n)}, \alpha \right).$$

The most comprehensive way to get a point estimate from this posterior through MAP estimation is to marginalize $Z^{(i)}$ and then find θ^* as following:

$$\theta^* = \arg\max_{\theta} \sum_{z^{(1)}, \ldots, z^{(n)}} p \left(\theta, z^{(1)}, \ldots, z^{(n)} \mid x^{(1)}, \ldots, x^{(n)}, \alpha \right). \tag{4.9}$$

However, such an estimate often does not have an analytic form, and even computing it numerically can be inefficient. One possible way to avoid this challenge is to change the optimization problem in Equation 4.9 to:

$$\theta^* = \arg\max_{\theta} \max_{z^{(1)}, \ldots, z^{(n)}} p \left(\theta, z^{(1)}, \ldots, z^{(n)} \mid x^{(1)}, \ldots, x^{(n)}, \alpha \right). \tag{4.10}$$

This optimization problem, which identifies the mode of the posterior both with respect to the parameters *and* the latent variables, is often more manageable to solve. For example, simulation methods such as MCMC algorithms can be used together with *simulated annealing* to find the mode of this posterior. The idea behind simulated annealing is to draw samples, through MCMC inference, from the posterior after a transformation so that it puts most of its probability mass on its mode. The transformation is gradual, and determined by a "temperature schedule," which slowly decreases a temperature parameter. That particular temperature parameter determines how peaked the distribution is—the lower the temperature is, the more peaked the distribution. Simulated annealing is discussed in detail in Section 5.6. The replacement of the marginal maximization problem (Equation 4.9) with the optimization problem in Equation 4.10 is a significant approximation. It tends to work best when the posterior has a peaked form—i.e., most of the probability mass of the posterior is concentrated on a few elements in the set of possible structures to predict.

Another approximation to the optimization problem in Equation 4.9 can be based on variational approximations. In this case, the posterior is approximated using a distribution q, which often has a factorized form:

$$p\left(\theta, z^{(1)}, \ldots, z^{(n)}\right) \approx q(\theta) \times \left(\prod_{i=1}^{n} q\left(z^{(i)}\right)\right).$$

The distribution $q(\theta)$ is also assumed to have a parametric form, and identifying each constituent of the distribution q (for each predicted structure and the parameters) is done iteratively using approximate inference methods such as mean-field variational inference. Then, the approximate MAP is simply:

$$\theta^* = \arg\max_{\theta} q(\theta).$$

where $q(\theta)$ is the marginal approximate posterior distribution over the parameters. A thorough discussion of variational approximation methods in Bayesian NLP is found in Chapter 6.

4.2.2   POSTERIOR APPROXIMATIONS BASED ON THE MAP SOLUTION

In cases where $\Theta \subset \mathbb{R}^K$, the mode of the posterior can be used to obtain an approximate distribution of the posterior. This approximation assumes that the posterior behaves similarly to a multivariate normal distribution with a mean at the posterior mode (note that the mode and the mean of the multivariate normal distribution are identical).

Let x be an observation from the likelihood $p(x \mid \theta)$ with a prior $p(\theta)$. This normal approximation to the posterior (also called "Laplace approximation") assumes that:

$$p(\theta \mid x) \approx f(\theta \mid \theta^*, \Sigma^*), \tag{4.11}$$

where

$$f(\theta \mid \theta^*, \Sigma^*) = \frac{1}{(2\pi)^{-K/2}\sqrt{|\det(\Sigma^*)|}} \exp\left(-\frac{1}{2}(\theta - \theta^*)^\top (\Sigma^*)^{-1}(\theta - \theta^*)\right),$$

is the density of the multivariate normal distribution with mean θ^* (the mode of the posterior) and covariance matrix Σ^* defined as inverse of the Hessian of the negated log-posterior at point θ^*:

$$(\Sigma^*)_{i,j}^{-1} = \frac{\partial^2 h}{\partial \theta_i \partial \theta_j}(\theta^*),$$

with $h(\theta) = -\log p(\theta \mid X = x)$. Note that the Hessian must be a positive definite matrix to serve as the covariance matrix of the distribution in Equation 4.11. This means that the Hessian has to be a symmetric matrix. A necessary condition is that the second derivatives of the log-posterior next to the mode are continuous.

The Laplace approximation is based on a second-order Taylor approximation of the log-posterior. A second-order Taylor approximation of the log-posterior around point θ^* yields:

$$\begin{aligned}
\log p(\theta \mid X = x) &= -h(\theta) \\
&\approx -h(\theta^*) - (\theta - \theta^*)^\top \nabla h(\theta^*) - \frac{1}{2}(\theta - \theta^*)^\top (\Sigma^*)^{-1}(\theta - \theta^*) \\
&= -h(\theta^*) - \frac{1}{2}(\theta - \theta^*)^\top (\Sigma^*)^{-1}(\theta - \theta^*),
\end{aligned} \tag{4.12}$$

where Equation 4.12 is true because θ^* is assumed to be the mode of the posterior, and therefore the gradient of h at θ^* equals 0. Equation 4.12 is proportional to the log-density of the multivariate normal distribution with mean θ^* and covariance matrix Σ^*. Therefore, when the second-order Taylor approximation is accurate, the posterior behaves like a multivariate normal variable around its mode.

The Laplace approximation for the posterior has not been widely used in the Bayesian NLP literature, and is given here for consumption by the interested reader. However, second-order Taylor approximation of posterior distributions has been used with models for text. For example, Ahmed and Xing (2007) improve the correlated topic model by using a tighter second-order approximation for the logistic normal distribution.

As pointed out earlier in this book, it is often the case that θ represents a multinomial distribution. In these cases, when using the Laplace approximation, it is better to change the parametrization of the prior, so that θ_i is defined on the real line (Gelman et al., 2003), because the Laplace approximation is dominated by a Gaussian distribution defined over the real line. One transformation that maps $(0, 1)$ to $(-\infty, \infty)$ is the logit transformation:

$$\text{logit}(u) = \log\left(\frac{u}{1-u}\right) \quad \forall u \in (0,1). \tag{4.13}$$

In Appendix A, there is a discussion of how to re-parametrize distributions using the Jacobian transformation.

4.2.3   DECISION-THEORETIC POINT ESTIMATION

Our discussion in this section is limited to the case where there are no latent variables in the model. Assume a prior $p(\theta)$ and a likelihood function $p(X = x|\theta)$. Decision-theoretic Bayesian analysis assumes the existence of a loss function $L(\hat{\theta}(x), \theta)$, which denotes the loss incurred to the decision maker by estimating θ with $\hat{\theta}(x)$, when observing x. The analysis then proceeds with the *Bayes risk*, which is defined as:

$$R\left(\hat{\theta}\right) = \int_\theta \sum_x L\left(\hat{\theta}(x), \theta\right) p(X = x|\theta)p(\theta)d\theta.$$

This analysis computes the average loss of estimating the parameters using the estimator function $\hat{\theta}(x)$, where the average is taken with respect to both the likelihood function and prior information about the parameters. The Bayes risk is a natural candidate for minimization in order to find an optimal set of parameters, in which the lowest average loss is incurred. For a complete discussion of the use of decision theory with Bayesian analysis, see Berger (1985).

Minimizing the Bayes risk can be done by choosing $\hat{\theta}(x)$ which minimizes the *posterior loss*:

$$E\left[L\left(\hat{\theta}(x), \theta\right)|X = x\right] = \int_\theta L\left(\hat{\theta}(x), \theta\right) p(\theta|X = x)d\theta$$
$$\propto \int_\theta L\left(\hat{\theta}(x), \theta\right) p(X = x|\theta)\, p(\theta)d\theta,$$

i.e., $\hat{\theta}(x) = \arg\min_{\theta'} E[L(\theta', \theta)|X = x]$.

Minimizing this expectation is not necessarily tractable in a general case, but it is often the case that choosing specific loss functions makes it possible to solve this expectation analytically. For example, if the parameter space is a subset of $\mathbb{R}^K$, and

$$L\left(\hat{\theta}(x), \theta\right) = \left\|\hat{\theta}(x) - \theta\right\|_2^2, \tag{4.14}$$

then the posterior loss minimizer is the mean value of the parameters under the posterior, i.e.[6]:

---

[6]To see that, consider that for any random variable T, the quantity $E[(T - \mu)^2]$ is minimized with respect to μ when $\mu = E[T]$.

$$\hat{\theta}(x) = \arg\min_{\theta'} E[L(\theta', \theta)|X = x] = E_{p(\theta|X=x)}[\theta], \qquad (4.15)$$

or, alternatively, when

$$L\left(\hat{\theta}(x), \theta\right) = \begin{cases} 1, & \text{if } \hat{\theta}(x) = \theta \\ 0, & \text{otherwise}, \end{cases}$$

then the posterior loss minimizer is the MAP estimator.

If the prior is also conjugate to the likelihood, then the expected value and the mode of the posteriors may even have an analytic solution.

In Bayesian NLP, it is uncommon to use Bayesian point estimation with non-trivial loss functions. Most often, either the mean value of the parameters under the posterior is computed, or MAP estimation is used. Loss functions in NLP are more often defined directly on the predicted structure space itself, conditioned on the input. Such loss functions are used, for example, with *minimum Bayes risk decoding* in parsing (Goodman, 1996) or machine translation (Kumar and Byrne, 2004, Tromble et al., 2008).

4.2.4   DISCUSSION AND SUMMARY

Bayesian point estimation refers to approaches to *summarize* the information in the posterior over the parameters. The most common approaches to Bayesian point estimation in NLP are computing the mean value of the posterior parameters and computing the maximum *a posteriori* estimation.

Several frequentist approaches, such as L_2 regularization and additive smoothing can be framed as Bayesian point estimation problems with a certain prior distribution. With a rich frequentist theory for L_2 regularization and similar methods, these interpretations can serve as an additional validation for these methods from a Bayesian point of view.

4.3   EMPIRICAL BAYES

As mentioned in Section 3.5, it is often the case that hyperpriors are defined over the hyperparameters in order to exploit dependencies in the parameter space. In this case, the posterior over the parameters for a model without any latent variables to predict (i.e., "model over X but not Z") is defined as:

$$p(\theta|X = x) = \frac{\int_\alpha p(X = x|\theta)p(\theta|\alpha)p(\alpha)d\alpha}{\int_\theta \int_\alpha p(X = x|\theta)p(\theta|\alpha)p(\alpha)d\alpha d\theta},$$

with $p(\alpha)$ being a distribution over the hyperparameters. This fully Bayesian approach places a second-stage prior on the hyperparameters, and when inferring the posterior, integrating out

α. Empirical Bayes takes a different approach to the problem of encoding information into the hyperparameters. Instead of using a prior $p(\alpha)$, in the empirical Bayes setting a fixed value for α is learned from observed data x. This hyperparameter, $\hat{\alpha}(x)$ can either be learned by maximizing the marginal likelihood $p(X = x|\alpha)$ or estimated through other estimation techniques. Then, predictions are made using a posterior of the form $p(\theta|X = x, \hat{\alpha}(x))$. One can also learn $\hat{\alpha}(x)$ from a dataset different from the one on which final inference is performed.

This idea of identifying a hyperparameter $\hat{\alpha}(x)$ based on the observed data is related to hyperparameter identification with conjugate priors (Section 3.1). Still, there are several key differences between hyperparameter identification with conjugate priors and empirical Bayes, as it is described in this section. First, empirical Bayes does not have to be done with conjugate priors. Second, identifying $\hat{\alpha}(x)$ is usually done using a different statistical technique than regular Bayesian inference (application of Bayes' rule), as is done with conjugate priors (see below, for example, about type II maximum likelihood). Third, empirical Bayes is usually just a preliminary stage to identify a set of hyperparameters, which can then be *followed* with Bayesian inference, potentially on a new set of data.

Similarly to the case with hierarchical priors, empirical Bayes is often used when the parameters of the model are not drawn once for the whole corpus, but are drawn multiple times for each instance in the corpus (see Section 3.5).

In this case, there are multiple observations $x^{(1)}, \ldots, x^{(n)}$, each associated with a set of parameters $\theta^{(i)}$ for $i = \{1, \ldots, n\}$. Empirical Bayes is similar to Bayesian point estimation, only instead of identifying a single parameter θ from the observed data, a single *hyperparameter* is identified.

This hyperparameter, $\hat{\alpha}(x^{(1)}, \ldots, x^{(n)})$, summarizes the information in the learned prior:

$$p\left(\theta^{(1)}, \ldots, \theta^{(n)}|\hat{\alpha}\left(x^{(1)}, \ldots, x^{(n)}\right)\right) = \prod_{i=1}^{n} p\left(\theta^{(i)}|\hat{\alpha}\left(x^{(1)}, \ldots, x^{(n)}\right)\right).$$

Although the traditional empirical Bayesian setting proceeds at this point to perform inference (after estimating $\hat{\alpha}\left(x^{(1)}, \ldots, x^{(n)}\right)$ with the posterior $p\left(\theta|\hat{\alpha}\left(x^{(1)}, \ldots, x^{(n)}\right)\right)$), it is sometimes preferable in NLP to apply a simple function on $\hat{\alpha}\left(x^{(1)}, \ldots, x^{(n)}\right)$ in order to identify a point estimate for the model. For example, one can find the mode of the estimated prior, $p\left(\theta^{(1)}, \ldots, \theta^{(n)}|\hat{\alpha}\left(x^{(1)}, \ldots, x^{(n)}\right)\right)$ or its mean.

Maximizing marginal likelihood is typically the most common approach to empirical Bayes in NLP. In that case, the following optimization problem—or an approximation of it—is solved:

$$\alpha\left(x^{(1)}, \ldots, x^{(n)}\right) = \arg\max_{\alpha} p\left(x^{(1)}, \ldots, x^{(n)}|\alpha\right). \tag{4.16}$$

There is an implicit marginalization of a set of parameters $\theta^{(i)}$ (or a single θ, if not each observed datum is associated with parameters) in the formulation in Equation 4.16. In addition, random variables $Z^{(i)}$, the latent structures, are also marginalized out if they are part of the model. In this setting, empirical Bayes is also referred to as *type II* maximum likelihood estimation. With latent variables, maximizing likelihood in this way is often computationally challenging, and algorithms such as variational EM are used. Variational approximations are discussed at length in Chapter 6.

Finkel and Manning (2009) describe a simple example of the use of empirical Bayes in NLP and an exploration of its advantages. They define a hierarchical prior for the purpose of domain adaptation. Their model is a log-linear model, in which there is a Gaussian prior with a *varying mean* over the feature weights (see discussion in Section 4.2.1)—instead of a regular L_2 regularization that assumes a zero-mean Gaussian prior. Each domain (among K domains) corresponds to a different mean for the Gaussian prior. In addition, they have a zero-mean Gaussian prior that is placed on the mean of all of the domain Gaussian priors. Such a hierarchical prior requires the model to share information between the models if the statistics available are sparse; if there is enough data for a specific domain, it will override this kind of information sharing.

The space of parameters is $\mathbb{R}^K$, and it parametrizes a conditional random field model. The hierarchical prior of Finkel and Manning is defined as follows:

$$
p\left(\overline{\theta}, \theta^{(1)}, \ldots, \theta^{(J)} | \sigma_1, \ldots, \sigma_J, \overline{\sigma}\right) = p\left(\overline{\theta} | \overline{\sigma}\right) \left(\prod_{i=1}^{J} p\left(\theta^{(j)} | \sigma_j, \overline{\theta}\right)\right),
$$

with each $p\left(\theta^{(j)} | \sigma_j, \overline{\theta}\right)$ being a multivariate normal variable with covariance matrix $\sigma_j^2 I$ and mean $\overline{\theta}$, and $p\left(\overline{\theta} | \overline{\sigma}\right)$ being a multivariate normal variable with mean zero and covariance matrix $\overline{\sigma}^2 I$.

In an empirical evaluation of their approach, Finkel and Manning tried their prior with named entity recognition (NER) and dependency parsing. For NER, each domain was represented by a different NER dataset from the CoNLL 2003 (Tjong Kim Sang and De Meulder, 2003), MUC-6 (Chinchor and Sundheim, 2003) and MUC-7 (Chinchor, 2001) shared tasks datasets. For this problem, their model performed better than just concatenating all of the datasets and training a single conditional random field with that large set of data. The performance gain (in F_1-measure) ranged from 2.66% to 0.43%, depending on the data set being tested.

For the parsing problem, Finkel and Manning used the OntoNotes data (Hovy et al., 2006), which includes parse trees from seven different domains. For this problem, the results were more mixed: in four of the cases the hierarchical model performed better than the rest of the tested methods, and in three cases, concatenating all of the domains into a single domain performed better than the rest of the methods being tested.

Finkel and Manning also show that their model is equivalent to the domain adaptation model of Daume III (2007). In Daume's model, the features in the base conditional random field are duplicated for each domain. Then, for each datum in each domain, two sets of features are used: one feature set associated with the specific domain the datum came from, and one feature set that is used for all of the domains.

4.4   ASYMPTOTIC BEHAVIOR OF THE POSTERIOR

At its core, Bayesian inference begins and ends with the application of Bayes' rule to invert the relationship between the parameters and the observed data. However, in the context of posterior summarization, one can use tools from frequentist analysis to discuss the behavior of the posterior summary as the size of the sample increases.

The most notable analysis of this kind is the one that discusses the multivariate normality of the posterior around the "true" parameter. This means that if we have a Bayesian model $p(X, \theta) = p(\theta)p(X \mid \theta)$, and a set of samples $x^{(1)}, \ldots, x^{(n)}$ where $x^{(i)}$ are drawn from $p(X|\theta_0)$ for some θ_0 in the parameter space, then under some regularity conditions (as Gelman et al. (2003) points out, these regularity conditions indicate mostly that the log-likelihood is continuous with respect to θ, and that θ_0 is not on the boundary of the parameter space), the posterior distribution acts like a multivariate normal distribution around θ_0 as the number of samples increases (i.e., "n goes to infinity"). This is shown by developing a Taylor series approximation of the log-posterior around θ_0. Such an approximation is described in Section 4.2.2. This general result of the normality of the posterior is also called the "Bayesian central limit theorem."

What happens when $x^{(i)}$ are sampled from a distribution which does not belong to the model family (i.e., the above θ_0 does not exist—the model family is "incorrect")? In this case, the role of θ_0 changes from the parameters according to which $x^{(i)}$ are drawn, to a set of parameters that minimize some distance between the true distribution and the model family. See Gelman et al. (2003) for more details, especially Appendix B for proof sketches.

What this type of result generally shows is that the prior has a much more important role when n is small. As n gets larger, the posterior becomes more and more concentrated around θ_0. In frequentist terminology, the posterior mode is a consistent estimator for θ_0.

4.5   SUMMARY

Bayesian point estimation is especially useful when a summary of the posterior is needed. In NLP, the most common reason for such a need is to maintain a lightweight model with a fixed set of parameters. Such a fixed set of parameters enables computationally efficient solutions for decoding.

Several common smoothing and regularization techniques can be interpreted as Bayesian point estimation with a specific prior. Additive smoothing, for example, can be interpreted as the mean of a posterior seeded by a Dirichlet prior. L_2 regularization can be interpreted as a maximum *a posteriori* solution with a Gaussian prior, and L_1 regularization can be interpreted as MAP solution with a Laplace prior.

Empirical Bayes estimation is another technique that is related to Bayesian point estimation. With empirical Bayes, a point estimate for the *hyperparameters* is identified. This point estimate can be subsequently followed with regular Bayesian inference (potentially on new set of data), or used to summarize the posterior over the parameters to identify a final point estimate for the parameters.

4.6 EXERCISES

4.1. Show that Equation 4.4 is true. (Hint: the maximizer of the log-posterior is also the maximizer of the posterior.)

4.2. Let θ be a value between [0, 1] drawn from the Beta distribution parametrized by (α, β). Use the Jacobian transformation (Appendix A) to transform the distribution over θ to the real line with a new random variable $\mu = \text{logit}(\theta)$. The logit transformation is defined in Equation 4.13.

4.3. Show that Equation 4.15 is true for the choice of $L\left(\hat{\theta}(x), \theta\right)$ as it appears in Equation 4.14.

4.4. Let $x^{(i)} \in \mathbb{R}^d$ and $y^{(i)} \in \mathbb{R}$ for $i \in \{1, \ldots, n\}$. With least squares ridge regression, our goal is to find a weight vector $\theta^* \in \mathbb{R}^d$ such that:

$$\theta^* = \arg\min_{\theta} \left(\sum_{i=1}^{n} \left(y^{(i)} - \theta \cdot x^{(i)} \right)^2 \right) + \lambda \left(\sum_{j=1}^{d} \theta_j^2 \right), \qquad (4.17)$$

where $\lambda > 0$ is a fixed value.

Describe a Bayesian statistical model $p(\theta, X)$ such that the above θ^* is the MAP solution for this model, i.e., $\theta^* = \arg\max_{\theta} p\left(\theta | x^{(1)}, \ldots, x^{(n)}\right)$. Here, $x^{(1)}, \ldots, x^{(n)}$ are assumed to be independently drawn from $p(X|\theta)$ (conditioned on a set of parameters drawn before them). The Bayesian model will require λ to be a hyperparameter. (Hint: You may use well-known distributions, such as the multivariate normal distribution and others in designing your model.)

4.5. Is there an analytical solution for the above MAP problem (or in other words, is there an analytical solution for Equation 4.17)? If so, write it down.

CHAPTER 5

Sampling Methods

When the posterior cannot be analytically represented, or efficiently computed, we often have to resort to approximate inference methods. One main thread of approximate inference relies on the ability to simulate from the posterior in order to draw structures or parameters from the underlying distribution represented by the posterior. The samples drawn from this posterior can be averaged to approximate expectations (or normalization constants). If these samples are close to the posterior mode, they can be used as the final output. In this case, the samples replace the need to find the highest scoring structure according to the model, which is often computationally difficult to do if one is interested in averaging predictions with respect to the inferred distribution over the parameters (see Section 4.1).

Monte Carlo (MC) methods provide a general framework ideal for drawing samples from a target distribution that satisfies certain conditions. While not specific to Bayesian statistics, an especially useful family of MC methods in the Bayesian context is the Markov Chain Monte Carlo (MCMC) methods. In general, these methods have an advantage in allowing sampling from a family of distributions that satisfy certain conditions (usually, that a distribution is computable up to a normalization constant). In Bayesian statistics, they are often used for posterior inference, because posterior distributions for various Bayesian models naturally meet these conditions. MCMC algorithms are especially useful in the Bayesian context for finding the normalization constant of the posterior, marginalizing out variables, computing expectations of summary statistics and finding the posterior mode.

It is important to keep in mind that Bayesian inference, at its core, manages uncertainty regarding the parameters and the remaining latent variables through the use of distributions. This means that the goal of Bayesian inference is to eventually find the posterior distribution in one form or another. Monte Carlo methods treat this problem slightly differently. Instead of directly representing the posterior distribution as a member of some (possibly approximate) family of distributions (such as with variational inference, see Chapter 6), MC methods instead permit indirect access to this posterior. Access to the posterior comes in the form of being able to draw from the posterior distribution, without necessarily needing a complete analytic representation for it.

The focus of this chapter is to provide an account of the way that Monte Carlo methods are used in Bayesian NLP. We cover some of the principal Markov chain Monte Carlo methods, and detail the design choices and the advantages and disadvantages for using them in the context of Bayesian NLP. We also cover some techniques used to assess the convergence of MCMC methods to the target distribution. Convergence here means that the MCMC sampler, which is iterative and outputs a sequence of samples, has finished its "burn-in" period, during which time it outputs samples that are not necessarily drawn from the target distribution. When the MCMC sampler has reached convergence, its output represents samples from the target distribution. It is often the case that poor assessment of an MCMC method implies that the output returned is invalid, and does not represent the underlying Bayesian model used.

This chapter is organized as follows. We begin by providing an overview of MCMC methods in Section 5.1 and then follow with an account of MCMC in NLP in Section 5.2. We then start covering several important MCMC sampling algorithms, such as Gibbs sampling (Section 5.3), Metropolis–Hastings (Section 5.4) and slice sampling (Section 5.5). We then cover other topics such as simulated annealing (Section 5.6); the convergence of MCMC algorithms (Section 5.7); the basic theory behind MCMC algorithms (Section 5.8); non-MCMC sampling algorithms such as importance sampling (Section 5.9); and finally, Monte Carlo integration (Section 5.10). We conclude with a discussion (Section 5.11) and a summary (Section 5.12).

5.1   MCMC ALGORITHMS: OVERVIEW

The basic idea of MCMC methods is intuitive. First, a space of states for the random variables of interest is defined; these random variables are those for which we want to draw samples. In Bayesian NLP, these random variables are usually the random variables over which the posterior is defined. Each state in the space corresponds to an assignment of values for all variables. Next, a strategy to explore this space is defined. Each type of MCMC method (whether it is Gibbs sampling, the Metropolis–Hastings or another MCMC method) has a different framework for defining this strategy. Once the strategy is defined, the algorithm works by exploring the space using the strategy until convergence is achieved, and a satisfactory number of samples has been obtained. The samples are collected as the state space is being explored.

If the MCMC method is sound, and the framework it offers is used correctly, there is a theoretical guarantee that the samples being drawn (i.e., the assignment to the random variables according to the state being explored) stem from the distribution the sampler was designed for, such as the posterior. The samples *are not* necessarily independent. As a matter of fact, in most cases with MCMC algorithms, there is a great dependence between states that were explored in proximity to each other, and thus, between the samples that the algorithm produces. In general, the farther apart the samples drawn are in the chain, the less correlated they are. This observation can be used to generate samples that are closer to being uncorrelated: if $S = \{y_1, \ldots, y_M\}$ is a set of correlated samples that were collected for some large M, then the subset $\{y_i \in S | i \bmod m = 0\}$ for some integer m will have samples with weaker correlation (the larger m is, the weaker the correlation). Less formally, we pick a subset of the samples drawn, every mth sample, for some m. This process is also called "thinning."

MCMC methods are iterative in nature, with each iteration moving from one state of the sample space to another state. Being iterative, they require some stopping criterion. This stopping criterion is of crucial importance with MCMC algorithms—choosing it carelessly could mean that the algorithm never converges, and therefore that all the samples drawn through the algorithm's execution are not really drawn from the desired posterior. Indeed, in the beginning period of an MCMC algorithm execution, random samples are drawn that are unrelated to the true posterior distribution, in a phase called the *burn-in* phase. It is sometimes possible to initialize the sampler a certain way so that its burn-in period is shorter. More information about the convergence of MCMC algorithms is discussed in Section 5.7.

It is important to note that MCMC algorithms are often used with Bayesian statistics, but that they can generally be used whenever there is a need to sample from a distribution, whether it is a Bayesian posterior or some other distribution that did not arise in a Bayesian context. MCMC algorithms are often mentioned in the Bayesian context because they are most useful when a distribution can be computed up to a normalization constant. This state naturally arises with the posterior of a Bayesian model, where the posterior is proportional to the joint distribution. While this joint distribution is usually easy to compute, the normalization constant that is required to turn this joint distribution into the posterior distribution is often more difficult to compute (see Chapter 3).

5.2   NLP MODEL STRUCTURE FOR MCMC INFERENCE

Introductory texts about Bayesian statistics usually consider the inference of the parameters with fully observed data. In NLP, however, most Bayesian statistics are used with latent variables, which means that the posterior is defined over parameters *and* some predicted structure. This predicted structure is usually a linguistic structure such as a parse tree, an alignment between a pair of trees or sentences or sequence denoting part-of-speech tags.

Since Bayesian NLP usually focuses on latent variable models, inference in this chapter focuses on Bayesian inference with latent variables. This means that the underlying statistical model used has the following structure:

$$p(\theta, X = x, Z = z \mid \alpha) = p(\theta|\alpha)p(Z = z|\theta)p(X = x|Z = z, \theta).$$

In addition, we consider n identically distributed samples (conditionally independent given the model parameters), with a prior at the top level (see Section 3.5). Therefore, the joint distribution values over all random variables in this process are defined as:

$$p\left(\theta, x^{(1)}, \ldots, x^{(n)}, z^{(1)}, \ldots, z^{(n)} \mid \alpha\right) = p(\theta \mid \alpha)\left(\prod_{i=1}^{n} p\left(z^{(i)}|\theta\right) P\left(x^{(i)}|z^{(i)}, \theta\right)\right).$$

Given that only $x^{(i)}$ for $i \in \{1, \ldots, n\}$ are observed, the posterior then has the form:

$$p\left(z^{(1)}, \ldots, z^{(n)}, \theta | x^{(1)}, \ldots, x^{(n)}\right).$$

MCMC sampling yields a stream of samples from this posterior, which can be used in various ways, including to find a point estimate for the parameters, to draw predicted structures from the posterior or even to find the maximum value of the posterior using simulated annealing (see Section 5.6). Often, the *collapsed* setting is of interest, and then samples are drawn from the posterior over the predicted structures only, integrating out the model parameters:

$$p\left(z^{(1)}, \ldots, z^{(n)} | x^{(1)}, \ldots, x^{(n)}\right) = \int_{\theta} p\left(z^{(1)}, \ldots, z^{(n)}, \theta | x^{(1)}, \ldots, x^{(n)}\right) d\theta.$$

In this case, the parameters are *nuisance* variables, because the inference procedure is not focused on them. Still, it is often the case that a summary of the parameters (in the style of Chapter 4) can be inferred from the samples drawn for the latent variables in the model.

5.2.1 PARTITIONING THE LATENT VARIABLES

Perhaps the most important choice when designing an MCMC sampler for a Bayesian NLP model is about the way in which the (latent) random variables of interest are partitioned. In their most general form, MCMC methods do not *require* the partitioning of the latent variables in the model. In fact, most of the introductory text to MCMC methods describes a single global state of all of the latent variables in the model (the state is a tuple with assignments for all $Z^{(i)}$ for $i \in \{1, \ldots, n\}$ and θ), and a chain that moves between states in this space. This state is often represented by a single random variable.

However, in NLP problems, treating the sample space with a single random variable without further refining it yields challenging inference problems, since this single random variable would potentially represent a complex combinatorial structure, such as a set of trees or graphs. Therefore, the set of latent variables is carved up into smaller subsets.

As mentioned earlier, NLP models are usually defined over discrete structures, and therefore the variables $Z^{(i)}$ commonly denote a structure such as a parse tree, an alignment or a sequence. We assume this type of structure for $Z^{(i)}$ for the rest of this section—i.e., a discrete compositional structure.

There are two common choices for partitioning the latent variables $Z^{(i)}$ in order to sample from the posterior:

- Keep each variable $Z^{(i)}$ as a single atomic unit. When moving between states, re-sample a whole $Z^{(i)}$ structure for some i, possibly more than one structure at a time. This is one type of *blocked* sampling where the atomic unit is a whole predicted structure. It is often the case that each $Z^{(i)}$ is sampled using a dynamic programming algorithm. See Section 5.3 for more details.

- Refine the predicted structure into a set of random variables, and sample each of them separately. This means, for example, that if $Z^{(i)}$ denotes a dependency tree, it will be refined to a set of random variables denoting the existence of edges in the tree. When moving between states, only one edge (or a small number of edges) is changed at a time. This is also often called *pointwise* sampling. See Section 5.3 for more details.

The parameters themselves, usually continuous variables, can also be refined into smaller constituents. For example, if the parameters are a product of Dirichlets (see Section 8.3.1 for an example), then each constituent can consist of a single Dirichlet distribution.

In the rest of this chapter, we assume a single random variable U, denoting the latent variables over which we perform the inference. For example, in the non-collapsed setting, $U = (\boldsymbol{Z}, \theta)$, with $\boldsymbol{Z}$ denoting the latent structures to be predicted. In the collapsed setting, on the other hand, $U = \boldsymbol{Z}$. Here, $\boldsymbol{Z}$ is a tuple of the form $(Z^{(1)}, \ldots, Z^{(n)})$. (Similarly, we use $\boldsymbol{X}$ to denote $(X^{(1)}, \ldots, X^{(n)})$.) The multivariate random variable U is also assumed to have a de-composable representation, such that $U = (U_1, \ldots, U_p)$. This decomposition partitions $(\boldsymbol{Z}, \theta)$ (in the non-collapsed setting) into smaller constituents. The random variable U_{-i} denotes the vector $(U_1, \ldots, U_{i-1}, U_{i+1}, \ldots, U_p)$.

5.3   GIBBS SAMPLING

The Gibbs sampling algorithm (Geman and Geman, 1984) is one of the most common MCMC algorithms used in the context of Bayesian NLP. In this setting, Gibbs sampling explores the state space, sampling u_i each time for some $i \in \{1, \ldots, p\}$. These u_i are drawn from the conditional distributions, $p(U_i \mid U_{-i}, \boldsymbol{X})$. The full algorithm is given in Algorithm 5.1.

Note that at each step, the "state" of the algorithm is a set of values for U. At each iteration, the distributions $p(U_i \mid U_{-i})$ condition on values u_{-i} from the *current* state, and modify the current state—by setting a new value for one of the U_i. The update to the current state of the algorithm is immediate when a new value is drawn for one of the variables. The Gibbs algorithm does not delay the global state update, and each new draw of a random variable is immediately followed by a global state update. (However, see Section 5.4 for information about using a "stale" state for parallelizing the Gibbs sampler.)

Algorithm 5.1 returns a single sample once the Markov chain has converged. However, once the Gibbs sampling has converged, a *stream* of samples can be produced repeatedly by changing the state according to the conditional distributions and traversing the search space, collecting a set of samples. All of these samples are produced from the target distribution $p(U|\boldsymbol{X})$. While these samples are not going to be independent of each other, the farther a pair of samples are from each other, the less correlated they are.

To follow the discussion in Section 5.2.1, the Gibbs sampler can be *pointwise* or *blocked* (Gao and Johnson, 2008). Pointwise sampling implies that the Gibbs sampler alternates between steps that make very local changes to the state, such as sampling a single part-of-speech tag, while blocked sampling implies that larger pieces of the structure are sampled at each step.

Input: Samplers for the conditionals $p(U_i|U_{-i}, X)$ of the distribution $p(U_1, \ldots, U_p|X)$.
Output: $u = (u_1, \ldots, u_p)$ drawn from $p(U_1, \ldots, U_p|X)$.

1: Initialize $u_1, \ldots, u_p$ with some value from their space of allowed values
2: **repeat**
3:    **for all** $i \leftarrow 1$ to p **do**
4:       Sample u_i from $p(u_i|u_{-i}, X)$
5:    **end for**
6: **until** Markov chain converged
7: **return** $u_1, \ldots, u_p$

Algorithm 5.1: The Gibbs sampling algorithm, in its "systematic sweep" form. Part of the input to the Gibbs algorithm is samplers for the conditional distributions derived from the target distribution. Such samplers are treated as black-box functions that draw samples from these conditionals (in line 4).

For example, a sentence-blocked sampler for part-of-speech tagging could sample the tags for a whole sentence using the dynamic programming forward-backward algorithm. A blocked sampler can also sample smaller constituents—for example, five part-of-speech tags at a time—again using the forward-backward algorithm applied to a window of five part-of-speech tags at a time.

In order to use a Gibbs sampler, one has to be able to draw samples for one variable in the model conditioned on a fixed value for all others. To achieve this, another MCMC algorithm can be used to sample from conditional distributions (see Section 5.11); however, it is often the case in Bayesian NLP models that these conditionals have an analytic form, and therefore are easy to sample from (while the whole posterior is intractable, and requires MCMC or some other approximate method).

Example 5.1   Consider the latent Dirichlet allocation model from Chapter 2. We denote the number of documents it models by N, the size of the vocabulary by V, and the number of words per document by M (in general, the number of words in a document varies, but for the sake of simplicity we assume all documents are of the same length). The full graphical model for LDA appears in Figure 2.1.

We will use the index i to range over documents, j to range over words in a specific document, k to range over the possible topics and v to range over the vocabulary. In addition, there are random variables $\theta^{(i)} \in \mathbb{R}^K$ which are the document topic distributions, $Z_j^{(i)}$ which denote the topic for the jth word in the ith document, $W_j^{(i)}$ which denote the jth word in the ith document and $\beta_k \in \mathbb{R}^V$ which denote the distribution over the vocabulary for the kth topic.

The joint distribution is factorized as follows:

$$
p\left(\theta, \beta, \mathbf{Z}, \mathbf{W} \mid \psi, \alpha\right) = \left(\prod_{k=1}^{K} p\left(\beta_k \mid \psi\right)\right)
$$
$$
\left(\prod_{i=1}^{N} p\left(\theta^{(i)} \mid \alpha\right) \prod_{j=1}^{M} p\left(Z_j^{(i)} \mid \theta^{(i)}\right) p\left(W_j^{(i)} \mid \beta, Z_j^{(i)}\right)\right). \tag{5.1}
$$

The random variables we need to infer are θ, β and $\mathbf{Z}$. One way to break the random variables into constituents (in conditional distributions) for a Gibbs sampler is the following:

- $p\left(\beta_k \mid \theta, \beta_{-k}, z, w, \psi, \alpha\right)$ for $k \in \{1, \ldots, K\}$. This is the distribution over the parameters of the LDA model that denote the probabilities over the vocabulary for each topic (conditioned on all other random variables). We denote by β_{-k} the set of $\{\beta_{k'} \mid k' \neq k\}$.

- $p\left(\theta^{(i)} \mid \theta^{(-i)}, \beta, z, w, \psi, \alpha\right)$ for $i \in \{1, \ldots, N\}$. This is the distribution over the topic distribution for the ith document, conditioned on all other random variables in the model. We denote by $\theta^{(-i)}$ the topic distributions for all documents other than the ith document.

- $p\left(Z_j^{(i)} \mid \theta, z_{-(i,j)}, w, \psi, \alpha\right)$ for $i \in \{1, \ldots, N\}$ and $j \in \{1, \ldots, M\}$. This is the distribution over a topic assignment for a specific word (jth word) in a specific document (ith document), conditioned on all other random variables in the model. We denote by $z_{-(i,j)}$ the set of all topic assignment variables other than $Z_j^{(i)}$.

At this point, the question remains as to what the form is of each of these distributions, and how we can sample from them. We begin with $p\left(\beta_k \mid \theta, \beta_{-k}, z, w, \psi, \alpha\right)$. According to Equation 5.1, the only factors that interact with β_k are denoted on the right-hand side of the following equation:

$$
p\left(\beta_k \mid \theta, \beta_{-k}, z, w, \psi, \alpha\right) \propto p(\beta_k \mid \psi) \left(\prod_{i=1}^{N} \prod_{j=1}^{M} p\left(w_j^{(i)} \mid \beta, z_j^{(i)}\right)^{I\left(z_j^{(i)}=k\right)}\right)
$$
$$
= \left(\prod_{v=1}^{V} \beta_{k,v}^{\psi-1}\right) \left(\prod_{i=1}^{N} \prod_{j=1}^{M} \prod_{v=1}^{V} \beta_k^{I\left(w_j^{(i)}=v \wedge z_j^{(i)}=k\right)}\right)
$$
$$
= \prod_{v=1}^{V} \beta_{k,v}^{\psi-1+\sum_{i=1}^{N} \sum_{j=1}^{M} I\left(w_j^{(i)}=v \wedge z_j^{(i)}=k\right)}. \tag{5.2}
$$

Denote by $n_{k,v}$ the quantity $\sum_{i=1}^{N} I(w_j^{(i)} = v \wedge z_j^{(i)} = k)$. In this case, $n_{k,v}$ denotes the number of times the word v is assigned to topic k in any of the documents based on the current state of the sampler. The form of Equation 5.2 is exactly the form of a Dirichlet distribution with the hyperparameter $\psi + n_k$, where n_k is the vector of $n_{k,v}$ ranging over v. This concludes the derivation of the conditional distribution, which is required to sample a new set of topic distributions β given the state of the sampler.

Consider $p\left(\theta^{(i)} \mid \theta^{(-i)}, \beta, z, w, \psi, \alpha\right)$. Following a similar derivation, we have:

$$
\begin{aligned}
p\left(\theta^{(i)} \mid \theta^{(-i)}, \beta, z, w, \psi, \alpha\right) &\propto p\left(\theta^{(i)} \mid \alpha\right) \prod_{j=1}^{M} p\left(z_j^{(i)} \mid \theta^{(i)}\right) \\
&= \prod_{k=1}^{K}\left(\theta_k^{(i)}\right)^{\alpha-1} \prod_{j=1}^{M} \prod_{k=1}^{K}\left(\theta_k^{(i)}\right)^{I\left(z_j^{(i)}=k\right)} \\
&= \prod_{k=1}^{K}\left(\theta_k^{(i)}\right)^{\alpha-1+\sum_{j=1}^{M} I\left(z_j^{(i)}=k\right)}.
\end{aligned}
\tag{5.3}
$$

Denote by $m_k^{(i)}$ the quantity $\sum_{j=1}^{M} I\left(z_j^{(i)} = k\right)$, i.e., the number of times in the ith document that a word was assigned to the kth topic. Then, it turns out that from Equation 5.3, $\theta^{(i)}$, conditioned on all other random variables in the model is distributed according to the Dirichlet distribution, with hyperparameters $\alpha + m^{(i)}$ where $m^{(i)}$ is the vector ranging over $m_k^{(i)}$ for all k.

The last distribution we have to consider is that of $p\left(Z_j^{(i)} \mid \theta, z_{-(i,j)}, w, \psi, \alpha\right)$. Again using the joint distribution from Equation 5.1, it holds that:

$$
p\left(Z_j^{(i)} = k \mid \theta, z_{-(i,j)}, w, \psi, \alpha\right) \propto p\left(Z_j^{(i)} = k \mid \theta^{(i)}\right) p\left(w_j^{(i)} \mid \beta, z_j^{(i)}\right) = \theta_k^{(i)} \beta_{k,w_j^{(i)}} \tag{5.4}
$$

Equation 5.4 corresponds to a multinomial distribution proportional to the topic distribution probability multiplied by the probability of generating the jth word in the document under the kth topic.

Note that this sampler is a pointwise sampler—it samples each coordinate of $Z^{(i)}$ separately. This example demonstrates a Gibbs sampler from a Dirichlet-multinomial family with non-trivial relationships between the multinomials. Such is the relationship in other more complex models in NLP (PCFGs, HMMs and so on). The structure of this Gibbs sampler will be similar in these more complex cases as well. This is especially true regarding the draw of θ. In more complex models, statistics will be collected from the current set of samples for the latent structures, and combined into hyperparameters for the posterior of the Dirichlet distribution.

In more complex cases, the draws of $Z^{(i)}$ could potentially rely on dynamic programming algorithms, for example, to draw a phrase-structure tree conditioned on the parameters (with PCFGs), or to draw a latent sequence (with HMMs)—see Chapter 8.

Input: Distribution $p(Z|X)$.
Output: $z^{(1)}, \ldots, z^{(n)}$ drawn from $p(Z^{(1)}, \ldots, Z^{(n)}|X)$.

- -

1: Initialize $z^{(1)}, \ldots, z^{(n)}$ with some value from their space of allowed values
2: **repeat**
3:     **for all** $i \in \{1, \ldots, n\}$ **do**
4:        Sample $z^{(i)}$ from $p(Z^{(i)}|z^{(1)}, \ldots, z^{(i-1)}, z^{(i+1)}, \ldots, z^{(n)}, X)$
5:     **end for**
6: **until** Markov chain converged
7: **return** $z^{(1)}, \ldots, z^{(n)}$

Algorithm 5.2: The collapsed observation-blocked Gibbs sampling algorithm, in its "systematic sweep" form.

5.3.1 COLLAPSED GIBBS SAMPLING

It is often the case that inference over the parameters is of no interest. The main focus is on directly inferring the predicted structures from the posterior distribution. In this case, the burn-in period of the Markov chain can be made shorter, if samples are drawn from the marginalized posterior, i.e.:

$$p(Z \mid X) = \int_\theta p(\theta, Z \mid X) d\theta.$$

Using Gibbs sampling with this marginalized posterior is also called *collapsed Gibbs sampling*. For the sake of discussion, we first consider an example of collapsed Gibbs sampling where we assume the posterior has a certain form without directly deriving it by performing Bayesian inference with a statistical model. Similar target distributions arise frequently, in one form or another, as posterior distributions in a Bayesian NLP model.

Example 5.2 Assume the following simple multinomial model:

- Draw $\theta \in [0, 1]^K$ from a Dirichlet distribution with hyperparameters $\alpha = (\alpha_1, \ldots, \alpha_K)$

- Draw $z^{(i)}$ from the multinomial distribution θ for $i = 1, \ldots, n$ (i.e., $z^{(i)}$ is a binary vector of length K with 1 in one coordinate and 0 in all others).

The joint distribution for this model is:

$$p\left(z^{(1)}, \ldots, z^{(n)}, \theta | \alpha\right) = p(\theta | \alpha) \prod_{i=1}^{n} p\left(z^{(j)} | \theta\right).$$

To derive a collapsed Gibbs sampler, the conditional distributions $p\left(Z^{(i)}|Z^{(-i)}\right)$ are required. Let e_k be the binary vector with 0 in all coordinates, except for the kth coordinate, where it is 1. The following holds:

$$p\left(Z^{(i)} = e_k|z^{(-i)}, \alpha\right) = \int_\theta p\left(Z^{(i)} = e_k, \theta|z^{(-i)}, \alpha\right) d\theta$$

$$= \int_\theta p\left(\theta|z^{(-i)}, \alpha\right) p\left(Z^{(i)} = e_k|z^{(-i)}, \theta, \alpha\right) d\theta$$

$$= \int_\theta p\left(\theta|z^{(-i)}, \alpha\right) p\left(Z^{(i)} = e_k|\theta, \alpha\right) d\theta \qquad (5.5)$$

$$= \int_\theta p\left(\theta|z^{(-i)}, \alpha\right) \theta_k d\theta$$

$$= \frac{\sum_{j \neq i} z_k^{(j)} + \alpha_k}{\sum_{k'=1}^{K} \left(\sum_{j \neq i}^{n} z_{k'}^{(j)} + \alpha_{k'}\right)} \qquad (5.6)$$

$$= \frac{\sum_{j \neq i} z_k^{(j)} + \alpha_k}{n - 1 + \sum_{k'=1}^{K} \alpha_{k'}}. \qquad (5.7)$$

Equation 5.5 is true because of the conditional independence of $Z^{(i)}$ given the parameter θ. Note that in Equation 5.5 the term $p\left(\theta|z^{(-i)}, \alpha\right)$ is a Dirichlet distribution with the hyperparameter $\alpha + \sum_{j \neq i} z^{(j)}$ (see Section 3.2.1), and that in the equation below $p\left(Z^{(i)} = e_k|\theta\right) = \theta_k$. Therefore, the integral is the mean value of θ_k according to a Dirichlet distribution with hyperparameters $\alpha + \sum_{j \neq i} z^{(j)}$, leading to Equation 5.6 (see Appendix B).

Example 5.2 exposes an interesting structure to a Gibbs sampler when the distribution being sampled is a multinomial with a Dirichlet prior. According to Equation 5.7:

$$p\left(Z^{(i)} = e_k|Z^{(-i)} = z^{(-i)}\right) = \frac{n_k + \alpha_k}{(n - 1) + \left(\sum_{k'=1}^{K} \alpha_{k'}\right)}, \qquad (5.8)$$

with $n_k = \sum_{j \neq i} z_k^{(j)}$, which is the total count of event k appearing in $z^{(-i)}$. Intuitively, the probability of a latent variable $Z^{(i)}$ taking a particular value is proportional to the number of times this value has been assigned to the rest of the latent variables, $Z^{(-i)}$. Equation 5.8 is essentially an additively smoothed (see Section 4.2.1) version of the maximum likelihood estimate of the parameters, when the estimation is based on the values of the variables being conditioned on. This kind of structure arises frequently when designing Gibbs samplers for models that have a Dirichlet-multinomial structure.

The following example, which is less trivial than the example above, demonstrates this point.

Example 5.3   Consider the LDA Example 5.1. It is often the case that the topic assignments $\mathbf{Z}$ are the only random variables that are of interest to do inference for.[1] The parameters β and the topic distributions θ can therefore be marginalized in this case when performing Gibbs sampling.

Therefore, we can place our focus on the random variables $\mathbf{Z}$ and $\mathbf{W}$. We would like to draw a value for $Z_j^{(i)}$ conditioned on $z_{-(i,j)}$ and $\mathbf{w}$. This means that we are interested in the distribution $p\left(Z_j^{(i)} \mid z_{-(i,j)}, \mathbf{w}\right)$. By Bayes' rule, we have the following:

$$p\left(Z_j^{(i)} = k \mid \mathbf{z}_{-(i,j)}, \mathbf{w}\right) \propto p\left(w_j^{(i)} \mid Z_j^{(i)}, \mathbf{z}_{-(i,j)}, \mathbf{w}_{-(i,j)}\right) p\left(Z_j^{(i)} = k \mid \mathbf{z}_{-(i,j)}\right). \quad (5.9)$$

For simplicity of notation, we do not explicitly condition on the hyperparameters α and ψ, though we always assume they exist in the background. We first tackle the first term. From the conditional independence assumptions in the model, it holds that for any k indexing a topic between 1 and K:

$$\begin{aligned}
p\left(w_j^{(i)} \mid Z_j^{(i)} = k, \mathbf{z}_{-(i,j)}, \mathbf{w}_{-(i,j)}\right) &= \int_{\beta_k} p\left(\beta_k, w_j^{(i)} \mid Z_j^{(i)} = k, \mathbf{z}_{-(i,j)}, \mathbf{w}_{-(i,j)}\right) d\beta_k \\
&= \int_{\beta_k} p\left(w_j^{(i)} \mid Z_j^{(i)} = k, \beta_k\right) p\left(\beta_k \mid Z_j^{(i)} = k, \mathbf{z}_{-(i,j)}, \mathbf{w}_{-(i,j)}\right) d\beta_k \\
&= \int_{\beta_k} p\left(w_j^{(i)} \mid Z_j^{(i)} = k, \beta_k\right) p\left(\beta_k \mid \mathbf{z}_{-(i,j)}, \mathbf{w}_{-(i,j)}\right) d\beta_k.
\end{aligned} \quad (5.10)$$

The last equality holds because $Z_j^{(i)}$ and β_k are conditionally independent when $W_j^{(i)}$ is not observed. Note also that β_k and $\mathbf{Z}_{-(i,j)}$ are *a priori* also independent of each other, and therefore:

---

[1]We follow the derivation of Griffiths (2002).

$$p\left(\beta_k \mid \mathbf{z}_{-(i,j)}, \mathbf{w}_{-(i,j)}\right) \propto p\left(\mathbf{w}_{-(i,j)} \mid \beta_k, \mathbf{z}_{-(i,j)}\right) p\left(\beta_k \mid \mathbf{z}_{-(i,j)}\right)$$
$$= p\left(\mathbf{w}_{-(i,j)} \mid \beta_k, \mathbf{z}_{-(i,j)}\right) p(\beta_k)$$
$$= \prod_{v=1}^{V} \prod_{i'=1}^{N} \prod_{j'=1,(i',j')\neq(i,j)}^{M} \beta_k^{I\left(Z^{(i,j)}=k \wedge w_j^{(i)}=v\right)} p(\beta_k)$$
$$= \prod_{v=1}^{V} \beta_k^{\sum_{i'=1}^{N} \sum_{j'=1,(i',j')\neq(i,j)}^{M} I\left(Z^{(i,j)}=k \wedge w_j^{(i)}=v\right)} p(\beta_k)$$
$$= \prod_{v=1}^{V} \beta_k^{\sum_{i'=1}^{N} \sum_{j'=1,(i',j')\neq(i,j)}^{M} I\left(Z^{(i,j)}=k \wedge w_j^{(i)}=v\right)+\psi-1} .$$

The above means that the distribution $p\left(\beta_k \mid \mathbf{z}_{-(i,j)}, \mathbf{w}_{-(i,j)}\right)$ has the form of a Dirichlet with parameters $\psi + n_{-(i,j),k}$, such that $n_{-(i,j),k}$ is a vector of length V, and each coordinate v equals the number of instances in $\mathbf{z}_{-(i,j)}$ and $\mathbf{w}_{-(i,j)}$ in which the vth word in the vocabulary was assigned to topic k (note that we exclude from the count here the jth word in the ith document).

Note that the term $p\left(w_j^{(i)} \mid Z_j^{(i)} = k, \beta_k\right)$ in Equation 5.10 is just $\beta_{k,w_j^{(i)}}$, and taking it with the above, means that Equation 5.10 is the mean value of a Dirichlet distribution with parameters $\psi + n_{-(i,j),k}$. This means that:

$$p\left(w_j^{(i)} = v \mid Z_j^{(i)} = k, \mathbf{z}_{-(i,j)}, \mathbf{w}_{-(i,j)}\right) = \frac{\psi + [n_{-(i,j),k}]_v}{V\psi + \sum_{v'} [n_{-(i,j),k}]_{v'}}. \tag{5.11}$$

We finished tackling the first term in Equation 5.9. We must still tackle $p\left(Z_j^{(i)} = k \mid \mathbf{z}_{-(i,j)}\right)$. First note that by Bayes' rule and the conditional independence assumptions in the model, it holds that:

$$p\left(Z_j^{(i)} = k \mid \mathbf{z}_{-(i,j)}\right) = \int_{\theta^{(i)}} p\left(\theta^{(i)}, Z_j^{(i)} = k \mid \mathbf{z}_{-(i,j)}\right) d\theta^{(i)}$$
$$= \int_{\theta^{(i)}} p\left(Z_j^{(i)} = k \mid \theta^{(i)}\right) p\left(\theta^{(i)} \mid \mathbf{z}_{-(i,j)}\right) d\theta^{(i)}. \tag{5.12}$$

A similar derivation as before shows that $p\left(\theta^{(i)} \mid \mathbf{z}_{-(i,j)}\right)$ is a Dirichlet distribution with parameters $\alpha + m_{-(i,j)}$ where $m_{-(i,j)}$ is a K-length vector such that $[m_{-(i,j)}]_{k'}$ is the number of times in $\mathbf{z}_{-(i,j)}$ such that words in the ith document (other than the jth word) were assigned to topic k'. The term $p\left(Z_j^{(i)} = k \mid \theta^{(i)}\right)$ is just $\theta_k^{(i)}$. Equation 5.12 is therefore again the mean value of a Dirichlet distribution: it is the kth coordinate of the mean value of a Dirichlet with parameters $\alpha + m_{-(i,j)}$. This means that:

$$p\left(Z_j^{(i)} = k \mid \mathbf{z}_{-(i,j)}\right) = \frac{\alpha + [m_{-(i,j)}]_k}{K\alpha + \sum_{k'} [m_{-(i,j)}]_{k'}}. \tag{5.13}$$

Taking Equations 5.9, 5.11 and 5.13, we get that in order to apply Gibbs sampling to LDA in the collapsed setting, we must sample at each point a single topic assignment for a single word in a document based on the distribution:

$$p\left(Z_j^{(i)} = k \mid \boldsymbol{z}_{-(i,j)}, \boldsymbol{w}\right) = \frac{\psi + [n_{-(i,j),k}]_{w_j^{(i)}}}{V\psi + \sum_{v'}[n_{-(i,j),k}]_{v'}} \times \frac{\alpha + [m_{-(i,j)}]_k}{K\alpha + \sum_{k'}[m_{-(i,j)}]_{k'}}.$$

It should not come as a surprise that the collapsed Gibbs sampler in the example above has a closed analytic form. This is a direct result of the Dirichlet distribution being conjugate to the multinomial distributions that govern the production of $Z^{(i)}$ and $W^{(i)}$. Even though the coupling of latent variables with the integration of the parameters may lead to non-analytic solutions for the posterior, the use of conjugate priors still often leads to analytic solutions for the conditional distributions (and for the Gibbs sampler, as a consequence).

To summarize this section, Algorithm 5.2 gives a collapsed example-blocked Gibbs sampler. It repeatedly draws a latent structure for each example until convergence.

5.3.2   OPERATOR VIEW

The operator view of Gibbs sampling is often used in NLP in place of explicitly partitioning the posterior variables into random variables $U_1, \ldots, U_p$, as described in Section 5.3. Denote the target distribution by $p(U|X)$ and its sample space by Ω. From an implementation perspective, the great advantage of the operator view is that it allows the modeler to design a correct Gibbs sampler without committing to a specific target distribution. If the design follows a few simple principles, then the sampler is guaranteed to be correct, no matter the underlying target distribution.

With the operator view, one defines a set of operators $\mathcal{O} = \{f_1, \ldots, f_M\}$, where each operator f_i is a function that maps an element $\omega \in \Omega$ to a set of neighbors $A \subseteq \Omega$. The sampler alternates between the operators, each time sampling one of the neighbors of the current state proportionally to its probability according to $p(U|X)$. This Gibbs algorithm is given in Algorithm 5.3. There, the notation $I(u' \in A)$ is for an indicator function that is 1 if $u' \in A$ and 0 otherwise. This indicator function is used to check whether u' belongs to the neighborhood of u according to the operator f_i. The term $Z(f_i, u)$ is a normalization constant that integrates or sums U over $f_i(\Omega)$ in order to ensure that $q(U')$ is a distribution. For example, if Ω is a discrete space, then this means that

$$Z(f_i, u) = \sum_{u'} p(U = u'|X)I(u' \in f_i(u)).$$

The algorithm could also randomly move between the operators, instead of systematically choosing an operator at each step.

Input: Operators $\mathcal{O} = \{f_1, \ldots, f_M\}$ and a target distribution $p(U \mid X)$.
Output: u drawn from $p(U \mid X)$.

- -

1: Initialize u to a random value
2: **repeat**
3:    **for all** $i \leftarrow 1$ *to* M **do**
4:       Sample u' from

$$q(u' \mid u) = \frac{p(u' \mid X)I(u' \in f_i(u))}{Z(f_i, u)} \qquad (5.14)$$

5:       Set $u \leftarrow u'$
6:    **end for**
7: **until** Markov chain converged
8: **return** u

Algorithm 5.3: The operator Gibbs sampling algorithm, in its "systematic sweep" form. The function $Z(f_i, u)$ denotes a normalization constant for the distribution $q(u')$. Note that it could be the case for the distribution $p(U \mid X)$ that its normalization constant is unknown.

The operators usually make local changes to the current state in the state space. For example, if the latent structure of interest is a part-of-speech tagging sequence, then an operator can make a local change to one of the part-of-speech tags. If the latent structure of interest is a phrase structure tree, then an operator can locally change a given node in the tree and its neighborhood. In these cases, the neighborhood returned by the operator is the set of states that are identical to the input state, other than some local changes.

In order to ensure that the operators do indeed induce a valid Gibbs sampler, there is a need for the operators to satisfy the following properties:

- Detailed balance—A sufficient condition for the detailed balance condition is the following: for each operator $f_i \in \mathcal{O}$ and each ω, detailed balance requires that if $\omega' \in f_i(\omega)$ then $f_i(\omega) = f_i(\omega')$. This ensures the detailed balance condition, meaning that for any u and u', it holds that:

$$p(u \mid X)q(u' \mid u) = p(u' \mid X)q(u \mid u'), \qquad (5.15)$$

where $q(u \mid u')$ and $q(u' \mid u)$ are defined in Equation 5.14. The reason Equation 5.15 holds is that the normalization constants for $q(u \mid u')$ and $q(u' \mid u)$ satisfy $Z(f_i, u) = Z(f_i, u')$ in case the sufficient condition mentioned above is satisfied.

- Recurrence—this implies that it is possible to get from any state in the search space to any other state. More formally, it means that for any $\omega, \omega' \in \Omega$, there is a sequence of operators $f_{a_1}, \ldots, f_{a_\ell}$ with $a_i \in \{1, \ldots, M\}$, such that $\omega' \in f_{i_M}(f_{i_{M-1}}(\ldots(f_{i_1}(\omega))))$, and this chain is possible with non-zero probability according to Equation 5.14.

Note that the symmetry condition implies that for every ω and f_i, it holds that $\omega \in f_i(\omega)$, i.e., an operator may not make changes at all to a given state. More generally, detailed balance and recurrence are formal properties of Markov chains that are important for ensuring the correctness of a sampler (i.e., that it actually samples from the desired target distribution), and the above two requirements from the operators are one way to satisfy them for the underlying Markov chain created by the Gibbs sampler.

There are several examples in the Bayesian NLP literature that make use of this operator view for Gibbs sampling, most notably for translation. For example, DeNero et al. (2008) used Gibbs sampling in this manner to sample phrase alignments for machine translation. They had several operators for making local changes to alignments: SWAP, which switches between the alignments of two pairs of phrases; FLIP, which changes the phrase boundaries; TOGGLE, which adds alignment links; FLIPTWO, which changes phrase boundaries in both the source and target language; and MOVE, which moves an aligned boundary either to the left or to the right. Similar operators have been used by Nakazawa and Kurohashi (2012) to handle the alignment of function words in machine translation. Ravi and Knight (2011) also used Gibbs operators to estimate the parameters of IBM Model 3 for translation. For a discussion of the issue of detailed balance with Gibbs sampling for a synchronous grammar model, see Levenberg et al. (2012).

It is often the case that an operator view of Gibbs sampling yields a sampler that is close to being a pointwise sampler, because the operators, as mentioned above, make local changes to the state space. These operators typically operate on latent *structures*, and not on the parameters. If the sampler is explicit, that is the parameters are not marginalized out, then the parameters can be sampled in an additional Gibbs step that samples from the conditional distribution of the parameters given the latent structure.

5.3.3 PARALLELIZING THE GIBBS SAMPLER

Each step in the Gibbs sampler can be quite expensive, especially when considering the collapsed example-blocked setting in NLP. It is therefore beneficial to parallelize the Gibbs algorithm on multiple processors (or multiple machines). The easiest means to parallelize the Gibbs algorithm would be to draw in parallel from the conditionals—each processor can be assigned a single conditional among the $p(U_i | U_{-i}, X)$ conditionals, and samples for U_i can be drawn on that processor.

Indeed, Geman and Geman (1984) suggested using this parallel Gibbs sampler (also called the synchronous Gibbs sampler), which is described in more detail in Algorithm 5.4. It turns out that making this simple change to the Gibbs algorithm—instead of making an immediate update to the state, the state is updated only after all conditionals have been sampled—actually

Input: Samplers for the conditionals $p(U_i|U_{-i}, X)$ for the distribution $p(U_1, \ldots, U_p|X)$.
Output: $u = (u_1, \ldots, u_p)$ approximately drawn from the above distribution.

1: Initialize $u_1, \ldots, u_p$ with some value from their space of allowed values
2: **repeat**
3:     **for all** $i \leftarrow 1$ *to* p (in parallel over i) **do**
4:         Sample u_i' from $p(u_i'|u_{-i}, X)$
5:     **end for**
6:     **for all** $i \leftarrow 1$ *to* p **do**
7:         $u_i \leftarrow u_i'$
8:     **end for**
9: **until** Markov chain converged
10: **return** $u_1, \ldots, u_p$

Algorithm 5.4: The parallel Gibbs sampling algorithm.

breaks the Gibbs algorithm. The stationary distribution (if it exists) for this sampler is not necessarily $p(U|X)$.

However, samplers similar in form have been used in practice (e.g., for the LDA model). For more information about parallelizing MCMC sampling for LDA, see Newman et al. (2009).

The difficulty of parallelizing sampling can be a reason to choose an inference algorithm which is more amenable to parallelization, such as variational inference. This is discussed further in Chapter 6.

Neiswanger et al. (2014) describe another method for parallelizing the Gibbs sampling algorithm (or any MCMC algorithm, for that matter). With their approach, the data that require inference is split into subsets, and Gibbs sampling is run separately on each subset to draw samples from the target distribution. Then, once all of the parallel MCMC chains have completed drawing samples, the samples are re-combined to get asymptotically exact samples.

5.3.4 SUMMARY

Gibbs sampling assumes a partition of the set of random variables of interest. It is an MCMC method that draws samples from the target distribution by alternating between steps for drawing samples from a set of conditional distributions for each of the random variables in each section of the partition. Among MCMC methods, Gibbs sampling is the most common one in Bayesian NLP.

Input: Distribution $p(U|X)$ computable up to its normalization constant, proposal distribution $q(U'|U)$.

Output: u drawn from p.

1: Initialize u with some value from its space of allowed values
2: **repeat**
3:     Randomly sample u' from $q(U'|u)$
4:     Calculate an acceptance ratio

$$\alpha = \min\left\{1, \frac{p(u'|X)q(u|u')}{p(u|X)q(u'|u)}\right\} \tag{5.16}$$

5:     Draw a value α' from a uniform distribution over $[0, 1]$
6:     **if** $\alpha' < \alpha$ **then**
7:         $u \leftarrow u'$
8:     **end if**
9: **until** Markov chain converged
10: **return** u

Algorithm 5.5: The Metropolis-Hastings algorithm.

5.4 THE METROPOLIS–HASTINGS ALGORITHM

The Metropolis–Hastings algorithm (MH) is an MCMC sampling algorithm that uses a *proposal* distribution to draw samples from the target distribution. Let Ω be the sample space of the target distribution $p(U|X)$ (for this example, U can represent the latent variables in the model). The proposal distribution is then a function $q(U'|U) \in \Omega \times \Omega \rightarrow [0, 1]$ such that each $u \in \Omega$ defines a distribution $q(U'|u)$. It is also assumed that sampling from $q(U'|u)$ for any $u \in \Omega$ is computationally efficient. The target distribution is assumed to be computable up to its normalization constant.

The Metropolis–Hastings sampler is given in Algorithm 5.5. It begins by initializing the state of interest with a random value, and then repeatedly samples from the underlying proposal distribution. Since the proposal distribution can be quite different from the target distribution, $p(U|X)$, there is a correction step following Equation 5.16 that determines whether or not to *accept* the sample from the proposal distribution.

Just like the Gibbs sampler, the MH algorithm *streams* samples. Once the chain has converged, one can continuously produce samples (which are not necessarily independent) by repeating the loop statements in the algorithm. At each step, u can be considered to be a sample from the underlying distribution.

We mentioned earlier that the distribution p needs to be computable up to its normalization constant. This is true even though Equation 5.16 makes explicit use of the values of p; the acceptance ratio always computes *ratios* between different values of p, and therefore the normalization constant is cancelled.

Accepting the proposed samples using the acceptance ratio pushes the sampler to explore parts of the space that tend to have a higher probability according to the target distribution. The acceptance ratio is proportional to the ratio between the probability of the next state and the probability of the current state. The larger the next state probability is, the larger the acceptance ratio is, and therefore it is more likely to be accepted by the sampler. However, there is an important correction ratio that is multiplied in: the ratio between the value of the proposed distribution in the current state and the value of the proposed distribution in the next state. This correction ratio controls for the bias that the proposal distribution introduces by having higher probability mass in certain parts of the state space over others (different than those of the target distribution).

It is important to note that the support of the proposal distribution should subsume (or be equal to) the support of the target distribution. This ensures that the underlying Markov chain is *recurrent*, and that all sample space will be explored if the sampler is run long enough. The additional property of *detailed balance* (see Section 5.3.2) is also important to ensure that the correctness of a given MCMC sampler is satisfied through the correction step using the acceptance ratio.

5.4.1   VARIANTS OF METROPOLIS–HASTINGS

Metropolis et al. (1953) originally developed the Metropolis algorithm, where the proposal distribution is assumed to be symmetric (i.e., $q(U'|U) = q(U|U')$). In this case, the acceptance ratio in Equation 5.16 consists only of the ratio between the distribution of interest at the next potential state and the current state. Hastings (1970) later generalized it to the case of an asymmetric q, which yielded the Metropolis–Hastings algorithm.

Another specific case of the Metropolis-Hastings algorithm is the one in which $q(U'|U) = q(U')$, i.e., the proposal distribution does not depend on the previous state. In this case, the MH algorithm reduces to an *independence sampler*.

An important variant of the Metropolis–Hastings given in Algorithm 5.5 is the component-wise MH algorithm. The component-wise MH algorithm is analogous to the Gibbs sampler, in that it assumes a partition over the variables in the target distribution, and it repeatedly changes the state of each of these variables using a collection of proposal distributions.

With the component-wise MH algorithm, one defines a set of proposal distributions $q_i(U'|U)$, where q_i is such that it allocates a non-zero probability mass only to transitions in the state space that keep U_{-i} intact, perhaps changing U_i. More formally, $q_i(U'_{-i}|U) > 0$ only if $U'_{-i} = U_{-i}$. Then, the component-wise MH algorithm alternates randomly or systematically, each time sampling from q_i and using the acceptance ratio:

$$\alpha_i = \min\left\{1, \frac{p(u'|X)q_i(u|u')}{p(u|X)q_i(u'|u)}\right\}, \tag{5.17}$$

to reject or accept the new sample. Each acceptance changes only a single coordinate in U.

The Gibbs algorithm can be viewed as a special case of the component-wise MH algorithm, in which

$$q_i(u'|u) = \begin{cases} p(u'_i|u_{-i}, X), & \text{if } u'_{-i} = u_{-i} \\ 0 & \text{otherwise.} \end{cases}$$

In this case, it holds that α_i from Equation 5.17 satisfies:

$$
\begin{aligned}
\alpha_i &= \min\left\{1, \frac{p(u'|X)q_i(u|u')}{p(u|X)q_i(u'|u)}\right\} \\
&= \min\left\{1, \frac{p(u'|X)p(u_i|u'_{-i}, X)}{p(u|X)p(u'_i|u_{-i}, X)}\right\} \\
&= \min\left\{1, \frac{p(u'_{-i}|X)p(u'_i|u'_{-i}, X)p(u_i|u'_{-i}, X)}{p(u_{-i}|X)p(u_i|u_{-i}, X)p(u'_i|u_{-i}, X)}\right\} \\
&= \min\left\{1, \frac{p(u'_{-i}|X)}{p(u_{-i}|X)}\right\} \\
&= 1,
\end{aligned}
$$

where the last equality comes from the fact that q_i changes only coordinate i in the state u, and the transition between the second and third inequality comes from the chain rule applied on $p(u|X)$ and $p(u'|X)$. Since $\alpha_i = 1$ for $i \in \{1, \ldots, p\}$, the MH sampler with the Gibbs proposal distributions is never going to reject any change to the state. For this reason, no correction step is needed for the Gibbs sampler, and it is removed.

5.5   SLICE SAMPLING

Slice sampling (Neal, 2003) is an MCMC method that is a specific, but interesting case of the Gibbs sampler. In its most basic form, the slice sampler is designed to draw samples from a univariate distribution.

To make the discussion concrete, assume that the target distribution is $q(\alpha)$ where α is a univariate random variable, that can appear, for example, in a hierarchical model as a hyperparameter (see Chapter 3). This means that $q(\alpha)$ can stand for distributions such as $p(\alpha|\theta, Z, X)$, or $p(\alpha|Z, X)$, if the parameters are collapsed.

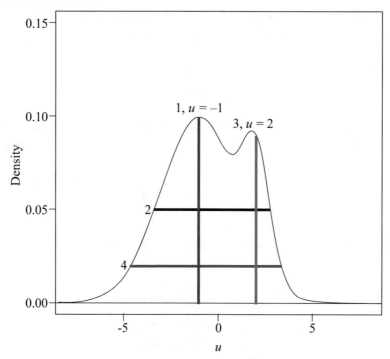

Figure 5.1: A demonstration of slice sampling for a univariate variable U. The density of U is given. The purple line (1) denotes the first sample we begin with, for which $u = -1$. We then sample a point across line 1 from a uniform distribution. Once we choose that point, we consider the black line (2), which intersects line 1 at that point. We uniformly sample a point on line 2, which yields the second sample, $u = 2$. Then we sample a random point on the blue line (3) that intersects line 2 at the new point, $u = 2$. We continue with that process of choosing points along vertically and horizontally intersecting lines (the red line, 4, intersects line 3). This amounts to a random walk on the graph of the density function of U.

The univariate slice sampler relies on the observation that sampling from a distribution can be done by uniformly sampling a point from the graph of the underlying distribution, and then projecting this point to the x-axis. Here, "graph" refers to the area that is bounded by the curve of the density function. The x-axis ranges over the values that α can receive, and the y-axis ranges over the actual density values. Figure 5.1 demonstrates that idea.

This idea of uniformly sampling the graph is where MCMC comes into play: instead of directly sampling from the graph, which can be computationally difficult, the slice sampler is an MCMC sampler for which the stationary distribution is a uniform distribution over the area (or volume) under the graph of the distribution of interest. Intuitively, the slice sampler is a Gibbs sampler that moves in straight lines along the x-axis and y-axis in a random walk.

More formally, the slice sampler introduces an auxiliary variable $V \in \mathbb{R}$ to $q(\alpha)$, and then defines two Gibbs sampling steps for changing the state (v, α). In the first step, α (given $V = v$) is drawn uniformly from the set $\{\alpha' | v \leq q(\alpha')\}$. This in essence corresponds to a move along the x-axis. The second step is perhaps more intuitive, where we draw v (given α) from a uniform distribution over the set $\{v | v \leq q(\alpha)\}$, corresponding to a move along the y-axis.

5.5.1   AUXILIARY VARIABLE SAMPLING

Slice sampling is a specific case of a general approach to sampling called "auxiliary variable sampling." This approach assumes the existence of a variable V, an auxiliary variable, such that together with U, it induces a joint distribution $p(U, V | X) = p(U | X) p(V | U, X)$. One can then proceed by using one of the MCMC algorithms to sample from $p(U, V | X)$. The samples from V are eventually ignored, and the samples from U are used as samples from the target distribution $p(U | X)$.

The choice of an auxiliary variable is not simple and depends on the model at hand; the selection should ensure that the MCMC sampler will tend to explore areas with higher probability mass. If Gibbs sampling is used in conjunction with the auxiliary variable, one should make sure that the conditionals $p(V | U, X)$ and $p(U | V, X)$ can be sampled from efficiently.

There is one interesting connection between explicit sampling (when the parameters of the model are sampled) and auxiliary variable methods. The parameters themselves can be thought of as an auxiliary variable for the "blocked posterior," since they introduce conditional independence assumptions between the latent structures that one is interested in sampling, and therefore, make sampling computationally easier.

5.5.2   THE USE OF SLICE SAMPLING AND AUXILIARY VARIABLE SAMPLING IN NLP

Slice sampling for a univariate continuous distribution is especially used in NLP for hyperparameter inference. For example, Johnson and Goldwater (2009) used slice sampling to sample the hyperparameters of a Pitman–Yor process, corresponding to the concentration and discount values. The slice sampler was used in conjunction with a vague Gamma prior placed on top of these hyperparameters. With a vague prior placed on the hyperparameters, slice sampling behaves almost as a search procedure for finding the best hyperparameter setting. This method can be compared, for example, to empirical Bayes in Section 4.3; other recent examples of using slice sampling for hyperparameter inference include Lindsey et al. (2012).

One of the thorough uses of auxiliary variable sampling in NLP was done by Blunsom and Cohn (2010a), who introduced an auxiliary variable sampler for synchronous grammars. This sampler obtains synchronous derivations given a pair of sentences. The goal was to obtain such derivations faster than a naïve dynamic programming algorithm with time complexity, which is cubic in both the source sentence length and the target sentence length.

The sampler by Blunsom and Cohn (2010a) introduces an auxiliary continuous variable for each possible span in a synchronous derivation. Then, when sampling a derivation given this set of continuous variables, the dynamic programming algorithm prunes away any span in the chart that has a probability lower than the corresponding value of the auxiliary variable. Blunsom and Cohn had to introduce a correction step, similar to the one that exists in Metropolis-Hastings, in order to make their sampler correct. The two alternative MCMC methods to auxiliary variable sampling that they discuss in their paper are reported to either mix very slowly (naïve Gibbs sampling) or are computationally inefficient (collapsed Gibbs sampling). See Section 5.7 for more information about the convergence of MCMC algorithms.

The slicer sampler of Blunsom and Cohn (2010a) led to a better BLEU score for translating Chinese to English, and also led to a higher log-likelihood of the model, compared to the naïve Gibbs sampling approach by Blunsom et al. (2009a). This could be partially attributed to the fact that the authors discovered that the Gibbs sampler is more sensitive to initialization. For more information, see Section 5.7. The authors also discovered that the Gibbs sampler tends to be trapped in modes of the distribution more often than the auxiliary variable sampler.

Van Gael et al. (2008) designed an inference algorithm for infinite hidden Markov models (Section 8.1.1) that combines dynamic programming with slice sampling (they called it a "beam sampler"). They tested their inference algorithm for predicting text from *Alice in Wonderland*. Still, their beam sampler did not have better predictive power on this problem than a Gibbs sampling algorithm. However, for other non-NLP and artificial data problems, they discovered that their beam sampler mixes faster than a Gibbs sampling algorithm.

Bouchard-côté et al. (2009) describe an auxiliary-variable sampler with the goal of pruning when running a dynamic programming algorithm, such as the inside-outside algorithm for PCFGs (Chapter 8). Their algorithm works by traversing the space of auxiliary variables, which are binary vectors indexed by spans and syntactic categories in the sentence, where each element in the vector denotes for each constituent whether it is pruned or not. At each point, once such binary vector is sampled, and the inside-outside algorithm is run while pruning the constituents according to the vector (therefore it runs much faster). Finally, all expectations computed from all of these steps are averaged together to achieve an approximate version of the expectations. This process is also related to Monte Carlo integration (Section 5.10).

5.6   SIMULATED ANNEALING

Simulated annealing is a method for biasing an MCMC sampler so that it will gradually focus on areas in the state space that consist of most of the probability mass of the distribution. It therefore can be used as a decoding method to find the maximum *a posteriori* solution for a given posterior distribution.

In its simplest form, simulated annealing explores the state space by starting with a high *temperature*, which corresponds to an exploratory phase of searching in the state space; as the sampler converges, the temperature is turned down, so that the search is more focused on the area the sampler has reached at that point.

If the target distribution is $p(U|X)$, then simulated annealing will instead strive to sample from the distribution:

$$\frac{p^{1/T_t}(U|X)}{Z(T_t)} \tag{5.18}$$

where $Z(T_t)$ is a normalization constant, integrating or summing $p^{1/T_t}(U|X)$ over U. The value T_t corresponds to the temperature, which starts at a high temperature, and slowly decreases to 1 as the iteration in the sampler, denoted t, increases. If one is interested in using simulated annealing for *optimization*, i.e., finding the posterior mode, then one can even decrease the temperature to 0, at which point the re-normalized posterior from Equation 5.18 concentrates most of its probability mass on a single point in the sample space.

For example, with Gibbs sampling, simulated annealing can be done by exponentiating the conditional distributions by $1/T_t$ and renormalizing, while increasing t at each iteration of the Gibbs sampler. For the Metropolis–Hastings algorithm, one needs to change the acceptance ratio so that it exponentiates $p(U|X)$ by $\frac{1}{T_t}$. There will be no need to compute $Z(T_t)$ in this case, since it is cancelled in the acceptance ratio that appears in Equation 5.16.

5.7 CONVERGENCE OF MCMC ALGORITHMS

Every MCMC algorithm execution goes through a period of "burn-in." In that phase, the Markov chain has not stabilized yet (or has not *mixed*), and the samples drawn are not drawn from the actual posterior. After the burn-in period, the Markov chain converges to the posterior distribution, at which point the samples being drawn are (dependent) samples from the posterior.

Characterizing the number of iterations before reaching convergence is generally a challenging problem with MCMC algorithms and specifically with Bayesian NLP models. There is some theory of convergence that provides the upper bounds on the number of iterations based on spectral decomposition of the *transition matrix* (Robert and Casella, 2005)—see Section 5.8— but this theory is difficult to apply to practical problems in NLP.

Most of the approaches to testing convergence are empirical, and based on heuristics. Some of the approaches include:

- **Visual inspection.** In the case of a single univariate parameter being sampled, one can manually inspect a traceplot that plots the value of the sampled parameter vs. the iteration number of the sampler. If we observe that the chain gets "stuck" in a certain range of the parameters, and then moves to another range, stays there for a while, and continuously moves between these ranges, this is an indication that the sampler has not mixed.

In NLP, the parameters are clearly multidimensional, and it is not always the case that we are sampling a continuous variable. In this case, a scalar function of the structure or multidimensional vector being sampled can be calculated at each iteration, and plotted instead. This will provide a uni-directional indication about the mixing of the chain: if the pattern mentioned above is observed, this is an indication that the sampler has not mixed.

One can also plot the mean of some scalar function $\frac{1}{t} \left(\sum_{i=1}^{t} f(u^{(i)}) \right)$ against t, where t is the sampler iteration and $u^{(i)}$ is the sample drawn at iteration i. This mean value should eventually plateau (by the law of large numbers), and if it has not, then that is an indication the sampler has not mixed. The scalar function, for example, can be the log-likelihood.

- **Validation on a development set.** In parallel to running the MCMC sampler, one could make predictions on a small annotated development set, if such a set exists for this end. In the explicit MCMC sampling setting, the parameters can be used to make predictions on this development set, and the sampler can be stopped when performance stops improving (performance is measured here according to the evaluation metric relevant to the problem at hand). If a collapsed setting is used, then one can extract a point estimate based on the current state of the sampler, and use it again to make predictions on a development set.

Note that with this approach, we are not checking for the convergence of the sampler on the "true posterior," but instead optimize our sampler so that it operates in a part of the state space that works well with the final evaluation metric.

- **Testing autocorrelation.** When the target distribution is defined over real values, one can use the autocorrelation to test for the diagonsis of an MCMC algorithm. Denote $p(\theta)$ as the target distribution. The autocorrelation with lag k is defined as:

$$\rho_k = \frac{\sum_{t=1}^{T-k} (\theta_t - \overline{\theta})(\theta_{t+k} - \overline{\theta})}{\sum_{t=1}^{T-k} (\theta_t - \overline{\theta})^2}, \tag{5.19}$$

where $\overline{\theta} = \frac{1}{T} \sum_{t=1}^{T} \theta_t$, θ_t is the tth sample in the chain and T is the total number of samples. The numerator in Equation 5.19 corresponds to an estimated covariance term, and the denominator to an estimated variance term. Autocorrelation tests rely on the idea that if the MCMC sampler has reached the stationary distribution, the autocorrelation value should be small as k increases. Thus, an indication of slow mixing or lack of convergence is large autocorrelation values even for relatively large k.

- **Other tests.** The Geweke test (Geweke, 1992) is a well-known method for checking whether an MCMC algorithm has converged. It works by splitting a chain of samples into two parts after an assumed burn-in period; these two parts are then tested to see whether they are similar to each other. If indeed the chain has reached the stationary state, then these two parts should be similar. The test is performed using a modification of the so-called z-test (Upton and Cook, 2014), and the score used to compare the two parts of the chain is called the Geweke z-score. Another test that is widely used for MCMC convergence diagnosis is the Raftery-Lewis test. It is a good fit in cases where the target distribution is defined over real values. It works by thresholding all elements in the chain against a certain quantile q, thus binarizing the chain into a sequence of 1s and 0s. The test then proceeds by estimating transition probabilities between these binary values, and uses these transition probabilities to assess convergence. For more details, see Raftery and Lewis (1992).

A valid criticism of the use of MCMC algorithms in NLP is that the algorithms are often used without a good verification of chain convergence. Since MCMC algorithms can be quite expensive in the context of Bayesian NLP, they are often run for a fixed number of iterations that are limited by the amount of time allotted for an empirical evaluation. This leads to high sensitivity of the reported results to starting conditions of the Markov chain, or even worse—a result that is based on samples that are not drawn from the true posterior. In this case, the use of MCMC algorithms is similar to a random search.

It is therefore encouraged to be more careful with Bayesian models, and monitor the convergence of MCMC algorithms. When MCMC algorithms are too slow to converge (an issue that can arise often with Bayesian NLP models), one should consider switching to a different approximate inference algorithm such as variational inference (Chapter 6), where convergence can be more easily assessed.

5.8   MARKOV CHAIN: BASIC THEORY

It is beyond the scope of this book to provide a full account of the theory behind Markov chains and MCMC methods. For a thorough investigation of Markov chain theory, see Robert and Casella (2005). Instead, we offer an informal exposition of the core ideas behind these methods. The first thing to note is that MCMC methods can be thought of as mechanisms to traverse the sample space, transitioning from one state to another at each iteration. With explicit posterior inference, for example, the search space includes pairs of parameters and latent structures for each observation: $(\theta, z^{(1)}, \ldots, z^{(n)})$.

We denote the sample space by Ω, and for simplicity, we assume it is finite (clearly, it is not finite with explicit posterior inference, when the parameters are continuous, or even with collapsed sampling, where the number of possible latent structures for a given observation is potentially infinite). Therefore, Ω can be enumerated as $\{s_1, \ldots, s_N\}$ where $N = |\Omega|$.

A *homogeneous* Markov chain is determined by a transition matrix T (or a "transition kernel"), such that T_{ij} denotes a probability of transition from s_i to state s_j according to this Markov chain. The matrix T, therefore, is a stochastic matrix, with non-negative elements where each column sums to 1:

$$\sum_{j=1}^{N} T_{ij} = 1 \ \forall i \in \{1, \ldots, N\}. \tag{5.20}$$

A non-homogeneous Markov chain would have a transition kernel per time step instead of a single T; all samplers and algorithms in this chapter are considered to be homogeneous chains.

There is an important algebraic property of Markov chains with respect to T. Let v be some distribution over Ω, i.e., a vector such that $v_i \geq 0$ and $\sum_i v_i = 1$. In this case, multiplying T by v (on the left)—i.e., computing vT—yields a distribution as well. To see this, consider that if $w = vT$ then:

$$\sum_{j=1}^{N} w_j = \sum_{j=1}^{N} \sum_{i=1}^{N} v_i T_{ij} = \sum_{i=1}^{N} v_i \times \underbrace{\left(\sum_{j=1}^{N} T_{ij} \right)}_{=1} = \sum_{i=1}^{N} v_i = 1,$$

because of Equation 5.20. Therefore, w is a distribution over the state space Ω. The distribution w is not an arbitrary distribution. It is the distribution that results from taking a single step using the Markov chain starting with the initial distribution v over states. More generally, vT^k for an integer $k \geq 0$ gives the distribution over Ω after k steps in the Markov chain. If we let $v^{(t)}$ be the distribution over Ω at time step t, then this means that:

$$v^{(t+1)} = v^{(t)}T = v^{(0)}T^{t+1}. \tag{5.21}$$

A key concept in Markov chains is that of a *stationary distribution*. A stationary distribution is a distribution such that if we use it to initiate the chain (i.e., use it as $v^{(0)}$), then the probabilities over the next state will still distribute according to the stationary distribution. Under some regularity conditions (irreducibility and aperiodicity, see Robert and Casella (2005) for more information), such a stationary distribution exists and is unique. In addition, under these regularity conditions, no matter what the initial distribution is, the Markov chain will eventually *mix* and arrive at the stationary distribution.

According to Equation 5.21, this means that if π is the stationary distribution, then

$$\pi T = \pi, \tag{5.22}$$

i.e., π is the eigenvector associated with eigenvalue 1. (This implicitly means that if T has a stationary distribution, then it has eigenvalue of 1 to begin with, which is also going to be the largest eigenvalue.)

This basic theory serves as the foundation for the proofs of samplers such as the Gibbs sampler and the Metropolis–Hastings algorithm. In these proofs, two key steps are taken:

- Proving that the chain induced by the sampler is such that it converges to a stationary distribution (i.e., satisfies the basic regularity conditions).

- Proving that the target distribution we are interested in sampling from is the stationary distribution of the Markov chain induced by the sampler (i.e., that it satisfies Equation 5.22).

5.9 SAMPLING ALGORITHMS NOT IN THE MCMC REALM

Markov chain Monte Carlo methods are not the only way to draw samples from a target distribution such as the posterior. MCMC methods are mostly necessary when it is possible to only calculate the target distribution up to its normalization constant. When it is possible to evaluate the target distribution, including the normalization constant, but it is difficult to sample from the distribution for some algorithmic or computational reason, methods such as rejection sampling can be useful and more efficient than MCMC methods.

We next describe rejection sampling (also known as the accept-reject algorithm), where we assume that the target distribution is $p(U|X)$. The rejection sampling algorithm assumes the existence of a proposal distribution $q(U)$ from which sampling is computationally feasible. This proposal distribution should satisfy:

$$p(U|X) \leq M q(U),$$

for some *known* $M > 0$—since M is directly used and evaluated in the rejection sampling algorithm. It is also assumed that for any u, one can *calculate* $p(u|X)$ (including its normalization constant). Then, in order to sample from $p(U|X)$, the procedure in Algorithm 5.6 is followed.

It can be shown that the probability of accepting y in each iteration is $1/M$. Therefore, rejection sampling is not practical when M is very large. This problem is especially severe with distributions that are defined over high dimensional data.[2]

The intuition behind rejection sampling is best explained graphically for the univariate case. Consider Figure 5.2. We see that $M q(u)$ serves as an envelope surrounding the target distribution $p(u)$.

To proceed with drawing a sample from $p(u)$, we can repeatedly sample points from this envelope defined by $M q(u)$, until we happen to hit a point which is within the graph of $p(u)$. Indeed, to sample points from the envelope, we sample a point from $q(u)$; this limits us to a point on the x-axis that corresponds to a point in the sample space. Now, we can proceed by just inspecting the line that stretches from the 0 y-axis coordinate to $M q(u)$ and draw a uniform

---

[2]This problem is partially tackled by *adaptive* rejection sampling. Adaptive rejection sampling is used when multiple samples $u^{(1)}, \ldots, u^{(m)}$ are needed from a distribution $p(u)$. It works by progressively tightening the proposal distribution $q(u)$ around the target distribution $p(u)$. See Robert and Casella (2005) for more details. Examples of using adaptive rejection sampling in Bayesian NLP are quite rare, but see for example Carter et al. (2012) and Dymetman et al. (2012) for its use in NLP.

Input: Distributions $p(U|X)$ and $q(U)$, a sampler for a distribution $q(U)$, and a constant M.
Output: u, a sample from $p(U|X)$.

1: Set accept to false
2: **repeat**
3:    Set u to be a sample from $q(U)$
4:    Draw $\alpha \in [0, 1]$ from a uniform distribution.
5:    **if** $\alpha \leq (p(u|X)/Mq(u))$ **then**
6:       Set accept to true.
7:    **end if**
8: **until** accept equals true
9: **return** u

Algorithm 5.6: The rejection sampling algorithm.

point on that line. If it falls below the graph of $p(u)$, then the sampler managed to draw a sample from $p(u)$. If it does not fall below the graph of $p(u)$, the process needs to be repeated.

In its general form, the main challenge behind the use of a rejection sampler is finding a bounding distribution $q(U)$ with its constant M. However, there is a specific case of rejection sampling in which these quantities can be easily identified. Consider the case in which one is interested in sampling from a more restricted subspace of the sample space Ω. Assume the existence of $p(u)$, and that the target distribution has the following form:

$$p'(u) = \frac{p(u)I(u \in A)}{Z},$$

where $A \subset \Omega$ and $I(u \in A)$ is the indicator function that equals 1 if $u \in A$ and 0 otherwise, and Z is a normalization constant that integrates or sums $p(u)$ over A. If $p(u)$ can be computed for each $u \in \Omega$ and efficiently sampled from, and the membership query $u \in A$ can be accomplished efficiently for any $u \in \Omega$, then rejection sampling can be used to sample from $p'(u)$, with a proposal distribution $p(u)$. In this case, $M = 1$, and in order to proceed with sampling from $p'(u)$, one has to sample from $p(u)$ until $u \in A$.

Cohen and Johnson (2013) use rejection sampling in this way in order to restrict Bayesian estimation of PCFGs to *tight* PCFGs, i.e., PCFGs for which their normalization constant (summing over all possible trees according to the grammar) sums to 1. Rejection sampling was used in conjunction with a Dirichlet prior. The Dirichlet prior was sampled, and then the resulting rule probabilities were inspected to see whether they were tight. If they were tight, these rule probabilities were accepted.

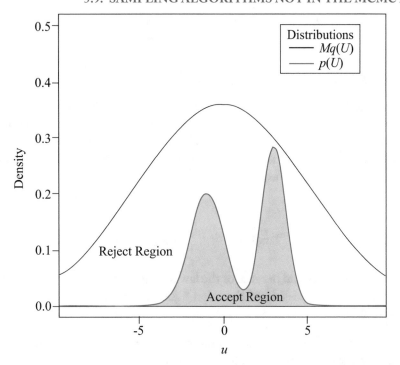

Figure 5.2: The plots of $Mq(U)$ (the envelope) and $p(U|X)$ (distribution of interest) for rejection sampling. Plot adapted from Andrieu et al. (2003).

Inverse Transform Sampling: Another non-MCMC method for sampling is inverse transform sampling (ITS). For a real-valued random variable X, the ITS method assumes that for a given $u \in \mathbb{R}$, we can identify the largest x such that $F(x) \leq u$, where F is the CDF of X (see Section 1.2.1). Then, ITS works by sampling u from a uniform distribution over $[0, 1]$, and then returning that largest x.

This inverse transform sampling method applies to sampling from multinomial distributions. In order to sample from such a distribution, we can apply the inverse transform sampling method on a random variable X that maps each event in the multinomial distribution to a unique integer between 1 and n, where n is the number of events for the multinomial.

A naïve implementation of ITS for the multinomial distribution will require linear time in n for each sample, where n is the number of events in the multinomial. There is actually a simple way to speed this up to $O(\log n)$ per sample from that multinomial, with a preprocessing step with asymptotic complexity $O(n)$. Once we map each event to an integer between 1 and n with a random variable X, we calculate the vector of numbers $\alpha_j = F(j) = \sum_{i=1}^{j} p(X = i)$ for $j \in \{1, \ldots, n\}$ and set $\alpha_0 = 0$. Now, in order to use the ITS, we draw a uniform variable u, and then apply a logarithmic-time binary search on the array represented by the vector $(\alpha_0, \ldots, \alpha_n)$

to find a j such that $u \in [\alpha_{j-1}, \alpha_j]$. We then return the multinomial event associated with index j.

5.10 MONTE CARLO INTEGRATION

Monte Carlo integration is a method to compute expectations of the form $I(f) = E_{p(U)}[f(U)]$ for some function f of the variables in a target distribution $p(U)$. It was one of the original motivations behind MC sampling methods. MC integration, in its simple form, relies on the observation that if $u^{(1)}, \ldots, u^{(M)}$ is a stream of samples from the target distribution, then this expectation can be approximated as:

$$I(f) = E_{p(U)}[f(U)] \approx \frac{1}{M} \sum_{i=1}^{M} f\left(u^{(i)}\right). \tag{5.23}$$

This approximation is valid because of the law of large numbers, which states that as $M \to \infty$, the sum on the right-hand-side of Equation 5.23 will converge to the desired expectation on the left-hand-side.

Importance Sampling: Importance sampling takes the idea in Equation 5.23, and suggests a way to approximate the expectation $I(f)$ by sampling using a proposal distribution $q(U)$. Therefore, importance sampling can be used when it is not easy to sample from p (but it is possible to calculate its value). Additionally, when choosing a specific proposal distribution under certain circumstances, importance sampling is more efficient than perfect Monte Carlo integration (i.e., when estimating $I(f)$ using samples from $p(U)$); this means the approximate integral tends to converge with fewer samples to $I(f)$.

Importance sampling relies on the following simple identity that holds for any distribution $q(U)$ such that $q(u) = 0$ only if $p(u) = 0$:

$$I(f) = E_{p(U)}[f(U)] = E_{q(U)}\left[f(U) \times \frac{p(U)}{q(U)}\right]. \tag{5.24}$$

Equation 5.24 is true, because the expectation operator folds a weighted sum/integration operation using $q(U)$, which in conjunction with the term $\frac{p(U)}{q(U)}$ leads to a re-weighting of the sum/integration operation using $p(U)$.

The implication of this is that $I(f)$ can be approximated as:

$$I(f) \approx \frac{1}{M} \sum_{i=1}^{M} f\left(u^{(i)}\right) \times \frac{p(u^{(i)})}{q(u^{(i)})} = \hat{I}(f),$$

where $u^{(i)}$ for $i \in \{1, \ldots, M\}$ are samples from $q(U)$.

As mentioned above, certain choices of $q(U)$ are preferable over others. One measure for the efficiency in the use of samples drawn from the proposal distribution is the variance of the quantity $f(U) \times \frac{p(U)}{q(U)}$ with respect to $q(U)$. This variance can be shown to be minimized when sampling from $q^*(U)$ such that:

$$q^*(u) = \frac{|f(u)|p(u)}{\int_u |f(u)|p(u)du},$$

where integration can be replaced by sum, if u is discrete. q^* itself is often hard to calculate or sample from. The reason it is optimal is related to the fact that it places large probability mass where both the magnitude of f and the mass/density of p are large (as opposed to just selecting a region with high probability mass according to p, but potentially insignificant small values of f). We want to sample points in the space that balance between being highly probable and also giving dominant values to f.

Going back to Equation 5.23, the samples drawn from p to estimate the integral can be generated using any MC method presented in this chapter, including MCMC methods. This means, for example, that we can repeatedly draw samples $u^{(i)}$ from the state space using a Gibbs sampler, and use them to estimate an integral of a specific function that we are interested in.

5.11   DISCUSSION

We will now briefly discuss some additional topics about sampling methods and their use in NLP.

5.11.1   COMPUTABILITY OF DISTRIBUTION VS. SAMPLING

We have seen that with MCMC that we do not need to be able to compute a probability distribution for a given assignment for the random variables in order to draw samples from it. For example, with MH sampling, all we need is to be able to compute the probability distribution up to a multilpicative constant. Still, being able to compute the probability distribution for every random variable assignment does not imply that it is easy to sample from it. This can be shown more formally, for example, by reducing the problem of finding a satisfying assignment for a uniquely satisfiable logical formula to the problem of sampling from a distribution that is fully calculable.

More specifically, the best well-known algorithm for finding the unique satisfying assignment for the above problem is exponential in its number of variables. Given such a formula, one can easily define a distribution $p(x)$ over assignments to the variables such that $p(x) = 1$ if and only if x is the satisfying formula. The distribution $p(x)$ can be calculated in linear time in the number of variables used. However, sampling from $p(x)$ is equivalent to finding a uniquely satisfying Boolean assignment.

5.11.2 NESTED MCMC SAMPLING

MCMC methods can be used in conjunction with each other. For example, one can use the Metropolis-within-Gibbs sampler, which is a Gibbs sampling algorithm where the sampling from the conditionals (or at least a few of them) takes a single Metropolis step instead of directly sampling from the conditional. In this case, there is no need to draw samples at each Gibbs step until the burn-in period has ended, as it is instead sufficient to take a single MH step to show that the sampler will theoretically converge to draw samples from the target distribution. See Robert and Casella (2005) for more details. Metropolis-within-Gibbs has been used for various problems in Bayesian NLP (Johnson et al., 2007b).

5.11.3 RUNTIME OF MCMC SAMPLERS

The runtime of MCMC methods depends on two factors that have a trade-off between them: the number of iterations it takes for the Markov chain to mix and the runtime of drawing samples from the proposal distributions or the conditional distributions (in the case of Gibbs sampling). In general, if possible, it is a good practice to run in a collapsed setting, and not sample variables that are not of interest for prediction (though there is evidence that samplers in the collapsed setting can actually run for longer periods of time than an explicit sampler; see, for example, Gao and Johnson (2008)).

Similarly, MCMC methods should converge in fewer iterations in the blocked setting compared to the pointwise setting. There is a trade-off here, since the blocked setting can make the sampler more expensive *per iteration* (requiring, for example, a dynamic programming algorithm to sample a whole latent structure for a given example), while the total number of iterations will be smaller than with a pointwise sampler. Empirically, it is often the case that blocked samplers have a shorter total running time.

5.11.4 PARTICLE FILTERING

Particle filtering, sometimes referred to as a sequential Monte Carlo method, is a sampling technique used to sequentially sample latent states based on observations. With particle filtering, we assume a sequential model with $Z = (Z_1, \ldots, Z_m)$ being a sequence of latent states and $X = (X_1, \ldots, X_m)$ being a sequence of observations. The independence assumptions are identical to the ones we make with hidden Markov models: X_i is independent of all other variables given Z_i, and Z_i is independent of all Z_j for $j < i - 1$ given Z_{i-1}.

The model, therefore, has the following structure, which is identical to the structure of a bigram hidden Markov model (see Section 8.1):

$$p(Z_1, \ldots, Z_m, X_1, \ldots, X_m) = p(Z_1)p(X_1|Z_1) \prod_{i=2}^{m} p(Z_i|Z_{i-1})p(X_i|Z_i). \quad (5.25)$$

The goal of particle filtering is to approximate the distribution $p(Z_i|X_1 = x_1, \ldots, X_i = x_i)$—i.e., to predict the latent state at position i in the sequence, conditioned on the observations up to that point. This means that we are interested in sampling Z_i from $p(Z_i|X_1 = x_1, \ldots, X_i = x_i)$ for $i \in \{1, \ldots m\}$. Particle filtering approaches this problem through the use of a sequence of importance sampling steps. The distribution p is assumed to be known.

First, particle filtering samples M "particles" from the distribution $p(Z_1|X_1)$. This distribution can be derived using a simple application of Bayes' rule on $p(X_1|Z_1)$ in tandem with the distribution $p(Z_1)$, both of which are components of the model in Equation 5.25. This leads to a set of particles $z_1^{(i)}$ for $i \in \{1, \ldots, M\}$.

In the general case, particle filtering samples M particles corresponding to Z_j in the jth step,. These M particles are used to approximate the distribution $p(Z_j|X_1, \ldots, X_j)$—each particle $z_j^{(i)}$ for $i \in \{1, \ldots, M\}$ is assigned a weight $\beta_{j,i}$, and the distribution $p(Z_j|X_1, \ldots, X_j)$ is approximated as:

$$p\left(Z_j = z|X_1 = x_1, \ldots, X_j = x_j\right) \approx \sum_{i=1}^{M} I\left(z_j^{(i)} = z\right)\beta_{j,i}. \qquad (5.26)$$

Particle filtering relies on a hierarchical construction of each distribution at each step j. Bayes' rule is applied for predicting a state conditioned on previous observations for $j \in \{1, \ldots, m\}$:

$$p\left(Z_j|X_1, \ldots, X_j\right) \propto \sum_z p\left(Z_{j-1} = z|X_1, \ldots, X_{j-1}\right) p\left(Z_j|Z_{j-1} = z\right) p\left(X_j|Z_j\right).$$

The quantity above exactly equals $E_{p(Z_{j-1}|X_1,\ldots,X_{j-1})}\left[p(Z_j|Z_{j-1} = z)p(X_j|Z_j)\right]$. We can therefore use importance sampling (see Section 5.10) to sample M particles from $p(Z_{j-1}|X_1, \ldots, X_{j-1})$, and for each such draw z, draw $z_j^{(i)}$ from $p(Z_j|Z_{j-1} = z)$, and set its weight $\beta_{j,i}$ to be proportional to $p(X_j = x_j|Z_j = z_j^{(i)})$. This leads to the approximation in Equation 5.26, which can be used in the next step of the particle filtering algorithm.

Particle filtering was used by Levy et al. (2009) to describe a model for incremental parsing. The motivation is psycholinguistic: the authors were interested in modeling human comprehension of language. The authors claim, based on prior work, that there is much evidence that shows that humans process language incrementally, and therefore it is beneficial to model the probability of a partial syntactic derivation conditioned on a prefix of a sentence. In the notation above, partial derivations are modeled whereas the latent random variables Z_i and X_i denote the words in a sentence, and the integer m denotes the length of the sentence. Levy et al.'s incremental parser was especially good in modeling the effect of human memory limitations in sentence comprehension.

Table 5.1: A list of Monte Carlo methods and the components they require in order to operate and sample from the posterior $p(U|X)$. The $\propto$ symbol denotes that we need to be able to calculate a quantity only up to a normalization constant.

Sampler	Need to Sample From	Need to Calculate
Gibbs sampler	$p(U_i|U_{-i}, X)$	None
Gibbs, operator view	Proportional to $p(U|X)$ in operator neighborhood	$\{f_1, \dots f_M\}$
MH sampler	$q(U'|U)$	$\propto p(U|X)$
Independence sampler	$q(U)$	$\propto p(U|X)$
Rejection sampler	$q(U)$ s.t. $p(U|X) \leq Mq(U)$	$M, p(U|X)$
Slice sampler	$q(\alpha|V)$ and $q(V|\alpha)$	Level sets
Importance sampler	$q(U)$	$q(U)$ and $p(U|X)$

Yang and Eisenstein (2013) also developed a sequential Monte Carlo method for normalizing tweets into English. The particles they maintain correspond to normalized tweets in English. The (non-Bayesian) model they used was composed of a conditional log-linear model that models the distribution over tweets given an English sentence, and a model over English sentences. These two models are multiplied together to get a joint distribution over tweets and English sentences.

5.12   CONCLUSION AND SUMMARY

Monte Carlo methods are an important machinery in Bayesian NLP. Most often they are used to sample either a set of parameters for the model, which can be followed by point estimation (see Chapter 4) or to directly sample the structures to be predicted. The samples are drawn from the posterior distribution.

An important family of Monte Carlo methods is the Markov chain Monte Carlo methods, which are based on traversing the sample space using a Markov chain, and converging to a stationary distribution that is identical to the target distribution such as the posterior distribution. They are often used in Bayesian NLP because they only require being able to compute the posterior distribution up to a normalization constant; this is natural in the Bayesian setting, in which the posterior is proportional to the joint model distribution. The joint distribution can be easily calculated in most cases, but computing the normalization constant for turning it into the posterior can be intractable. Table 5.1 describes a summary of the sampling algorithms that were mentioned in this chapter.

In various sections in this chapter (such as in Example 5.1), we gave a detailed account of how to derive specific samplers for specific models. We derived the sampler from the basic principles that need to be followed for the sampler family, such as the Gibbs algorithm. It is important to note that often NLP researchers do not follow such detailed derivations, and instead leave much of the derivation to intuition. This intuition is developed over time, after heavy use of specific families of sampling algorithms; similar intuitions, develop for algorithms such as the expectation-maximization algorithm. However, such intuition can often also be misleading, especially with respect to the finer details of the sampling algorithm. For researchers who just begin to use sampling algorithms, it is highly recommended to derive sampling algorithms from basic principles, at least until they develop more sound intuition about the sampling algorithms they use.

5.13   EXERCISES

5.1.   Consider the Bayesian LDA model, with its graphical model in Figure 2.1. Construct a Gibbs sampler for it, that alternates between sampling the topic distributions $\theta^{(i)}$, the topic parameters β and then word topics $z_j^{(i)}$. The index i here ranges over N documents. You can also use generative story 2.1.

5.2.   Construct an example of a target distribution to sample from, and a proposal distribution, such that the Metropolis-Hastings has a very low rejection rate, but actually mixes very slowly.

5.3.   Let T be a transition matrix, such as the one described in Section 5.8. We say that T satisfies the detailed balance condition with distribution π if:

$$\pi_i T_{ij} = \pi_j T_{ji},$$

for all i and j. Show that when the detailed balance condition is satisfied, π is the stationary distribution. Is the reverse true as well?

5.4.   The following two questions prove the correctness of a Gibbs sampler for a simple model. (The exercise is based on Section 3 in Casella and George (1992).) Consider a probability distribution $p(X, Y)$ over two binary random variables X, Y, with the following probability table:

		X	
values		0	1
Y	0	p_1	p_2
	1	p_3	p_4

such that $\sum_{i=1}^{4} p_i = 1$ and $p_i \geq 0$ for $i \in \{1, \ldots, 4\}$.

Write down two matrices $A_{y|x}$ and $A_{x|y}$ (in terms of p_i), both of size 2×2 such that:

$$[A_{y|x}]_{ij} = p(Y = i | X = j)$$
$$[A_{x|y}]_{ij} = p(X = i | Y = j)$$

where i and j ranges over $\{0, 1\}$.

5.5.   Assume that we are interested in sampling from $p(X)$. Assume that we are sampling a chain $x_0 \rightarrow y_1 \rightarrow x_1 \rightarrow y_2 \ldots$ using the matrices $A_{x|y}$ and $A_{y|x}$ from the previous question. Compute the transition probability of $p(x_i | x_{i-1})$, marginalizing y_i, and write it down as a transition matrix $A_{x|x'}$. Compute the eigenvector of $A_{x|x'}$, which is associated with eigenvalue 1 (by solving $\pi A_{x|x'} = \pi$ with respect to π) and show that π is the marginal distribution $p(X)$.

5.6. The Gibbs sampler is a correct sampler: given the conditional distributions of the target distribution, running it will converge to the target distribution. For two random variables X and Y, this means that the conditional distributions $p(X \mid Y)$ and $p(Y \mid X)$ uniquely identify the joint distribution $p(X, Y)$. Prove that analytically (i.e., show that $p(X, Y)$ can be expressed in terms of the conditional distributions). Hint: can you express $p(X)$ (or $p(Y)$) in terms of the conditionals?

CHAPTER 6

Variational Inference

In the previous chapter, we described some of the core algorithms used for drawing samples from the posterior, or more generally, from a probability distribution. In this chapter, we consider another approach to approximate inference—variational inference.

Variational inference treats the problem of identifying the posterior as an *optimization problem*. When this optimization problem is solved, the output is an approximate version of the posterior distribution. This means that the objective function that variational inference aims to optimize is a function over a family of distributions. The reason this is an *approximate* inference is that this family of distributions is usually not inclusive of the true posterior, and makes strong assumptions about the form of the posterior distribution.

The term "variational" here refers to concepts from mathematical analysis (such as the calculus of variations) which focus on the maximization and minimization of functionals (mappings from a set of functions to real numbers). This kind of analysis has been used frequently in physics (e.g., quantum mechanics). Very commonly, it is used in the context of minimizing energy through a functional that describes the state of physical elements.

Section 6.1 begins the discussion of variational inference in this chapter, by describing the basic variational bound used in variational inference. We then discuss mean-field variational inference, the main type of variational inference used in Bayesian NLP (Sections 6.2–6.3). We continue with a discussion of empirical Bayes estimation with variational approximations (Section 6.4). In the next section (Section 6.5), we discuss various topics related to variational inference in Bayesian NLP, covering topics such as initialization of variational inference algorithms, convergence diagnosis, variational inference decoding, the relationship between variational inference and KL minimization, and finally, online variational inference. We conclude with a summary (Section 6.6). There is also a treatment of variational inference in the context of neural networks and representation learning in Chapter 9.

6.1 VARIATIONAL BOUND ON MARGINAL LOG-LIKELIHOOD

Consider a typical scenario in which the observations are represented by the random variables $X^{(1)}, \ldots, X^{(n)}$. These observations are (deterministic or probabilistic) functions of the latent structure $Z^{(1)}, \ldots, Z^{(n)}$. These latent structures are the targets for prediction.

On top of the latent structure and the observations, there is a prior $p(\theta|\alpha)$ over the parameters θ such that $\alpha \in A$ is the hyperparameter. This prior is a top-level prior (Section 3.5), but we later address the same scenario when parameters are drawn for each observation and latent structure. The joint probability distribution for this typical scenario is:

$$p(\theta, \mathbf{Z}, \mathbf{X}|\alpha)$$

$$= p\left(\theta, Z^{(1)}, \ldots, Z^{(n)}, X^{(1)}, \ldots, X^{(n)}|\alpha\right) = p(\theta|\alpha)\left(\prod_{i=1}^{n} p\left(Z^{(i)}|\theta\right)p\left(X^{(i)}|Z^{(i)}, \theta\right)\right).$$

As mentioned in Section 3.1.2, in order to compute the posterior, one needs to compute the following marginalization constant:

$$p\left(x^{(1)}, \ldots, x^{(n)}|\alpha\right) = \int_{\theta} \sum_{z^{(1)}, \ldots, z^{(n)}} p(\theta|\alpha)\left(\prod_{i=1}^{n} p\left(z^{(i)}|\theta\right)p\left(x^{(i)}|z^{(i)}, \theta\right)\right)d\theta.$$

The computation of this integral-sum combination is intractable, because of the coupling between the integral and the sum over a potentially exponential space. This intractability is problematic even when the chosen prior is a conjugate prior, but choosing a conjugate prior is still important, because it can make algorithms, such as variational EM, simpler (see Section 3.1.2).

The computation of this marginal distribution is not just helpful in directly computing the posterior (when dividing the joint distribution by the marginal distribution). In addition, the likelihood of the observed data can be derived from the values of this marginal distribution (called "the evidence") for fixed values of the observations.

There is a partial remedy to this issue, if we consider the *log*-likelihood of the data. This remedy is obtained by approximating the log-likelihood, instead of having to compute it directly, which is intractable, as mentioned earlier.

Let $q(\theta, \mathbf{Z}) = q(\theta, Z^{(1)}, \ldots, Z^{(n)})$ be some distribution over the parameters and the latent structure. Consider the following inequalities:

$$\log p(\mathbf{X}|\alpha) =$$

$$\log\left(\int_{\theta} \sum_{z^{(1)}, \ldots, z^{(n)}} q(\theta, z^{(1)}, \ldots, z^{(n)}) \times \left(\frac{p(\theta|\alpha)\left(\prod_{i=1}^{n} p(z^{(i)}|\theta)p(x^{(i)}|z^{(i)}, \theta)\right)}{q(\theta, z^{(1)}, \ldots, z^{(n)})}\right)d\theta\right) \quad (6.1)$$

$$\geq \int_{\theta} \sum_{z^{(1)}, \ldots, z^{(n)}} q(\theta, z^{(1)}, \ldots, z^{(n)}) \times \log\left(\frac{p(\theta|\alpha)\left(\prod_{i=1}^{n} p(z^{(i)}|\theta)p(x^{(i)}|z^{(i)}, \theta)\right)}{q(\theta, z^{(1)}, \ldots, z^{(n)})}\right)d\theta \quad (6.2)$$

$$= E_q\left[\log\left(\frac{p(\theta|\alpha)\left(\prod_{i=1}^{n} p(Z^{(i)}|\theta)p(x^{(i)}|Z^{(i)}, \theta)\right)}{q(\theta, \mathbf{Z})}\right)\Big|\alpha\right] \quad (6.3)$$

$$= \mathcal{F}(q, x^{(1)}, \ldots, x^{(n)}|\alpha).$$

Equation 6.1 is the result of multiplying and dividing $p(X|\alpha)$ by the distribution $q(\theta, Z)$, then marginalizing over the parameters and latent variables—after expressing $p(X|\alpha)$ through the full joint distribution with a sum over the latent variables. This by itself has no effect on the log-likelihood. Equation 6.2 is the result of applying Jensen's inequality (see Appendix A), which switches between the order of the sum and integration in the application of the log function. Last, Equation 6.3 is the result of folding the sum and integration into an expectation with respect to $q(\theta, Z)$. The bound $\mathcal{F}$ is sometimes referred to as "ELBO," short for "evidence lower bound."

Consider what happens when the distribution q actually equals the posterior, i.e.,

$$q(\theta, Z) = p(\theta, Z|X, \alpha).$$

In that case, it can be shown, using of the definition of conditional probability, that the inequality in Equation 6.1 becomes an equality, and

$$\log p(X|\alpha) = \mathcal{F}\left(q, x^{(1)}, \ldots, x^{(n)}|\alpha\right).$$

Since, in that case, the bound $\mathcal{F}\left(q, x^{(1)}, \ldots, x^{(n)}|\alpha\right)$ is tight, this means that the posterior distribution maximizes the lower bound, and $\mathcal{F}\left(q, x^{(1)}, \ldots, x^{(n)}|\alpha\right)$ equals the marginal log-likelihood. Because finding the posterior for Bayesian NLP problems, in the general case, is intractable, it follows that optimizing $\mathcal{F}\left(q, x^{(1)}, \ldots, x^{(n)}|\alpha\right)$ with respect to q, in the general case, is intractable (if we could do it, we would have been able to find the true posterior).

This is where variational inference plays an important role in removing the intractability of this optimization problem. Variational inference implies that this optimization problem is still being solved, but with a compromise: we maximize the bound with respect to a certain family of distributions $\mathcal{Q}$. The family $\mathcal{Q}$ is chosen so that, at the very least, finding a local maximum for the following maximization problem is tractable:

$$\max_{q \in \mathcal{Q}} \mathcal{F}\left(q, x^{(1)}, \ldots, x^{(n)}|\alpha\right). \tag{6.4}$$

Since the true posterior usually does not belong to $\mathcal{Q}$, this is an approximate method. Clearly, the closer that one of the distributions in $\mathcal{Q}$ is to the true posterior (or, the more expressive the distributions in $\mathcal{Q}$ are), the more accurate this approximate solution is.

The approximate posterior in the solution is not only due to the restriction inherent in choosing $\mathcal{Q}$. Another reason is that even with "tractable" $\mathcal{Q}$, the above optimization problem is non-convex, and therefore, there is inherent difficulty in finding the global maximum for it. Mean-field variational inference is one algorithm that treats this issue by applying coordinate ascent on a factorized approximate posterior family (Section 6.3).[1] The maximization problem, however, stays non-convex.

---

[1]Coordinate ascent is a method for maximizing the value of a real-valued function $f(y_1, \ldots, y_n)$. It works by iterating through the different arguments of f, at each point maximizing f with respect to a specific variable y_i while holding y_j for

6.2   MEAN-FIELD APPROXIMATION

Mean-field approximation defines an approximate posterior family which has a factorized form. Just as in the case of Gibbs sampling (Chapter 5), mean-field variational inference requires a partition of the latent variables in the model (the most common choice for such a partition is a separation of the parameters from the latent structures being predicted).

Once the latent variables $Z^{(1)}, \ldots, Z^{(n)}$ and θ are carved up into p random variables, $U_1, \ldots, U_p$, the factorized form of the approximate posterior is such that it assumes independence between each of U_i. More specifically, each member q of the family $\mathcal{Q}$ is assumed to have the form:

$$q\left(U_1, \ldots, U_p\right) = \prod_{i=1}^{p} q\left(U_i\right). \tag{6.5}$$

See Section 5.2.1 for more discussion about the ways to partition the latent variables of a Bayesian model.

One of the most natural approximate posterior families $\mathcal{Q}$ is one that *decouples* between the parameters θ and the random variables of each of the latent structures $\boldsymbol{Z} = \left(Z^{(1)}, \ldots, Z^{(n)}\right)$. With a top-level prior placement, a typical approximate posterior has the form:

$$q(\theta, \boldsymbol{Z}) = q(\theta)q(\boldsymbol{Z}).$$

Therefore, $\mathcal{Q}$ is the set of all distributions such that θ and the latent structures $Z^{(i)}$ (for $i = 1, \ldots, n$) are all independent of each other. This approximation for the posterior family belongs to the family of mean-field approximations.

When a new set of parameters is drawn for each example (Section 3.5), leading to a set of parameters $\theta^{(1)}, \ldots, \theta^{(n)}$, it is more typical to use a mean-field approximation that assumes independence between each of $\theta^{(i)}$ and $Z^{(i)}$ such that the approximate posterior has the form:

$$\left(\prod_{i=1}^{n} q(z^{(i)})\right) \times \left(\prod_{i=1}^{n} q(\theta^{(i)})\right). \tag{6.6}$$

The approximation in Equation 6.6 is the most naïve mean-field approximation, where all variables in the model are assumed to be independent of each other (parameters and latent structures).

It is important to note, however, that this naïve mean-field approximation in this case is not very useful by itself. When considering the bound in Equation 6.3, with this factorization of the posterior family, we actually end up with n separate optimization sub-problems for each observation, and these sub-problems do not interact with each other. Interaction between these

$j \neq i$ fixed with values from the previous steps. The value of the assignment to y_i at each step is guaranteed to increase the value of f, and under some circumstances, converge to the maximizer of f.

sub-problems, however, can be introduced by following a *variational expectation-maximization algorithm*, that estimates joint hyperparameters for all $\theta^{(i)}$, in the style of empirical Bayes. For a discussion of empirical Bayes, see Section 4.3. For more details about variational EM, see Section 6.4.

The factorized posterior family q does not have to follow the above naïve factorization, and more structured approximations can certainly be used. The way that the posterior is factorized depends on the modeler choice for carving up the variables on which the inference is done. In addition, each factor in q can either be parametric (by defining "variational parameters" that control this factor) or can be left as nonparametric (see Section 1.5.1 for the difference between a parametric model family and a nonparametric one). In many cases it can be shown that even when a factor is left as nonparametric (to obtain a tighter approximation, without confining the factor to a special form), the factor that gives the tightest approximation actually has a parametric form. See Section 6.3.1.

Mean-field methods actually originate in statistical physics. The main motivation behind them in statistical physics (or statistical mechanics) is to reduce the complexity of stochastically modeling interactions between many physical elements by considering much simpler models. Mean-field methods are now often used in machine learning, especially with inference for graphical models (Wainwright and Jordan, 2008).

6.3 MEAN-FIELD VARIATIONAL INFERENCE ALGORITHM

Finding the optimal solution, q (for Equation 6.3), even with a more constrained set of distributions $\mathcal{Q}$, can be computationally intractable in the general case. The main problem is that the functional $\mathcal{F}$ often leads to a non-convex optimization problem. The optimization tools currently available for non-convex functions are quite limited for the problems that arise in Bayesian NLP, and in most cases, these optimization algorithms come with a guarantee to converge to a *local* maximum of the optimization problem in Equation 6.4.

Computational intractability here can be formally stated: for many problems (such as the case with PCFGs, Cohen and Smith 2010a), it can be shown that an algorithm for finding the global maximum of $\mathcal{F}$ can be used to solve an NP-hard decision problem.

The family of variational inference algorithms finds a local maximum for the optimization problem in Equation 6.4. It does so by choosing an approximate posterior family such that the computation of the evidence lower bound can be performed efficiently. For example, the family of approximate posteriors can be made parametric so that both the evidence lower bound and its gradient are computed efficiently. In that case, gradient-based optimization algorithms can be used to find a local maximum for the bound.

Most commonly in Bayesian NLP, variational inference is used in the context of the mean-field approximation mentioned in Section 6.2 with a coordinate ascent algorithm, where the "coordinates" being optimized, each in their own turn, correspond to each factor that appears in

Input: Observed data $x^{(1)}, \ldots, x^{(n)}$, a partition of the latent variables into $U_1, \ldots, U_p$ and a set of possible distributions for $U_1, \ldots, U_p$: $\mathcal{Q}_1, \ldots, \mathcal{Q}_p$.
Output: Factorized approximate posterior $q(U_1, \ldots, U_p)$.

1: Initialize $q^*(U_i)$ from $\mathcal{Q}_i$ for $i = 1, \ldots, p$
   $q^*(U_1, \ldots, U_p) \leftarrow \left(\prod_{i=1}^{p} q^*(U_i) \right)$
2: **repeat**
3:    **for** $i \in \{1, \ldots, p\}$ **do**
4:       Set $\mathcal{Q}^* = \{q^*(U_1)\} \times \ldots \times \{q^*(U_{i-1})\} \times \mathcal{Q}_i \times \{q^*(U_{i+1})\} \times \ldots \times \{q^*(U_p)\}$
5:       $q^*(U_i) \leftarrow$ the factor $q(U_i)$ in

$$\arg \max_{q \in \mathcal{Q}^*} \mathcal{F}(q, x^{(1)}, \ldots, x^{(n)} | \alpha) \tag{6.7}$$

6:    **end for**
7:    $q^*(U_1, \ldots, U_p) \leftarrow \left(\prod_{i=1}^{p} q^*(U_i) \right)$
8: **until** the bound $\mathcal{F}(q^*, x^{(1)}, \ldots, x^{(n)} | \alpha)$ converged
9: **return** q^*

Algorithm 6.1: The mean-field variational inference algorithm. Its input are observations, a partition of the random variables that the inference is done on, and a set of distribution families, one set per element in the partition. The algorithm then iterates (with iterator i) through the different elements in the partition, each time maximizing the variational bound for the observations with respect to $\mathcal{Q}_i$, while holding $q^*(U_j)$ for $j \neq i$ fixed.

the factorization in Equation 6.5. Algorithm 6.1 provides the skeleton for the coordinate ascent mean-field variational inference algorithm.

The optimization problem in Equation 6.7 is not always easy to solve, but fortunately, the solution has a rather general formula. It can be shown that $q^*(U_i)$ maximizing Equation 6.7 equals:

$$q^*(U_i) = \frac{\exp \left(E_{q_{-i}} [\log p(X, U_1, \ldots, U_p)] \right)}{Z_i}, \tag{6.8}$$

where q_{-i} is a distribution over U_{-i} defined as:

$$q_{-i}(U_1, \ldots, U_{i-1}, U_{i+1}, \ldots, U_p) = \prod_{j \neq i} q(U_j),$$

and Z_i is a normalization constant that integrates or sums the numerator in Equation 6.8 with respect to U_i. For example, if U_i is discrete, then $Z_i = \sum_u E_{q_{-i}}[\log p(X, U_1, \ldots, U_i = u, \ldots, U_p)])]$. This general derivation appears in detail in Bishop (2006), but in Section 6.3.1 we derive a specific case of this formulation for the Dirichlet-Multinomial family.

The following decisions need to be made by the modeler when actually implementing Algorithm 6.1.

- **Partitioning of the latent variables** This issue is discussed at length in Chapter 5 and in Section 6.2. The decision that the modeler has to make with respect to this issue is how to carve up the random variables into a set of random variables that have minimal interaction, or that offer some computational tractability for maximizing the variational bound with respect to each of members of this set of random variables.

- **Choosing the parametrization of each factor (Q_i)** Determining the parametrization of each of the factors requires a balance between richness of the parametrization (so we are able to get a tighter bound) and tractability (see below). It is often the case that even when Q_i is left nonparametric (or when it includes the set of all possible distributions over the sample space of U_i), the solution to the coordinate ascent step is actually a distribution from a parametric family. Identifying this parametric family can be done as part of the derivation of the variational EM algorithm, so that the variational distributions can be represented computationally (and optimized with respect to their parameters, also referred to as "variational parameters").

- **Optimizing the bound at each step of the coordinate ascent** At each step of the mean-field variational inference algorithm, we have to find the factor in q that maximizes the variational bound while maintaining all other factors fixed according to their values from the previous iterations. If the parametrization of each factor is chosen carefully, then sometimes closed-form solutions for these mini-maximization problems are available (this is especially true when the prior is conjugate to the likelihood). It is also often the case that a nested optimization problem needs to be solved using optimization techniques such as gradient descent or Newton's method. Unfortunately, sometimes the nested optimization problem itself is a non-convex optimization problem.

Recent work, such as the work by Kucukelbir et al. (2016), tries to minimize the decision making which is not strictly related to modeling and data collection. The work by Kucukelbir et al. proposes an automatic variational inference algorithm, which uses automatic differentiation, integrated into the Stan programming language Carpenter et al. (2015).

6.3.1 DIRICHLET-MULTINOMIAL VARIATIONAL INFERENCE

The following example demonstrates the decisions that the modeler has to make when deriving a variational inference algorithm. We derive in this section a mean-field variational inference algorithm which is commonly used for Dirichlet-Multinomial models.

Consider the case where the likelihood is a collection of multinomials, which is often the case with NLP models such as probabilistic context-free grammars and hidden Markov models. In such a case, the model family is parametrized by $\theta = (\theta^1, \ldots, \theta^K)$ such that each θ^k is in the probability simplex of dimension $N_k - 1$ for some natural number N_k:

$$\theta_i^k \geq 0 \qquad\qquad \forall k \in \{1, \ldots, K\}, \forall i \in \{1, \ldots, N_k\}$$

$$\sum_{i=1}^{N_k} \theta_i^k = 1 \qquad\qquad \forall k \in \{1, \ldots, K\}.$$

For example, in the case of PCFGs, K would be the number of nonterminals in the grammar, N_k would be the number of rules for each nonterminal and θ_i^k would correspond to the probability of the ith rule for the kth nonterminal. See Section 8.2 for more details about this formulation. Let $f_i^k(x, z)$ be a function that counts the times that event i from multinomial k fires in (x, z).

The most common choice of a conjugate prior for this model is a product-of-Dirichlet distribution, such that:

$$p(\theta|\alpha) \propto \prod_{k=1}^{K} \prod_{i=1}^{N_k} \left(\theta_i^k\right)^{\alpha_i^k - 1},$$

with $\alpha = (\alpha^1, \ldots, \alpha^K)$ and $\alpha^k \in \mathbb{R}^{N_k}$ such that $\alpha_i^k \geq 0$ for all i and k.

Assuming a top-level prior, and with $X^{(1)}, \ldots, X^{(n)}$ being the observed random variables and $Z^{(1)}, \ldots, Z^{(n)}$ being the latent structures, the likelihood is:

$$\prod_{j=1}^{n} p\left(x^{(j)}, z^{(j)}|\theta\right) = \prod_{j=1}^{n} \prod_{k=1}^{K} \prod_{i=1}^{N_k} \left(\theta_i^k\right)^{f_i^k(x^{(j)}, z^{(j)})}$$

$$= \prod_{k=1}^{K} \prod_{i=1}^{N_k} \left(\theta_i^k\right)^{\sum_{j=1}^{n} f_i^k(x^{(j)}, z^{(j)})},$$

with $f_i^k(x, z)$ being the count of event i from multinomial k in the pair (x, z). We denote in short:

$$f_{k,i} = \sum_{j=1}^{n} f_i^k\left(x^{(j)}, z^{(j)}\right).$$

We will be interested in mean-field variational inference such that q remains nonparametric (for now), factorized into $q(\theta)$ and $q(Z)$. That, in essence, is the tightest approximation one can use, while assuming independent parameters and latent structures for the approximate posterior family. In that case, the functional $\mathcal{F}\left(q, x^{(1)}, \ldots, x^{(n)} | \alpha\right)$, following Equation 6.3 (which gives the bound on the marginal log-likelihood), looks like the following:

$$
\begin{aligned}
\mathcal{F}\left(q, x^{(1)}, \ldots, x^{(n)} | \alpha\right) & \\
& = E_q\left[\log\left(p(\theta|\alpha) \times \prod_{k=1}^{K}\prod_{i=1}^{N_k}\left(\theta_i^k\right)^{f_{k,i}}\right)\right] - E_q[\log q(\theta)] - E_q[\log q(\mathbf{Z})] \\
& = \sum_{k=1}^{K}\sum_{i=1}^{N_k} E_q\left[\left(f_{k,i} + \alpha_i^k - 1\right) \times \log\left(\theta_i^k\right)\right] + H(q(\theta)) + H(q(\mathbf{Z})),
\end{aligned}
$$

where $H(q(\theta))$ denotes the entropy of the distribution $q(\theta)$, and $H(q(\mathbf{Z}))$ denotes the entropy of the distribution $q(\mathbf{Z})$ (for the definition of entropy, see Appendix A).

If we consider Algorithm 6.1 for this case, then we iterate between stages: (a) assuming $q(\theta)$ is fixed, we optimize the bound in the above equation with respect to $q(\mathbf{Z})$ and (b) assuming $q(\mathbf{Z})$ is fixed, we optimize the bound in the above equation with respect to $q(\theta)$.

Assume the case where $q(\theta)$ is fixed. In that case, $f_{k,i}$ depends only on the latent assignments $z^{(1)}, \ldots, z^{(n)}$ and not on the parameters, and therefore it holds that:

$$
\begin{aligned}
\mathcal{F}\left(q, x^{(1)}, \ldots, x^{(n)} | \alpha\right) & = \sum_{k=1}^{K}\sum_{i=1}^{N_k} E_q\left[\left(f_{k,i} + \alpha_i^k - 1\right) \times \psi_i^k\right] + H(q(\mathbf{Z})) + \text{const} \\
& = \sum_{k=1}^{K}\sum_{i=1}^{N_k} E_q\left[\psi_i^k f_{k,i} - \log A(\psi)\right] + H(q(\mathbf{Z})) + \text{const}, \quad (6.9)
\end{aligned}
$$

with ψ having the same vector structure like θ and α such that

$$
\psi_i^k = E_{q(\theta)}\left[\log\left(\theta_i^k\right)\right],
$$

and

$$
\log A(\psi) = \sum_{z^{(1)}} \cdots \sum_{z^{(n)}} \exp\left(\sum_{k=1}^{K}\sum_{i=1}^{N_k} \psi_i^k f_{k,i}\right).
$$

Note that the term $\log A(\psi)$ can be added to Equation 6.9 because it does not depend on the latent structures, since we sum them out in this term. It does, however, depend on $q(\theta)$, but it is assumed to be fixed. If we carefully consider Equation 6.9, we note that it denotes the negated KL-divergence (Appendix A) between $q(\mathbf{Z})$ and a log-linear model over $\mathbf{Z}$ with sufficient statistics $f_{k,i}$ and parameters ψ_i^k. Therefore, when $q(\theta)$ is fixed, the functional $\mathcal{F}$ is maximized when we choose $q(Z)$ to be a log-linear distribution with the sufficient statistics $f_{k,i}$ and parameters $\psi_i^k = E_{q(\theta)}[\log(\theta_i^k)]$.

The meaning of this is that even though we *a priori* left $q(Z)$ to be in a nonparametric family, we discovered that the tightest solution for it resides in a parametric family, and this family has a very similar form to the likelihood (the main difference between the approximate posterior family and the likelihood is that with the approximate posterior family we also require normalization through $\log Z(\psi)$ because ψ does not necessarily represent a collection of multinomial distributions).

What about the opposite case, i.e., when $q(Z)$ is fixed and $q(\theta)$ needs to be inferred? In that case, it holds that:

$$\mathcal{F}\left(q, x^{(1)}, \ldots, x^{(n)}|\alpha\right) \propto \sum_{k=1}^{K} \sum_{i=1}^{N_k} \left(E_q\left[f_{k,i}\right] + \alpha_i^k - 1\right) \times E_{q(\theta)}\left[\log \theta_i^k\right] - H(q(\theta)). \quad (6.10)$$

If we carefully consider the equation above, we see that it is proportional to the KL-divergence between $q(\theta)$ and a product of Dirichlet distributions (of the same form as the prior family) with hyperparameters $\beta = (\beta^1, \ldots, \beta^K)$ such that $\beta_i^k = E_q[f_{k,i}] + \alpha_i^k$. This is again a case where we leave $q(\theta)$ nonparametric, and we discover that the tightest solution has a parametric form. In fact, not only is it parametric, it also has the same form as the prior family.

The final variational inference algorithm looks like this:

- Initialize in some way $\beta = (\beta^1, \ldots, \beta^K)$.

- Repeat until convergence:

    - Compute $q(z^{(1)}, \ldots, z^{(n)})$ as the log-linear model mentioned above with parameters $\psi_i^k = E_{q(\theta)}[\log(\theta_i^k)|\beta]$.

    - Compute $q(\theta)$ as a product of Dirichlet distributions with hyperparameters $\beta_i^k = E_q[f_{k,i}|\psi] + \alpha_i^k$.

Consider the computation of $E_{q(\theta)}\left[\log\left(\theta_i^k\right)|\beta\right]$ and $E_q[f_{k,i}|\psi]$. It is known that for a given Dirichlet distribution, the expected log value of a single parameter can be expressed using the digamma function, meaning that:

$$E_{q(\theta)}\left[\log\left(\theta_i^k\right)|\beta\right] = \Psi\left(\beta_i^k\right) - \Psi\left(\sum_{i=1}^{N_k} \beta_i^k\right),$$

with Ψ representing the digamma function. The digamma function cannot be expressed analytically, but there are numerical recipes for finding its value for a given parameter. See Appendix B for more details about the digamma function and its relationship to the Dirichlet distribution.

On the other hand, computing $E_q[f_{k,i}|\psi]$ can be done using an algorithm that heavily depends on the structure of the likelihood function. For PCFGs, for example, this expectation can be computed using the inside-outside algorithm. For HMMs, it can be done using the forward-backward algorithm. See Chapter 8 for more details. Note that this expectation is computed for each observed example separately, i.e., we calculate $E_q[f_i^k(x^{(j)}, z^{(j)})|\psi]$ for $j \in \{1, \ldots, n\}$ and then aggregate all of these counts to get $E_q[f_{k,i}|\psi]$.

Whenever we are simply interested in the posterior over $q(Z)$, the above two update steps collapse to the following update rule for the variational parameters of $q(Z)$:

$$(\psi_i^k)^{\text{new}} \leftarrow \Psi\left(E_q\left[f_{k,i}|\psi^{\text{old}}\right] + \alpha_i^k\right) - \Psi\left(\sum_{i=1}^{N_k} E_q\left[f_{k,i}|\psi^{\text{old}}\right] + \alpha_i^k\right). \qquad (6.11)$$

Note that for these updates, the variational parameters ψ_i^k need to be initialized first. Most often in the Bayesian NLP literature, when variational inference is used, the final update rule forms such as the one above are described. The log-linear model parametrized by ψ_i^k can be re-parameterized using a new set of parameters $\mu_i^k = \exp(\psi_i^k)$ for all k and i. In this case, the update becomes:

$$\left(\mu_i^k\right)^{\text{new}} \leftarrow \frac{\exp\left(\Psi(E_q[f_{k,i}|\mu^{\text{old}}] + \alpha_i^k)\right)}{\exp\left(\Psi(\sum_{i=1}^{N_k} E_q[f_{k,i}|\mu^{\text{old}}] + \alpha_i^k)\right)}. \qquad (6.12)$$

Note that now we have a similar update to the EM algorithm, where we compute expected counts, and in the M-step, we normalize them. The main difference is that the counts are passed through the filter of the exp-digamma function, $\exp(\Psi(x))$. Figure 6.1 plots the exp-digamma function and compares it against the function $x - 0.5$. We can see that as x becomes larger, the two functions get closer to each other. The main difference between the two functions is that at values smaller than 0.5, for which the exp-digamma function returns positive values which are very close to 0, while $x - 0.5$ returns negative values. Therefore, one way to interpret the update Equation 6.12 is as the truncation of low expected counts during the E-step (lower than 0.5). Higher counts are also subtracted a value of around 0.5, and the higher the count is in the E-step, the less influential this decrease will be on the corresponding μ parameter.

6.3.2   CONNECTION TO THE EXPECTATION-MAXIMIZATION ALGORITHM

The variational inference algorithm in the previous section, in spirit, resembles the expectation-maximization (EM) algorithm of Dempster et al. (1977), which is set up in the frequentist setting. The goal of the EM algorithm is to estimate the parameters of a given model from incomplete data.

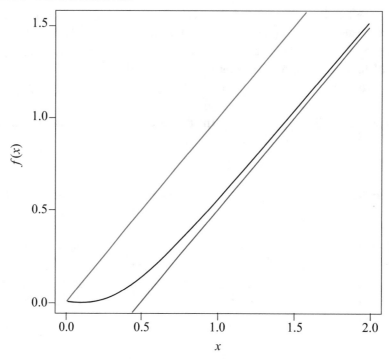

Figure 6.1: A plot of the function $f(x) = \exp(\Psi(x))$, the exp-digamma function (in the middle in black) compared to the functions $f(x) = x$ (at the top in blue) and $f(x) = x - 0.5$ (at the bottom in red). Adapted from Johnson (2007b).

The EM algorithm iterates between two steps: the E-step, in which the posterior over the latent structures is computed, and the M-step, in which a new set of parameters is computed, until the marginal log-likelihood converges. It can be shown that the EM algorithm finds a local maximum of the marginal log-likelihood function. The M-step is performed by maximizing the expected log-likelihood of all variables in the model. The expectation is taken with respect to a product distribution: the product of the empirical distribution over the observed data and the posterior induced in the E-step. For more detailed information about the expectation-maximization algorithm, see Appendix A.

There is actually a deeper connection between the EM algorithm and the variational inference algorithm presented in Algorithm 6.1. The variational inference algorithm reduces to the EM algorithm when the inputs to the variational inference algorithm and the prior in the model are chosen carefully.

Consider the case where the set of latent variables is partitioned into two random variables: in terms of Algorithm 6.1, U_1 corresponds to a random variable over the parameters, and U_2

corresponds to a variable over the set of all latent structures in the model (usually, it would be $Z^{(1)}, \ldots, Z^{(n)}$). Hence, the posterior has the form $q(\theta, \mathbf{Z}) = q(\theta)q(\mathbf{Z})$.

Consider also $\mathcal{Q}_1$ to represent the set of all distributions that place their whole probability mass on a single point on the parameter space. This means that $\mathcal{Q}_1$ includes the set of all the distributions $q(\theta|\mu)$ (parameterized by $\mu \in \Theta$) such that

$$q(\theta|\mu) = \begin{cases} 1, & \text{if } \theta = \mu \\ 0 & \text{otherwise,} \end{cases}$$

$\mathcal{Q}_2$, on the other hand, remains nonparametric, and just includes the set of all possible distributions over the latent structures. Last, the prior chosen in the model is chosen to be $p(\theta) = c$ (for some constant c) for all $\theta \in \Theta$, i.e., a uniform non-informative prior (possibly improper).

The functional $\mathcal{F}$ now in essence depends on the assignment μ (selecting $q(\theta|\mu)$) and the $q(\mathbf{Z})$. We will express this functional as:

$$\mathcal{F}\left(q(\mathbf{Z}), \mu, x^{(1)}, \ldots, x^{(n)}\right) = E_{q(\mathbf{Z})}\left[\log\left(\frac{p(\mu|\alpha)p(\mathbf{Z}, \mathbf{X} = (x^{(1)}, \ldots, x^{(n)})|\mu)}{q(\mathbf{Z})}\right)\right].$$

If we assume a non-informative constant prior, then maximizing the bound with respect to $q(\mathbf{Z})$ and μ can be done while ignoring the prior:

$$\mathcal{F}\left(q(\mathbf{Z}), \mu, x^{(1)}, \ldots, x^{(n)}\right) \propto E_{q(\mathbf{Z})}\left[\log\left(\frac{p(\mathbf{Z}, \mathbf{X} = \left(x^{(1)}, \ldots, x^{(n)}\right)|\mu)}{q(\mathbf{Z})}\right)\right].$$

This functional is exactly the same bound that the expectation-maximization algorithm maximizes. Maximizing the right-hand side with respect to $q(\mathbf{Z})$ while keeping μ fixed yields the posterior $q(\mathbf{Z}) = p(\mathbf{Z}|\mathbf{X} = (x^{(1)}, \ldots, x^{(n)}), \mu)$, which in turn yields the E-step in the EM algorithm. On the other hand, maximizing the right-hand side with respect to μ yields the M-step—doing so maximizes the bound with respect to the parameters, which keeps $q(\mathbf{Z})$ fixed. See Appendix A for a derivation of the EM algorithm.

6.4   EMPIRICAL BAYES WITH VARIATIONAL INFERENCE

In the empirical Bayes setting (Section 4.3), parameters are drawn for each observed instance. There, the typical approach to mean-field variational inference would be to use an approximate posterior family such that all latent structures and all parameter sets are independent of each other (see Equation 6.6).

The variational inference algorithm (Algorithm 6.1) in this case actually separately solves each pair of problems for each instance i, finding the posterior $q\left(\theta^{(i)}\right)$ and $q\left(\mathbf{Z}^{(i)}\right)$. Therefore,

Input: Observed data $x^{(1)}, \ldots, x^{(n)}$, the bound $\mathcal{F}(q^*, x^{(1)}, \ldots, x^{(n)} | \alpha)$.
Output: Factorized approximate posteriors $q(\theta^{(i)})$ and $q(Z^{(i)})$ for $i \in \{1, \ldots, n\}$ and an estimated hyperparameter α.

- -

1: Initialize α'
2: **repeat**
3:    Maximize $\mathcal{F}(q^*, x^{(1)}, \ldots, x^{(n)} | \alpha')$ with respect to q^*
4:       using Algorithm 6.1 with factorization as in Equation 6.6
5:    $\alpha' \leftarrow \arg\max_{\alpha'} \mathcal{F}(q^*, x^{(1)}, \ldots, x^{(n)} | \alpha')$
6: **until** the bound $\mathcal{F}(q^*, x^{(1)}, \ldots, x^{(n)} | \alpha')$ converges
7: **return** (α', q^*)

Algorithm 6.2: The mean-field variational expectation-maximization algorithm (empirical Bayes).

when using this kind of mean-field approximation, we require an additional estimation step, which integrates all the solutions for these sub-problems into a re-estimation step of the prior.

This is the main idea behind the variational EM algorithm. Variational EM is actually an expectation-maximization algorithm, in which the hyperparameters for a prior family are estimated based on data, and in which the E-step is an *approximate* E-step that finds a posterior based on a variational inference algorithm, such as the one introduced in Algorithm 6.1. The approximate posterior is identified over Z and θ, while the M-step maximizes the marginal log-likelihood with respect to the hyperparameters.

The variational EM algorithm, with mean-field variational inference for the E-step, is given in Algorithm 6.2.

6.5   DISCUSSION

We turn now to a discussion about important issues regarding the variational inference algorithms presented in this chapter—issues that have a crucial effect on the performance of these algorithms, but do not have well-formed theory.

6.5.1   INITIALIZATION OF THE INFERENCE ALGORITHMS

The need to properly initialize the variational parameters in variational inference is a problematic issue, mostly because it does not have a well-established theory, yet it has been shown that initialization may greatly affect the results when using variational inference.

For example, with the Dirichlet-multinomial family mean-field variational inference algorithm in Section 6.3.1, one has to decide how to initialize β (or alternatively, if the algorithm is started on the second step in the loop instead of the first step, when computing the expectations of the features $f_{k,i}$, one would have to decide how to initialize the parameters of the log-linear model $q\left(z^{(1)}, \ldots, z^{(n)}\right)$).

The variational bound that $\mathcal{F}$ represents, for a general model, is a non-convex function (with respect to the approximate posterior q), and therefore Algorithm 6.1 does not have any guarantees in terms of converging to the global maximum of the variational bound. One approach for tackling this issue is quite similar to the solution that is often used for the EM algorithm in the form of random restarts. The variational inference algorithm is run repetitively from different starting points, and we eventually choose the run that gives the maximal value to the variational bound.

This method will not necessarily lead to optimal results with respect to the evaluation metric used. The aim of maximizing the variational bound is to obtain higher log-likelihood for the observed data. Log-likelihood here is used as a proxy for the underlying evaluation metric, such as the parsing evaluation metric (Black et al., 1991) or part-of-speech accuracy. However, being just a proxy, it does not fully correlate with the evaluation metric. Even if we were able to globally maximize the log-likelihood, this problem would persist.

For this reason, random restarts, which aim at maximizing the variational bound, are sometimes replaced with a more specific initialization technique which is based on some intuition that the modeler has about the relationship between the data and the model. For example, a common technique for unsupervised dependency parsing, is to initialize EM (Klein and Manning, 2004) or variational inference (Cohen et al., 2009) with parameters that tend to prefer attachments for words that are close, in their position in the text, to each other. This is a very useful bias for unsupervised dependency parsing in general (Eisner and Smith, 2005, Spitkovsky et al., 2010).

Other initialization techniques include initialization based on a simpler model, sometimes a model which induces a concave log-likelihood function (Gimpel and Smith, 2012). Many of the techniques used to initialize EM for various models can also be used effectively for variational inference.

6.5.2   CONVERGENCE DIAGNOSIS

Checking for convergence of the variational inference algorithm (or more specifically, the bound $\mathcal{F}\left(q^*, x^{(1)}, \ldots, x^{(n)} | \alpha\right)$ in Algorithm 6.1 or Algorithm 6.2) is relatively easy, since all quantities in the bound $\mathcal{F}$ are computable. However, it is important to note that unlike EM, variational inference does not guarantee an increase in the log-likelihood of the data after each iteration. While both EM and variational inference are coordinate ascent algorithms, EM finds a local maximum for the log-likelihood function, and variational inference finds a local maximum for the variational bound only. (Both algorithms use a similar bounding technique, based on

Jensen's inequality, but the EM's bound for the log-likelihood is tight because no assumptions are made for the approximate posterior family. This means that the bound for EM equals the log-likelihood at its maximal value.)

6.5.3   THE USE OF VARIATIONAL INFERENCE FOR DECODING

There are several ways to use the output of variational inference and variational EM in order to actually predict or estimate parameters. In the non-empirical-Bayes variational inference setting, once $q(\theta)$ is estimated, this posterior can be summarized as a point estimate following the techniques in Chapter 4. Afterward, decoding can proceed using this point estimate. In addition, one can follow maximum *a posteriori* decoding directly using $q(Z)$ and identify

$$\left(z^{(1)},\ldots,z^{(n)}\right) = \arg \max_{\left(z^{(1)},\ldots,z^{(n)}\right)} q\left(Z = \left(z^{(1)},\ldots,z^{(n)}\right)\right).$$

A similar route can be followed in the empirical Bayesian setting, decoding $z^{(i)}$ by computing $\arg \max_z q\left(Z^{(i)} = z\right)$.

With variational EM, the hyperparameters α that are being eventually estimated can be used to get a summary for the parameter's point estimate. For example, given these hyperparameters α, one can use the mean value of the posterior over the parameters as a point estimate θ^*

$$\theta^* = E[\theta|\alpha] = \int_\theta \theta p(\theta|\alpha)d\theta,$$

or alternatively, $\theta^* = \arg \max_\theta p(\theta|\alpha)$ (corresponding to maximum *a posteriori* estimate). See Chapter 4 for a discussion. If the hyperparameters α have the same structure as the parameters (i.e., for each hyperparameter in the ith coordinate, α_i, maps directly to a parameter θ_i), then the hyperparameters themselves can be used as a point estimate. The hyperparameters may not adhere, perhaps, to constraints on the parameter space (i.e., it could be the case that $\alpha \notin \Theta$), but they often do yield *weights*, which can be used in decoding the underlying model.

Cohen and Smith (2010b) used this technique, and estimated the hyperparameters of a collection of logistic normal distributions for grammar induction. The Gaussian means were eventually used as parameters for a weighted grammar they used in decoding.

The above approach is especially useful when there is a clear distinction between a training set and a test set, and the final performance measures are reported on the test set, as opposed to a setting in which inference is done on all of the observed data.

When this split between a training and test set exists, one can use a different approach to the problem of decoding with variational EM. Using the hyperparameters estimated from the training data, an extra variational inference step can be taken on the test set, thus identifying the posterior over latent structures for each of the training examples (using mean-field variational inference). Based on these results, it is possible to follow the same route mentioned in the beginning of this section, finding the highest scoring structure according to each of the posteriors and using these as the predicted structure.

6.5.4   VARIATIONAL INFERENCE AS KL DIVERGENCE MINIMIZATION

Consider Equation 6.3 again, restated below:

$$
\begin{aligned}
\log p(X|\alpha) &= \\
&= E_q\left[\log\left(\frac{p(\theta|\alpha)\left(\prod_{i=1}^{n} p(Z^{(i)}|\theta)p(x^{(i)}|Z^{(i)},\theta)\right)}{q(\theta,Z)}\right)\middle|\alpha\right] \\
&= \mathcal{F}\left(q, x^{(1)}, \ldots, x^{(n)}|\alpha\right).
\end{aligned}
$$

The bound $\mathcal{F}$ actually denotes the Kullback-Leibler (KL) divergence (see Appendix A) between q and the posterior. As mentioned in the beginning of this chapter, finding an approximate posterior is done by minimizing $\mathcal{F}$. Therefore, minimization of the bound $\mathcal{F}$ corresponds to finding a posterior q from the family of posteriors $\mathcal{Q}$ which minimizes $\mathrm{KL}(q, p)$.

KL divergence is not a symmetric function, and unfortunately, this minimization of the KL divergence is done in the "reverse direction" from what is desirable. In most, "more correct," KL divergence minimization problems (such as maximum likelihood estimation), the free distribution that is optimized should represent the second argument to the KL divergence, while the "true" distribution (the true posterior, in the case of variational inference), should represent the first argument. In the reverse direction, $\min_q \mathrm{KL}(q, p)$, one could find solutions that are not necessarily meaningful. Still, with this approach, the KL divergence would get its minimum when $p = q$ (and then it would be 0), which is a desirable property.

A discussion regarding KL divergence minimization direction for variational inference, with graphical models, is given by Koller and Friedman (2009).

6.5.5   ONLINE VARIATIONAL INFERENCE

Standard variational inference and variational EM algorithms work in a batch mode. This means that the available learning data is pre-determined, statistics are then computed from all datapoints (E-step), and finally an update to the parameters is made (M-step). Expectation-maximization works in a similar way.

An alternative to these batch algorithms is online algorithms. With online algorithms, each datapoint is first processed, then followed by an update to the parameters. The motivation behind online algorithms is a scenario in which an "infinite" stream of datapoints is fed to an algorithm, and the inference algorithm needs to update its internal state. This internal state can be used to make predictions until more data in the infinite stream arrives. This setting is especially appealing for large-scale data and real-world applications, in which a statistical model is continuously updated as more data is being presented to it (for example, from the web).

Variational inference and variational EM can be converted into an online algorithm as well, relying on ideas from the literature regarding online EM (Cappé and Moulines, 2009, Liang and Klein, 2009, Neal and Hinton, 1998, Sato and Ishii, 2000). The idea behind this conversion is to make an update to the parameters once the posterior of an example is computed. The current parameters are then interpolated (with some mixture coefficient $\lambda \in [0, 1]$) using the statistics computed for the example.

Batch algorithms and online algorithms, as described above are two extremes in a wide spectrum of approaches. As a middle ground, one can use a so-called "mini-batch" online algorithm, in which several examples are processed at a time using the current set of parameters, and only then followed by an update to the parameters.

Online variational inference that relies on such ideas has been used, for example, for the LDA model (Hoffman et al., 2010), as well as for unsupervised learning of syntax (Kwiatkowski et al., 2012a). It has also been used for nonparametric models, such as the hierarchical Dirichlet process (Wang et al., 2011). Such models are described in Chapter 7.

6.6   SUMMARY

Variational inference is just one of the workhorses used in Bayesian NLP inference. The most common variant of variational inference used in NLP is that of mean-field variational inference, the main variant discussed in this chapter.

Variational expectation-maximization can be used in the empirical Bayes setting, using a variational inference sub-routine for the E-step, while maximizing the variational bound with respect to the hyperparameters in the M-step.

6.7 EXERCISES

6.1. Consider the model in Example 5.1. Write down a mean-field variational inference algorithm to infer $p\left(\theta|x^{(1)},\dots,x^{(n)}\right)$.

6.2. Consider again the model in Example 5.1, only now change it such that there are multiple parameter draws, and $\theta^{(1)},\dots,\theta^{(n)}$ drawn for each example. Write down a mean-field variational inference algorithm to infer $p\left(\theta^{(1)},\dots,\theta^{(n)}|x^{(1)},\dots,x^{(n)}\right)$.

6.3. Show that Equation 6.8 is true. Also, show that Equation 6.10 is true.

6.4. Let $\theta_1,\dots,\theta_K$ represent a set of K parameters, where K is fixed. In addition, let $p(X|\theta_i)$ represent a fixed distribution for a random variable X over sample space Ω such that $|\Omega| < \infty$. Assume that $p(x|\theta_i) \neq p(x|\theta_j)$ for any $x \in \Omega$ and $i \neq j$. Define the following model, parametrized by μ:

$$p(X|\mu,\theta_1,\dots,\theta_K) = \sum_{k=1}^{K} \mu_k\, p(X|\theta_k),$$

where $\sum_{k=1}^{K} \mu_k = 1$ and $\mu_k \geq 0$. This is a mixture model, with mixture components that are fixed.

What is the log-likelihood for n observations, $x^{(1)},\dots,x^{(n)}$, with respect to the parameters μ? Under what conditions is the log-likelihood convex, if at all (with respect to μ)?

6.5. Now assume that there is a symmetric Dirichlet prior over μ, hyperparametrized by $\alpha > 0$. Compute the marginal log-likelihood n observations, $x^{(1)},\dots,x^{(n)}$, integrating out μ. Is this a convex function with respect to α?

CHAPTER 7

Nonparametric Priors

Consider a simple mixture model that defines a distribution over a fixed set of words. Each draw from that mixture model corresponds to a draw of a cluster index (corresponding to a mixture component) followed by a draw from a cluster-specific distribution over words. Each distribution associated with a given cluster can be defined so that it captures specific distributional properties of the words in the vocabulary, or identifies a specific category for the word. If the categories are not pre-defined, then the modeler is confronted with the problem of choosing the number of clusters in the mixture model. On one hand, if there is not a sufficiently large number of components, it will be difficult to represent the range of possible categories; indeed, words that are quite dissimiliar according to the desired categorization may end up in the same cluster. The opposite will happen if there are too many components in the model: much of the slack in the number of clusters will be used to represent the noise in the data, and create overly fine-grained clusters that should otherwise be merged together.

Ideally, we would like the number of clusters to grow as we increase the size of the vocabulary and the observed text in the data. This flexibility can be attained with nonparametric Bayesian modeling. The size of a nonparametric Bayesian model can potentially grow to be quite large (it is unbounded), as a function of the number of data points n; but for any set of n data points, the number of components inferred will always be finite.

The more general approach to nonparametric Bayesian modeling is to use a nonparametric prior, often a stochastic process (roughly referring to a set of random variables indexed by an infinite, linearly ordered set, such as the integers), which provides a direct distribution over a set of functions or a set of distributions, instead of a distribution over a set of parameters. A typical example of this in Bayesian NLP would be the Dirichlet process. The Dirichlet process is a stochastic process that is often used as a nonparametric prior to define a distribution over distributions. Each distribution drawn from the Dirichlet process can later be used to eventually draw the observed data. For those who are completely unfamiliar with nonparametric Bayesian modeling this may seem a bit vague, but a much more thorough discussion of the Dirichlet process follows later in this chapter.[1]

Nonparametric priors are often generalizations of parametric priors, in which the number of parameters is taken to infinity for the specific parametric family. For example, the nonparametric Griffiths-Engen-McCloskey distribution can be thought of as a multinomial with an infinite number of components. The Dirichlet process is the limit of a series of Dirichlet distri-

---

[1]For a description of a very direct relation between the k-means clustering algorithm and the Dirichlet process, see Kulis and Jordan (2011).

butions. A Gaussian process is a generalization of the multivariate Gaussian distribution, only instead of draws from the Gaussian process being vectors indexed by a finite set of coordinates, they are indexed by a continuous value (which can be interpreted, for example, as a temporal axis).

The area of Bayesian nonparametrics in the Statistics and Machine Learning literature is an evolving and highly active area of research. New models, inference algorithms and applications are frequently being developed in this area. Traditional parametric modeling is in a more stable state compared to Bayesian nonparametrics, especially in natural language processing. It is therefore difficult to comprhensively review the rich, cutting-edge literature on this topic; instead, the goal of this chapter is to serve as a preliminary peek into the core technical ideas behind Bayesian nonparametrics in NLP.

The Dirichlet process plays a pivotal role in Bayesian nonparametrics for NLP, similar to the pivotal role that the Dirichlet distribution plays in parametric Bayesian NLP modeling. Therefore, this chapter focuses on the Dirichlet process, and as such has the following organization. We begin by introducing the Dirichet process and its various representations in Section 7.1. We then show how the Dirichlet process can be used in an nonparametric mixture model in Section 7.2. We next show in Section 7.3 how hierarchical models can be constructed with the Dirichlet process as the foundation for solving issues such as the selection of the number of topics for the latent Dirichlet allocation model. Finally, we discuss the Pitman-Yor process, for which the Dirichlet process is a specific case (Section 7.4), and then follow with a brief discussion of other stochastic processes that are used in Bayesian nonparametrics.

7.1   THE DIRICHLET PROCESS: THREE VIEWS

The Dirichlet process (Ferguson, 1973) defines a distribution over distributions. The parameters controlling a Dirichlet process are a *concentration parameter* (also called a strength parameter) s, and a *base distribution* G_0, which functions as the "mean" of the Dirichlet process, in a manner that will be described below. We denote the support of G_0 by Θ. We use Θ because often G_0 is a function $G_0 \colon \Theta \to [0, 1]$ such that Θ defines some parameter space for a parametric model. Such is the case, for example, with the Dirichet process mixture model (see Section 7.2).

Each draw $G \sim \mathrm{DP}(G_0, s)$ from such a Dirichlet process is a distribution with its support being a discrete subset of the support of G_0. Each draw G from the Dirichlet process satisfies the following condition: for every finite partition $A_1, \ldots, A_r$ of Θ, with each A_i being measurable, it holds that the random vector $(G(A_1), \ldots, G(A_r))$ distributes as follows:

$$(G(A_1), \ldots, G(A_r)) \sim \mathrm{Dirichlet}(sG_0(A_1), \ldots, sG_0(A_r)).$$

This property is both necessary and sufficient, and actually serves as one of several equivalent definitions of the Dirichlet process. This definition also results in the fact that any draw G from the Dirichlet process is actually a discrete distribution—i.e., any draw G is such that $G(\theta) = 0$ for all $\theta \in \Theta \setminus \Theta_0$, where Θ_0 is a countable set. The base distribution G_0 functions

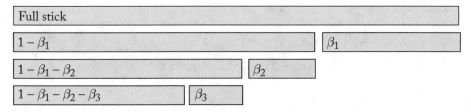

Figure 7.1: A graphical depiction of the stick breaking process. The rectangles on the right (in blue) are the actual probabilities associated with each element in the infinite multinomial. The process of breaking the stick repeats ad infinitum, leading to an infinite vector of β_i variables. At each step, the left part of the stick is broken into two pieces.

as the "mean," where the expected value $E[G(A)]$ (where expectation is taken with respect to G) equals $G_0(A)$ for any measurable set A. The concentration parameter, on the other hand, controls the variance in the Dirichlet process as follows:

$$\mathrm{Var}(G(A)) = \frac{G_0(A)(1 - G_0(A))}{s + 1}.$$

The larger s is, the closer draws G from the Dirichlet process to G_0.

The mathematical definition of the Dirichlet process above, as fundamental as it may be, is not constructive.[2] In the next two sections we provide two other perspectives on the Dirichlet process that are more constructive, and therefore are also more amenable to use in Bayesian NLP with approximate inference algorithms.

7.1.1 THE STICK-BREAKING PROCESS

The stick-breaking process (Figure 7.1) is a constructive representation of the Dirichlet process due to Sethuraman (1994). To define the stick-breaking process, we first need to define the Griffiths–Engen–McCloskey (GEM) distribution. Let $v_k \sim \mathrm{Beta}(1, s)$ for $k \in \{1, 2, \ldots\}$, i.e., a sequence of i.i.d. draws from the Beta distribution with hyperparameters $(1, s)$ for $s > 0$. (The Beta distribution defines a probability distribution over the interval $[0, 1]$.) Define

$$\beta_k = v_k \prod_{j=1}^{k-1}(1 - v_j). \tag{7.1}$$

In this case, the infinite vector $(\beta_1, \beta_2, \ldots)$ is said to be drawn from the GEM distribution with concentration parameter s.

Draws from the GEM distribution can be thought of as draws of "infinite multinomials," because the following is satisfied for every draw β from the GEM distribution:

[2]By that we mean that it does not describe the Dirichlet process in a way amenable to model specification, or inference.

Hyperparameters: G_0, s.
Variables: $\beta_i \geq 0$, θ_i for $i \in \{1, 2, \ldots\}$.
Output: Distribution G over a discrete subset of the sample space of G_0.

- -

- Draw $\beta \sim \text{GEM}(s)$.

- Draw $\theta_1, \theta_2, \ldots \sim G_0$.

- The distribution G is defined as:

$$G(\theta) = \sum_{k=1}^{\infty} \beta_k I(\theta = \theta_k). \qquad (7.4)$$

Generative Story 7.1: The generative story for drawing a distribution from the Dirichlet process.

$$\beta_k \geq 0 \; \forall k \in \{1, 2, \ldots\}, \qquad (7.2)$$

$$\sum_{k=1}^{\infty} \beta_k = 1. \qquad (7.3)$$

Since the components of this infinite multinomial sum to one, the components must decay quickly, so that the tail $\sum_{i=m}^{\infty} \beta_i$ goes to 0 as m goes to infinity. This is guaranteed by the iterative process through which a unit "stick" is broken to pieces, each time further breaking the residual part of the stick (Equation 7.1).

Based on the stick-breaking representation, a draw of a distribution $G \sim \text{DP}(G_0, s)$ from the Dirichet process can be represented using generative story 7.1. First, an infinite non-negative vector that sums to 1 is drawn from the GEM distribution (line 1). This corresponds to an infinite multinomial over "atoms," which are drawn next from the base distribution (line 2). Each atom is associated with an index in the infinite vector (line 3). This means that every draw from the Dirichlet process has the structure in Equation 7.4 for some atoms θ_k and coefficients β.

The stick-breaking process also demonstrates again the role of the s parameter. The larger s is, the less rapidly the parts of the stick decay to zero (in their length, taken with respect to the unit length). This is evident in Equation 7.1, when considering the fact that $v_k \sim \text{Beta}(1, s)$. The larger s is, the smaller each v_k is compared to $1 - v_k$, and therefore, more of the probability mass is preserved for other pieces in the stick.

The stick-breaking process also demonstrates that any draw from the Dirichlet process is a distribution defined over a *discrete* (or finite) support. The distribution in Equation 7.4 assigns positive weight to a discrete subset of the sample space of G_0.

7.1.2 THE CHINESE RESTAURANT PROCESS

As implied by the stick-breaking representation in Section 7.1.1, one way to view the Dirichlet process is as draws of infinite multinomial distributions over a countable set of atoms, drawn from the base distribution G_0. The Chinese Restaurant Process (CRP) representation of the Dirichlet process describes how to draw samples from these multinomials.

The CRP by itself defines a prior over *partitions*. Similarly to the Dirichlet process, it is controlled by a concentration hyperparameter s. Each $y^{(i)}$ drawn from the CRP is associated with an integer index (denoting a cluster assignment). The CRP then defines a distribution for drawing $y^{(i)}$ conditioned on the draws $y^{(1)}, \ldots, y^{(i-1)}$. The first draw is assigned with index 1. Now, let $y^{(1)}, \ldots, y^{(i-1)}$ be draws from the CRP and define $y_i^* = \max_{j \leq i-1} y^{(j)}$ (i.e., y_i^* is the cluster with largest index that was assigned to the first $i - 1$ instances in the samples from the CRP). Then, in order to draw $y^{(i)}$ conditioned on $y^{(1)}, \ldots, y^{(i-1)}$ we use the following distribution:

$$p\left(Y^{(i)} = r | y^{(1)}, \ldots, y^{(i-1)}, s\right) = \begin{cases} \dfrac{\sum_{j=1}^{i-1} I(y^{(j)} = r)}{i - 1 + s}, & \text{if } r \leq y_i^* \\[2ex] \dfrac{s}{i - 1 + s}, & \text{if } r = y_i^* + 1. \end{cases} \qquad (7.5)$$

This distribution definition, together with the chain rule, immediately leads to the following distribution over assignments of each $y^{(i)}$ to an integer:

$$p\left(y^{(1)}, \ldots, y^{(n)} | s\right) = p\left(y^{(1)} | s\right) \underbrace{\prod_{i=2}^{n} p\left(y^{(i)} | y^{(1)}, \ldots, y^{(i-1)}, s\right)}_{\text{Equation 7.5}},$$

with $p\left(y^{(1)} | s\right) = 0$ for any value other than $y^{(1)} = 1$.

In the CRP metaphor, when a new "customer," indexed by i, enters the restaurant, it sits at a table with other customers with a probability proportional to the number of the current occupants at that table, or starts a new table with a probability proportional to s. Here, the role of s is evident again—the larger s is, the more "new tables" are opened. In the CRP metaphor, $y^{(i)}$ denotes the table assignment for the ith customer, and y_i^* denotes the number of "occupied tables" before the ith customer is seated. Figure 7.2 depicts this posterior distribution in a graphical manner.

It is important to note that the set of random variables $Y^{(i)}$ for $i \in \{1, \ldots, n\}$ in the Chinese restaurant process is a set of exchangeable random variables (see also Section 1.3.3). This

Hyperparameters: G_0, s.
Variables: $Y^{(i)}$, ϕ_i for $i \in \{1, \ldots, n\}$.
Output: $\theta^{(i)}$ for $i \in \{1, \ldots, n\}$ drawn from $G \sim \mathrm{DP}(G_0, s)$.

- Draw $y^{(1)}, \ldots, y^{(n)} \sim \mathrm{CRP}(s)$.

- Draw $\phi_1, \ldots, \phi_{y_n^*} \sim G_0$.

- Set each $\theta^{(i)}$ to $\phi_{y^{(i)}}$ for $i \in \{1, \ldots, n\}$.

Generative Story 7.2: The Dirichlet process represented using the Chinese restaurant process.

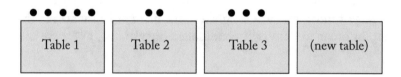

Figure 7.2: A graphical depiction of the posterior distribution of the Chinese restaurant process. Each black circle is a "customer" that sat next to one of the tables. In the picture, 3 tables are open in the restaurant with 10 customers. For $\alpha = 1.5$, there is a probability of $\dfrac{5}{5+2+3+1.5} = \dfrac{5}{11.5}$ for a new customer to go to the first table, probability of $\dfrac{2}{11.5}$ to go the second table, $\dfrac{3}{11.5}$ for the third table and $\dfrac{1.5}{11.5}$ to go to a new table.

means that the joint distribution over $Y^{(1)}, \ldots, Y^{(n)}$ is the same as the distribution over a permutation of these random variables. In the CRP metaphor, the order in which the customers enter the restaurant does not matter.

This view of the Dirichlet process demonstrates the way that the number of parameters grows as more data is available (see beginning of this chapter). The larger the number of samples is, the more "tables" are open, and therefore, the larger the number of parameters used when performing inference.

The Chinese restaurant process induces a distribution over partitions of $Y^{(i)}$, and therefore it is only a function of the counts of customers that are seated next to a certain table. More formally, the CRP distribution is a function of the integer count vector N of length m with $m = y_n^*$ (the total number of tables used for n customers) and $N_k = \sum_{i=1}^{n} I(Y^{(i)} = k)$ (the count of customers for each table $k \in \{1, \ldots, m\}$) and is defined as follows:

$$p(N|s) = \frac{s^m \left(\prod_{k=1}^{m}(N_k - 1)!\right)}{\prod_{i=0}^{n-1}(i + s)}.$$

With the CRP process, one can use a generative story 7.2 to define a representation for the Dirichlet process. An equivalent procedure for generating $\theta^{(1)}, \ldots, \theta^{(n)}$ from $G \sim \mathrm{DP}(G_0, s)$ is to draw a partition from the CRP, assigning each "table" in the partition a draw from G_0 and then setting $\theta^{(i)}$ to be that draw from G_0 according to the table the ith customer is seated in.

The CRP has a strong connection to the GEM distribution. Let π be a draw from the GEM distribution with concentration parameter s. Let $U_1, \ldots, U_N$ be a set of random variables that take integer values such that $p(U_i = k) = \pi_k$. These random variables induce a partition over $\{1, \ldots, N\}$, where each set in the partition consists of all U_i that take the same value. As such, for a given N, the GEM distribution induces a partition over $\{1, \ldots, N\}$. The distribution over partitions that the GEM distribution induces is identical to the distribution over partitions that the CRP induces (with N customers) with concentration parameter s.

7.2   DIRICHLET PROCESS MIXTURES

Dirichlet process mixture models (DPMMs) are a generalization of the finite mixture model. Just like a finite mixture model, the Dirichlet process mixture associates each of the observations with a cluster. The number of clusters, as expected, is potentially unbounded—the more data observed, the more clusters will be inferred. Each cluster is associated with a parameter, drawn from the base distribution, which is defined over the space Θ. There is a probability distribution $p(X|\theta)$, where $\theta \in \Theta$. Generative story 7.3 defines the generative process of the Dirichlet process mixture model.

Note the similarity to a regular non-Bayesian parametric mixture model. If G were a fixed distribution over a finite number of elements (K) in Θ (instead of a countable set), then the last two steps in the above generative process would correspond to a (non-Bayesian) mixture model. In this case, placing a prior (which can be parametric) on G would turn the model into a Bayesian finite mixture model.

7.2.1   INFERENCE WITH DIRICHLET PROCESS MIXTURES

In this section, we describe the two common methods for inference with DPMMs: MCMC and variational.

MCMC Inference for DPMMs

One way to define posterior inference for DPM is to identify the posterior distribution $p\left(\theta^{(1)}, \ldots, \theta^{(n)} | X, G_0, s\right)$. The most straightforward way to do so is to use a Gibbs sampler that samples from the conditional distributions $p\left(\theta^{(i)} | \theta^{(-i)}, X, G_0, s\right)$, for $i \in \{1, \ldots, n\}$ (Neal, 2000).

Hyperparameters: G_0, s.
Latent variables: $\theta^{(i)}$ for $i \in \{1, \ldots, n\}$.
Observed variables: $X^{(i)}$ for $i \in \{1, \ldots, n\}$.
Output: $x^{(1)}, \ldots, x^{(n)}$ for $i \in \{1, \ldots, n\}$ drawn from the Dirichlet process mixture model.

- Draw $G \sim \text{DP}(G_0, s)$.

- Draw $\theta^{(1)}, \ldots, \theta^{(n)} \sim G$.

- Draw $x^{(i)} \sim p(X^{(i)} | \theta^{(i)})$ for $i \in \{1, \ldots, n\}$.

Generative Story 7.3: The generative story for the Dirichlet process mixture model. The distribution G_0 is the base distribution such that its sample space is a set of parameters for each of the mixture components.

The first observation we make is that $\theta^{(i)}$ is independent of $X^{(-i)}$ conditioned on $\theta^{(-i)}$. Therefore, we seek conditional distributions of the form $p\left(\theta^{(i)} | \theta^{(-i)}, x^{(i)}, G_0, s\right)$. It holds for this conditional that[3]:

$$
\begin{aligned}
p\left(\theta^{(i)} | \theta^{(-i)}, x^{(i)}, G_0, s\right) & \\
\propto\ & p\left(\theta^{(i)}, x^{(i)} | \theta^{(-i)}, G_0, s\right) \\
=\ & \frac{1}{n-1+s} \sum_{j \neq i} I\left(\theta^{(j)} = \theta^{(i)}\right) p\left(x^{(i)} | \theta^{(j)}\right) + \frac{s}{n-1+s} G_0\left(\theta^{(i)}\right) p\left(x^{(i)} | \theta^{(i)}\right) \\
=\ & \frac{1}{n-1+s} \sum_{j \neq i} I\left(\theta^{(j)} = \theta^{(i)}\right) p\left(x^{(i)} | \theta^{(j)}\right) \\
& + \frac{s}{n-1+s} \left(\int_\theta G_0(\theta) p(x^{(i)} | \theta) d\theta \right) p\left(\theta^{(i)} | x^{(i)}\right),
\end{aligned}
\tag{7.6}
$$

where $p(\theta | X)$ is the posterior distribution over the parameter space for the distribution $p(\theta, X) = G_0(\theta) p(X | \theta)$, i.e., $p(\theta | X) \propto G_0(\theta) p(X | \theta)$. The transition to Equation 7.6 can be justified by the following:

$$
G_0\left(\theta^{(i)}\right) p\left(x^{(i)} | \theta^{(i)}\right) = G_0\left(\theta^{(i)}\right) \frac{p\left(\theta^{(i)} | x^{(i)}\right) p\left(x^{(i)}\right)}{G_0\left(\theta^{(i)}\right)} = p\left(\theta^{(i)} | x^{(i)}\right) p\left(x^{(i)}\right),
$$

[3]This can be shown by exchangeability, and assuming that the ith sample is the last one that was drawn.

and

$$p\left(x^{(i)}\right) = \int_\theta G_0(\theta) p\left(x^{(i)} \mid \theta\right) d\theta. \tag{7.7}$$

This is where the importance of the conjugacy of G_0 to the likelihood becomes apparent. If indeed there is such a conjugacy, the constant in Equation 7.7 can be easily computed, and the posterior is easy to calculate as well. (This conjugacy is not *necessary* for the use of the Dirichlet process mixture model, but it makes it more tractable.)

These observations yield a simple posterior inference mechanism for $\theta^{(1)}, \ldots, \theta^{(n)}$: for each i, given $\theta^{(-i)}$, do the following:

- With probability proportional to $p\left(x^{(i)} | \theta^{(j)}\right)$ for $j \neq i$, set $\theta^{(i)}$ to $\theta^{(j)}$

- With probability proportional to $s\left(\int_\theta G_0(\theta) p(x^{(i)}|\theta) d\theta\right)$ set $\theta^{(i)}$ to a draw from the distribution $p(\theta|x^{(i)})$.

This sampler is a direct result of Equation 7.6. The probability of $\theta^{(i)}$ given the relevant information can be viewed as a composition of two types of events: an event that assigns $\theta^{(i)}$ an existing $\theta^{(j)}$ for $j \neq i$, and an event that draws a new $\theta^{(i)}$.

The above two steps are iterated until convergence. While the sampler above is a perfectly correct Gibbs sampler (Escobar, 1994, Escobar and West, 1995), it tends to mix quite slowly. The reason is that each $\theta^{(i)}$ is sampled separately—local changes are made to the seating arrangements, and therefore it is hard to find a *global* seating arrangement with high probability. Neal (2000) describes another Gibbs algorithm that solves this issue. This algorithm samples the assignment to tables, and changes atoms for all customers sitting at a given table at once. He also suggests a specification of this algorithm to the conjugate DPM case, where G_0 is conjugate to the likelihood from which $x^{(i)}$ are sampled. For a thorough investigation of other scenarios in which Gibbs sampling or other MCMC algorithms can be used for Dirichlet process mixture models, see Neal (2000).

Variational Inference for DPMMs

The DPM can be represented using the stick-breaking process, which enables the development of a variational inference algorithm for it (Blei and Jordan, 2004). The stick-breaking representation for DPM is displayed in generative story 7.4.

The variational inference algorithm of Blei and Jordan treats this model with infinite components by using variational distributions that are finite, and more specifically, correspond to a *truncated* stick-breaking distribution.

The variational distribution for the DPMM needs to account for the latent variables π (derived from β), θ_i and $z^{(i)}$. The main point behind Blei and Jordan's variational inference algorithm is to use a truncated stick approximation for the π distribution. Since the π distribution comes from a GEM distribution, it is constructed from v_i for $i \in \{1, 2, \ldots\}$, which is drawn

Hyperparameters: G_0, s.
Latent variables: π, θ_j for $j \in \{1, \ldots\}$, $Z^{(i)}$ for $i \in \{1, \ldots, n\}$.
Observed variables: $X^{(i)}$ for $i \in \{1, \ldots, n\}$.
Output: $x^{(i)}, \ldots, x^{(n)}$ generated from the Dirichlet process mixture model.

- Draw $\pi \sim \text{GEM}(s)$.

- Draw $\theta_1, \theta_2, \ldots \sim G_0$.

- Draw $z^{(i)} \sim \pi$ for $i \in \{1, \ldots, n\}$ such that $z^{(i)}$ is an integer.

- Draw $x^{(i)} \sim p(x^{(i)} | \theta_{z^{(i)}})$ for $i \in \{1, \ldots, n\}$.

Generative Story 7.4: The generative story for the DPMM using the stick-breaking process. The distribution G_0 is the base distribution such that its sample space is a set of parameters for each of the mixture components.

from the Beta distribution, as explained in Section 7.1.1. Therefore, to define a variational distribution over π, it is sufficient to define a variational distribution over $\nu_1, \nu_2, \ldots$.

Blei and Jordan suggest using a mean-field approximation for ν_i, such that $q(\nu_i)$ for $i \in \{1, \ldots, K - 1\}$ is a Beta distribution (just like the true distribution for ν_i) and:

$$q(\nu_K) = \begin{cases} 1 & \nu_K = 1 \\ 0 & \nu_K \neq 1. \end{cases}$$

Since $q(\nu_K)$ puts its whole probability mass on ν_K being 1, there is no need to define variational distributions for ν_i for $i > K$. Such $q(\nu_K)$ implies that $\pi_i = 0$ for any $i > K$ according to the variational distribution over ν_i. The variational stick is truncated at point K.

Other Inference Algorithms for DPMMs

A rather unique way of performing inference with DPMMs was developed by Daume (2007). Daumé was interested in identifying the cluster assignment for a DPM that maximizes the probability according to the model—the maximum *a posteriori* (MAP) assignment. His algorithm is a search algorithm that keeps a queue with possible partial clusterings and values attached to them (tables, dishes and customers associated with them). If the function that attaches values to these clusterings (the scoring function) satisfies some properties (i.e., it is *admissible*, meaning it always overestimates the probability of the best clustering that agrees with a partial clustering in the queue), and if the beam size used during the search is ∞, then the search algorithm is guaranteed to find the MAP assignment for the clustering. Daumé also provides a few admissible

Constants: K and n.

Hyperparameters: G_0 base measure defined over Θ, s, a model family $F(X|\theta)$ for $\theta \in \Theta$.

Latent variables: $Z^{(1)}, \ldots, Z^{(n)}$.

Observed variables: $X^{(1)}, \ldots, X^{(n)}$.

Output: A set of n points drawn from a mixture model.

- -

- Generate $\theta_1, \ldots, \theta_K \sim G_0$.

- Draw $\pi \sim \text{Dirichlet}(\alpha/K)$ (from a symmetric Dirichlet).

- For $j \in \{1, \ldots, n\}$ ranging over examples:
  - Draw $z^{(j)}$ from π for $j \in \{1, \ldots, n\}$.
  - Draw $x^{(j)}$ from $F(X|\theta_{z_j})$ for $j \in \{1, \ldots, n\}$.

Generative Story 7.5: An approximation of the Dirichlet process mixture model using a finite mixture model.

scoring functions; he tested his algorithm on a character recognition problem and the clustering of documents from the NIPS conference.

7.2.2 DIRICHLET PROCESS MIXTURE AS A LIMIT OF MIXTURE MODELS

Another DPM construction exists that provides more intuition about its structure. Consider generative story 7.5. It can be shown that as K becomes large, this model is a good approximation of the Dirichlet process. It can also be shown that as K becomes large, the number of components actually used for a fixed number of datapoints, n, becomes independent of K (approximately $O(\alpha \log n)$—see also the exercises).

7.3   THE HIERARCHICAL DIRICHLET PROCESS

The distributions drawn from a Dirichlet process, as mentioned in Section 7.1.1, have a countable (or finite) support. The Dirichlet process selects a countable set of *atoms* from the base distribution, and then places weights on these atoms.

It is often desirable to create some hierarchy over this set of atoms drawn from a Dirichlet process. For example, in the spirit of the latent Dirichlet allocation model, a corpus of documents (modeled as bags of words) can be represented by an infinite, countable set of topics corresponding to multinomials over the vocabulary (see Section 2.2); each document might have a different set of probabilities assigned to each of these topics.

This means that the set of atoms—corresponding to multinomial distributions over the vocabulary—should be shared across all of the documents. However, the distribution of selecting each of these multinomials (corresponding to topic distribution in LDA) should be different for each document, similar to the LDA model.

Note that the number of topics assumed to exist in the corpora is infinite, but still countable. This is a reasonable modeling assumption if one thinks of each topic as a concept in the real world. While clearly the number of such concepts may grow over time, it should remain countable.

However, any reasonable prior distribution over topics, i.e., over vocabulary multinomials, is a continuous distribution (consider, for example, the Dirichlet distribution). Therefore, if we draw for each document a distribution over possible topics, $G^{(j)} \sim \mathrm{DP}(G_0, s)$, $j \in \{1, \ldots, n\}$, there almost surely will be no atoms at the intersection of the support of $G^{(j)}$ and $G^{(j')}$. The support of each of these infinite multinomials is countable, and therefore has negligible cardinality compared to the cardinality of the continuous space from which the support is being drawn. This issue is problematic because it violates the countable-topic-world assumption mentioned earlier. A solution to this problem (presented in more generality, and described also for other problems outside of NLP) is suggested by Teh et al. (2006).

The authors suggest having a hierarchical prior where $G_0 \sim \mathrm{DP}(H, s)$—this means that the base distribution G_0 for the Dirichlet process is itself a draw from the Dirichlet process. Now G_0 has a countable support, and therefore atom sharing will occur between the distributions $G^{(j)}$. With this model, a draw of G_0 represents a draw of the set of all possible topics that could emerge in the text, and $G^{(j)}$, for each document, re-weights the probability of these topics.

The full hierarchical Dirichlet process for the bag-of-word LDA-style model is the following. Assume H is some prior distribution over topics, which can now be continuous. For example, H can be a Dirichlet distribution over the probability simplex of a dimension the size of the vocabulary.

Then, in order to generate n documents, each of length ℓ_j, $j \in \{1, \ldots, n\}$, we follow generative story 7.6. The observed random variables are $X^{(j)}$, where $X^{(j)}$ is a vector of length ℓ_j, with $X_i^{(j)}$ being the ith word in document j.

Inference with the HDP   The original paper by Teh et al. (2006) suggested to perform inference with the HDP using MCMC sampling (Chapter 5). The authors suggest three sampling schemes for the hierarchical Dirichlet process:

- Sampling using the Chinese restaurant franchise representation: the HDP can be described in terms similar to that of the Chinese restaurant process. Instead of having a single restaurant, there would be multiple restaurants, each representing a draw from a base distribution, which is by itself a draw from a Dirichlet process. With this sampling scheme, the state space consists of indices for tables assigned to each customer i in restaurant j, and indices for dishes serves at table t in restaurant j.

Constants: ℓ_j for $j \in \{1, \ldots, n\}$ a sequence of lengths for n documents.

Hyperparameters: H, s, s^*.

Latent variables: $G_0, G^{(j)}, \theta^{(j)}, G_0$.

Observed variables: $X^{(j)}$.

Output: A set of n documents. The jth document has ℓ_j words, $x^{(j)}, \ldots, x_{\ell_j}^{(j)}$.

- - - - - - - - - -

- Generate $G_0 \sim \mathrm{DP}(H, s)$.

- For $j \in \{1, \ldots, n\}$ ranging over documents:

    - Draw $G^{(j)} \sim \mathrm{DP}(G_0, s^*)$ denoting the topic distribution for document j

    - For $i \in \{1, \ldots, \ell_j\}$ ranging over words in the document:

        - Draw $\theta_i^{(j)} \sim G_j$, representing a topic.

        - Draw $x_i^{(j)} \sim \mathrm{Multinomial}(\theta_i^{(j)})$, a word in the document.

Generative Story 7.6: The generative story for an LDA-style model using the Dirichlet process.

- Sampling using an augmented representation: in the sampling scheme mentioned above, the base distribution of the first DP in the HDP hierarchy (G_0) is assumed to be integrated out, which can complicate matters for certain models, such as HMMs, where there are additional dependencies between the Dirichlet processes. Therefore, Teh also describes an MCMC sampling scheme in which G_0 is not integrated out. This sampler resembles the previous one, only now the state space also includes bookkeeping for G_0.

- Sampling using direct assignment: in the previous two samplers, the state space is such that assignments of customers to dishes is indirect, through table dish assignment. This can make bookkeeping complicated as well. Teh suggests another sampler, in which customers are assigned to dishes directly from the first draw of the HDP, G_0. This means that the state space is now assignments to a dish (from the draw of G_0) for each customer i in restaurant j and a count of the number of customers with a certain dish k in restaurant j.

Alternatives to MCMC sampling for the HDP have also been suggested. For example, Wang et al. (2011) developed an online variational inference algorithm for the HDP. Bryant and Sudderth (2012) developed another variational inference algorithm for the HDP, based on a split-merge technique. Teh et al. (2008) extended a collapsed variational inference algorithm, originally designed for the LDA model, to the HDP model.

7.4 THE PITMAN–YOR PROCESS

The Pitman–Yor process (Pitman and Yor, 1997), sometimes also called the "two-parameter Poisson-Dirichlet process" is closely related to Dirichlet process, and it also defines a distribution over distributions. The Pitman-Yor process uses two real-valued parameters—a strength parameter s that plays the same role as in the CRP, and a discount parameter $d \in [0, 1]$. In addition, it also makes use of a base distribution G_0.

The generative process for generating a random distribution from the Pitman–Yor process is almost identical to the generative process described in Section 7.1.2. This means that for n observations, one draws a partition over the integers between 1 to n, and each cluster in the partition is assigned an atom from G_0.

The difference between the Dirichlet process and the Pitman–Yor process is that the Pitman–Yor process makes use of a generalization of the Chinese restaurant process, and it modifies Equation 7.5 such that:

$$p\left(Y^{(i)} = r | y^{(1)}, \ldots, y^{(i-1)}, s, d\right) =$$

$$\begin{cases} \dfrac{\left(\sum_{j=1}^{i-1} I(y^{(j)} = r)\right) - d}{i - 1 + s}, & \text{if } r \leq y_i^* \\ \dfrac{s + y_i^* d}{i - 1 + s}, & \text{if } r = y_i^* + 1 \end{cases}.$$

The discount parameter d plays a role in controlling the expected number of tables that will be generated for n "customers." With $d = 0$, the Pitman–Yor process reduces to the Dirichlet process. With larger d, more tables are expected to be used for n customers. For a more detailed discussion, see Section 7.4.2.

This modified Chinese restaurant process again induces a distribution that is a function of the integer count vector N of length m with $m = y_n^*$ and $N_k = \sum_{i=1}^n I(Y^{(i)} = k)$. It is defined as follows:

$$p(N|s, d) = \frac{\prod_{k=1}^m \left((d(k-1) + s) \times \prod_{j=1}^{N_k-1}(j - d)\right)}{\prod_{i=0}^{n-1}(i + s)}. \tag{7.8}$$

The Pitman–Yor process also has a stick-breaking representation, which is very similar to the stick-breaking representation of the Dirichlet process. More specifically, a PY with a base distribution G_0, a strength parameter s and a discount parameter d, will follow the same generative process in Section 7.1.1 for the Dirichlet process, only v_k are now drawn from Beta$(1 - d, s + kd)$ (Pitman and Yor, 1997). This again shows that when $d = 0$, the Pitman–Yor process reduces to the Dirichlet process.

The Pitman–Yor process can be used to construct a hierarchical Pitman–Yor process, similar to the way that the Dirichlet process can be used to create an HDP (Section 7.3). The hierarchy is constructed from Pitman-Yor processes, instead of Dirichlet processes—with an additional discount parameter. Such a hierchical PY process was used, for example, for dependency parsing by Wallach et al. (2008).

7.4.1   PITMAN–YOR PROCESS FOR LANGUAGE MODELING

Language modeling is one of the most basic and earliest problems in natural language processing. The goal of a language model is to assign a probability to an utterance, a sentence or some text. Language models are used, for example, to ensure the output of a machine translation system is coherent, or speech recognition to assess the plausbility of an utterance, as it is decoded from a given speech signal.

If $x_1 \cdots x_m$ is a string, corresponding to a sentence over some vocabulary, then one can imagine a model that progressively generates word by word, each time conditioning on the words generated up to that point. The words being conditioned on are "the context" in which the new word is being generated. Mathematically, this is a simple use of the chain rule, that defines the probability of $x_1 \cdots x_m$ as:

$$p(x_1 \cdots x_m) = p(x_1) \prod_{i=2}^{n} p(x_i | x_1 \cdots x_{i-1}). \tag{7.9}$$

The most common and successful language models are n-gram models, which simply make a Markovian assumption that the context necessary to generate x_i is the $n-1$ words that preceeded x_i. For example, for a bigram model, where $n = 2$, the probability in Equation 7.9 would be formulated as:

$$p(x_1 \cdots x_m) = p(x_1) \prod_{i=2}^{n} p(x_i | x_{i-1}).$$

Naturally, a Bayesian language model would place a prior over the probability distributions that generate a new word given its context. Teh (2006b) uses the Pitman–Yor process as a prior over these distributions. In the terminlogy of the paper, let an n-gram distribution such as $p(w|w_1 \cdots w_{n-1})$ be $G_{w_1 \cdots w_{n-1}}(w)$ and let $\pi(w_1 \cdots w_r) = w_2 \cdots w_r$, i.e., π is a function that takes a sequence of words and removes the "earliest" word. Then, Teh defines a hierarchical prior over the n-gram distributions $G_{w_1 \cdots w_r}$ ($r \leq n-1$) as:

$$G_{\emptyset} \sim \mathrm{PY}\left(d_0, a_0, G_0\right) \qquad \qquad \textit{base case}$$
$$G_{w_1 \cdots w_r} \sim \mathrm{PY}\left(d_r, a_r, G_{\pi(w_1 \cdots w_r)}\right) \qquad \qquad \textit{recursive case for } 1 \leq r \leq n-1.$$

Here, G_0 is the base distribution such that $G_0(w) = 1/V$ where V is the vocabulary size (i.e., it is a uniform distribution over the vocabulary). In addition, there is a uniform prior on the discount parameters, and a Gamma$(1, 1)$ prior over all concentration parameters.

Because of the hierarchical structure of this prior, a word that has been drawn for a certain context $w_1 \cdots w_r$ is more likely to be drawn again for all other contexts that share an identical suffix to $w_1 \cdots w_r$.

This hierarchical definition of a prior is reminiscent of back-off smoothing or interpolation with lower order models, both of which are common smoothing techniques for n-gram language model estimations (Rosenfeld, 2000). As a matter of fact, Teh (2006a) shows that his hierarchical prior can be viewed as a generalization of the interpolated Kneser–Ney estimator for n-gram language models (Chen and Goodman, 1996, Kneser and Ney, 1995).

Teh designs an inference scheme for predicting the probability of a word given the context in which it appears (i.e., the words that came before it), and proceeds to compute the perplexity of text based on his language model. The inference algorithm is a Gibbs sampler that uses the Chinese restaurant process representation.

Teh reports that the Gibbs implementation of the Pitman-Yor language model (PYLM) performs better than interpolated Kneser–Ney, but worse than "modified Kneser–Ney," (MKN) which is an improved variant of Kneser–Ney, by Chen and Goodman (1996). Teh hypothesized that the reason PYLM does worse than MKN is that the inferred estimates of the hyperparameters are not optimal for prediction. He overcomes this limitation by designing a cross-validation scheme for finding these hyperparameter estimates for PYLM. (MKN's parameters are also optimized using cross-validation.) Indeed, the perplexity result he reports using this cross-validation scheme with PYLM, compared to MKN, is lower, and is overall the best among all of the baselines that he compares (such as interpolated Kneser–Ney and a hierarchical Dirichlet model, for different n-gram sizes).

Noji et al. (2013) used the Pitman–Yor process for combining an n-gram language model with a topic model. Their work builds and extends the model of Wallach (2006), which also combines an n-gram language model with a topic model, but in the parametric setting (with Dirichlet priors).

7.4.2   POWER-LAW BEHAVIOR OF THE PITMAN–YOR PROCESS

The PY process reduces to a Dirichlet process when the discount parameter is 0. In this case, it can be shown that the expected number of tables, with the CRP representation, is approximately $s \log n$, with n being the number of customers (usually corresponding to the number of observations), and s being the concentration parameter for the Dirichlet process.

With $d > 0$, the number of expected tables actually changes in a critical manner: from a logarithmic number of tables, the expected number of tables becomes sn^d. This means that the expected number of tables follows a *power-law*, so that the number of expected tables as a function of n is proportional to a power of n.

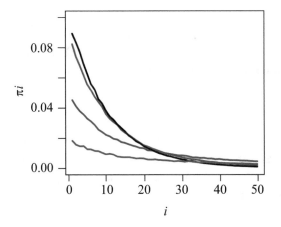 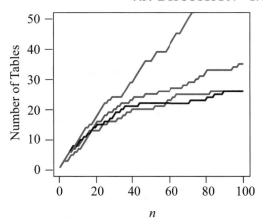

Figure 7.3: Left plot: average of π_i as a function of i according to 5,000 samples from a Pitman–Yor process prior. The value of the concentration parameter s is 10 in all cases. The value of the discount parameters are $d = 0$ (black; Dirichlet process), $d = 0.1$ (red), $d = 0.5$ (blue) and $d = 0.8$ (purple). Right plot: the average of number of tables obtained as a function of the number of customers n over 5,000 samples from the Chinese restaurant process. The concentration and the discount parameters are identical to the left plot.

This power-law behavior fits natural languge modeling very well. For example, with a Pitman-Yor unigram language model, each table corresponds to a word *type*, and n corresponds to word tokens. Therefore, the expected number of tables gives the expected number of word types in a corpus of size n. As Zipf (1932) argued, this setting fits a power-law behavior.

Figure 7.3 demonstrates the behavior of the Dirichlet process vs. the Pitman–Yor process when $d \neq 0$. First, it shows that π_i, the length of the i part of the stick (in the stick-breaking process representation of DP and PYP) has an exponential decay when $d = 0$ (i.e., when we use the Dirichlet process) vs. a heavier tail when we use the Pitman–Yor process. With $d \neq 0$, it can be shown that $\pi_i \propto (i)^{-\frac{1}{d}}$. The figure also shows the average number of tables opened when sampling from the Chinese restaurant process for DP and PYP. The number of tables grows logarithmically when using $d = 0$, but grows faster when $d > 0$.

7.5 DISCUSSION

This chapter has a large focus on the Dirichlet process, its derivatives and its different representations. While the Dirichlet process plays an important role in Bayesian nonparametric NLP, there are other stochastic processes used as nonparametric Bayesian priors.

The machine learning literature has produced many other nonparametric Bayesian priors for solving various problems. In this section we provide an overview of some of these other nonparametric models. We do not describe the posterior inference algorithms with these priors, since they depend on the specifics of the model in which they are used. The reader should consult with the literature in order to understand how to do statistical inference with any of these priors. Indeed, the goal of this section is to inspire the reader to find a good use for the described priors for natural language processing problems, as these priors have not often been used in NLP.

7.5.1   GAUSSIAN PROCESSES

Gaussian processes (GPs) is a stochastic process commonly used to model temporal and/or spatial observed data. A Gaussian process is a set of random variables $\{X_t | t \in T\}$ that are indexed by some set T (T, for example, can denote time), such that each finite subset of this set of random variable distributes according to the multivariate normal distribution.

The Gaussian process, therefore, is defined using an expectation function $\mu : T \to \mathbb{R}$ and a covariance function $\text{Cov}(t, t')$ that denotes the covariance between X_t and $X_{t'}$. Every subvector of the random variables, $X = (X_{t_1}, \ldots, X_{t_n})$ is normally distributed, such that $E[X] = (\mu(t_1), \ldots, \mu(t_n))$ and covariance matrix Σ such that $\Sigma_{ij} = \text{Cov}(t_i, t_j)$.

When instantiating all values of X_t to a certain value, one can think of the Gaussian process as a function: each $t \in T$ is mapped to a real-value. This is the main inspiration for using Gaussian processes in the Bayesian setting: they are used to define priors over real-valued functions. Each draw from a Gaussian process yields a specific function that maps the values of T to real-values. The "mean function" of this prior is μ. For more detailed information about the use of Gaussian processes in machine learning, see Rasmussen and Williams (2006).

Gaussian processes are not heavily used in NLP. There is some work that uses these processes for classification and sequence labeling; for example, the work of Altun et al. (2004) uses a Gaussian process prior over a *compatibility* function that measures the match of an observation to a certain label. Altun et al. test their model on the problem of named entity recognition, and show error reduction compared to a conditional random field model.

More recent work that makes use of GPs in N LP focuses on regression problems. For example, Preoţiuc-Pietro and Cohn (2013) use Gaussian processes to model temporal changes in Twitter data. The goal is to predict trends in time (in Twitter), as indicated by the surrogate of the volume of a hashtag. The regression function $f(t)$ is assumed to be drawn from a Gaussian process prior, where t denotes the time and $f(t)$ denotes the volume (i.e., each X_t in the process denotes a random value for $f(t)$). The authors also made use of the predictions in an additional classification step to predict the hashtags of given tweets.

7.5.2   THE INDIAN BUFFET PROCESS

The Indian buffet process (IBP) describes a stochastic process for drawing infinite binary matrices (Griffiths and Ghahramani, 2005). It also uses a restaurant metaphor, similar to the CRP, only customers can have multiple dishes based on their popularity with other customers. The IBP is controlled by a hyperparameter α.

The metaphor for the IBP is the following. There is a restaurant with an infinite number of dishes, ordered in a long buffet-style line. The first customer enters, and takes a serving from the first r_1 dishes, where r_1 is drawn from Poisson(α). When the ith customer enters, she samples a dish according to its popularity, serving herself a dish k with probability m_k / i, where m_k is the number of customers that previously served themselves dish k. After reaching the end of all previously sampled dishes, she serves herself r_i new dishes, where r_i is drawn according to Poisson(α / i).

The description of the above process implies that the IBP defines a distribution over infinite binary matrices. Each draw M of such a binary matrix (where the columns and rows are indexed with a natural number, corresponding to the customer index) has $M_{ik} = 1$ if customer i served himself the kth dish, and 0 otherwise.

7.5.3   NESTED CHINESE RESTAURANT PROCESS

The nested Chinese restaurant process (Blei et al., 2010) gives a prior of infinitely branching trees with an infinite depth. The nested CRP assumes the existence of an infinite number of Chinese restaurants, each with an infinite number of tables. There is a main "root" restaurant, and each table points to exactly one other restaurant. Each table in each of the other restaurants also points to another restaurant. Each restaurant is referenced exactly once, and therefore the restaurants have a tree structure, where the nodes are the referenced restaurants (or referencing tables) and edges denote that one restaurant references the other.

The nested CRP induces a distribution over paths in this infinite tree—each draw from the nested CRP is such a path. We assume M tourists, coming to a city with the Chinese restaurants described above, starting at the root restaurant, choosing a table, and then moving to the next restaurant as referenced by that table. This is repeated ad-infinitum. With M tourists, there will be M infinite paths in the tree, which can be described as a subtree of the infinite tree with a branching factor of at most M.

Blei et al. (2010) use the nested CRP to describe a hierarchical LDA model. The infinite tree over all tables is assumed to be a hierarchical topic distribution. This means that each node in the tree is associated with a distribution over the vocabulary of words in the documents. The generative story uses a draw from the nested CRP (of an infinite path) instead of the usual topic distribution. Then, to draw the words in the document, we first draw a path from a nested CRP, and then for each word we first draw a level in that infinite path, and then the word from the vocabulary distribution associated with the node in that level of the path.

7.5.4   DISTANCE-DEPENDENT CHINESE RESTAURANT PROCESS

As mentioned in Section 7.1.2, the Chinese restaurant process defines a probability distribution over partitions. The metaphor is that customers are arranged in seats next to tables, where the ith customer is seated next to a table with a probability proportional to the number of customers already sitting next to the table. Some probability mass is allocated for seating a customer next to a new, empty table.

The key observation that Blei and Frazier (2011) made is that the CRP defines the seating arrangement based on the *tables*, more specifically, according to the number of people seated at a table. They suggest an alternative view, in which a customer is seated with another customer.

More formally, let f be a "decay function" that needs to be positive, non-increasing with $f(\infty) = 0$. In addition, let D be an $n \times n$ matrix such that D_{ij} denotes a distance between customer i and customer j. We assume that $D_{ij} \geq 0$. Then, if $Y^{(i)}$ for $i \in \{1, \ldots, n\}$ is a random variable denoting who customer i sits with, the distance-based CRP assumes that:

$$p\left(Y^{(i)} = j | D, s\right) \propto \begin{cases} f\left(D_{ij}\right), & \text{if } i \neq j \\ s, & \text{if } i = j, \end{cases}$$

where s plays a similar role to a concentration parameter.

The seating arrangement of each customer next to another customer induces a seating arrangement next to tables, similar to the CRP, by assigning a table to all customers who are connected to each other through some path.

Note that the process that Blei and Fraizer suggest is not sequential. This means that customer 1 can pick customer 2 and customer 2 can pick customer 1, and more generally, that there can be cycles in the arrangement. The distance-based CRP is not sequential in the sense of the original CRP. In addition, the order in which the customers enter the restaurant does matter, and the property of exchangeability is broken with the distance-dependent CRP (see also Section 7.1.2).

However, it is possible to recover the traditional sequential CRP (with concentration parameter s) by assuming that $D_{ij} = \infty$ for $j > i$, $D_{ij} = 1$ for $j < i$, $f(D) = 1/d$ with $f(\infty) = 0$. In this case, customers can only join customers that have a lower index. The total probability of joining a certain table will be proportional to the sum of the distances between a customer and all other customers sitting at that table, which in the above formulation will just be the total number of customers sitting next to that table.

There has been relatively little use of distance-dependent CRPs in NLP, but examples of such use include the use of distance-dependent CRP for the induction of part-of-speech classes (Sirts et al., 2014). Sirts et al. use a model that treats words as customers entering a restaurant, and at each point, the seating of a word at a table depends on its similarity to the other words at the table with respect to distributional and morphological features. The tables represent the part-of-speech classes.

Another example for the use of distance-dependent CRPs in NLP is by Titov and Klementiev (2012). In this example, the distance-dependent CRP is used to induce semantic roles in an unsupervised manner.

7.5.5   SEQUENCE MEMOIZERS

Sequence memoizers (Wood et al., 2009) are hierarchical nonparametric Bayesian models that define non-Markovian sequence models. Their idea is similar to the one that appears in Section 7.4.1. A sequence of distributions over predicted tokens at each step are drawn from the Pitman–Yor process. To predict the kth token given context $x_1 \cdots x_{k-1}$, the distribution $G_{x_1 \cdots x_{k-1}}$ is drawn from a Pitman–Yor process with base distribution $G_{x_2 \cdots x_{k-1}}$. The distribution $G_{x_2 \cdots x_{k-1}}$, in turn, is drawn from a Pitman–Yor distribution with base distribution $G_{x_3 \cdots x_{k-1}}$ and so on.

Wood et al. describe a technique to make posterior inference with sequence memoizers efficient. To do so, they use a specific sub-family of the Pitman–Yor process, in which the concentration parameter is 0. This enables marginalizing out the distributions $G_{x_i \cdots x_{k-1}}$ for $i > 1$, and constructing the final predictive distribution $G_{x_1 \cdots x_{k-1}}$. It also enables an efficient representation of the sequence memoizer, which grows linearly with the sequence length.

Sequence memoizers were mostly used for language modeling, as a replacement for the usual n-gram Markovian models. They were further improved by Gasthaus and Teh (2010), introducing a richer hyperparameter setting, and a representation that is memory efficient. Inference algorithms for this improved model are also described by Gasthaus and Teh (2010). The richer hyperparameter setting allows the modeler to use a non-zero concentration value for the underlying Pitman–Yor process. They were also used by Shareghi et al. (2015) for structured prediction.

7.6   SUMMARY

This chapter gave a glimpse into the use of Bayesian nonparametrics in the NLP literature. Some of the important concepts that were covered include the following.

- The Dirichlet process, which serves as an important building block in many Bayesian nonparametric models for NLP. Three equivalent constructions of the Dirichlet process were given.

- Dirichlet process mixtures, which are a generalization of a finite mixture model.

- The Hierarchical Dirichlet process, in which several Dirichlet processes are nested together in the model, in order to be able to "share atoms" between the various parts of the model.

- The Pitman–Yor process, which is a generalization of the Dirichlet process.

- Some discussion of other Bayesian nonparametric models and priors.

In Chapter 8, other examples of models and uses of Bayesian nonparametrics are given, such as the HDP probabilistic context-free grammar and adaptor grammars.

7.7 EXERCISES

7.1. Show that the Chinese restaurant process describes a joint distribution over an exchangeable set of random variables.

7.2. Let Z_n be a random variable denoting the total number of tables open after n customers were seated in a Chinese restaurant process arrangement (with concentration α). Show that as n becomes large, $E[Z_n] \approx \alpha \log n$.

7.3. Consider Equations 7.2–7.3. Show that indeed a draw β from the GEM distribution satisfies them. You will need to use the definition of β from Equation 7.1.

7.4. In Section 7.2.1, a Gibbs sampler is given to sample $\theta^{(1)}, \ldots, \theta^{(n)}$ from the Dirichlet process mixture model. Write down the sampler for the case in which G_0 is a Dirichlet distribution over the $p - 1$ dimensional probability simplex, and $p(X|\theta)$ is a multinomial distribution over p elements.

7.5. Alice derived the sampler in the previous question, but discovered later that a better choice of G_0 is a renormalized Dirichlet distribution, in which none of the coordinates in $\theta \sim G_0$ can be larger than $1/2$ (assume $p > 2$). Based on rejection sampling (Section 5.9), derive a Gibbs sampler for such G_0. Consult with Section 3.1.4 as needed.

CHAPTER 8

Bayesian Grammar Models

One of the most successful applications of the Bayesian approach to NLP is probabilistic models derived from grammar formalisms. These probabilistic grammars play an important role in the modeling toolkit of NLP researchers, with applications pervasive in all areas, most notably, the computational analysis of language at the morphosyntactic level.

In order to apply Bayesian statistics to inference with probabilistic grammars, we must first place a prior over the parameters of the grammar. Probabilistic context-free grammars, for example, can have a Dirichlet prior on their rule multinomial probabilities. More complex models can also be used. For example, one can use nonparametric priors such as the Dirichlet process with probabilistic context-free grammars (PCFGs) to break the independence assumptions that PCFGs make.

Most of the work done with probabilistic grammars in the Bayesian setting is done in an unsupervised setting, where only strings are available to the learner, and the goal is to infer a posterior over derivation trees, or even to induce the structure of the grammar. Still, there are a few exceptions, where Bayesian learning is used with grammars in a supervised setting—some of these exceptions are mentioned in this chapter.

Most of this chapter is devoted to a specific grammar model, probabilistic context-free grammars, and its use in the Bayesian setting, both parametric and nonparametric. There are several reasons for this focus.

- Probabilistic context-free grammars are the simplest cases of grammar formalisms in which the rewrite rules have a context-free format of the form $a \rightarrow \alpha$ where a is a "non-terminal" and α is some object that can replace a in a partial derivation. Such a rule structure is common with many other formalisms that have a "context-free backbone."[1] Examples include linear context-free rewriting systems—which are now being revisited in NLP and generalize many grammar formalisms used in NLP (Kallmeyer and Maier, 2010, Vijay-Shanker et al., 1987)—combinatory categorial grammars (Steedman and Baldridge, 2011), and even formalisms where the language is not a set of strings, such as graph rewriting grammars (Rozenberg and Ehrig, 1999). They also generalize sequence models, such as hidden Markov models.

---

[1]If a grammar has a "context-free backbone," it does not necessarily mean that the language it generates is context-free. It just means that its production rules do not require context on the left-hand side.

- There is a large body of work on probabilistic context-free grammars and their derivatives. This means that being well-acquainted with this grammar formalism is important for any NLP researcher.

- PCFGs offer a generic way to derive and communicate about statistical models in NLP. They offer a sweet spot between tractability and expressivity, and as such, their use is not limited to just syntactic parsing. Many models in NLP can be captured in terms of PCFGs.

In Section 8.1 we cover the use of hidden Markov models, a fundamental sequence labeling model that is used in NLP and outside of it. In Section 8.2 we provide a general overview of PCFGs and set up notation for the rest of this chapter. In Section 8.3 we begin the discussion of the use of PCFGs with the Bayesian approach. We then move to nonparametric modeling of grammars, covering adaptor grammars in Section 8.4, and the hierarchical Dirichlet process PCFGs in Section 8.5. We then discuss dependency grammars in Section 8.6, synchronous grammars in Section 8.7 and multilingual learning in Section 8.8, and conclude with some suggestions for further reading in Section 8.9.

8.1 BAYESIAN HIDDEN MARKOV MODELS

Hidden Markov models are important models that are used in many NLP applications for sequence modeling. HMMs are usually not thought of as "grammar models," but they are actually a special case of probabilistic context-free grammars. This is clarified later in Section 8.2.3. A hidden Markov model is represented by a tuple $H = (\mathcal{T}, \mathcal{N}, \diamond, \theta)$ where:

- $\mathcal{T}$ is a finite set of symbols called the *emission symbols*.

- $\mathcal{N}$ is a finite set of symbols called the *states*, such that $\mathcal{T} \cap \mathcal{N} = \emptyset$.

- A special state symbol $\diamond \in \mathcal{T}$ called "the stop state" or "the sink state."

- θ is a vector of parameters such that it defines for every $s, s' \in \mathcal{N}$ and every $o \in \mathcal{T}$ the following non-negative parameters:

  - Initial state probabilities: θ_s. It holds that $\sum_{s \in \mathcal{N}} \theta_s = 1$.

  - Emission probabilities: $\theta_{o|s}$ for all $s \in \mathcal{N} \setminus \{\diamond\}$ and $o \in \mathcal{T}$. It holds that $\sum_{o \in \mathcal{T}} \theta_{o|s} = 1$.

  - Transition probabilities: $\theta_{s'|s}$ for all $s \in \mathcal{N} \setminus \{\diamond\}$ and $s' \in \mathcal{N}$. It holds that $\sum_{s \in \mathcal{N}} \theta_{s|s'} = 1$.

Hidden Markov models define a probability distribution over pairs (x, z) such that $x = x_1 \cdots x_m$ is a string over $\mathcal{T}$, and $z = z_1 \cdots z_m$ is a sequence of states from $\mathcal{N}$ such that $z_i \neq \diamond$. This distribution is defined as follows:

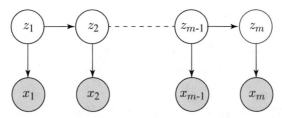

Figure 8.1: A hidden Markov model depicted graphically as a chain structure. The shaded nodes correspond to observations and the unshaded nodes correspond to the latent states. The sequence is of length m, with latent nodes and observations indexed 3 through $m - 2$ reprsented by the dashed line.

$$p(x, z | \theta) = \theta_{z_1} \theta_{x_1 | z_1} \left(\prod_{i=2}^{m} \theta_{z_i | z_{i-1}} \theta_{x_i | z_i} \right) \theta_{\diamond | z_m}.$$

HMMs have basic inference algorithms called the forward and backward algorithms. These are dynamic programming algorithms that can be used to compute feature expectations given an observation sequence. For example, they can compute the expected number of times that a certain emission $o|s$ fires in the sequence, or alternatively, this pair of algorithms can compute the expected number of times a certain transition $s|s'$ fires. For a complete description of these algorithms, see Rabiner (1989). These algorithms are an analog to the inside and outside algorithms for PCFGs (see Section 8.2.2).

A graphical depiction of a hidden Markov model is given in Figure 8.1. The chain structure graphically denotes the independence assumptions in the HMM. Given a fixed set of parameters for the HMM and a state z_i, the observation x_i is conditionally independent of the rest of the nodes in the chain. In addition, given a fixed set of parameters for the HMM and a state z_{i-1}, the state z_i is conditionally independent of all previous states z_j, $j < i - 1$.

Hidden Markov models can be defined with higher order—in which case the probability distribution over a given state depends on more states than just the previous one. A trigram HMM, for example, has the probability over a given state depend on the two previous states. The algorithms for inference with trigram HMMs (or higher order HMMs) are similar to the inference algorithms that are used with vanilla bigram HMMs.

8.1.1   HIDDEN MARKOV MODELS WITH AN INFINITE STATE SPACE

With an HMM, the problem of selecting the number of latent states to use (when the states do not correspond to a known set of states, such as with supervised part-of-speech tagging) can be solved using the usual set of tools for controlling for model complexity. For example, with

Constants: ℓ, s_0, s_1
Latent variables: $\beta, \pi_0, \pi_i, \theta_i$ for $i \in \{1, \ldots\}$, Z_j for $j \in \{1, \ldots, \ell\}$
Observed variables: X_j for $j \in \{1, \ldots, \ell\}$

- Generate a base infinite multinomial $\beta \sim \text{GEM}(s_0)$

- Generate $\pi_i \sim \text{DP}(s_1, \beta)$ for $i \in \{0, 1, \ldots\}$

- Generate $\theta_i \sim G_0$ for $i \in \{1, \ldots\}$

- Generate $z_1 \sim \pi_0$

- Generate $x_1 \sim F(\cdot|\theta_{z_1})$

- For $j \in \{2, \ldots, \ell\}$

  - Generate $z_j \sim \pi_{z_{j-1}}$
  - Generate $x_j \sim F(\cdot|\theta_{z_j})$

Generative Story 8.1: The generative story of the infinite hidden Markov model.

held-out data validation, one can increasingly add more states, each time performing inference on the data, and checking the behavior of the log-likelihood function on the held-out data.

Another way to overcome the requirement to predefine the number of latent states in an HMM is the use of nonparametric modeling, and more specifically, the hierarchical Dirichlet process (Section 7.3). This allows the modeler to define an infinite state space (with a countable number of latent states). During inference with sequence observations, the underlying number of states that is used for explaining the data will grow with the amount of data available.

Hierarchical Dirichlet process hidden Markov models (HDP-HMM) are a rather intuitive extension, which combines HMMs with the HDP. Here we provide a specification of the HDP-HMM in the general form that Teh (2006b) gave, but also see the infinite HMM model by Beal et al. (2002).

The first model component that Teh assumes is a parametric family $F(\cdot|\theta)$ (for $\theta \in \Theta$) for generating observations and a base distribution G_0 used as a prior over the space of parameters Θ. For example, θ could be a multinomial distribution over a set of observation symbols $\mathcal{T}$, and G_0 could be a Dirichlet distribution over the $(|\mathcal{T}| - 1)$th probability simplex. In order to generate a sequence of observations of length ℓ, we use generative story 8.1.

The generative process assumes a discrete state space, and works by first generating a base distribution β, which is an infinite multinomial distribution over the state space. It then draws another infinite multinomial distribution for each state. That infinite multinomial corresponds to a transition distribution from the state it is indexed by to other states (so that each event in the infinite multinomial is also mapped to one of the states). Then the emission parameters are drawn for each state using G_0, which is a base distribution over parameter space Θ. In order to actually generate the sequences, the generative process proceeds by following the usual Markovian process while using the transition and emission distributions. Inference with this infinite HMM model is akin to inference with the Hierarchical Dirichlet process (Section 7.3). For the full details, see Teh (2006b). See also Van Gael et al. (2008).

8.2   PROBABILISTIC CONTEXT-FREE GRAMMARS

One of the most basic, generic model families that is available in NLP is probabilistic context-free grammars (PCFGs). Probabilistic context-free grammars augment context-free grammars (CFGs) with a probabilistic interpretation. CFGs are a grammar formalism that provides a mechanism to define context-free languages (the language of a grammar is the set of strings that can be generated by the grammar). They also associate each string in such a language with one or more grammar derivations in the form of a *phrase-structure tree*, such as the one in Figure 8.2. This phrase-structure tree is a labeled tree, with labels on nodes denoting the syntactic category of the substring they span in their yield (NP for noun phrase, VP for verb phrase, and so on). The yield, read from left to right, represents the sentence for which this derivation was created. A collection of such trees in a specific language is referred to as a "treebank."

More formally, a context-free grammar is a tuple $G = (\mathcal{T}, \mathcal{N}, S, \mathcal{R})$ where:

- $\mathcal{T}$ is a finite set of symbols called the *terminal symbols*. These include the symbols that appear at the yield of the phrase-structure trees the CFG generates.

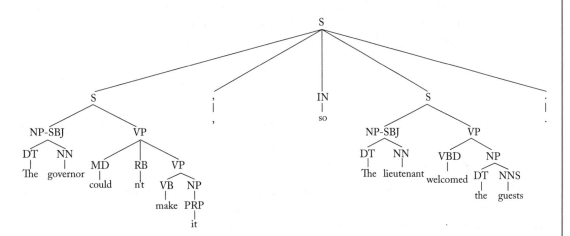

Figure 8.2: An example of a phrase-structure tree in English inspired by the Penn treebank (Marcus et al., 1993).

- $\mathcal{N}$ is a finite set of *nonterminal symbols,* which label nodes in the phrase-structure tree. We require that $\mathcal{T} \cap \mathcal{N} = \emptyset$.

- $\mathcal{R}$ is a finite set of *production rules.* Each element $r \in \mathcal{R}$ has the form of $a \to \alpha$, with $a \in \mathcal{N}$ and $\alpha \in (\mathcal{T} \cup \mathcal{N})^*$. We denote by $\mathcal{R}_a$ the set $\{r \in \mathcal{R} \mid r = a \to \alpha\}$, i.e., the rules associated with nonterminal $a \in \mathcal{N}$ on the left-hand side of the rule.

- S is a designated start symbol which always appears at the top of the phrase-structure trees.

In their most general form, CFGs can also have rules of the form $a \to \varepsilon$ where ε is the "empty word." Of special interest in natural language processing are CFGs which are in *Chomsky normal form.* With Chomsky normal form grammars, only productions of the form $a \to t$ (for $a \in \mathcal{N}$ and $t \in \mathcal{T}$) or $a \to b\,c$ (for $a, b, c \in \mathcal{N}$) are allowed in the grammar. The original definition of Chomsky normal form also permits a rule $S \to \varepsilon$, but in most uses of CFGs in Bayesian NLP, this rule is not added to the grammar. For simplification, we will not introduce ε rules to the grammars we discuss. (Still, ε rules are useful for modeling specific components of linguistic theories, such as empty categories or "gaps.")

Chomsky normal form is useful in NLP because it usually has simple algorithms for basic inference, such as the CKY algorithm (Cocke and Schwartz, 1970, Kasami, 1965, Younger, 1967). The simplicity of CNF does not come at the expense of its expressive power—it can be shown that any context-free grammar can be reduced to a CNF form that generates equivalent grammar derivations and the same string language. Therefore, our focus is on CFGs in CNF form.[2]

A probabilistic context-free grammar attaches a set of parameters θ to a CFG G (these are also called *rule probabilities*). Here, θ is a set of $|\mathcal{N}|$ vectors. Each θ_a for $a \in \mathcal{N}$ is a vector of length $|\mathcal{R}_a|$ in the probability simplex. Each coordinate in θ_a corresponds to a parameter $\theta_{a \to b\,c}$ or a parameter $\theta_{a \to t}$. With probabilistic context-free grammars, the following needs to be satisfied:

$$\theta_{a \to b\,c} \geq 0 \qquad\qquad a \to b\,c \in \mathcal{R} \qquad (8.1)$$
$$\theta_{a \to t} \geq 0 \qquad\qquad a \to t \in \mathcal{R} \qquad (8.2)$$
$$\sum_{b,c:a \to b\,c \in \mathcal{R}} \theta_{a \to b\,c} + \sum_{t:a \to t \in \mathcal{R}} \theta_{a \to t} = 1 \qquad\qquad \forall a \in \mathcal{N}. \qquad (8.3)$$

This means that each nonterminal is associated with a multinomial distribution over the possible rules for that nonterminal. The parameters θ define a probability distribution $p(Z|\theta)$ over phrase-structure trees. Assume z is composed of the sequence of rules $r_1, \ldots, r_m$ where $r_i = a_i \to b_i\, c_i$ or $r_i = a_i \to x_i$. The distribution $P(Z|\theta)$ is defined as:

---

[2]Note that it is not always possible to convert a PCFG to a PCFG in CNF form while retaining the same distribution over derivations and strings, and approximations could be required. See also Abney et al. (1999).

$$p(Z = (r_1, \ldots, r_m)|\theta) = \left(\prod_{i=1}^{m} \theta_{r_i}\right). \tag{8.4}$$

Not every assignment of rule probabilities that satisfies the above constraints (Equations 8.1–8.3)yields a valid probability distribution over the space of trees. Certain rule probabilities lead to PCFGs that are "inconsistent"—this means that these PCFGs allocate non-zero probability to trees of infinite length. For example, for the grammar with rules $S \rightarrow S\ S$ (with probability 0.8) and $S \rightarrow$ buffalo (with probability 0.2), there is a non-zero probability to generate trees with an infinite yield. For a comprehensive discussion of this issue, see Chi (1999).

In most cases in the Bayesian NLP literature, the underlying symbolic grammar in a PCFG is assumed to be known. It can be a hand-crafted grammar that is compatible with a specific NLP problem, or it can be a grammar that is learned by reading the rules that appear in the parse trees in a treebank.

With PCFGs, the observations are typically the yield of the sentence appearing in a derivation z. This means that PCFGs define an additional random variable, X, which ranges over strings over $\mathcal{T}$. It holds that $X = \text{yield}(Z)$ where $\text{yield}(z)$ is a deterministic function that returns the string in the yield of z. For example, letting the derivation in Figure 8.2 be z, it holds that $\text{yield}(z)$ is the string "The governor could n't make it, so the lieutenant welcomed the guests."

The distribution $p(Z|x, \theta)$ is the conditional distribution for all possible derivation trees that have the yield x. Since X is a deterministic function of Z, Equation 8.4 defines the distribution $p(X, Z|\theta)$ as follows:

$$p(x, z|\theta) = \begin{cases} p(z|\theta) & \text{yield}(z) = x \\ 0 & \text{yield}(z) \neq x. \end{cases}$$

In this chapter, the words in string x will often be denoted as $x_1 \cdots x_m$ where m is the length of x, and each x_i is a symbol from the terminal symbols $\mathcal{T}$.

Another important class of models related to PCFGs is that of weighted context-free grammars. With weighted CFGs, $\theta_{a \rightarrow bc}$ and $\theta_{a \rightarrow t}$ have no sum-to-1 constraints (Equation 8.2). They can be of arbitrary non-negative weight. Weighted PCFGs again induce distribution $p(Z|\theta)$, by defining:

$$p(z|\theta) = \frac{\prod_{i=1}^{m} \theta_{r_i}}{A(\theta)}, \tag{8.5}$$

where $A(\theta)$ is a normalization constant that equals:

$$A(\theta) = \sum_z \prod_{i=1}^{m} \theta_{r_i}.$$

For consistent PCFGs, $A(\theta) = 1$. For any assignment of rule probabilities (i.e., assignment of weights that satisfy Equations 8.1–8.2), it holds that $A(\theta) \leq 1$. For weighted CFGs, it is not always the case that $A(\theta)$ is a finite real number. The function $A(\theta)$ can also diverge to infinity for certain grammars with certain weight settings, since the sum is potentially over an infinite number of derivations with different yields.

8.2.1 PCFGS AS A COLLECTION OF MULTINOMIALS

It is common to factorize a set of parameters in a Bayesian NLP generative model into a set of multinomial distributions. In general, θ is a vector that consists of K subvectors, each of length N_k for $k \in \{1, \dots, K\}$. This means that the following is satisfied:

$$\theta_{k,k'} \geq 0 \qquad \forall k \in \{1, \dots, K\} \ and \ k' \in \{1, \dots, N_k\}$$
$$\sum_{k'=1}^{N_k} \theta_{k,k'} = 1 \qquad \forall k \in \{1, \dots, K\}.$$

With PCFGs, K equals the number of nonterminals in the grammar, and N_k is the size of $\mathcal{R}_a$ for the nonterminal a associated with index $k \in \{1, \dots, K\}$. We denote by $\theta_{k,k'}$ the event k' in the kth multinomial.

With this kind of abstract model, each multinomial event corresponds to some piece of structure. With PCFGs, these pieces of structures are production rules. Let $f_{k,k'}(x, z)$ be the number of times that production rule k' for nonterminal $k \in \{1, \dots, K\}$ fires in the pair of string and phrase-structure tree (x, z). The probabilistic model defined over pairs of strings and phrase structure trees is:

$$p(x, z|\theta) = \prod_{k=1}^{K} \prod_{k'=1}^{N_k} \theta_{k,k'}^{f_{k,k'}(x,z)}. \tag{8.6}$$

If we consider $x = \left(x^{(1)}, \dots, x^{(n)}\right)$ and $z = \left(z^{(1)}, \dots, z^{(n)}\right)$ being generated from the likelihood in Equation 8.6, independently (given the parameters), then it can be shown the likelihood of these data is:

$$p(x, z|\theta) = \prod_{k=1}^{K} \prod_{k'=1}^{N_k} \theta_{k,k'}^{\sum_{i=1}^{n} f_{k,k'}(x^{(i)}, z^{(i)})}.$$

Input: A probabilistic context-free grammar G with weights θ, a string $x = x_1 \cdots x_m$, a nonterminal $a \in \mathcal{N}$, a pair of endpoints (j, j'), inside probability chart "in."

Output: A sampled tree, headed by nonterminal a spanning words x_j through $x_{j'}$, based on the inside-outside chart.

1: **if** $j = j'$ **then**
2:    $z \leftarrow$ a tree with a root a and the word x_j below a
3:    **return** z
4: **end if**
5: **for all** rules $a \rightarrow b\, c \in \mathcal{R}$ ranging over $b, c \in \mathcal{N}$ **do**
6:    **for** $q \leftarrow j$ to $j' - 1$ **do**
7:       Let sampleMult$(a \rightarrow b\, c, q)$ be $\theta_{a \rightarrow b\, c} \times \text{in}(b, j, q) \times \text{in}(c, q + 1, j')$
8:    **end for**
9: **end for**
10: Normalize s: Let sampleMult$(a \rightarrow b\, c, q)$ be $\dfrac{\text{sampleMult}(a \rightarrow b\, c, q)}{\sum_{a \rightarrow b\, c, q} \text{sampleMult}(a \rightarrow b\, c, q)}$
11: Sample from the multinomial sampleMult an event $(a \rightarrow b\, c, q)$.
12: $z_{\text{left}} \leftarrow$ SamplePCFG$(G, \theta, x, b, (j, q), \text{in})$
13: $z_{\text{right}} \leftarrow$ SamplePCFG$(G, \theta, x, c, (q + 1, j'), \text{in})$
14: $z \leftarrow$ a
                        $\diagup \diagdown$
                   z_{left} z_{right}
15: **return** z

Algorithm 8.1: A recursive algorithm SamplePCFG for sampling from a probabilistic context-free grammar (in Chomsky normal form) conditioned on a fixed string and fixed parameters.

8.2.2   BASIC INFERENCE ALGORITHMS FOR PCFGS

Bayesian inference over PCFGs often requires computing marginal quantities for a given sentence, such as the probability of a certain nonterminal spanning a substring in a sentence (called the "inside probability") or the total probability of a string according to a given PCFG.

The inference algorithms for identifying these quantities are usually based on dynamic programming. It is often the case in the Bayesian setting that these dynamic programming algorithms are used with *weighted* grammars, as previously mentioned, i.e., the parameters assigned to the rules in the grammar do not have to satisfy Equation 8.2. These kinds of weighted grammars appear, for example, with variational updates rules such as in Equation 6.11. More discussion of this appears in Section 8.3.3.

The first basic inference algorithm we tackle in this section is the *inside algorithm*. The inside algorithm comes to compute, for a given sentence $x_1 \cdots x_m$, its total probability (or weight) according to a PCFG (in CNF form), i.e.:

$$\mathrm{in}(S, 1, m) = \sum_{z:\mathrm{yield}(z)=x_1\cdots x_m} p(z|\theta).$$

Here, $p(Z|\theta)$ is a PCFG distribution parametrized by weights θ with start symbol S. The use of the notation $\mathrm{in}(S, 1, m)$, with the arguments 1 and m, is deliberate: this quantity can be calculated for other nonterminals and other spans in the sentence. Generally, it holds that:

$$\mathrm{in}(a, i, j) = \sum_{z \in A(a,i,j)} p(z|\theta),$$

where $A(a, i, j) = \{z | \mathrm{yield}(z) = x_i \cdots x_j, h(z) = a\}$. This means that the inside probability of a nonterminal a for span (i, j) is the total probability of generating the string $x_i \cdots x_j$, starting from nonterminal a. The function $h(z)$ returns the root of the derivation z. Note that in this formulation we allow for the root to be arbitrary nonterminal, not just S. The probability $p(z|\theta)$ is defined as usual, as the product of all rules in the derivation.

The inside quantities can be computed through a recursive procedure, using quantities of the same form. The following is the recursive definition:

$$\mathrm{in}(a, i, i) = \theta_{a \to x_i} \qquad\qquad a \in \mathcal{N}, a \to x_i \in \mathcal{R}, 1 \le i \le m$$

$$\mathrm{in}(a, i, j) = \sum_{k=i}^{j} \sum_{a \to b\, c \in \mathcal{R}} \theta_{a \to b\, c} \times \mathrm{in}(b, i, k) \times \mathrm{in}(c, k+1, j) \qquad a \in \mathcal{N}, 1 \le i < j \le m.$$

The intermediate quantity $\mathrm{in}(a, i, j)$ is to be interpreted as the total weight of all trees in which the nonterminal a spans words $x_i \cdots x_j$ at positions i through j. There are various execution models for computing the recursive equations above. One simple way is to use bottom-up dynamic programming, in which the chart elements $\mathrm{in}(a, i, j)$ are computed starting with those that have small width of $j - i + 1$ and ending with the final element $\mathrm{in}(S, 1, n)$ which has a width of n. One can also use an agenda algorithm, such as the one that was developed by Eisner et al. (2005)—see also Smith (2011).

Another important quantity of interest is the *outside probability* which is computed using the outside algorithm. The outside quantity calculates the probability of generating an "outer" part of the derivation. More formally, we define $\mathrm{out}(a, i, j)$ for any $i < j$ indices in a given string and a a nonterminal as:

$$\mathrm{out}(a, i, j) = \sum_{z \in B(a, i, j)} p(z|\theta),$$

where $B(a, i, j) = \{z | \mathrm{yield}(z) = x_1 \cdots x_{i-1} y x_{j+1} \cdots x_n, y \in \mathcal{T}^*, head\ of\ y\ in\ z\ is\ a\}$. This means that the outside probability is the total probability of generating the partial derivation $x_1 \cdots x_{i-1} a x_{j+1} \cdots x_n$ where a is the nonterminal not being fully rewritten yet to a string. Similarly to the inside probability, the outside probability can also be computed recursively as follows (this time top-down):

$$\mathrm{out}(S, 1, n) = 1$$
$$\mathrm{out}(a, 1, n) = 0 \qquad\qquad\qquad\qquad\qquad\qquad\qquad a \in \mathcal{N}, a \neq S$$
$$\mathrm{out}(a, i, j) = \sum_{k=1}^{j-1} \sum_{b \to c\, a \in \mathcal{R}} \theta_{b \to c\, a} \times \mathrm{in}(c, k, i-1) \times \mathrm{out}(b, k, j)$$
$$+ \sum_{k=j+1}^{n} \sum_{b \to a\, c \in \mathcal{R}} \theta_{b \to a\, c} \times \mathrm{in}(c, j+1, k) \times \mathrm{out}(b, i, k) \quad a \in \mathcal{N}, 1 \le i < j \le n.$$

The most important use of the inside and outside algorithms is to compute *feature expectations* of nonterminals spanning certain positions for a given sentence. More formally, if the following indicator is defined:

$$I(\langle a, i, j \rangle \in z) = \begin{cases} 1 & \textit{if a spans words i through j in z} \\ 0 & \textit{otherwise,} \end{cases}$$

then the inside and outside probabilities assist in computing:

$$E\left[I(\langle a, i, j \rangle \in Z) | x_1 \cdots x_m\right] = \frac{\sum_{z, \mathrm{yield}(z) = x_1 \cdots x_m} p(z|\theta) I(\langle a, i, j \rangle \in z)}{p(x_1 \cdots x_m | \theta)},$$

because it can be shown that:

$$E\left[I(\langle a, i, j \rangle \in Z) | x_1 \cdots x_m\right] = \frac{\mathrm{in}(a, i, j) \times \mathrm{out}(a, i, j)}{\mathrm{in}(S, 1, n)}.$$

Similarly, expectations of the form $E[I(\langle a \to b\, c, i, k, j \rangle \in Z) | x_1 \cdots x_m]$ can also be computed. Here, $I(\langle a \to b\, c, i, k, j \rangle \in z)$ is 1 if the rule $a \to b\, c$ is used in z such that a spans words i to j and below it b spans words i to k and c spans words $k + 1$ to j. It can be shown that:

$$E\left[I(\langle a \rightarrow b\,c, i, k, j\rangle \in Z)|x_1 \cdots x_m\right] = \frac{\theta_{a \rightarrow b\,c} \times \text{in}(b, i, k) \times \text{in}(c, k+1, j) \times \text{out}(a, i, j)}{\text{in}(S, 1, n)}.$$

(8.7)

Last, expectations of the form $E[I(\langle a \rightarrow x_i, i\rangle \in Z)|x_1 \cdots x_m]$ can be similarly defined as:

$$E\left[I(\langle a \rightarrow x_i, i\rangle \in Z)|x_1 \cdots x_m\right] = \frac{\theta_{a \rightarrow x_i} \times \text{out}(a, i, i)}{\text{in}(S, 1, n)}.$$

(8.8)

The inside probabilities have an important role in PCFG sampling algorithms as well. The inside probabilities are used in a sampling algorithm that samples a single tree z from the distribution $p(Z|x_1 \cdots x_m, \theta)$. The sampling algorithm is given in Algorithm 8.1. The algorithm assumes the computation (for a fixed θ) of the inside chart of the relevant sentence is available. It then proceeds by recursively sampling a left child and right child for a given node, based on the inside chart.

The above pair of inside and outside algorithms are used with PCFGs in Chomsky normal form. There are generalizations to these algorithms that actually work for arbitrary grammars (without ε rules). For example, the Earley algorithm can be used to compute feature expectations of the form above (Earley, 1970).

The Computational Complexity of Basic Inference with PCFGs

The inside and the outside algorithms for Chomsky normal form grammars have an asymptotic complexity of $O(Gm^3)$, where m is the length of the string and G is the size of the grammar (the total length of all of its production rules). This means that in the worst case, the asymptotic complexity could be cubic in the number of nonterminals, $O(N^3 m^3)$, with N being the number of nonterminals, since the size of a grammar can be cubic in the number of nonterminals. Using the "folding trick," an optimization technique for improving the complexity of dynamic programming algorithms (Burstall and Darlington, 1977, Johnson, 2007a), the complexity of the inside and outside algorithms can be further reduced to $O(N^2 m^3 + N^3 m^2)$.

It is important to note that once the inside and outside charts have been computed for a given string, conditioned on a specific set of parameters, we can efficiently draw as many trees as we want based on this chart and Algorithm 8.1, without re-computing the inside-outside chart. The worst-case asymptotic complexity of Algorithm 8.1, as described in the figure, is linear in the grammar size and is quadratic in the length of the string. (Note that the running time is random, and balanced trees will be sampled faster than unbalanced trees.) The algorithm can be sped up by computing lines 6–8 just once in an outer loop, prior to the execution of the sampling algorithm. Finally, the algorithm can be sped up further by using a logarithmic-time sampling algorithm for multinomial sampling (see Section 5.9 for more information). These modifications will be important only if multiple trees are sampled using the same inside chart.

8.2.3   HIDDEN MARKOV MODELS AS PCFGS

HMMs can be captured using a right-branching PCFG. More specifically, using the notation in Section 8.1, define a PCFG such that:

- The nonterminal symbols are $((\mathcal{N} \setminus \diamond) \times \{0, 1\}) \cup \{S\}$.

- The terminal symbols are $\mathcal{T}$.

- For each pair of states $s, s' \in \mathcal{N} \setminus \{\diamond\}$ there is a rule $(s, 0) \rightarrow (s, 1)(s', 0)$ with probability $\theta_{s'|s}$.

- For each state $s \in \mathcal{N} \setminus \{\diamond\}$ there is a rule $(s, 0) \rightarrow (s, 1)$ with probability $\theta_{\diamond|s}$.

- For each pair of a state and an observation symbol, $s \in \mathcal{N} \setminus \diamond$, $o \in \mathcal{T}$, there is a rule $(s, 1) \rightarrow o$ with probability $\theta_{o|s}$.

- For each state $s \in \mathcal{N} \setminus \{\diamond\}$ there is a rule $S \rightarrow (s, 0)$ with probability θ_s.

This PCFG induces a distribution over derivations that are equivalent to sequences of states. To produce the state sequence from a given derivation, one must traverse the derivation from the top symbol S, and then visit the nonterminal nodes in the tree by always picking the right child from a given node.

Basic inference with PCFGs can be used to compute feature expectations for HMMs as well. In fact, the inside and outside dynamic programming algorithms can be viewed as generalizations of the forward and backward algorithms. Running the inside and outside algorithms on sequential structures, however, leads to computational complexity that is cubic in the length of the sequence, while the forward and backward algorithms are linear in the length of the sequence (and quadratic in the number of states). The forward and backward algorithms are linear in the length of the sequence because they exploit the linear structure of the sequence—they do not require computing an inside chart with two endpoints, denoting a span in the string, but instead can maintain a dynamic programming chart with a single endpoint (the other endpoint is assumed to be either the last word or the first word).

8.3   BAYESIAN PROBABILISTIC CONTEXT-FREE GRAMMARS

The next natural step, once PCFGs are defined, is to introduce them in a Bayesian context. This is the focus of this section.

8.3.1   PRIORS ON PCFGS

A conjugate product-of-Dirichlets distribution is a natural choice as a prior for the parameters of PCFGs, which can be viewed as a collection of multinomials. This prior over θ is defined as:

$$p(\theta|\alpha) \propto \prod_{a \in \mathcal{N}} \left(\prod_{a \rightarrow b\,c \in \mathcal{R}(a)} \theta_{a \rightarrow b\,c}^{(\alpha_{a \rightarrow b\,c} - 1)} \right) \times \left(\prod_{a \rightarrow t \in \mathcal{R}(a)} \theta_{a \rightarrow t}^{(\alpha_{a \rightarrow t} - 1)} \right). \qquad (8.9)$$

Here, α is a vector of hyperparameters that decomposes the same way that θ does. Each $\alpha_{a \rightarrow b\,c}$ is non-negative. See Chapter 3 for a definition of the missing normalization constant in Equation 8.9.

There is also room for exploring different granularities for the hyperparameters α. For example, instead of having a hyperparameter associated with a rule in the grammar, there can be a symmetric Dirichlet defined per nonterminal $a \in \mathcal{N}$ by using a single hyperparameter α_a for each $a \in \mathcal{N}$, or perhaps even a single hyperparameter α for all rules in the grammar.

The distribution in Equation 8.9 is conjugate to the distribution defined by a PCFG in Equation 8.4. Let us assume the complete data scenario, in which derivations from the grammar, $z^{(1)}, \ldots, z^{(n)}$, are observed. Denote the yields of these derivations by $x^{(1)}, \ldots, x^{(n)}$. The posterior,

$$p\left(\theta|\alpha, z^{(1)}, \ldots, z^{(n)}, x^{(1)}, \ldots, x^{(n)}\right),$$

is a product-of-Dirichlet distribution with hyperparameters $\alpha + \sum_{j=1}^{n} f\left(x^{(j)}, z^{(j)}\right)$ where f is a function that returns a vector indexed by grammar rules such that $f_{a \rightarrow b\,c}(x, z)$ counts the number of times rule $a \rightarrow b\,c$ appears in (x, z) and $f_{a \rightarrow t}(x, z)$ counts the number of times rule $a \rightarrow t$ appears in (x, z).

As mentioned earlier, not all assignments of rule probabilities to a PCFG (or more generally, a multinomial generative distribution) lead to a consistent PCFG. This means that the Dirichlet prior in Equation 8.9 potentially assigns a non-zero probability mass to inconsistent PCFGs. This issue is largely ignored in the Bayesian NLP literature, perhaps because it makes little empirical difference.

8.3.2   MONTE CARLO INFERENCE WITH BAYESIAN PCFGS

Section 8.2.2 gives a basic algorithm for sampling from a PCFG given its parameters θ. As pointed out by Johnson et al. (2007a), this algorithm can be used in a rather straightforward way for an explicit sentence-blocked Gibbs sampler with a product-of-Dirichlets prior. Johnson et al. explore MCMC inference with such a model, where $x^{(1)}, \ldots, x^{(n)}$ is a set of observed sentences, and the target prediction is a set of derivations $z^{(1)}, \ldots, z^{(n)}$. The symbolic grammar itself is assumed to be known. Johnson et al. use a top-level product-of-Dirichlets prior for the PCFG model, as specified in Equation 8.9 for CNF grammars.

This Gibbs sampler that Johnson et al. design alternates between sampling a derivation $z^{(i)}$ from $p\left(Z^{(i)}|x^{(i)}, \theta\right)$ and then sampling θ from $p\left(\theta|z^{(1)}, \ldots, z^{(n)}, x^{(1)}, \ldots, x^{(n)}, \alpha\right)$. The latter distribution is also a Dirichlet distribution, because of the conjugacy of the product-of-Dirichlet distribution to the PCFG likelihood. See Section 8.3.1 and Chapter 5 for more detail. The samples from $p(Z^{(i)}|x^{(i)}, \theta)$ are drawn using Algorithm 8.1.

Using the terminology from Chapter 5, this Gibbs sampler is an explicit sentence-blocked sampler. As such, it tends to converge slowly and also requires re-parsing the entire corpus of input strings before making updates to θ. Johnson et al. designed a Metropolis–Hastings algorithm (or Metropolis-within-Gibbs, to be more exact) that tackles these two issues.

This sampler is collapsed, and samples directly from the posterior $p(Z|X, \alpha)$, marginalizing out θ. A sentence-blocked Gibbs sampler in the collapsed setting uses the following conditionals:

$$p\left(z^{(i)}|x^{(1)}, \ldots, x^{(n)}, z^{(-i)}, \alpha\right) = \frac{p\left(x^{(i)}|z^{(i)}\right) p\left(z^{(i)}|z^{(-i)}, \alpha\right)}{p\left(x^{(i)}|z^{(-i)}, \alpha\right)}. \qquad (8.10)$$

The distribution $p\left(X^{(i)}|Z^{(i)}\right)$ is just a deterministic distribution that places its whole probability mass on the string yield $\left(Z^{(i)}\right)$. The quantity $p\left(z^{(i)}|z^{(-i)}, \alpha\right)$ can also be computed by relying on the conjugacy of the prior to the PCFG likelihood (see exercises). However, there is no known efficient way to compute $p(x^{(i)}|z^{(-i)}, \alpha)$. This means that the conditional distribution can only be computed up to a normalization constant, making it a perfect candidate for MCMC sampling.

Therefore, Johnson et al. approach the problem of sampling from the conditional distribution in Equation 8.10 by sampling from a proposal distribution and then making a Metropolis-Hastings correction step. Their algorithm is given in Algorithm 8.2.

There is no need to re-calculate $\theta'_{a \rightarrow \beta}$ from scratch after each tree draw. One can keep one global count, together with the current state of the sampler (which consists of a tree per sentence in the corpus), and then just subtract the counts of a current tree, and add back the counts of a newly drawn tree.

Inferring sparse grammars   Johnson et al. report that Bayesian inference with PCFGs and a Dirichlet prior does not give a radically different result than a plain EM algorithm without Bayesian inference. They tested their Bayesian inference with a simple grammar for analyzing the morphology of one of the Bantu languages, Sesotho.

They discovered that their MCMC inference was not very sensitive to the hyperparameters of the Dirichlet distribution (in terms of the F_1-measure of morphological segmentation and exact segmentation), except for when $\alpha < 0.01$, in which case performance was low. On the other hand, small α values (but larger than 0.01) lead to relatively sparse posterior over θ. Therefore, small values of α can be used to estimate a sparse θ, leading to an *interpretable* model, which has a small number of grammar rules that are actually active. The performance of their model sharply peaks as α is decreased to a value around 0.01. This peak is followed by a slow decrease in performance, as α is decreased further to significantly smaller values.

Input: A PCFG, a vector α ranging over rules in the PCFG, a set of strings from the language of the grammar $x^{(1)}, \ldots, x^{(n)}$.

Output: $z = (z^{(1)}, \ldots, z^{(n)})$ trees from the posterior defined by the grammar with a Dirichlet prior with hyperparameters α.

1: Initialize the trees $z^{(1)}, \ldots, z^{(n)}$ randomly
2: **repeat**
3:   **for** $i \to 1$ to n **do**
4:     Calculate for each rule $a \to \beta \in \mathcal{R}$

$$\theta'_{a\to\beta} = \frac{\sum_{j\neq i} f_{a\to\beta}(x^{(j)}, z^{(j)}) + \alpha_{a\to\beta}}{\sum_{\beta:a\to\beta\in\mathcal{R}} \sum_{j\neq i} f_{a\to\beta}(x^{(j)}, z^{(j)}) + \alpha_{a\to\beta}}.$$

5:     Draw z from the PCFG distribution $p(Z|X = x^{(i)}, \theta')$.
6:     Set $z^{(i)}$ to be z with probability

$$\min\left\{1, \frac{p(Z^{(i)} = z|x^{(i)}, z^{(-i)}, \alpha)\, p(z^{(i)}|x^{(i)}, \theta')}{p(Z^{(i)} = z^{(i)}|x^{(i)}, z^{(-i)}, \alpha)\, p(Z^{(i)} = z|x^{(i)}, \theta')}\right\}$$

7:   **end for**
8: **until** reaching convergence
9: **return** $z^{(1)}, \ldots, z^{(n)}$

Algorithm 8.2: An algorithm for sampling from the posterior of a PCFG with Dirichlet prior: $p(z|x, \alpha) = \int_\theta p(z, \theta|x, \alpha)d\theta$.

8.3.3   VARIATIONAL INFERENCE WITH BAYESIAN PCFGS

Mean-field variational inference for PCFGs (with product-of-Dirichlet prior) can be viewed as a special case of the variational inference algorithm given for the Dirichlet-Multinomial family in Section 6.3.1. The part that must be specialized for PCFGs is the one that calculates the feature expectations $E_q[f_{k,i}|\psi^{\text{old}}]$ in Equation 6.11.

These feature expectations can be computed using Equation 8.7 and Equation 8.8. More specifically, to compute the expectation of feature $f_{k,i}$ where k represents nonterminal a and i represents rule $a \to b\,c$, one would have to sum expectations of the form $E[I(\langle a \to b\,c, i, k, j\rangle \in Z)|x_1 \cdots x_m]$ over all possible i, k, j. Expectations for rules of the form $a \to x_i$ can be computed directly using Equation 8.8.

The conjugacy of the product-of-Dirichlet distribution to the PCFG likelihood function makes the derivation of a mean-field variational inference algorithm more straightforward, but the product-of-Dirichlet is not the only possible prior for PCFG variational inference. For example, Cohen et al. (2009) use a product of logistic normal distributions as a prior over a PCFG grammar. For inference, they used a first-order Taylor approximation for the normalization constant of the logistic normal prior—a normalization constant for which computing the expectation for the variational bound is not trivial.

8.4   ADAPTOR GRAMMARS

Probabilistic context-free grammars make strong independence assumptions: the probability of a partial derivation below a given node is conditionally independent of everything rewritten above that node, if the identity of the nonterminal at that node is known. These strong independence assumptions enable the simple basic inference mechanisms for deriving, for example, feature expectations, as described in Section 8.2.2.

Still, these independence assumptions can be too strong for modeling language. This has been noted in the parsing literature, especially for treebank-driven parsing in a supervised setting; myriad solutions have been suggested to overcome this issue, and adaptor grammars also address that issue.

Adaptor grammars are a type of syntactic model, and they are most suitable for a learning scenario in which only strings are available (without examples of phrase-structure trees, i.e., in an unsupervised setting). Adaptor grammars define distributions over phrase-structure trees, similarly to PCFGs. The distribution over phrase-structure trees they define is based on a PCFG. For a given phrase-structure tree, denote by $\mathrm{Subtrees}(z)$ the tuple $(z'_1, \ldots, z'_m)$ where z'_i denotes the subtree of the ith immediate child of z. In addition, for a given phrase-structure tree z, denote by $h(z) \in \mathcal{N}$, its root nonterminal and by $r(z) \in \mathcal{R}$, the rule that appears at the top of the tree. (The left-hand side of $r(z)$ is always $h(z)$.)

We will assume the existence of a PCFG with the notation from Section 8.2. Then, adaptor grammars define the following set of statistical relationships on distributions H_a and G_a for $a \in \mathcal{N}$, where both G_a and H_a are distributions over phrase-structure trees with root $a \in \mathcal{N}$:

$$\forall a \in \mathcal{N} : G_a \ such \ that \ G_a(z) = \theta_{a \to \beta} \prod_{i=1}^{m} H_{h(z'_i)}(z'_i) \tag{8.11}$$

$$where \ h(z) = a \ and \ r(z) = a \to \beta \ and \ \mathrm{Subtrees}(z) = (z'_1, \ldots, z'_m)$$

$$\forall a \in \mathcal{N} : H_a \ such \ that \ H_a \sim C_a(G_a). \tag{8.12}$$

Here, C_a is an *adaptor*, which defines a distribution over a set of distributions. Each distribution in this set is defined over phrase-structure trees. The distribution G_a serves as the "base distribution" for the adaptor. As such, each distribution in the set of distributions mentioned above, on average, bears some similarity to G_a. In the most general form of adaptor grammars, the actual adaptor is left unspecified. This means that any distribution over phrase-structure tree distributions (that is based on G_a) can be used there. If C_a places all of its probability mass on G_a

(this means that Equation 8.12 is replaced with $H_a = G_a$), then what remains from the above statistical relationships is the definition of a regular PCFG.

The final distribution over phrase-structure trees from which we draw full trees is H_S. The key idea with adaptor grammars is to choose C_a, so that we break the independence assumptions that PCFGs have, which can be too strong for modeling language. Using a Pitman–Yor process for the adaptors, C_a serves as an example for breaking these independence assumptions. In Section 8.4.1, this use of the Pitman–Yor process is described.

An adaptor grammar makes a distinction between the set of the "adapted non-terminals" (denoted $\mathcal{A}$) and the set of non-adapted non-terminals (which are $\mathcal{N} \setminus \mathcal{A}$). For the non-adapted non-terminals, C_a refers only to the probabilistic identity mapping, that maps G_a to a distribution that is set on G_a with probability 1.

8.4.1 PITMAN–YOR ADAPTOR GRAMMARS

A Pitman–Yor Adaptor Grammar (PYAG) is a statistical model that defines a distribution over phrase-structure tree distributions that satisfy the relationships in Equations 8.11–8.12 while using a Pitman–Yor process for C_a with strength parameters s_a and discount parameters d_a for $a \in \mathcal{N}$. The set of adapted nonterminals $\mathcal{A}$ is assumed to be "non-recursive" in the sense that a nonterminal $a \in \mathcal{A}$ can never appear in a derivation with an ancestor being an a as well. If these cases are not avoided, a PYAG can be ill-defined (see exercises).

A draw from a PYAG defines a distribution $H_S(Z)$ over phrase-structure trees. The support of $H_S(Z)$ (i.e., the phrase-structure trees with non-zero probability) is subsumed by the tree language of the underlying context-free grammar. The generative model of a PYAG for generating $z^{(1)}, \ldots, z^{(n)}$, a set of phrase-structure trees, is given in generative story 8.2.

Without loss of generality, we can actually assume that all nonterminals are adapted, i.e., $\mathcal{A} = \mathcal{N}$, since the Pitman–Yor process with a discount parameter $d_a = 1$ reduces to the identity function. Note the added step of generating PCFG parameters from the Dirichlet distribution in generative story 8.2. This step appears in the original formulation of PYAG from Johnson et al. (2007b), to make the model fully Bayesian. The distribution H_S is itself a random variable, and therefore can be marginalized out. In this manner, one can reveal the distribution that a PYAG induces directly on phrase-structure trees, similarly to the way PCFGs do.

It is possible to write down an analytic expression that specifies the distribution that an adaptor grammar defines on Z (a set of n phrase-structure trees). However, understanding adaptor grammars in terms of the Chinese restaurant process is more revealing and easier to grasp, so we begin first by describing the generative process for generating a phrase-structure tree $z^{(i)}$ based on the previous trees $z^{(1)}, \ldots, z^{(i-1)}$.

Once the PCFG parameters θ are drawn, phrase-structure trees can be consecutively generated from

$$p\left(Z^{(i)} | z^{(1)}, \ldots, z^{(i-1)}, s, d, \theta\right). \tag{8.13}$$

Constants: Context-free grammar, adaptors C_a for $a \in \mathcal{N}$
Hyperparameters: $\alpha > 0$, $s_a > 0$ strength parameters and discount parameters $d_a, a \in \mathcal{A}$
Latent variables: θ_a for $a \in \mathcal{N}$, H_a for $a \in \mathcal{A}$, $Z^{(1)}, \ldots, Z^{(n)}$ grammar derivations
Observed variables: $X^{(1)}, \ldots, X^{(n)}$ strings

- -

- Generate PCFG parameters $\theta \sim \text{Dirichlet}(\alpha)$ for the underlying CFG (see Equation 8.9).

- Generate H_S from the following PYAG Equations 8.11–8.12 with C_a being a Pitman-Yor process with strength parameter s_a and discount parameter d_a for $a \in \mathcal{A}$ (for $a \in \mathcal{N} \setminus \mathcal{A}$, C_a is the probabilistic identity mapping).

- For $i \in \{1, \ldots, n\}$, generate $z^{(i)} \sim H_S$.

- For $i \in \{1, \ldots, n\}$, set $x^{(i)} = \text{yield}(z^{(i)})$.

Generative Story 8.2: The generative story of the Pitman-Yor adaptor grammar.

Trees from Equation 8.13 are generated top-down beginning with the start symbol S. Any non-adapted nonterminal $a \in \mathcal{N} \setminus \mathcal{A}$ is expanded by drawing a rule from $\mathcal{R}_a$. There are two ways to expand $a \in \mathcal{A}$.

- With probability $(n_z - d_a)/(n_a + s_a)$ we expand a to subtree z (a tree rooted at a with a yield in $\mathcal{T}^*$), where n_z is the number of times the tree z was previously generated as a subtree in $z^{(1)}, \ldots, z^{(i-1)}$ and n_a is the total number of subtrees (tokens) previously generated with their root being a.

- With probability $(s_a + k_a d_a)/(n_a + s_a)$, a is expanded as in a PCFG by a draw from θ_a over $\mathcal{R}_a$, where k_a is the number of subtrees (types) previously generated with root a in $z^{(1)}, \ldots, z^{(i-1)}$.

The counts n_z, n_a and k_a are all functions of the previously generated phrase-structure trees $z^{(1)}, \ldots, z^{(n)}$.

The state of an adaptor grammar, i.e., an assignment to all latent structures, can be described using a set of *analyses*. Assume that we use an adaptor grammar to draw $x^{(1)}, \ldots, x^{(n)}$ and their corresponding phrase-structure trees $z^{(1)}, \ldots, z^{(n)}$. In addition, denote by $z(a)$ the list of subtrees that were generated by the adaptor grammar and are headed by nonterminal a. This means that $z(a) = ((z(a))^{(1)}, \ldots, (z(a))^{(k_a)})$ with:

$$\sum_{i=1}^{k_a} n_{z(a)^{(i)}} = n_a.$$

Adaptor grammars can be viewed as defining a distribution over a set of *analyses*. An analysis u is a pair (z, ℓ) where z is a phrase structure tree and ℓ is a function. Let Nodes(z) be the set of nodes in the phrase-structure z. We define $\ell \in \text{Nodes}(z) \rightarrow \mathbb{N}$ to be the following. For any $q \in \text{Nodes}(z)$, $l(q)$, let a be the nonterminal at node q. Then $\ell(q)$ is the index in $z(a)$ of the subtree q dominates. If q dominates the subtree z', then this means that $z' = z(a)^{(\ell(q))}$.

Note that $z(a)$ for $a \in \mathcal{N}$ is a deterministic function of $u^{(1)}, \ldots, u^{(n)}$. Therefore, the distribution that an adaptor grammar defines over analyses can now be readily defined in terms of $u = (u^{(1)}, \ldots, u^{(n)})$ where the phrase structure in $u^{(i)}$ corresponds to the tree $z^{(i)}$. More specifically, it holds:

$$p(u|s, d, \alpha) = \prod_{a \in \mathcal{N}} \left(\frac{B(\alpha_a + f(z(a)))}{B(\alpha_a)} \right) \times \text{PY} \left(m(a)|s_a, d_a \right), \tag{8.14}$$

with $f(z(a))$ being a vector indexed by the rules in the grammar that have a on the left-hand side, and $f_{a \rightarrow \beta}(z(a))$ denoting the total count of $a \rightarrow \beta$ in all subtrees in the list $z(a)$. In addition, $m(a)$ is a vector of the same length as $z(a)$, such that $m_i(a) = n_{z(a)^{(i)}}$. Therefore, $m(a)$ is a vector of integers, and the term $\text{PY}(m(a)|s_a, d_a)$ is computed according to the distribution of the Pitman-Yor process, defined in Equation 7.8 and repeated here:

$$\text{PY} \left(m(a)|s_a, d_a \right) = \frac{\prod_{k=1}^{k_a} \left((d_a(k-1) + s_a) \times \prod_{j=1}^{m_k(a)-1} (j - d_a) \right)}{\prod_{i=0}^{n_a-1} (i + s_a)}.$$

The function $B(y)$ is defined for a vector of integers y as (see also Equation 2.3):

$$B(y) = \frac{\Gamma \left(\sum_{i=1}^{|y|} y_i \right)}{\prod_{i=1}^{|y|} \Gamma(y_i)}.$$

8.4.2   STICK-BREAKING VIEW OF PYAG

Analogously to the stick-breaking process representation for the Pitman–Yor process (or the Dirichlet process), there is a stick-breaking representation for adaptor grammars (Cohen et al., 2010).

This stick-breaking process for describing adaptor grammars was developed to enable variational inference. This variational inference algorithm is based on the truncated stick-breaking variational inference algorithm for the Dirichlet process that was developed by Blei and Jordan (2004). See the next section for more details.

The generative process that the stick-breaking process for adaptor grammars follows is described in generative story 8.3.

Constants: Context-free grammar
Hyperparameters: $\alpha > 0$, $s_a > 0$ strength parameters and discount parameters d_a, $a \in \mathcal{A}$
Latent variables: π_a for $a \in \mathcal{A}$ infinite multinomials, θ_a for $a \in \mathcal{N}$, $Z^{(1)}, \dots, Z^{(n)}$ grammar derivations, $Z_{a,i}$ for $a \in \mathcal{A}$ and $i \in \mathbb{N}$
Observed variables: $X^{(1)}, \dots, X^{(n)}$ strings

- -

- For each $a \in \mathcal{A}$, draw $\theta_a \sim \text{Dirichlet}(\alpha_a)$.

- For all $a \in \mathcal{A}$, define G_a as follows:

  - Draw $\pi_a \mid s_a, d_a \sim \text{GEM}(s_a, d_a)$.
  - For $i \in \{1, \dots\}$, grow a tree $z_{a,i}$ as follows:
    - Draw $a \to b_1 \dots b_m$ from $\mathcal{R}_a$.
    - $z_{a,i} = $

    - While yield$(z_{a,i})$ has nonterminals:
      - Choose an unexpanded nonterminal b from the yield of $z_{a,i}$.
      - If $b \in \mathcal{A}$, expand b according to G_b (defined on previous iterations of step 2).
      - If $b \in \mathcal{N} \setminus \mathcal{A}$, expand b with a rule from $\mathcal{R}_b$ according to Multinomial(θ_B).
  - For $i \in \{1, \dots\}$, define $G_a(z_{a,i}) = \pi_{a,i}$

- For $i \in \{1, \dots, n\}$ draw z_i as follows:

  - If $S \in \mathcal{A}$, draw $z^{(i)} \mid G_S \sim G_S$.
  - If $S \notin \mathcal{A}$, draw $z^{(i)}$ as in line 4.

- Set $x^{(i)} = \text{yield}(z^{(i)})$ for $i \in \{1, \dots, n\}$.

Generative Story 8.3: The generative story for adaptor grammars with the stick-breaking representation.

8.4.3   INFERENCE WITH PYAG

This section discusses the two main approaches for the following inference schemes with adaptor grammars: sampling and variational inference.

MCMC Inference   Consider the distribution defined over analyses as defined in Equation 8.14. The inference usually considered with adaptor grammars is one such that it infers parse trees (phrase-structure trees) for a given set of strings $x = (x^{(1)}, \ldots, x^{(n)})$.

The distribution over phrase structure trees can be derived from the distribution over analyses by marginalizing out the phrase-structure trees. More specifically, we are interested in $p(Z|x, s, d, \alpha)$. However, computing this posterior is intractable.

In order to perform inference, Johnson et al. (2007b) suggest using a compononent-wise Metropolis–Hastings algorithm. They first specify how to create a static PCFG, a snapshot of the adaptor grammar, based on a specific state of the adaptor grammar. This snapshot grammar includes all rules in the underlying context-free grammar and rules that rewrite a nonterminal directly to a string, corresponding to subtrees that appear in the history derivation vectors $z(a)$ for $a \in \mathcal{N}$. All of these rules are assigned probabilities according to the following estimate:

$$\theta'_{a \to \beta} = \left(\frac{k_a d_a + s_a}{n_a + d_a} \right) \left(\frac{f_{a \to \beta}(z(a)) + \alpha_{a \to \beta}}{k_a + \sum_{a \to \beta \in \mathcal{R}_a} \alpha_{a \to \beta}} \right) + \sum_{i : \text{yield}(z(a)^{(i)}) = \beta} \frac{n_{z(a)^{(i)}} - s_a}{n_a + d_a}. \quad (8.15)$$

The first two multiplied terms are responsible for selecting a grammar rule from the underlying context-free grammar. The term to the right of the sum is the MAP estimate of the rules added to the snapshot grammar, in the form of a nonterminal rewriting to a string.

This snapshot grammar is created, and then used with a Metropolis–Hastings algorithm, such that the proposal distribution is based on the snapshot grammar with the θ' estimates from Equation 8.15 (i.e., we use the snapshot grammar to define a distribution over the analyses, conditioning on the strings in the corpus). The target distribution is the one specified in Equation 8.14. Note that the real target distribution needs a normalization constant, corresponding to the probability of the strings themselves according to the adaptor grammar, but this constant is canceled in the MH algorithm, when calculating the probability of rejecting or accepting the update.

Sampling with their MH algorithm is component-wise—each analysis $u^{(i)}$ is sampled based on the snapshot grammar. At this point, the acceptance ratio is calculated, and if the MH sampler decides to accept this sample for $u^{(i)}$, the state of the sampler is updated, and the snapshot grammar is re-calculated.

Variational Inference   Cohen et al. (2010) describe a variational inference algorithm based on the stick-breaking representation for adaptor grammars described in Section 8.4.2. The main idea in their variational inference algorithm is similar to the idea that is used for variational inference algorithms with the Dirichlet process mixture (see Section 7.2). Each nonparametric stick

Constants: n, number of samples
Hyperparameters: $\alpha \geq 0, \alpha^{\text{type}} \geq 0, \alpha^{\text{emission}} \geq 0, \alpha^{\text{binary}} \geq 0$ concentration parameters
Parameters: $\beta, \theta_k^{\text{type}}, \theta_k^{\text{emission}}, \theta_k^{\text{binary}}$—distributions over a discrete of finite set
Latent variables: $Z^{(1)}, \ldots, Z^{(n)}$
Observed variables: $X^{(1)}, \ldots, X^{(n)}$

- -

- Draw β, an infinite column vector, from the GEM distribution with hyperparameter α. The infinite vector β indices correspond to nonterminal symbols in the grammar.

- For each grammar symbol $k \in \{1, 2, \ldots\}$

  - Draw $\theta_k^{\text{type}} \sim \text{Dirichlet}(\alpha^{\text{type}})$.
  - Draw $\theta_k^{\text{emission}} \sim \text{Dirichlet}(\alpha^{\text{emission}})$.
  - Draw $\theta_k^{\text{binary}} \sim \text{DP}(\alpha^{\text{binary}}, \beta\beta^\top)$.

- For $i \in \{1, \ldots, n\}$ draw a tree $z^{(i)}$ (and a string $x^{(i)}$) as follows:

  - While the yield of $z^{(i)}$ is not all terminal symbols:
    - Pick an unexpanded node in $z^{(i)}$. Denote its nonterminal by k.
    - Draw a rule type from θ_k^{type}
    - If the rule type is "emission," expand this node by drawing a rule from $\theta_k^{\text{emission}}$.
    - If the rule type is "binary," expand this node by drawing a rule from θ_k^{binary}.
  - Set $x^{(i)}$ to be the yield of the fully expanded $z^{(i)}$.

Generative Story 8.4: The generative story for the HDP-PCFG model.

for each adapted nonterminal (and the corresponding strength and concentration parameters) is associated with a variational distribution, which is a truncated stick—i.e., it is a distribution that follows a finite version of the GEM distribution (see Equation 7.1).

One major advantage of the truncated stick-breaking variational inference algorithm for adaptor grammars over MCMC inference is that its E-step can be parallelized. On the other hand, its major disadvantage is the need to select a fixed subset of strings for each adapted nonterminal to which the variational distributions may assign non-zero probability to. A specific subset of strings, for a specific adapted nonterminal is selected from the set of strings that can be the yield of a subtree dominated by that nonterminal. Cohen et al. use heuristics in order to select such subset for each adapted nonterminal.

Online and Hybrid Methods   Zhai et al. (2014) have developed an inference algorithm for adaptor grammars that combines MCMC inference and variational inference. The inference algorithm in this case is an online algorithm. The training data is processed in mini-batches. At each mini-batch processing step, the algorithm updates the posterior so that it reflects the information in the new data. During this update, MCMC inference is used to estimate the sufficient statistics that are needed in order to make an update to the current posterior.

The main motivation behind such an inference algorithm, and more generally online algorithms, is the ability to process an ongoing stream of data, without the need to either iteratively go through the data several times, or keep it all in memory.

8.5   HIERARCHICAL DIRICHLET PROCESS PCFGS (HDP-PCFGS)

With parametric priors on PCFGs, such as the one described in Section 8.3.1, the symbolic grammar is fixed, and as a consequence, the number of nonterminals in the grammar is fixed as well. Liang et al. (2007) introduced a PCFG model that overcomes this limitation by using nonparametric Bayesian modeling. Their goal is to automatically decide, through Bayesian nonparameteric modeling, on the number of nonterminals that is needed to accurately represent the data.

Their model, which is based on the hierarchical Dirichlet process (see Chapter 7), lets the number of syntactic categories grow as more trees are observed, and the prior over the grammar includes an infinite (countable) number of nonterminals. The parameters of the model, θ, are an infinite vector with the following subvectors (k in the following varies over an infinite set of nonterminals).

- θ_k^{type} for $k \in \{1, \ldots\}$ – for each k, a multinomial of fixed length, which gives the distribution over "rule types" that are available in the grammar for nonterminal k. Since Liang et al.'s experiment with grammars in Chomsky normal form, the available rule types are "emission" and "binary" for preterminal rules and binary rules. Therefore, the size of this multinomial for HDP-PCFGs is 2.

- $\theta_k^{\text{emission}}$ for $k \in \{1, \ldots\}$ – for each k, this is a multinomial distribution over the terminal symbols in the grammar. It corresponds to rule probabilities for rewriting a nonterminal to a word.

- θ_k^{binary} for $k \in \{1, \ldots\}$ – this is an *infinite* multinomial distribution over pairs of nonterminals. It can therefore also be seen as a doubly-infinite matrix indexed by pairs of nonterminals. Each $\theta_{k,k_1,k_2}^{\text{binary}}$ gives the probability of a binary rule that rewrites a nonterminal k to the pair of nonterminals k_1 and k_2 on the right-hand side.

The generative story of their model (HDP-PCFG) is given in generative story 8.4. Note the prior distribution for binary rule probabilities, which is denoted by $\text{DP}(\alpha^{\text{binary}}, \beta\beta^\top)$. The vector β is an infinite vector, with all positive elements that sum to one. Therefore, $\beta\beta^\top$ is a doubly-infinite matrix with coordinate k, k' being $\beta_k\beta_{k'}$, such that the sum over all elements in this matrix is 1 as well. It can be viewed as a distribution over the right-hand sides of binary rules. A draw from the DP prior that uses $\beta\beta^\top$ as a base distribution is a doubly-infinite matrix of the same form (in which all elements sum to 1), and this matrix corresponds to all possible binary rule expansions of pairs of nonterminals from the countable set of nonterminals available in β.

The generative process above is actually missing an essential detail about the generation of the top root symbol. Liang et al. did not address this issue in their model description, but it can be easily overcome by adding an additional initial step that draws a root nonterminal for the tree from a distribution generated from $\mathrm{DP}(\alpha^{\mathrm{root}}, \beta)$.

The HDP-PCFG model is a hierarchical Dirichlet process model because of the Dirichlet process draw of binary rules on top of the draw of β from the GEM distribution. The draw of β provides the basic set of nonterminals and is a building block in constructing the rule probabilities for binary rules.

This model demonstrates again the importance of "atom sharing" with the hierarchical Dirichlet process (see Section 7.3). The top draw from the GEM distribution of a countable set of atoms ensures that there is a non-zero probability for the nonterminals to be shared in the binary rules.

Liang et al. developed an inference algorithm for their HDP-PCFG model that is based on the truncated stick-breaking representation that Blei and Jordan (2004) developed for the goal of performing inference with a Dirichlet process mixture model. Liang's et al. algorithm is based on mean-field variational inference, such that the binary rule parameters, the emission parameters, the rule type parameters (for a finite, truncated, subset of symbol $k \in \{1, \ldots K\}$), the distribution over $Z^{(i)}$ and the distribution over β are factorized: each component above has its own variational distribution.

8.5.1 EXTENSIONS TO THE HDP-PCFG MODEL

PCFGs, by themselves, are rather weak models for modeling language, or its syntax, to be more precise. Reading a PCFG grammar off a treebank and using it as it is (using any kind of reasonable estimation technique, Bayesian or frequentist), leads to rather poor results.

Indeed, it has been noted in the literature that PCFGs by themselves can be too weak to model syntax in natural language. One of the biggest problems is that the syntactic categories that appear in various treebanks, by themselves, do not provide sufficient contextual information on their own for the derivation steps. This is true whenever a grammar is extracted from a treebank by considering a node and its immediate children. To remedy this, one can refine the syntactic categories in this extracted grammar with latent states (Cohen, 2017, Matsuzaki et al., 2005, Prescher, 2005). This means that each nonterminal in the grammar is indexed with an integer that denotes its state—and this state is never observed.

In the frequentist use of L-PCFGs, the goal of the learner is to estimate the parameters of this latent-variable PCFG, without ever observing the latent states. The statistical parsing model itself is still a PCFG, but now the data is incomplete, because it does not include the additional information about the latent states of each syntactic node. This changes the expressive power of a vanilla PCFG model extracted from the treebank, since now the probability of each derivation is a sum-of-products of possible derivations—the derivations now include latent states, and the sum is taken with respect to all possible combinations of latent states for that derivation. With a vanilla PCFG, the probability of a derivation is just the product of the rules that appear in that derivation.

However, the problem of choosing the number of latent states associated with each non-terminal, though, is not trivial. Previous work only attempted to use a fixed number of states, and later estimation algorithms for latent-variable PCFGs used techniques such as coarse-to-fine EM (Petrov et al., 2006) and other automatic splitting techniques (Dreyer and Eisner, 2006), threshold singular values using spectral methods (Cohen and Collins, 2014, Cohen et al., 2013) and other estimation algorithms based on the method of moments (Cohen et al., 2014).

In the Bayesian context, Liang et al. extended the HDP-PCFG model to a grammar refinement model, where Bayesian nonparametrics help choose the number of latent states to refine the nonterminals in a PCFG. Instead of having an infinite set of nonterminals that are never observed, they designed a model like the HDP-PCFG extending a fixed set of known nonterminals and binary rules, such that an infinite set of atoms refines these nonterminals and rules.

Let $\mathcal{N}$ be a fixed set of nonterminals. Then, the refinement extension of the HDP-PCFG draws distributions of the following form.

- For each nonterminal $a \in \mathcal{N}$, an infinite multinomial β_a is drawn from a GEM distribution.

- For each nonterminal $a \in \mathcal{N}$ and $k \in \{1, 2, \ldots\}$, an infinite multinomial $\theta_{a,k}^{\text{emission}}$ is drawn. The index k ranges over the nonterminal refinements.

- For each rule $a \to b \ c$ and $k \in \{1, 2, \ldots\}$, a doubly-infinite matrix $\theta_{a \to b \ c, k}^{\text{binary}}$ is drawn from a Dirichlet process with $\beta_b \beta_c^\top$ being the base distribution.

The parameters above are very similar to the parameters drawn for the vanilla HDP-PCFG, only they are indexed with nonterminals from the fixed set, or a rule from the fixed set of rules. In addition, the authors also add parameters for unary rules.

8.6   DEPENDENCY GRAMMARS

Dependency grammar (Tesnière, 1959, Tesnière et al., 2015) refers to linguistic theories that describe syntax using directed trees (in the graph theoretic sense). In these trees, words are

Figure 8.3: A dependency tree with latent states. The first line denotes the latent states and the second line denotes the words generated from these latent states.

vertices and edges that denote syntactic relationships. For the use of dependency grammar and dependency parsing in natural language processing, see Kübler et al. (2009).

8.6.1   STATE-SPLIT NONPARAMETRIC DEPENDENCY MODELS

Finkel et al. (2007) devised several nonparametric Bayesian models, based on the hierarchical Dirichlet process, for dependency trees. At the core of their models is the idea to generate a dependency tree with the nodes being latent states originating in a set of atoms from a Dirichlet process. Each such atom is a distribution over words, or observations. Once a latent state has been generated, it then generates its observations.

Let Z denote a random variable that ranges over dependency trees, such that z_i denotes the state of node i in the tree. These states are taken from some discrete set. In addition, let X denote the observations generated by each state, ranging over some vocabulary. Then, x_i denotes the observation generated by state z_i. The list of children of a node i is denoted by $c(i)$, and $Z_{c(i)}$ denotes a vector of latent states ranging over the children of node i. A graphical example of this formulation of dependency trees is given in Figure 8.3. In this figure, $Z_{c(3)} = (1, 2, 1)$ and $c(2) = (1)$. If i is a leaf node, then $c(i) = \emptyset$, therefore, $c(1) = c(4) = c(6) = \emptyset$. (The nodes are numbered according to their order in the sentence, i.e., the node 1 is "The," node 2 is "king," node 3 is "welcomed" and so on.)

Finkel et al. suggests three progressively advanced models for generating $z^{(1)}, \ldots, z^{(n)}$ and their corresponding $x^{(1)}, \ldots, x^{(n)}$ given the model parameters. The models that Finkel et al. suggest assume knowledge of the actual tree structure. The goal of their models is to populate this tree structure with latent states and observations. Their models are based on a probabilistic decomposition of a top-down generation of the latent states, each time generating the children states of a node conditioned on the parent state. If node 1 is the root of Z, a dependency tree with m nodes, then:

$$p(z, x) = p(z_1) \times \left(\prod_{i:c(i) \neq \emptyset} p(z_{c(i)}|z_i) \right) \times \left(\prod_{i=1}^{m} p(x_i|z_i) \right). \tag{8.16}$$

With their first model, "independent children," it holds that:

$$p\left(z_{c(i)}|z_i\right) = \prod_{j \in c(i)} p\left(z_j|z_i\right). \tag{8.17}$$

The independent children model is not realistic for modeling natural language, because it assumes independence assumptions that are too strong (all siblings are conditionally independent given the parent). For this reason, Finkel et al. suggest two additional models. In their second model, "Markov children," a child node is assumed to be conditionally independent of the rest of the children given the parent and its sibling. More specifically, if $c(i) = (j_1, \ldots, j_r)$, then:

$$p\left(z_{c(i)}|z_i\right) = p\left(z_{j_1}|z_i\right) \times \left(\prod_{k=2}^{r} p\left(z_{j_k}|z_{j_{k-1}}, z_i\right)\right). \tag{8.18}$$

Finkel et al. do not specify in which order they generate the children, which is necessary to know to complete the model. Their last model, "simultaeneous children," assumes that all children are generated as one block of nodes. This means that $p(z_{c(i)}|z_i)$ is not decomposed.

The main idea in Finkel's et al. model is to use nonparametric distributions for Z_i. The latent states are assumed to obtain an integer value $\{1, 2, \ldots\}$. The prior over the latent state distributions is constructed using the hierarchical Dirichlet process (see Section 7.3).

For the independent children model, the generative process is the following. First, a basic distribution over the integers is drawn from $\text{GEM}(s_0)$, where s_0 is a concentration parameter. Then, for each $k \in \{1, 2, \ldots\}$, a distribution $\pi_k \sim \text{DP}(\pi, s_1)$ is drawn. The distributions π_k (for $k \geq 2$) are used for the conditional distributions $p(Z_j|Z_i)$ in Equation 8.17—i.e., $p(z_j|Z_i = k) = \pi_{k,z_j}$. (Note that π_1 is used for the distribution $p(Z_1)$ as it appears in Equation 8.16.) In addition, for generating the observations X, a multinomial distribution ϕ_k is generated from a Dirichlet distribution. Then the observation distributions in Equation 8.16 are set such that $p(x_i|Z_i = k) = \phi_{k,x_i}$.

For their simultaneous children model, Finkel et al. draw a distribution over the latent states for all children from $\text{DP}(s_2, G_0)$, where G_0 is defined to be the independent children distribution from 8.17 drawn from the prior described above. This draw defines $p(Z_{c(i)}|Z_i)$ for each node i in the dependency tree. According to Finkel et al., the use of the independent children distribution as a base distribution for the simultaneous children distribution promotes consistency—if a certain sequence of children states has high probability, then similar sequences of latent states (i.e., sequences that overlap with the high probability sequence) will also have high probability.

The prior over the latent state distributions for the Markov children model (Equation 8.18) makes similar use of the hierarchical Dirichlet process. With this model, $\pi_{k\ell}$ are generated, corresponding to distributions over latent states conditioning on a pair of latent states, a parent and a sibling, with the parent being assigned to latent state k and the sibling being assigned to latent state ℓ. The observations are handled identically to the independent children model.

8.7 SYNCHRONOUS GRAMMARS

The term "synchronous grammars" broadly refers to grammars that define multiple-string languages (languages which are sets of tuples of strings), most commonly two languages. Usually this means that such grammars are defined over two sets of vocabularies, $\mathcal{T}_1$ and $\mathcal{T}_2$ (each for a different language, for example French and English), and their grammar rules generate a *synchronous* derivation: a derivation that can be decomposed into two parse trees over two strings in the languages. Different parts of the parse trees are aligned to each other. Naturally, there are probabilistic extensions to synchronous grammars.

The most common type of probabilistic synchronous grammars in NLP is synchronous PCFGs. The rules in such a grammar have a fixed nonterminal set $\mathcal{N}$, and rules of the form $a \rightarrow \langle \alpha, \beta \rangle$ where $a \in \mathcal{N}$ and $\alpha \in (\mathcal{N} \cup \mathcal{T}_1)^*$ and $\beta \in (\mathcal{N} \cup \mathcal{T}_2)^*$. The right-hand side α corresponds to one language while β corresponds to the other. In addition, there is an alignment function for each rule that maps between nonterminals in α and nonterminals in β. Different restrictions on α and β coupled with restrictions on the alignments yield different families of synchronous PCFGs. For example, with inversion-transduction grammars (Wu, 1997), $\alpha = \alpha_1 \cdots \alpha_m$ is a string over the nonterminals and vocabulary, and β is either the same string with elements from $\mathcal{T}_1$ in α replaced with elements from $\mathcal{T}_2$ or the α reversed (α reversed is $\alpha_m \cdots \alpha_1$) with elements from $\mathcal{T}_1$ replaced with elements from $\mathcal{T}_2$. The identical nonterminals in α and β are aligned to each other.

The natural application for synchronous grammars is machine translation. Synchronous grammars are typically used for *syntax-based machine translation*, in which the nonterminals carry some syntactic interpretation (such as denoting noun phrases or verb phrases), and hierarchical phrase-based translation, in which the nonterminals usually do not have a syntactic interpretation. For more information about synchronous grammars and their relation to machine translation, see Williams et al. (2016). Much of the work about synchronous grammars in a Bayesian context was done with the aim of learning the grammar rules themselves (synchronous grammar induction) for machine translation, usually through nonparametric Bayesian modeling. This includes work by Blunsom et al. (2009b), Blunsom et al. (2009a), Neubig et al. (2011), Sankaran et al. (2011) and Levenberg et al. (2012). Yamangil and Shieber (2010) made use of synchronous grammar induction algorithms for the problem of sentence compression. Earlier work that learns the grammar rules of a synchronous grammar (for phrase-based machine translation) without necessarily using nonparametric modeling includes work by Zhang et al. (2008).

There are extensions of other Bayesian grammars to the synchronous setting. For example, Huang et al. (2011) extended adaptor grammars (Section 8.4) to synchronous adaptor grammars, and used them to solve a transliteration problem. The grammar they used maps syllables in one language to the other, with certain nonterminals being adapted to capture groups of syllables that are transliterated to other groups of syllables in the target language.

8.8   MULTILINGUAL LEARNING

This chapter focuses on structured models where the underlying backbone model is a well-known formalism or grammar, such as a hidden Markov model or a probabilistic context-free grammar. However, over the years, many researchers have developed creative generative models to solve specific problems in natural language processing. The basic building blocks for these models are a set of probability distributions such as the multinomial distribution (Chapter 3) or the Dirichlet distribution. These blocks are assembled together, just like Lego pieces, into one model. In this section, we provide an example for one such thread of models aimed at multilingual learning.

Multilingual learning is a broad umbrella term for the use of language data in multiple languages to estimate models for each of the languages that can be used to solve problems in NLP, such as parsing or part-of-speech tagging. Multilingual learning usually exploits some weak or strong alignment between the corpora in the different languages.

8.8.1   PART-OF-SPEECH TAGGING

One of the early uses of Bayesian learning in the context of multilingual learning was introduced by Snyder et al. (2008). The model Snyder et al. introduced learns bilingual part-of-speech tag models in an unsupervised manner.

The generative story for the bilingual POS tagging model is described in generative story 8.5. As expected in a Bayesian context, the generative story starts by drawing the parameters of the model from a prior distribution—the emission and transition parameters. The emission parameters are multinomial distributions over the set of words in each language that condition on a specific POS tag. The transition parameters generate new tags based on previous ones. The tag generation is based on an alignment between the sentences in the two languages.[3] The main novelty that the model of Snyder et al. introduces is based on the idea that the POS tags of two aligned words provide information about each other. Whenever two words are aligned in the two sentences, their POS tags are coupled through a "coupling distribution" ω.

In principle, this model can also be used in a frequentist setting, and estimated with an algorithm such as the expectation-maximization algorithm (Appendix A). However, there are several advantages to using a Bayesian model in this setup. First, all parameters for the different languages are drawn from the same prior distribution. This means that this prior distribution *ties* all of these languages together through one universal distribution. This prior distribution itself is parametrized, and this hyperparameter can be thought of as describing a property of all languages used in the data (such as the level of the sparsity in the transition and emission parameters).

---

[3]The alignments are assumed to be fixed and observed. The alignments are generated using the machine translation tool GIZA++ (Och and Ney, 2003).

Hyperparameters: $\alpha_0, \alpha_1, \alpha_0', \alpha_1', \alpha_\omega > 0$
Constants: N and N', lengths of sentences
Parameters: $\phi_t \in \mathbb{R}^{|V|}$, $\theta_t \in \mathbb{R}^{|T|}$ for $t \in T$, $\phi_t' \in \mathbb{R}^{|V'|}$, $\theta_t' \in \mathbb{R}^{|T'|}$ for $t \in T'$, ω
Latent variables: $y_1, \ldots, y_N \in T$, $y_1', \ldots, y_{N'}' \in T'$ POS tags for two languages
Observed variables: $x_1, \ldots, x_N \in V$, $x_1', \ldots, x_{N'}' \in V'$, words for first and second language, a alignment between words

---

- (First language) Draw transition multinomial distribution over tags ϕ_t for each $t \in T$ from a Dirichlet distribution with hyperparameter α_0.

- (First language) Draw emission multinomial distribution over vocabulary θ_t for each $t \in T$ from a Dirichlet distribution with hyperparameter α_1.

- (Second language) Draw transition multinomial distribution over tags ϕ_t' for each $t \in T'$ from a Dirichlet distribution with hyperparameter α_0'.

- (Second language) Draw emission multinomial distribution over vocabulary θ_t' for each $t \in T'$ from a Dirichlet distribution with hyperparameter α_1'.

- Draw a multinomial distribution ω over $T \times T'$ from a Dirichlet distribution

- Define the distribution for four tags $y, y_0 \in T$ and $y', y_0' \in T'$

$$p(y, y' | y_0, y_0') \propto \phi_{y_0,y} \phi_{y_0',y'}' \omega_{y,y'}.$$

- Let $a_0 = \{i \mid \neg \exists j (i,j) \in a\}$ be the unaligned indices in a for the first language

- Let $a_0' = \{j \mid \neg \exists i (i,j) \in a\}$ be the unaligned indices in a for the second language

- Draw tags $y_1, \ldots, y_N$ and $y_1', \ldots, y_{N'}'$ from the distribution

$$p(y_1, \ldots, y_N, y_1', \ldots, y_{N'}') = \prod_{i \in a_0} \phi_{y_{i-1},y_i} \prod_{j \in a_0'} \phi_{y_{j-1}',y_j'} \prod_{(i,j) \in a} p(y_i, y_j' \mid y_{i-1}, y_{j-1}').$$

- (First language) For each $i \in [N]$, emit a word x_i from the multinomial θ_{y_i}.

- (Second language) For each $j \in [N']$, emit a word x_j' from the multinomial $\theta_{y_j'}$.

Generative Story 8.5: *Continues.*

Generative Story 8.5: *Continued.* The generative story for the bilingual part-of-speech tagging model of Snyder et al. The alignment a is a set of pairs of indices that align a word in one language to a word in the other language. The alignment does not have to be fully specified (i.e., words in both languages can be unaligned). Each word is aligned to at most one word. The set of words (vocabulary) in each language is V and V', respectively. The set of part-of-speech tags in each language is T and T', respectively. The generative story describes a draw for a single pair of sentences. The parameters ϕ_t, θ_t, θ'_t and ϕ'_t are also latent variables, and integrated out during inference.

The inference mechanism that Snyder et al. used to sample POS tags and words based on the POS tags is reminiscent of hidden Markov models (HMMs). The model of Snyder et al. relies on an alignment to generate pairs of tags together, but the information these tags condition on is the same type of information bigram HMMs use—the previous tags before them in the sequence.

Snyder et al. (2009b) further extended their model to introduce a fully multilingual model: a model for POS tagging that models more than two languages. They do so by introducing a new ingredient into their model—superlingual tags which are coarse tags that are presupposed to be common to all languages, but are latent. These superlingual tags are generated from a nonparametric model (Chapter 7).

8.8.2   GRAMMAR INDUCTION

The problem of grammar induction in NLP is an umbrella term for the unsupervised learning of syntax in language in various forms. It can refer to the learning of an actual grammar with its rules (such as a context-free grammar), the estimation of the parameters of an existing grammar (production probabilities) from strings only, or to the induction of parse trees from a set of strings, not necessarily with an explicit grammar formalism.

In the context of multilingual learning, Snyder et al. (2009a) described a Bayesian model for multilingual grammar induction. Their model relies on a tree-edit model that aligns a pair of trees (corresponding to parse trees) for two sentences in two languages (translations of each other). This tree-edit model (also known as unordered tree alignment by Jiang et al. (1995)) helps to capture cross-lingual syntactic regularities.

The generative story for their model is a generalization of the constituent-context model (CCM) of Klein and Manning (2004). The main novelty is the multilingual (or bilingual, to be more precise) setup. Once the model parameters are drawn, the model works by drawing, a pair of aligned parse trees, one for each language, from a uniform distribution. Next begins the phase of sentence-pair generation, in which *constituents, distituents, constituent contexts* and *distituent contexts* are drawn. These elements are substrings of the observed part-of-speech tag sequences observed in the data (on which the grammar induction process is based) in various forms. Constituents, for example, are substrings that are dominated by some node in a parse tree. Any substring that is not a constituent is a distituent.

The model that Snyder et al. introduce inherits, in a Bayesian context, a property that the CCM model has: the model *overgenerates* the observed data. This happens because constituents, distituents and contexts all consist of overlapping strings, and as such different parts of the observed data are generated multiple times.

The model of Snyder et al. introduces another novelty when compared to the CCM model. For all aligned nodes in the pair of parse trees generated at the beginning, it generates a *Giza score*. This is a score that generates another part of the observed data (other than the POS tags sequences in the two languages) that is based on word alignments between the paired sentences created using GIZA++ (Och and Ney, 2003). Let a and b be a pair of aligned nodes in the two generated parse trees. Let m be the number of pairs of words (one word for each language) that are aligned according to the GIZA++ alignments and are dominated by the nodes a and b in each tree. In addition, let n be the number of pairs of words in the sentence where one of the words is aligned by a or b, but the other is not dominated by b or a. Then the Giza score is $m - n$.

The Giza scores matches how well a pair of substrings is aligned according to GIZA++. The higher the score is of a given pair of nodes, the more likely they should be aligned. As such, the Giza score generation component in the model is a way to ensure that posterior inference will look for trees that are aligned in a way that matches the Giza score.

8.9 FURTHER READING

The topics that are presented in this chapter are by no means an exhaustive representation of the rich literature that has evolved for grammar learning and estimation in a Bayesian framework. Here we provide some additional highlights of the literature.

Context-free grammars are central to NLP and to syntactic models of language in linguistics and the theory of formal languages. It has long been argued that their expressive power is too limited for representing the syntax of natural languages. The goal of modeling language through a grammar formalism is to identify a grammar that generates a language that is as close as possible to natural language. This means that, on the one hand, it should generate any sentence possible in a language; on the other hand, it should not *overgenerate*—otherwise it is a not a good model for natural language. (A grammar that just generates V^* for some vocabulary V of English words is easy to describe using a few rules, but clearly will overgenerate as a model for English.)

The most prominent property that is present in many languages but that is difficult to represent using context-free grammars is that of crossing or intercalating dependencies, often arising from free word order. This property appears in language in different ways, and to accommodate it, alternative grammar formalisms have been suggested, most notably those often referred to as "mildly context-sensitive" (MCS) grammars.

These formalisms are so-called because if their grammars were represented using production rules like in CFGs, this would require that the left-hand side include some additional context (it would not be just a single nonterminal), without using the full expressive power of constext-sensitive rules. Typically, such rules engender infinite sets of nonterminal symbols, or an infinite set of rules (and therefore the languages they generate are no longer context-free).

Two most common examples of "near context-free" MCS grammar formalisms that have been applied in Bayesian NLP are tree adjoining grammars (Joshi and Schabes, 1997, TAG) and combinatory categorial grammars (Steedman, 2000, CCG). These two formalisms are weakly equivalent (Weir, 1988). This means that any language that can be generated using a TAG can also be represented using a CCG and vice versa. However, they do not have the same strong generative capacity. Each formalism represents a different set of derivations, and it is not always possible to create one-to-one mappings between the derivations of one to the derivations of the other, even when two such grammars generate the same language.

MCS grammars have analogues to the CKY and the inside-outside algorithm, but with increased computational complexity. For the near context-free TAG and CCG, the complexity of the parsing algorithm is $O(n^6)$, where n is the length of the sentence.

The concepts that are relevant to the use of Bayesian statistics with these grammars are similar to those already described in this chapter for CFG. The parameters in the grammar are represented as a set of multinomials, and inference proceeds from there. Some previous studies that used such grammars in a Bayesian context include the use of CCG for Bayesian grammar induction (Bisk and Hockenmaier, 2013, Huang et al., 2012, Kwiatkowski et al., 2012b), the use of TAG for parsing with Bayesian nonparametric methods (Yamangil and Shieber, 2013) and others.

In principle, the concepts that are relevant to the use of Bayesian statistics with these grammars are similar to those already described in this chapter. The parameters in the grammar are represented as a set of multinomials, and inference proceeds from there. Some previous studies that used such grammars in a Bayesian context include the use of CCG for Bayesian grammar induction (Bisk and Hockenmaier, 2013, Huang et al., 2012), the use of TAG for parsing with Bayesian nonparametric methods (Yamangil and Shieber, 2013) and others. Formalisms in the form of automata have also been used in Bayesian NLP, such as for semantic parsing Jones et al. (2012).

In addition, Cohn et al. (2010) developed a Gibbs sampling using a Bayesian nonparametric model to learn tree substitution grammars (TSG). Tree substitution grammars are another type of formalism with a context-free backbone, in which a context-free rule can substitute a nonterminal in a partial derivation with a whole subtree. The yield of these subtrees consists of either nonterminals or terminals. The nonparametric model of Cohn et al. controls the size of the fragments that are learned in the TSG. The expressive power of TSG does not necessarily supersede that of a CFG, but it can be a better model for language since it can generate frequent sub-structures without direct compositionality as in CFGs, leading to better generalization for language data. A similar nonparametric model for inducing TSGs was developed by Post and Gildea (2009) and Post and Gildea (2013).

It is also important to note that the use of grammar models in NLP with Bayesian statistics is not limited to the unsupervised setting. Shindo et al. (2012), for example, developed a symbol refinement tree substitution model with a Bayesian component, and reported state-of-the-art parsing results with their model. Here, symbol refinement refers to latent states that refine the syntactic categories that appear in the treebank, in the style of Matsuzaki et al. (2005), Prescher (2005) and Petrov et al. (2006). See also Section 8.5.1.

Finally, if we are willing to step away from the more "traditional" uses of Bayesian statistics with grammars, then we can find cases in which Bayesian approaches are used to perform inference about the underlying *structure* of the grammar. Stolcke and Omohundro (1994), for example, show how to use a "Bayesian model merging" procedure to learn the structure of a grammar. Their idea is based on the idea of model merging (Omohundro, 1992). Model merging works by building an initial model for each data point available, and then merging these models iteratively, by coalescing substructures from the current set of models available. The "merge" operations are applied according to the fitness score of the new model after the merging operation. For their grammar learning, Stolcke and Omohundro used the posterior distribution of a Bayesian model given the data. For this, they used a prior that decomposes the structure from the parameters. The probability of a structure is inversely proportional to its exponentiated size, and therefore higher for simpler models.

8.10 SUMMARY

Probabilistic grammars are the most commonly used generic model family in NLP. As such, given the fact that most probabilistic grammars are generative models, this enabled a large focus of Bayesian NLP to be on development of Bayesian models and inference algorithms for these grammars. The focus of this chapter was on probabilistic context-free grammars and their use with Bayesian analysis, both parametric and nonparametric. Consequently, we covered the basics of inference with PCFGs, their use with their Dirichlet priors and nonparametric models such as adaptor grammars and the hierarchical Dirichlet process PCFGs.

8.11   EXERCISES

8.1.   Consider the exponential model family which is discussed in Section 3.4. Show that the model defined by Equation 8.5 is an exponential model, and define the different components of the exponential model based on the notation from Section 8.2.

8.2.   Consider the context-free grammar with rules $S \rightarrow S\,a$, $S \rightarrow S\,b$ and $S \rightarrow c$ where S is a nonterminal and a, b, c are terminal symbols. Can you find the probability assignment to its rules such that the grammar is not consistent (or not "tight")? If not, show that such an assignment does not exist. (See also Section 8.3.1.)

8.3.   In Equations 8.7–8.8 we show how to compute feature expectations for nonterminals spanning certain positions in a string, and similarly for a rule. These two can be thought of as features of "height" 1 and height 2, respectively. Write the equations of computing expectations for features of height 3.

8.4.   Show that the prior in Equation 8.9 is conjugate to the PCFG distribution in Equation 8.5. Identify the missing normalization constant of the posterior.

8.5.   Consider the context-free grammar with rules $S \rightarrow S\,a$ and $S \rightarrow a$. In Section 8.4.1 we mentioned that a PYAG could not adapt the nonterminal S with this CFG as the base grammar. Can you explain why a PYAG, in the form of generative story 8.2, could be ill-defined if we were allowed to adapt S?

CHAPTER 9

Representation Learning and Neural Networks

In recent years, new techniques for representation learning have become important in NLP literature. Such representation learning happens in a continuous space, in which words, sentences and even paragraphs are represented by dense, relatively short, vectors. Representation learning is also intended to sidestep the problem of feature design, which is used with traditional statistical techniques that pre-dated the current use of representation learning (such as with linear models). Continuous data representations of the data are directly extracted from simple, raw forms of data (such as indicator vectors which represent word co-occurrence in a sentence) and these data representations act as a substitute for feature templates used as part of linear models.

The most common tool in this area of representation learning is neural networks. Loosely speaking, these networks are complex functions that propagate values (linear transformation of input values) through nonlinear functions (such as the sigmoid function or the hyperbolic tangent function) and these values produce outputs that can then be further propagated in the same way to the upper layers of the network. Such propagation in a neural network architecture enables creation of models that are more expressive than linear ones. As mentioned above, one of the main strengths of neural networks is that they often do not require direction extraction of explicit features from the data, as lower layers in the network perform such "feature extraction." In addition, they are able to describe complex nonlinear decision rules for classification. The complexity of their decision rules makes them "data hungry"—see more in Section 9.1.

In NLP, the term "neural" has become an umbrella term to describe the use of learning in continuous spaces (and representing symbolic information in such spaces) in combination with nonlinear functions. This term does not necessarily refer to the strict use of neural networks as introduced in the past, but rather more generally to computation graphs or the use of nonlinear functions such as the sigmoid function.

While the increasing use of neural networks is partially rooted in the growing importance of new techniques for representation learning in NLP, it has also become a standard tool for a wide array of problems in NLP that do not necessarily require complex representation learning. For example, neural networks are now also popular for classification for fixed-dimension inputs (for example, one might use a feed-forward neural network to perform document classification with a bag-of-words model).

There are several connections between the Bayesian approach and the use of neural networks. First, one can place a prior on the weights of a neural network (or, alternatively, on the parameters of a representation learning model). More indirectly, through generative modeling, the modeler may introduce continuous latent variables over which we can find the posterior distribution given the data.

This chapter serves as a basic anchor for current methods in representation learning common in NLP and the goal of the chapter is to provide a basic introduction to this area, specifically in a Bayesian context. Thus, the chapter makes connections between representation learning, neural networks and the Bayesian approach, when possible.

9.1   NEURAL NETWORKS AND REPRESENTATION LEARNING: WHY NOW?

The Three Waves of Neural Networks   The seed ideas behind modern neural networks date back to the 1940s,[1] during which McCulloch and Pitts (1943) proposed a linear model with a threshold as a way for classification, with Rosenblatt (1958) proposing the perceptron algorithm to learn the weights of such a linear model. These early ideas served later as the foundations for the connectionism movement. They also started the first wave of interest in neural networks, which significantly diminished with criticism against the perceptron and its weak capacity to learn complex functions such as the XOR function. This criticism culminated in a book called "Perceptrons," published by Minsky and Papert (1969).

The second wave of popularity for neural networks started in the 1980s with the resurgence of connectionism to the field of Cognitive Science. While previous work in the field of Cognitive Science has focused on symbolic models, connectionism proposed that better modeling for cognition should be coupled with artificial neural networks, so as to more closely relate to the way the brain works in the context of neuroscience. During the rising popularity of connectionism, important achievements were made with neural networks, such as the successful use of the backpropagation algorithm (LeCun et al., 1989, Rumelhart et al., 1988). This wave has also introduced some work in the area of language learning (Elman, 1991, Harris, 1992, Neco and Forcada, 1997).

The use of neural networks in academia has declined in the mid-1990s with the rising success of probabilistic modeling (such as kernel methods and graphical models) as a complimentary approach to neural networks to solve certain problems in machine learning while also providing adequate theoretical foundations (Goodfellow et al., 2016).

The third and current wave of popularity of neural networks started in the mid 2000s. A community of proponents of neural networks continued to work on these models before this wave; with limited funding and support from the machine learning community, they managed to demonstrate the successful application of neural networks on several problems, including

---

[1]The three-wave historical perspective described here is based on the description in the book by Goodfellow et al. (2016).

image classification (and other problems in computer vision), speech recognition and language modeling. In this third wave, neural network modeling is often called "deep learning," which refers to the need to train a significant number of hidden layers placed between the input and output layers of a neural network to achieve state-of-the-art performance for several problems.

One of the reasons neural networks are being revisited in their current form in machine learning is the the scale of the data that is now being collected and the discovered importance of that scale for precise modeling—both in academia and in industry. Large amounts of data are now being collected. While the performance of linear models plateaued on these data (meaning, there were more data than needed to exploit the full power of such models), this has not been the case for neural networks. Instead, neural networks continued to improve modeling performance as more data arrived. This is not a surprise, as the decision surfaces and decision rules that neural networks yield are complex, especially the deep ones that consist of multiple hidden layers and therefore can exploit these data for better generalization.[2] As mentioned above, this quality of neural networks has improved the state of computer vision, language modeling and other areas of machine learning.

The ability to use large-scale data would have not been possible without advancements in high-performance computing, which also contributed to the rise of neural networks in their current form. The use of neural networks was found to be especially suitable with Graphics Processing Units (GPUs) as opposed to the standard Central Processing Units (CPUs) found in computers. While GPUs were originally developed to more efficiently render graphics, they have gradually taken on a more general form to perform matrix and vector operations more efficiently and in a parallel manner, which is a good match for deep learning calculations and other scientific applications, especially when the speed of CPUs has seemed to develop more slowly than in the past.

The Third Wave in NLP   This third wave of popularity of neural networks did not overlook the NLP community. Furthermore, the NLP community has recently rediscovered the usefulness of learning representations for words for various NLP problems (Turian et al., 2010). Within this line of research, words are no longer represented as symbolic units, but instead projected to a Euclidean space, usually based on co-occurrence statistics with other words. These projections are often referred to as "word embeddings." This discovery has marked a significant shift in the NLP community, such that most recent NLP work represent words as vectors (see also Section 9.2). This shift also comes hand-in-hand with the use of neural networks, which are a very good fit for working with continuous representations (such as word embeddings). The

---

[2]There are a variety of ways to discuss the complexity of a decision rule, such as the one entailed by a neural network. For example, if a "nonlinear" neural network performs a binary classification over a two-dimensional space, the curve that separates the positive examples from negative examples may have a complex pattern. This is in opposition to a linear classifier, where there would be a single straight line in the plane separating the two types of examples. One of the theoretical properties of neural networks that indicate the complexity of their decision surfaces is that a neural network with one hidden layer can approximate a large set of functions, as described by Funahashi (1989), Cybenko (1989) and Hornik et al. (1989) (this property is often referred to as "universal approximation").

concept of word embeddings is rooted in older work that grounds text in vector space models (for example, Hofmann 1999a, Mitchell and Lapata 2008, Turney and Pantel 2010).

NLP work with neural networks has already been seeded in preliminary stages of the third wave. Bengio et al. (2003), for example, has created a neural language model and Henderson and Lane (1998) have completed earlier work that featured the use of neural networks for syntactic parsing (see also Henderson 2003 and Titov and Henderson 2010). Collobert et al. (2011) pushed neural networks more prominently into the awareness of the NLP community when they showed how a variety of NLP problems (including part-of-speech tagging, chunking, named entity recognition and semantic role labeling) can all be framed as classification problems with neural networks. The researchers proposed that the use of their framework did not require much feature engineering, as opposed to the techniques available at that time. Arguably, this is indeed one of the great advantages of neural networks and representation-learning algorithms.

In the early days of neural networks in modern NLP, there was an extensive use of off-the-shelf models such as seq2seq (Section 9.4.3) and pre-trained word embeddings (Section 9.2) that did not make much use of intermediate structures. Even when the prediction was a complex structure for a specific NLP problem, seq2seq models were used with a process of "stringification"—the reduction of such a structure to a string so that off-the-shelf neural tools could be used to learn string mappings. Since then, intermediate structures have become more important in neural NLP literature and seq2seq models have been further extended to process trees and even graphs. The exact balance between the use of intermediate structures and the use of shallow stringification remains a moving target.

The use of the Bayesian approach, as presented in this book, is focusing on discrete structures. To some extent, the approach presented this way and neural networks have somewhat of a mismatch between them. The Bayesian approach has been, as mentioned in Chapter 2, mostly used in the context of generative models, while neural network architectures are usually used to define discriminative models (though, in principle, they can also be used to describe generative models). In addition, learning with neural networks can be quite complex, and becomes even more complicated when placing a prior on their parameters and finding the posterior. Still, this has not deterred many researchers from exploring and interpreting neural networks in a Bayesian context, as we discuss in this chapter.

Since the expansion of their use in the past decade, neural networks have become synonomous with both the usual generic architectures that have been used before (such as feedforward networks and recurrent neural networks), and also with complex computation graphs that propagate and handle vectors, matrices and even tensors as their values and weights. In some sense, the engineering of a good model with neural networks for NLP has become the design and search for the architecture, in the form of a computation graph, that behaves best.[3] This search is done both manually (by careful thinking about the problem and trial and error with

---

[3]Some argue that this need for "manual" architecture design has replaced the manual feature engineering that is required with linear models. See also Section 9.5.2.

different architectures) as well as automatically (by tuning hyperparameters, and more recently, by automatically searching for an architecture; see Section 9.5).

These computation graphs can be readily used to optimize an objective function, as is standard in machine learning (Section 1.5.2). The most common objective function used is still the log-likelihood, often referred to as "cross entropy" in the neural network literature (in an equivalent form). There are generic algorithms, such as backpropagation (see Section 9.3.1) that can optimize these objective functions for arbitrary computation graphs while relying on principles such as automatic differentiation. Indeed, with the advent of automatic differentiation, that allows us to specify a function and then automatically compute its derivatives and gradients, it is not surprising that several software packages were introduced, such as Torch (Collobert et al., 2002), TensorFlow (Abadi et al., 2016) DyNet (Neubig et al., 2017) and Theano (Al-Rfou et al., 2016), that allow the user to define a computation graph and the way data is fed into it. After that, learning is done as a blackbox using automatic differentiation and the backpropagation algorithm (Section 9.3.1).

9.2 WORD EMBEDDINGS

Perhaps one of the most important advances made in NLP in recent years is the widespread use of *word embeddings* as a substitute for symbolic representations of words. A word embedding is a vectoric representation of a word. For a vocabulary V and an integer k, a word embedding function of dimension k is a function that maps V to $\mathbb{R}^k$.

Word embeddings tend to cluster together when the words they denote behave similarly. The notion of "behavior" in this case usually remains underspecified, but could refer to syntactic categorization (i.e., words most often associated with the same part of speech will cluster together) or semantic association (words that are semantically related cluster together). The similarity between word embedding vectors is often measured through such measures as the dot product or cosine similarity.[4]

Most prominently, word embeddings assist with the treatment of words which do not appear in the training data of a given problem (such as parsing or part-of-speech tagging). The word embedding function can be learned by exploiting co-occurence data on a large corpus (without any annotation), and thus the vocabulary over which the word embedding function is constructed is larger than the one that the training data consists of, and covers a significant amount of the words in the test data, including "unseen words." The reliance on co-occurrence statistics is based on the *distributional hypothesis* (Harris, 1954) which states that co-occurrence of words in similar contexts implies that they have similar meanings (i.e., "you shall know a word

---

[4]The cosine similarity between two vectors $u \in \mathbb{R}^d$ and $v \in \mathbb{R}^d$ is calculated as $\dfrac{\sum_{i=1}^d u_i v_i}{\sqrt{\sum_{i=1}^d u_i^2} \cdot \sqrt{\sum_{i=1}^d v_i^2}}$. This quantity provides the cosine of the angle between u and v.

by the company it keeps;" Firth 1957[5]). Since words that tend to "behave similarly" end up close to one another in the embedding space, word embeddings can greatly alleviate the problem of unseen words by exploiting information from the words that do appear in the training data. Instead of using the word symbol as a feature in the model, we can use its vector, which exploits such similarities.

In this section, we mostly cover a specific type of word embedding model, the *skip-gram* model, which has served as the basis for many other models. We also cover this model because it has a Bayesian version (Section 9.2.2).

9.2.1 SKIP-GRAM MODELS FOR WORD EMBEDDINGS

A skip-gram model is a conditional model that generates the context surrounding a pivot word conditioned on that pivot word (Mikolov et al., 2013a). Each sample from such a model includes the pivot word together with the context surrounding it. For a context size $c \in \mathbb{N}$ and a vocabulary V, the model has the form:

$$\prod_{j=-c, j \neq 0}^{c} p(w_j \mid w_0),$$ (9.1)

where $w_0 \in V$ is the pivot word such that the sequence of words in the sample is $(w_{-c}, w_{-c+1}, \ldots, w_0, w_1, \ldots w_c) \in V^{2c+1}$. Let $w_1, \ldots, w_N$ be a sequence of words in a corpus. If we take a frequentist approach in skip-gram model estimation, for example, through maximum likelihood estimation (see Chapter 1), then we would aim to maximize the following objective function:[6]

$$\frac{1}{N} \sum_{i=1}^{N} \sum_{j=-c, j \neq 0}^{c} \log p\left(w_{i+j} \mid w_i\right).$$ (9.2)

While the skip-gram model has strong similarities to the n-gram model, in which a word is generated conditioned on a fixed number of previous words in the text, there is a significant difference in the underlying generative process. For a given corpus with skip-gram modeling, we will generate each word multiple times, since we generate the *context* (and not the pivot word), as a word appears in several contexts of various pivot words. Therefore, the skip-gram model is not a generative model of a corpus—instead words are generated multiple times.

---

[5]While this quote is widely used in NLP in the context of justifying the use of co-occurrence statistics to derive word embeddings across a dictionary of *different* words, it is arguable whether this was Firth's original intention—he may have been referring to identifying the specific sense of an ambiguous word compared to its other senses by its "habitual collocation."

[6]The indices in Equation 9.2 may be negative or may exceed the number of words in the text. We assume the text is padded by c symbols in its beginning and in its end to accommodate for this.

Another point of departure of the skip-gram model from the common n-gram model is the way that we model the factors of the form $p(w_j \mid w_0)$ in Equation 9.1. With representation learning models such as skip-gram (Mikolov et al., 2013a), this probability is modeled as

$$p\left(w_j \mid w_0, u, v\right) = \frac{\exp\left(u(w_0)^\top v(w_j)\right)}{\displaystyle\sum_{w \in V} \exp\left(u(w_0)^\top v(w)\right)}, \qquad (9.3)$$

where $u: V \to \mathbb{R}^k$ and $v: V \to \mathbb{R}^k$ are functions which map words to a word embedding—one for the pivot words, and the other for context. We estimate these functions, and they act as the parameters of this model. The goal of learning is to maximize the objective in Equation 9.2 with respect to u and v, and as such, to find embeddings for words both as contexts (u) and as pivot words (v).

This model learns parameters that lead to a high-valued dot product for embeddings of frequently co-occuring pivot and context words (as the probability is pushed to the maximum in such cases). Therefore, through the contexts, words that are similar to each other in their co-occurrence patterns map to vectors that are close to each other in the Euclidean space.

Unfortunately, the model in Equation 9.3 is impractical to use because computation of the right-hand side requires the summation over the whole vocabulary (in the denominator). The vocabulary size can be quite large, in the order of hundred thousands of word types, and therefore computing this denominator is expensive. Calculation of the gradient of the log-likelihood objective function over examples in the form of words paired with their contexts is intractable in the vanilla form.

Mikolov et al. (2013b) proposed a technique called "negative sampling" to resolve this issue. Replacing Equation 9.3, negative sampling uses the following model to estimate $p(w_j \mid w_0, u, v)$:

$$p\left(w_j \mid w_0, u, v\right) = \sigma\left(u(w_0)^\top v(w_j)\right) \prod_{w \in \text{neg}(w_0)} \sigma\left(-u(w_0)^\top v(w)\right),$$

where $\sigma(z) = \dfrac{1}{1 + e^{-z}}$ (the sigmoid function) and $\text{neg}(w_0)$ is a set of "negative" word sample—i.e., words that are unlikely to be in the context of w_0. These words are sampled from a unigram distribution (estimated using the frequency count from a corpus) raised to a power $\alpha = \dfrac{3}{4}$ ($\alpha <$ 1 is a hyperparameter of the method, which results in the unigram distribution "flattening" compared to its original form). Skip-gram modeling of the above form coupled with negative sampling is often referred to as one of the word2vec models (Mikolov et al., 2013a,b). A second proposed model of word2vec is the continuous bag-of-words model (CBOW), which predicts a word from the context—in reverse from the skip-gram model. The model gets its name from the way context is represented—as an average of word embeddings which appear in the context. In this case, word order in the text is lost, similar to the case with the bag-of-words model in the

Latent Dirichlet Allocation model (Section 2.2). An alternative to the use of negative sampling with the CBOW model is *hierarchical softmax* (Mikolov et al., 2013a), for which the sum over the vocabulary becomes logarithmic in the size of the vocabulary. With the hierarchical softmax, the probability of a word is modeled as a path in a binary tree with the leaves being the words in the vocabulary.

9.2.2 BAYESIAN SKIP-GRAM WORD EMBEDDINGS

As mentioned in the beginning of this chapter, representing discrete objects as continuous vectors is central to current techniques in representation learning and neural networks. Therefore, when these techniques are coupled with the Bayesian approach, they often make use of the Gaussian distribution as a prior or to represent a latent state. As described in Section 9.3.2, a Gaussian distribution (Section B.5) can be used to model the distribution from which neural network parameters are drawn, or alternatively, it can be used to model a latent continuous variable (Section 9.6.1). This is also the case with Bayesian word embeddings.

Barkan (2017) proposed a simple Bayesian model, based on word2vec. His motivation was to provide a more robust inference procedure for word embeddings, so that it is less sensitive to hyperparameter tuning and provides a *density* over vectors for a given word instead of a single vector. With this model, there is a Gaussian prior for each vector defined by the embedding functions u and v, which play the role of parameters in the model. The model defines a joint distribution over the embedding vectors and binary indicator variables that tell whether a pair of words—a token and its context—co-occur together in a specific position in the corpus.

More specifically, this Bayesian model sets a prior over u and v in the following way:

$$p(u, v \mid \tau) = \left(\prod_{w \in V} p(u(w) \mid \tau) \right) \times \left(\prod_{w \in V} p(v(w) \mid \tau) \right), \qquad (9.4)$$

where both $p(u(w))$ and $p(v(w))$ are multivariate Gaussian distributions with mean value 0 and covariance matrix $\tau^{-1} I$ where I is the $k \times k$ identity matrix.

Let $C(i)$ be a multiset of the words that appear in the context of w_i in a corpus $(w_1, \ldots, w_N)$. We define the random variable D_{iw} where $i \in [N]$ ($[N] = \{1, \ldots, N\}$) and $w \in V$ that receives the value r if w appears in $C(i)$ $r \geq 1$ times and -1 if $w \notin C(i)$. We then define the likelihood of the model as:

$$\prod_{i=1}^{N} \prod_{w \in V} p\left(D_{iw} \mid u, v\right), \qquad (9.5)$$

where

$$p\left(D_{iw} = d \mid u, v\right) = \sigma\left(du(w_i)^{\top} v(w)\right),$$

with $\sigma(z) = \dfrac{1}{1 + e^{-z}}$ (the sigmoid function). The full joint model is defined as the product of Equations 9.4 and 9.5. The product in Equation 9.5 can be split over terms $w \in C(i)$ and

$w \notin C(i)$. Clearly, there are many more terms of the latter kind, leading to intractability of computing their product (or the sum of their logarithms). Barkan (2017) uses negative sampling for that set of terms, similar to `word2vec`.

Until now our discussion has focused on defining a word embedding function that maps a word to a vector (or potentially a distribution over vectors). However, words do not stand alone, and can be interpreted differently depending on their context, both syntactically ("I can can the can") or semantically (compare the use of the word "bank" in "the bank of the river is green and flowery" vs. "the bank increased its deposit fees"). A subsequent question that arises is whether we can define a word embedding function that also takes as an argument the context of the word. Recent work (Devlin et al., 2018, Peters et al., 2018) suggests that is possible, and can lead to state-of-the-art results in a variety of NLP problems.

There is an earlier Bayesian connection to contextual embeddings. Bražinskas et al. (2017) propose a Bayesian skip-gram contextualized model, through which word embeddings are represented as distributions. In this model, the context of a word c is generated while conditioning on the word itself w, with a latent variable z (the embedding) in between. The distribution that defines the model is:

$$p(c \mid w) = \int_z p(z \mid w) p(c \mid z) dz.$$

While $p(z \mid w)$ is modeled using a Gaussian, $p(c \mid z)$ is modeled using a neural network. The latent variable z can indicate, for example, a word sense or a syntactic category the word belongs to in that context.

Inference in this model is intractable, and the authors use variational inference with a mean-field approximation such that each factor represents a distribution z for a given word and its context in the data. See also Chapter 6 and Section 9.6.1. This work is inspired by the *Gaussian embeddings* of Vilnis and McCallum (2015) (where a word embedding is represented using a Gaussian distribution), with two key differences. First, the work of Vilnis and McCallum (2015) does not provide contextualized embeddings (i.e., we eventually get a single distribution per word independent of its context as an output). In addition, the original work about Gaussian embeddings does not define a generative model through which posterior inference can be done in a Bayesian setting. Instead, finding the distribution for each word is done by directly optimizing an objective function that is based on KL-divergence terms.

9.2.3 DISCUSSION

Whereas our discussion in the previous sections focused on pre-trained embeddings, word embeddings can be either pre-trained or trained (generic vs. task-specific). With pre-trained embeddings, we use a large corpus to estimate the word embeddings with techniques such as `word2vec` and others. Trained embeddings, on the other hand, are estimated in conjunction with the specific NLP problem we are trying to solve, such as machine translation or summarization. While pre-trained embeddings have the advantage that they can be used in conjunction with large corpora—it is usually easy to find large amounts of unlabeled text data—trained embeddings have the advantage that the learned vectors are tuned specifically to the problem at hand, often with less data because annotated corpora for specific tasks tend to be smaller. Trained embeddings may be initialized as pre-trained in the beginning of the training procedure of a neural network (which often uses the *backpropagation* algorithm; see Section 9.3.1).

The idea of embedding words in a Euclidean space can be generalized further, and sentences, paragraphs and even whole documents can be embedded as vectors. Indeed, this is one of the main ideas behind encoder-decoder models, which are discussed in Section 9.4.3. In addition, like in the word2vec model, models for embedding larger chunks of text have been developed (Le and Mikolov, 2014).

9.3 NEURAL NETWORKS

In their modern incarnation, neural networks are complex nested functions that describe correspondingly complex decision spaces for classification and regression. At their core, these functions are composed of two components.

- Linear functions: these functions take as inputs either the basic inputs on which the neural network operates or alternatively, values already calculated by the neural network.

- Nonlinear activation functions: these are functions through which the linear functions are passed to the next level of the neural network.

Logistic regression (Section 4.2.1), for example, can be re-formulated as a neural network. Figure 9.1 describes such a neural network in graphical terms. The input to the network is $x \in \mathbb{R}^d$ for some fixed dimensionality d. We multiply each vector coordinate x_i, $i \in [d]$, by a weight w_i and then add a bias term. This linear term is now passed through the logistic function (or a sigmoid) to calculate the final output of the neural network.

The power of neural networks comes from their expressivity for complex decision surfaces.[7] With the logistic regression example, we can continue and build a hierarchy of functions that take as inputs a previous layer of *activation* values, compute their linear transformation of them and propagate them to the next layer. In this case, the logistic regression output model above will be replaced with multiple outputs that serve as the input to the next layer. This is demonstrated in Figure 9.2.

More specifically, in such a neural network, also referred to as *feed-forward neural network*, we would have a set of weight matrices $W^{(i)}$ for $i \in \{1, \ldots, L\}$ where L is the number of layers in the network, and a set of bias vectors $b^{(i)}$ for $i \in \{1, \ldots, L\}$. Each matrix $W^{(i)}$ is in $\mathbb{R}^{d_i \times d_{i-1}}$ where d_i denotes the number of desired units in the ith layer. The vectors $b^{(i)}$ are in $\mathbb{R}^{d_i}$. For $i = 0$, the number of units corresponds to the dimension of the input $x \in \mathbb{R}^d$ to the neural network (i.e., $d_0 = d$). Finally, we also have a set of activation functions $g^{(i)} \colon \mathbb{R}^{d_i} \to \mathbb{R}^{d_i}$ for

---

[7]Complex decision surfaces can be obtained with linear models through *kernelization*. See Murphy (2012).

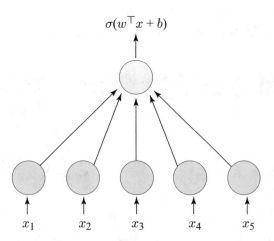

Figure 9.1: An example of a neural network representing a logistic regression model. The function σ denotes the sigmoid function. The weights of the neural network are $w \in \mathbb{R}^5$ and the bias term is $b \in \mathbb{R}$.

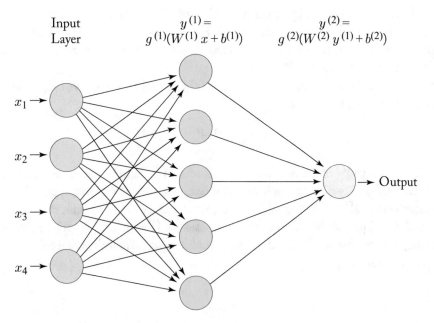

Figure 9.2: An example of a feed-forward neural network with one hidden layer. The dimension of the input is $d_0 = 4$, and $L = 2$ such that $d_1 = 5$ and $d_2 = 1$.

Table 9.1: Example of activation functions commonly used with neural networks in NLP. The function $I(\Gamma)$ for a statement Γ is the indicator function (1 if Γ is true and 0 otherwise). Functions $g \colon \mathbb{R} \to \mathbb{R}$ map the linear combination of the values from the current layer (x) to a new value.

Name	Value $g(x)$	Derivative
Identity	$g(x) = x$	$g'(x) = 1$
Step function	$g(x) = I(x \geq 0)$	$g'(x) = 0$ for $x \neq 0$ (undefined) for $x = 0$
Logistic function (sigmoid)	$g(x) = \dfrac{1}{1 + e^{-x}}$	$g'(x) = g(x)(1 - g(x))$
Hyperbolic tangent (tanh)	$g(x) = \dfrac{e^x - e^{-x}}{e^x + e^{-x}}$	$g'(x) = 1 - g(x))^2$
Rectified linear unit (ReLU)[8]	$g(x) = xI(x \geq 0)$	$g'(x) = I(x \geq 0)$
Softplus	$g(x) = \log(1 + e^x)$	$g'(x) = \dfrac{1}{1 + e^{-x}}$

$1 \leq i \leq L$. These functions usually operate coordinate-wise on their input (but do not have to, such as the case with pooling or normalization). For example, $g^{(i)}$ could be returning the value of the sigmoid function on each coordinate. Table 9.1 gives examples of prototypical activation functions used with neural networks.

Now we can recursively define the outputs of the neural network. We begin with $y^{(0)} = x$ and then define for $i \in \{1, \ldots, L\}$,

$$y^{(i)} = g^{(i)}\left(W^{(i)} y^{(i-1)} + b^{(i)}\right). \tag{9.6}$$

The final output $y^{(L)}$ of the neural network is often a scalar, and in the case of classification, might denote a probability distribution over a discrete space of outputs that is calculated by using a logistic function for $g^{(L)}$. For example, in the case of binary classification, the neural network defines a conditional probability model over outcomes $\{0, 1\}$ with $y^{(L)} = p(1 \mid x, W^{(i)}, b^{(i)}, i \in [L])$ where $[L]$ denotes the set $\{1, \ldots, L\}$. The parameters of this model are naturally the weight matrices and the bias vectors.

---

[8]A variant of ReLU, called "leaky ReLU" is sometimes used instead of the vanilla ReLU activation function (Maas et al., 2013). With leaky ReLU, $g(x) = xI(x \geq 0) + \alpha x I(x < 0)$ for a small value of α (such as 0.001). This solves the problem of "dead neurons," which are never updated because they always have a negative pre-activation value; as a result, their gradient update is 0.

9.3.1   FREQUENTIST ESTIMATION AND THE BACKPROPAGATION ALGORITHM

Given that now we have defined a conditional probability model over the space of y conditioned on x, we can proceed with the frequentist approach to estimate the weight matrices and the bias vectors by maximizing an objective function of the parameters of this model and the data. This can be done, for example, by maximizing the log-likelihood of the data (Section 1.5.2). In this case, we assume that we receive a set $(x^{(k)}, z^{(k)})$ where $k \in \{1, \dots, N\}$ as input to the estimation algorithm; we then aim to find (see Section 1.5.2):

$$\left(W^{(i)}, b^{(i)}\right)_{i=1}^{L} = \arg \max_{(W^{(i)}, b^{(i)})_{i=1}^{L}} \underbrace{\sum_{k=1}^{N} \log p\left(z^{(k)} \mid x^{(k)}, W^{(i)}, b^{(i)}, i \in [L]\right)}_{\mathcal{L}((W^{(i)}, b^{(i)})_{i=1}^{L})}. \qquad (9.7)$$

This maximization problem usually does not have a closed-form solution which is just a simple function of the training data. Therefore, we need to use optimization techniques which require the calculation of the gradient of $\mathcal{L}\left((W^{(i)}, b^{(i)})_{i=1}^{L}\right)$. This optimization technique will "follow" the gradient of the function with respect to the parameters, which provides the direction in which the function is increasing. This way it will find a local maximum of $\mathcal{L}\left((W^{(i)}, b^{(i)})_{i=1}^{L}\right)$ with respect to the parameters of the neural network (see Section A.3). The computation of the gradient leads to "update rules" that iteratively update the parameters until convergence to a local maximum.[9]

To compute the gradient, we first note that when $g^{(i)}$ operates coordinate-wise on its inputs, the jth output coordinate $y_j^{(i)}$ for $i \in \{1, \dots, L\}$ $(y_j^{(i)})$ has the following form:

$$y_j^{(i)} = g_j^{(i)}\left(a_j^{(i)}\right), \qquad\qquad \textit{activation values} \qquad (9.8)$$

$$a_j^{(i)} = \sum_{\ell=1}^{d_i} W_{j\ell}^{(i)} y_\ell^{(i-1)} + b_j^{(i)} \qquad\qquad \textit{pre-activation values.} \qquad (9.9)$$

The definition $a^{(i)}$ is such that $a^{(i)} \in \mathbb{R}^{d_i}$. These vectors are also referred to as the "pre-activation" values. We would like to compute the gradient of $y^{(L)}$ with respect to $W_{st}^{(r)}$ and $b_s^{(r)}$ where $r \in [L]$, $s \in [d_r]$ and $t \in [d_{r-1}]$. For simplicity, we will assume that $d_L = 1$ (i.e., the neural network has a single output).

To compute this derivative, we will use the chain rule several times. We begin by defining the terms $\delta_s^{(r)}$ for $r \in [L]$ and $s \in [d_r]$:

$$\delta_s^{(r)} = \frac{\partial y_1^{(L)}}{\partial a_s^{(r)}}. \qquad (9.10)$$

---

[9]While most neural network packages now provide automatic ways to optimize objective functions and calculate their gradient, we give in this section a derivation of the way to calculate these gradients for completeness.

Using the chain rule (in Equation 9.11), we get a recursive formula for computing $\delta_s^{(r)}$:

$$\delta_1^{(L)} = \left(g_1^{(L)}\right)' \left(a_1^{(L)}\right) \qquad \textit{base case}$$

$$\delta_s^{(r)} = \sum_{\ell=1}^{d_{r+1}} \frac{\partial y_1^{(L)}}{\partial a_\ell^{(r+1)}} \frac{\partial a_\ell^{(r+1)}}{\partial a_s^{(r)}} \qquad\qquad (9.11)$$

$$= \sum_{\ell=1}^{d_{r+1}} \delta_\ell^{(r+1)} \frac{\partial a_\ell^{(r+1)}}{\partial a_s^{(r)}} \qquad r \in \{L-1, \ldots, 1\}, s \in [d_L], \qquad (9.12)$$

where $\left(g_j^{(i)}\right)'(z)$ denotes the value of the derivative of $g_j^{(i)}(z)$ for $z \in \mathbb{R}$.

To fully compute $\delta_s^{(r)}$, we need to be able to compute $\dfrac{\partial a_\ell^{(r+1)}}{\partial a_s^{(r)}}$. Based on Equations 9.8–9.9 the following relationship holds:

$$a_\ell^{(r+1)} = \sum_{k=1}^{d_r} W_{\ell k}^{(r+1)} g_k^{(r)} \left(a_k^{(r)}\right) + b_\ell^{(r+1)}.$$

As such,

$$\frac{\partial a_\ell^{(r+1)}}{\partial a_s^{(r)}} = W_{\ell s}^{(r+1)} \left(g_s^{(r)}\right)' \left(a_s^{(r)}\right).$$

Plugging this into Equation 9.12 we get:

$$\delta_s^{(r)} = \sum_{\ell=1}^{d_{r+1}} \delta_\ell^{(r+1)} \left(g_s^{(r)}\right)' \left(a_s^{(r)}\right) W_{\ell s}^{(r+1)} \qquad r \in \{L-1, \ldots, 1\}, s \in [d_L]. \quad (9.13)$$

Now, we can calculate the derivatives for $y_1^{(L)}$ with respect to the weights and bias terms by using Equation 9.10:

$$\frac{\partial y_1^{(L)}}{\partial W_{st}^{(r)}} = \frac{\partial y_1^{(L)}}{\partial a_s^{(r)}} \frac{\partial a_s^{(r)}}{\partial W_{st}^{(r)}} = \delta_s^{(r)} y_t^{(r-1)} \qquad\qquad (9.14)$$

$$\frac{\partial y_1^{(L)}}{\partial b_s^{(r)}} = \frac{\partial y_1^{(L)}}{\partial a_s^{(r)}} \frac{\partial a_s^{(r)}}{\partial b_s^{(r)}} = \delta_s^{(r)}. \qquad\qquad (9.15)$$

Note that $\delta_s^{(r)}$ can be computed by first propagating all of the inputs into the neural network to get the ys and the as. This is called the "forward" step. Then, working backward from the top layer, we can compute the terms $\delta_s^{(r)}$ based on the ys and the as, in a "backward" step. The backpropagation algorithm gets its name from Equation 9.13: we backpropagate the $\delta_s^{(r)}$ terms from the top layer downwards to the first layer.

Calculation of the Objective Function In the case of the log-likelihood objective in Equation 9.7, for example, if we assume $z^{(k)} \in \{0, 1\}$ and the conditional probability is modeled as:

$$y_1^{(L)} = p\left(z^{(k)} = 1 \mid x^{(k)}, W^{(i)}, b^{(i)}, i \in [L]\right),$$

then each summand in the log-likelihood objective function can be expressed as the following function of the outputs:

$$\log p\left(z^{(k)} \mid x^{(k)}, W^{(i)}, b^{(i)}, i \in [L]\right) = \log\left((y_1^{(L)})^{z^{(k)}}(1 - y_1^{(L)})^{1-z^{(k)}}\right)$$

$$= \underbrace{z^{(k)} \log y_1^{(L)} + \left(1 - z^{(k)}\right) \log\left(1 - y_1^{(L)}\right)}_{\mathcal{L}\left(k, (W^{(i)}, b^{(i)})_{i=1}^L\right)}. \quad (9.16)$$

By the chain rule, the derivative of each of these terms as in Equation 9.16 with respect to $W_{st}^{(r)}$ is:

$$\frac{\partial \mathcal{L}\left(k, (W^{(i)}, b^{(i)})_{i=1}^L\right)}{\partial W_{st}^{(r)}} = \begin{cases} \frac{1}{y_1^{(L)}} \frac{\partial y_1^{(L)}}{\partial W_{st}^{(r)}} & \text{if } z^{(k)} = 1 \\ -\frac{1}{y_1^{(L)}} \frac{\partial y_1^{(L)}}{\partial W_{st}^{(r)}} & \text{if } z^{(k)} = 0, \end{cases}$$

where $\dfrac{\partial y_1^{(L)}}{\partial W_{st}^{(r)}}$ is taken from Equation 9.14. We can similarly use Equation 9.15 to calculate the gradient of the objective function with respect to the bias terms.

Intuition Behind the Backpropagation Algorithm As mentioned in the beginning of this section, the goal of the backpropagation algorithm is to compute the gradient of the neural network output as a function of the weights and the bias terms of the network (the parameters), or the gradient of the objective function as a function of the outputs, to be more precise. Equation 9.10 defines the $\delta_s^{(r)}$ term, which provides the "amount of change" in the network output as a function of the change in the pre-activation in layer r to neuron s in that layer ($a_s^{(r)}$). The derivation of Equation 9.10, which is based on the chain rule, shows that this amount of change can be expressed as the weighted average of the amount of change of the activation with respect to each pre-activation ℓ in layer $r + 1$ times the amount of change to the pre-activation of neuron ℓ as a function of the amount of change to $a_s^{(r)}$. Therefore, the pre-activations in layer

$r + 1$ are used as *intermediate* variables; the change in upper layers of the network as a function of changes in pre-activations in lower layers can be expressed through these intermediate pre-activations. For more intuition on the chain rule, see Appendix A.2.2. It is important to note that while the chain rule was our main tool to derive the backpropagation algorithm in this section, automatic differentiation for complex functions requires more than just a simple application of the chain rule. These implementation details are now often hidden when using off-the-shelf packages (such as PyTorch and Tensorflow) for neural network modeling. There are also strong connections between the backpropagation algorithm and the inside-outside algorithtm described in Chapter 8. See Eisner (2016) for more details.

Initialization with the Backpropagation Algorithm   Most objective functions used in conjunction with neural networks are non-convex and have multiple exterma. This non-convexity arises when there are latent layers in the neural network, as commonly happens with unsupervised learning (this happens because the latent layers introduce higher-order multiplicative terms of interaction between different parameters of the neural networks). Therefore, initialization of neural network weights with the backpropagation algorithm, which essentially optimizes the objective function in a gradient-descent style, is crucial. In addition, if the weights are not chosen in a suitable way at the beginning of the algorithm, the gradients may quickly explode or vanish (Section 9.4.2).

Various examples of initialization techniques exist. For example, one can initialize the weights of the neural network by sampling from a Gaussian variable with mean zero and variance that is inversely proportional to the square-root of the number of connections in the network (Glorot and Bengio, 2010). Alternatively, instead of initializing each weight separately through sampling, Saxe et al. (2014) proposed jointly initializing all weights in a given layer by using an orthonormal matrix that preserves the size of the vector being input to the layer to prevent the gradient from exploding or vanishing. For more details, see also Eisenstein (2019).

9.3.2   PRIORS ON NEURAL NETWORK WEIGHTS

The most natural way to treat neural networks in the Bayesian setting is to put a prior on the weights of the neural network, with its architecture being fixed. This has been the mainstay of framing neural network learning in a Bayesian context. Indeed, MacKay (1992) applied a Gaussian prior on the weights of a single-layered neural network. This prior uses mean 0 and a hyperparameter α that controls the variance. In turn, this hyperparameter has a prior placed on it and leads, together with the Gaussian prior, to a hierarchical model (Section 3.5).

MacKay then proceeds to optimize the neural network weights by finding approximate maximizers of the posterior function, including over α. He discovered that using a single α hyperparameter for all weights in the neural network led to relatively poor generalization, as the role of each neuron in the neural network is different. To fix this, he set a separate variance hyperparameter for each type of weights: input, hidden-layer and output weights. The use of the Bayesian framework in MacKay's case was mainly for the regularization of the weights in the neural network. Since MacKay's work, the Gaussian distribution has been used often as a prior for neural network weights in a Bayesian context (Neal, 2012).

Indeed, this idea of putting a prior on the weights in the form of a Gaussian distribution has been further developed by Graves (2011). The author studied Gaussian and Laplacian distributions as the priors, and used variational inference to derive the posterior over the weights, where the approximate posterior is assumed to be a Gaussian or a delta distribution (i.e., putting all its mass on a single point). He did not optimize the variational bound using coordinate ascent as described in Chapter 6, but instead calculated the expectations defined by the variational bound using numerical integration by stochastically sampling weights from the approximate posterior over them. As Graves points out, it may at first seem absurd to replace posterior inference, which requires complex integration with neural networks, with variational inference where the approximate posterior expectations are also intractable; however, the approximate posterior is more amenable to numerical integration and can be more easily accessed.

Another way to identify the posterior over the parameters of a neural network is by using Stochastic Gradient Langevin Dynamics (SGLD; Welling and Teh 2011). In this case, we perform stochastic gradient steps on the parameters of the neural network, where the calculated gradient consists of the gradient of the log-probability of the prior together with the gradient of the log-likelihood function with respect to the parameters:[10]

$$F(\theta) = \frac{1}{n}\nabla_\theta \log p(\theta) + \sum_{i=1}^{n} \nabla_\theta \log p\left(x^{(i)} \mid \theta\right),$$

where $x^{(1)}, \ldots, x^{(n)}$ consist of the observed data points and θ denote the parameters of the model.

The gradient of the log-likelihood function can be computed using the backpropagation algorithm if it is indeed modeled by a neural network. The update made to the parameters is in the direction of this gradient together with additional noise sampled from a multidimensional Gaussian distribution:

$$\theta_{t+1} \leftarrow \theta_t - \mu_t F(\theta_t) + \xi_t,$$

where ξ_t is a sample from a multivariate Gaussian with mean zero, θ_t is the set of parameters at timestep t in the set of updates to the parameters and μ_t is a learning rate.

It can be shown that when running these gradient updates, as t increases, the distribution over the parameters (given the Gaussian noise, we have a distribution over θ_t so it can be treated as a random variable) eventually converges to the true posterior over the parameters (Teh et al., 2016). This convergence requires the learning rate to become closer to 0 as t increases (see also Section 4.4). In NLP, for example, Shareghi et al. (2019) used SGLD for the problem of dependency parsing. See more about stochastic gradient descent in Section A.3.1.

---

[10]It is possible also to calculate this gradient in "batches." See more in Section A.3.1.

9.4   MODERN USE OF NEURAL NETWORKS IN NLP

In their current form in NLP, neural networks have become complex, and they use more advanced architectures, particularly convolutional neural networks (CNNs) and recurrent neural networks (RNNs).

9.4.1   RECURRENT AND RECURSIVE NEURAL NETWORKS

RNNs (Elman, 1990) were developed originally as models for time series where the time steps are discrete. As such, they are a good fit for modeling natural language in its linear form, where the time dimension is exchanged, for example, for a position in a given sentence (or a sentence index in a document). In their vanilla form, recurrent neural networks work by maintaining a state that is updated at each step by feeding both the state and a new input (for example, the next word in the sentence) to a nonlinear function.

More formally, the recurrent neural network maintains a state $h^{(t)} \in \mathbb{R}^d$ for time step $t \geq 0$ and receives input $x^{(t)} \in \mathbb{R}^k$ at time step t. In an example of a generic form, the recurrent network updates $h^{(t)}$ ($t \geq 1$) are as follows (Pascanu et al., 2013):

$$h^{(t)} = W_{\text{rec}}g\left(h^{(t-1)}\right) + W_{\text{in}}x^{(t)} + b, \tag{9.17}$$

where $W_{\text{rec}} \in \mathbb{R}^{d \times d}$, $W_{\text{in}} \in \mathbb{R}^{d \times k}$, $b \in \mathbb{R}^d$ and $g \colon \mathbb{R}^d \to \mathbb{R}^d$ is a coordinate-wise activation function.[11] The state $h^{(0)}$ can be chosen arbitrarily, and as such, its definition is left underspecified. Figure 9.3a provides a schematic representation of a recurrent neural network as described in Equation 9.17.

The computation of a recurrent neural network can be "unrolled" (Figure 9.3b) and represented as a set of feed-forward calculations. For each step, there is a latent layer for computing $h^{(t)}$. The main difference between such unrolled RNN and a feed-forward network as presented in Equation 9.6 is that the network parameters in the case of RNNs are all tied: we use a single set of weights and bias terms for all layers. In addition, with a vanilla feed-forward network there is no new input for each latent layer. Instead, the input is fed at the beginning. That being said, there is nothing in principle that prevents us from tying certain parameters in a feed-forward neural network (which is actually done in practice) or feeding new inputs at certain latent layers of the network.

Given the unrolled representation of the RNN, backpropagation can be used to compute the gradient of any output with respect to the parameters. Let $W_{\text{rec}}^{(t)}$, $W_{\text{in}}^{(r)}$ and $b^{(t)}$ be the weights in the unrolled network. The gradient with respect to the parameters W_{rec}, W_{in} and b is just the sum of the gradients of the corresponding parameter with respect to each layer. This is due to

---

[11]The notation rec stands for "recurrent" and in for "input."

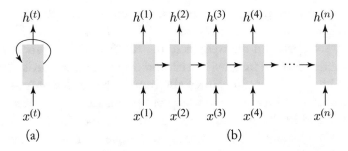

Figure 9.3: (a) A representation of a recurrent neural network; (b) an unrolled representation of the network.

the chain rule which states that for an objective $\mathcal{L}$ and a parameter θ in the RNN it holds that:

$$\frac{\partial \mathcal{L}}{\partial \theta} = \sum_{t=1}^{T} \frac{\partial \mathcal{L}}{\partial \theta^{(t)}} \cdot \frac{\partial \theta^{(t)}}{\partial \theta},$$

where T is the number of timesteps unrolled and $\theta^{(t)}$ is the corresponding unrolled parameter in timestep t. As $\frac{\partial \theta^{(t)}}{\partial \theta} = 1$ (because $\theta^{(t)} = \theta$), it holds that the derivative of $\mathcal{L}$ with respect to θ is the sum of all derivatives in the unrolled network with respect to $\theta^{(t)}$. This variant of gradient computation which is based on backpropagation is also referred to as "backpropagation through time" (Werbos, 1990).

While RNNs focus on cases in which the network represents a sequence (the input to the recurrent unit is the output of the recurrent unit from the previous step), we can extend this idea further and have several "history" vectors that are fed into a unit at an upper level. This can be done, for example, using a tree structure. Networks with this form of generalization of RNNs are referred to as *Recursive Neural Networks* (Pollack, 1990).

The computation of Recursive Neural Networks, with the sharing of parameters at different nodes in the network, can be unrolled similarly to the way it is done with RNNs using a directed acyclic graph representing the full computation. This unrolled form can be used to compute the gradient for the optimization of a training objective. This technique of backpropagation calculation is called "backpropagation through structure" (Goller and Kuchler, 1996), and it is a generalization of backpropagation through time.

RNNs enable the solution for a problem with natural language inputs: they are generally of varying length, and in many applications (e.g., classification), we need a fixed-size vector to apply the final classification step. An RNN can be used to "read" the input, token by token, and the internal state that it maintains can be used in the last time step as a representation for the whole input, which is fed to a classifier, for example. CNNs (Section 9.4.4) also tackle this issue of fixed-size vectors for natural language inputs.

One can adapt RNN training to the Bayesian setting. For example, Fortunato et al. (2017) used "Bayes by backprop" in a way that is similar to the work of Graves (2011), mentioned in Section 9.3.2. They set a prior on the weights of the RNN, and then proceed with variational Bayes to infer a posterior over the weights. The backpropagation algorithm is used as a subroutine in their variational inference procedure. They also introduce the idea of "posterior shattering," in which the approximate posterior at each step of optimization is conditioned on the mini-batch of datapoints used in that step. This reduces the variance in the learning process. Gal and Ghahramani (2016c) framed a regularization technique for neural networks, dropout, in a Bayesian manner. For more details see Section 9.5.1.

9.4.2   VANISHING AND EXPLODING GRADIENT PROBLEM

Activation functions such as the sigmoid and tanh tend to "squash" a large range of values into smaller ranges. Indeed, the sigmoid maps $\mathbb{R}$ to the interval $[0, 1]$. As such, when we apply the backpropagation algorithm on a neural network that is deep (or, alternatively, when we apply backpropagation through time or through structure for a long sequence or a large graph), we may get small gradient values for certain parameters. This may cause the gradient to underflow or, alternatively, leads to a very slow convergence of the optimization algorithm (Pascanu et al., 2013).

Consider the case of RNNs again, such as those described in Equation 9.17. Let us assume that there is an objective function $\mathcal{L}$ that decomposes over the different timesteps, such that $\mathcal{L} = \sum_{t=1}^{T} \mathcal{L}_t$.

In this case, it holds that the derivative of $\mathcal{L}_t$ with respect to any parameter θ:

$$\frac{\partial \mathcal{L}_t}{\partial \theta} = \sum_{k=1}^{t} \left(\frac{\partial \mathcal{L}_t}{\partial h^{(t)}} \frac{\partial h^{(t)}}{\partial h^{(k)}} \frac{\partial^+ h^{(k)}}{\partial \theta} \right),$$

where $\dfrac{\partial^+ h^{(k)}}{\partial \theta}$ refers to the "immediate derivative" (Pascanu et al., 2013) of $h^{(k)}$ with respect to θ, in which $h^{(k-1)}$ is taken to be a constant with respect to θ (so we do not apply further the chain rule for $h^{(k-1)}$ when taking its derivative with respect to θ). The derivative $\dfrac{\partial h^{(t)}}{\partial h^{(k)}}$ can be shown to be:

$$\frac{\partial h^{(t)}}{\partial h^{(k)}} = \prod_{i=t}^{k-1} \frac{\partial h^{(i)}}{\partial h^{(i-1)}} = \prod_{t=i}^{k-1} W_{\text{rec}}^{\top} \text{diag} \left(g'(h^{(i-1)}) \right), \tag{9.18}$$

where diag is a function that takes as an input a vector (coordinate-wise derivatives of the activation function, in this case) and turns it into a diagonal matrix with the values of the vector on the diagonal. Note that $\dfrac{\partial h^{(t)}}{\partial h^{(k)}}$ is shorthand for a matrix that takes the derivative of a specific coordinate of $h^{(t)}$ with respect to a specific coordinate of $h^{(k)}$. This is a gradient formulation that unravels the backpropagation equations in full.

The vanishing gradient problem arises, for example, when the largest singular value of W_{rec} is small, and as such the norm of the right-hand side of Equation 9.18 reaches 0 quickly. This will happen if that singular value λ is smaller than $\frac{1}{\gamma}$ where γ is an upper bound on $||\text{diag}(g'(h^{(i-1)}))||$. In this case, following Equation 9.18, it holds that:[12]

$$\left\|\left\|\frac{\partial h^{(t)}}{\partial h^{(k)}}\right\|\right\| \leq ||W_{\text{rec}}^{\mathsf{T}}|| \cdot \left\|\text{diag}\left(g'(h^{(i-1)})\right)\right\| < \frac{1}{\gamma}\gamma < 1. \tag{9.19}$$

Equation 9.19 indicates that it could be the case that there exists $\mu < 1$ such that $||\frac{\partial h^{(t)}}{\partial h^{(k)}}|| < \mu$ for all timesteps k. In this case, it holds that

$$\left\|\left\|\frac{\partial \mathcal{L}_t}{\partial h^{(t)}} \cdot \frac{\partial h^{(t)}}{\partial h^{(k)}}\right\|\right\| = \left\|\left\|\frac{\partial \mathcal{L}_t}{\partial h^{(t)}} \cdot \prod_{i=t}^{k-1} \frac{\partial h^{(i)}}{\partial h^{(i-1)}}\right\|\right\| \leq \mu^{t-k}\left\|\left\|\frac{\partial \mathcal{L}_t}{\partial h^{(t)}}\right\|\right\|.$$

The above equation shows that the contribution to the gradient of terms in further timesteps reaches 0 exponentially fast as the timestep increases. While the vanishing gradient happens whenever $\mu < 1$, the opposite problem *may* happen if the largest singular value of W_{rec} is too large. In this case, the gradient becomes larger and larger until it "explodes" and convergence becomes erratic, or there is an overflow. "Gradient clipping" (in which the gradient is clipped if it is larger than a certain threshold value) is often used to overcome this problem. The intuition behind the reason of the problem of vanishing gradients and the exploding gradient is in our multiplication of the gradients through the backpropagated terms. Multiplying too many of these terms together may lead to such problems.

Long Short-Term Memory Units and Gated Recurrent Units   One way to solve the problem of the vanishing gradient in recurrent and deep networks is to use an abstraction of a neuron called a Long Short-Term Memory (LSTM) cell, developed by Hochreiter and Schmidhuber (1997) and depicted in Figure 9.4. An LSTM cell maintains an internal cell state at time step $c^{(t)}$ as well as an output state $\alpha^{(t)}$. These two states are vectors determined by the following two equations:

$$c^{(t)} = f^{(t)} \odot c^{(t-1)} + i^{(t)} \odot z^{(t)} \qquad \qquad \textit{cell memory} \qquad (9.20)$$

$$\alpha^{(t)} = o^{(t)} \odot \tanh\left(c^{(t)}\right) \qquad \qquad \textit{hidden state output,} \qquad (9.21)$$

---

[12]The matrix norms are taken with respect to the spectral norm, which corresponds to the largest singular value of the matrix.

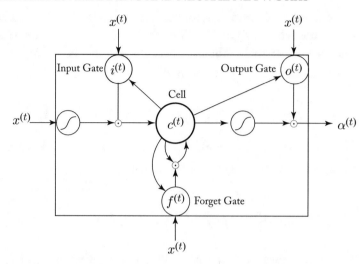

Figure 9.4: A diagram depicting an LSTM cell, with an input $x^{(t)}$ at timestep t (all $x^{(t)}$ in the diagram refer to the same vector). There are three gates: output gate, input gate and forget gate. The cell also maintains an internal state ($c^{(t)}$) and outputs a state $\alpha^{(t)}$. Different operations are used, such as the sigmoid (denoted by the curve operator) and Hadamard product (denoted by $\odot$).[13]

where $\odot$ denotes vector coordinate-wise multiplication (Hadamard product) and the values of $f^{(t)}, i^{(t)}, z^{(t)}$ and $o^{(t)}$ are determined by the following additional equations:

$$i^{(t)} = \sigma\left(W^i x^{(t)} + U^i \alpha^{(t-1)} + b^i\right) \qquad \textit{input gate}$$

$$f^{(t)} = \sigma\left(W^f x^{(t)} + U^f \alpha^{(t-1)} + b^f\right) \qquad \textit{forget gate}$$

$$z^{(t)} = \tanh\left(W^z x^{(t)} + U^z \alpha^{(t-1)} + b^z\right)$$

$$o^{(t)} = \sigma\left(W^o x^{(t)} + U^o \alpha^{(t-1)} + b^o\right) \qquad \textit{output gate,}$$

where $c^{(t)}, \alpha^{(t)}, i^{(t)}, f^{(t)}, z^{(t)}, o^{(t)} \in \mathbb{R}^d$ are vectors maintained by the LSTM cell (as such, σ above denotes a coordinate-wise application of the sigmoid function as described in Table 9.1), $W^i, W^f, W^z, W^o \in \mathbb{R}^{d \times k}$ are the weight matrices of the LSTM and b^i, b^f, b^z, b^o are the bias parameters. When considering the LSTM, we see the following structure. The vector $c^{(t)}$, which represents the state of the LSTM cell, is an interpolation between the previous state and $z^{(t)}$, which depends directly on the input. This means that the internal state $c^{(t)}$ can be updated by "forgetting" some of the previous information in the state as the previous state is multiplied against a forget gate $f^{(t)}$) and includes a certain level of information from the input (as $z^{(t)}$

is multiplied against an "input gate" $i^{(t)}$). Finally, $\alpha^{(t)}$ is the output of the LSTM cell, which multiplies a transformation of the internal state against an "output gate" $o^{(t)}$.

The reason that LSTM is less prone to the vanishing gradient problem is that its internal state $c^{(t)}$ in Equation 9.20 does not include a nonlinear, possibly squashing, function applied on the state itself, causing the "squashing" to compound. Information is additively combined into a new cell state from the previous timestep. Some information is potentially forgotten (through the forget gate which is multiplied against $c^{(t-1)}$) and some information is added by incorporating $z^{(t)}$. LSTM is constructed in a way that allows long range dependencies to propagate through the updates of the state of the cell.

LSTMs are part of a family of neural network units that make use of gates. Another example of such a unit is the Gated Recurrent Unit (GRUs), originally developed for machine translation (Cho et al., 2014). GRUs maintain the gates and states that are defined by the following equations:

$$
\begin{aligned}
r^{(t)} &= \sigma(W^r x^{(t)} + U^r \alpha^{(t-1)}) & \text{\textit{reset gate}} \\
z^{(t)} &= \sigma(W^z x^{(t)} + U^z \alpha^{(t-1)}) & \text{\textit{update gate}} \\
\alpha^{(t)} &= z^{(t)} \odot \alpha^{(t-1)} + (1 - z^{(t)}) \odot \beta^{(t-1)} & \text{\textit{output}} \quad (9.22) \\
\beta^{(t)} &= \tanh\left(W^\beta x^{(t)} + U^\beta (r^{(t)} \odot \alpha^{(t-1)})\right).
\end{aligned}
$$

The reset and update gates, $r^{(t)}$ and $z^{(t)}$, control how much of the information from the previous hidden state is maintained in the next state $\alpha^{(t)}$. In principle, the number of parameters used by a GRU would be lower than the number of parameters used by an LSTM.

LSTMs and GRUs are an abstract form of a cell that may take part in a RNN, and one can stack them up (with the output of one LSTM cell being fed as an input to another) or combine them in other ways. Indeed, neural encoder-decoders (in the next section) build on this idea. See also Graves (2012) for early work on using recurrent neural models for sequence modeling.

9.4.3   NEURAL ENCODER-DECODER MODELS

Neural encoder-decoder models are recurrent neural network models that read a sequence of symbols (usually represented as vectors) and then output a sequence of symbols. This model is one of the generic neural network architectures that is now widely used by the NLP community. This neural network architecture is also often referred to as "sequence-to-sequence models" or seq2seq for short.

Such a model consists of two main components, usually LSTM cells, an encoder and a decoder, that are "stitched" together to feed the output of one as an input for the other. More

---

[13]Figure adapted from https://tex.stackexchange.com/questions/332747/how-to-draw-a-diagram-of-long-short-term-memory.

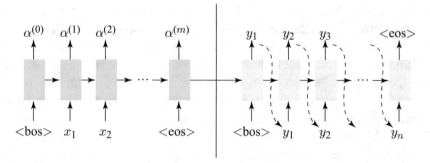

Figure 9.5: An unrolled diagram for an encoder-decoder model. The left part is the encoder, the right part is the decoder. The encoder also returns an output state $\alpha^{(t)}$ at each position t. The decoder, on the other hand, outputs a symbol at each step, until it reaches the end-of-sentence symbol. The output in the previous step is used as an input for the next step. The output symbol is determined by the output state in each position. The blocks themselves "contain" the "cell memory" (in LSTM, this is $c^{(t)}$; see Equation 9.20). The markers bos and eos are beginning-of-sequence and end-of-sequence markers.

specifically, the encoder part is an LSTM[14] cell that receives the sequential input and maintains an internal state, and the decoder part also consists of a cell that (a) receives as an input the encoder's last state after reading the sequence; (b) outputs a symbol; (c) receives as an input its output from the previous position in the sequence and continues the process. Figure 9.5 gives a diagram of an encoder-decoder model.

In their modern version, neural encoder-decoder models were first introduced for machine translation (Cho et al., 2014, Sutskever et al., 2014), rooted in a two-decade-old endeavour to treat machine translation in a connectionist framework (Castano and Casacuberta 1997, Neco and Forcada 1997; see also Kalchbrenner and Blunsom 2013). Since then, these models have been widely used for many other types of problems that require transduction of a sequence of symbols to another sequence, such as summarization (or more generally, generation), question answering and syntactic and semantic parsing.

The neural encoder-decoder model of Cho et al. (2014), which has become the base for other variants, models a distribution of the form $p(y_1, \ldots, y_n \mid x_1, \ldots, x_m)$, mapping an input sequence of symbols $x_1 \ldots x_m$ to an output sequence $y_1 \ldots y_n$. The model works by first computing a (global) vector c of the input sequence by running it through a recurrent unit (GRU or LSTM, for example). That vector c is the cell memory of the last step in the input scan (see Equation 9.20 for LSTM). The decoder, in turn, also uses a recurrent unit (for example, LSTM)

---

[14]While we generally make reference to LSTM cells composing the encoder-decoder model, a natural variant is one in which we use a GRU cell. This variant is common in NLP.

to define the following probability of generating an output symbol:

$$p(y_t \mid y_1, \ldots, y_{t-1}, x_1, \ldots, x_m) = g\left(\overline{\alpha}^{(t)}, y_{t-1}, c\right), \tag{9.23}$$

where g is a probabilistic function (parameterized by some weights, for example, by using a softmax function that combines its arguments into a probability), $\overline{\alpha}^{(t)}$ (Equation 9.21) is the output state of the decoder recurrent unit at position t, y_{t-1} is the output symbol in the previous decoder state and c is the context vector as defined above. The total probability of $y_1 \ldots y_n$ is naturally defined as the product of the factors in Equation 9.23.[15]

Many variants for encoder-decoder models have been suggested, the most prominent being the one that includes an "attention mechanism" (Bahdanau et al., 2015). The attention mechanism aims to solve the problem of locality in predicting the output sequence. At each position in the output, there is usually a specific part of the input that is most relevant to predicting the relevant output symbol. The attention mechanism works by using all LSTM hidden state outputs across the input sequence as an input to the output cell. This is in contrast to only using the last state of the encoder as the input to the decoder. Figure 9.6 depicts the mechanism. Through "attention weights," the mechanism creates a soft alignment between the input sequence elements and the output sequence elements. This was found to be highly useful for neural machine translation, as an example, in line with the importance of word alignment modeling in traditional machine translation models, such as phrase-based ones.

More formally, let t be an index in the encoder sequence and s be an index in the decoder sequence. In addition, let $\alpha^{(s)}$ be defined as in Equation 9.21 (or in Equation 9.22 for GRUs) for the encoder (over a sequence of length n), and let $\overline{\alpha}^{(t-1)}$ be the corresponding state at index $t-1$ for the decoder. We also assume the existence of a parameterized similarity function $\text{sim}(\alpha, \overline{\alpha})$ between encoder and decoder states. We compute the coefficients:

$$\beta_t(s) = \frac{\exp(\text{sim}(\overline{\alpha}^{(t-1)}, \alpha^{(s)}))}{\sum_{s'=1}^{n} \exp(\text{sim}(\overline{\alpha}^{(t-1)}, \alpha^{(s')}))}.$$

We now compute a weighted context vector, defined as:

$$d^{(t)} = \sum_{s=1}^{n} \beta_t(s)\alpha^{(s)},$$

and use this context vector as an input to the decoder cell at index t, in addition to the output from the decoder at index $t-1$, which is also input at index t. The context vector $d^{(t)}$ allows the decoder to focus on a specific index in the encoder states when predicting the output. Since $\beta_t(s)$ are potentially parameterized, the neural network can learn how to set these coefficients to focus on relevant parts of the encoder states.

---

[15]The encoder-decoder model of Sutskever et al. (2014) has some differences, for example, in the fact that c is not used as the input for all decoding steps, but just as the input for the first decoder step.

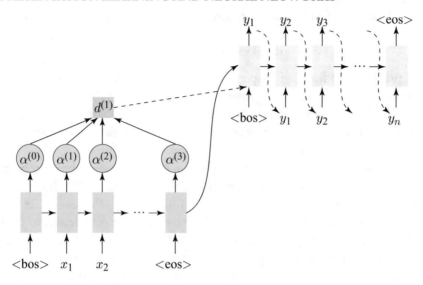

Figure 9.6: An unrolled diagram for a neural encoder-decoder model with an attention mechanism. The context vector $d^{(t)}$ is created at each time step as a weighted average of the states of the encoder, and is fed into the decoder at each position. There is a connection through $d^{(t)}$ between each element of the encoder and each element of the decoder.

There is a variety of similarity scores that can be used, such as the dot product between α and $\overline{\alpha}$, or a parameterized dot-product in the form of $\alpha^{\top} W \overline{\alpha}$ where W are additional parameters in the neural network. One can also concatenate the two input vectors to the similarity function, for example as $v^{\top} \tanh (W [\alpha; \overline{\alpha}])$ (with v and W being parameters of the neural network). See Luong et al. (2015) for a thorough investigation of scoring functions for attention-based models.

The encoder component in the encoder-decoder model usually scans an input sequence token by token. It is sometimes advisable to scan the input in the reverse direction, to bias the encoder to encode the beginning of the sentence as more salient. To help overcome the problem of long-range dependencies, one may also use a *BiLSTM* encoder (Huang et al., 2015), in which the input sequence is scanned both left-to-right and right-to-left. A diagram of a BiLSTM encoder is given in Figure 9.7.

In addition, it may be preferable for the model to *copy* a word from the input sequence to the output sequence. This is especially true in the context of machine translation, in which named entities in one language may be unseen words might be written in an identical manner in the target language. For that end, Gu et al. (2016) introduced the notion of a "copying mechanism," which copies words from the input sequence based on the attention vectors. The total probability of outputting a specific word becomes a mixture between the probability according to a softmax

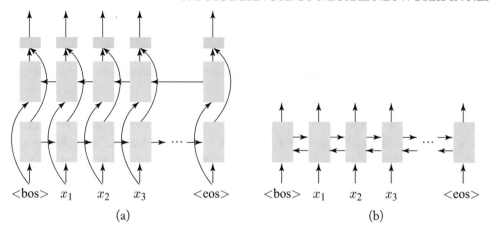

Figure 9.7: Diagrams for a bidirectional encoder. (a) With bidirectional encoders, there are two LSTM encoders that read the input left-to-right and right-to-left. As such, the final representation at each position is as such a combination of the state of the two encoders at the relevant position, reading from both directions; (b) a common schematic representation used to describe (a).

over the output vocabulary and a softmax (based on the attention weights) over the words in the input.

From a technical perspective, neural encoder-decoder models are relatively easy to implement with current computation graph software packages, which makes them even more attractive as a modeling option. There are also quite a few existing off-the-shelf packages for `seq2seq` models that are widely popular, such as OpenNMT (Klein et al., 2017) and Nematus (Sennrich et al., 2017).

9.4.4 CONVOLUTIONAL NEURAL NETWORKS

CNNs are a type of neural network architecture that is biologically inspired by the visual processing system. This architecture has shown great success in computer vision and image processing problems, and we begin our discussion with an example from image processing.

Consider the case in which a researcher is interested in building a classifier that classifies an image into two classes. The binary label indicates whether there is a chair appearing in the image or not. If the image is of a fixed size, one can build a feed-forward network, mapping the inputs to the output with a neuron per input pixel in the image, and a corresponding weight(s) associated with it. However, the number of parameters that would be required for a neural network that has a set of weights for each pixel in the image would be prohibitive. In addition, generalization to "unseen chairs" will require a large amount of data. Ideally, we would want to have the network learn certain characteristics of a chair in an abstract manner, and identify them in the image in a way which is invariant to the position of the chair in the picture. More generally, we want to identify different abstract features in the image that can be used further for classification.

CNNs aim at tackling these issues by reducing the number of parameters that the network needs to learn so that each small region of the image uses a fixed set of parameters. For example, we may have a sliding window of dimensions 4×4 scanning an image of dimensions 128×128. The window may scan the image, moving pixel by pixel, or with larger steps (controlled by a parameter called the "stride size"). At each scanning point in the window, we yield a single number which is the dot product between a vector of a set of weights and the pixel values in the window. This number could potentially be further run through a nonlinear activation unit.

The result of this process is a new "meta-pixel" per sliding window position in the original image. We may have several types of sliding windows, resulting in several new matrices with meta-pixels. Each such matrix, corresponding to a specific sliding window *filter* (with a different set of weights associated with that filter) could detect some specific property of the image.

As such, the first layer of a CNN may include a set of filters, each leading to a new matrix in dimensions that are smaller than the original image. Each of these filter outputs can be further run through a set of new sliding windows, narrowing down the number of meta-pixels, until reaching a small number that can be used for classification at the final neuron.

CNNs are often also interlaced with layers of pooling, such as max-pooling, most often used to obtain a fixed-size vector after convolution. This means that each matrix, the result of a specific filter, is run through some transformation, such as max or average, leading to a single number. Max-pooling, for example, would select the largest value in the matrix result of a specific filter. The result of this pooling can be further convolved again with a sliding window. In the case of natural language, the matrices on which convolution is applied may be of different dimensions across training examples. This variability happens, for example, because sentence length may vary from one example to another. In that case, pooling also helps reducing such variable-size matrix to a fixed-dimension matrix. This is described later in this section.

While CNNs have demonstrated great success in vision tasks, including image understanding and classification (Krizhevsky et al., 2012), it took some time for them to become a standard tool in the neural network NLP toolkit. Originally, CNNs performed convolution with a sliding window, reminiscent of n-gram modeling, over a matrix, representing an image. The natural way to treat, say, a sentence, in a similar manner is to create a matrix where each column corresponds to a word in the sentence (in the form of a word embedding), and the columns are indexed by the position of the word in the sentence. As such, we apply convolution on a single dimension.

This was the approach that Kalchbrenner et al. (2014) took when they showed how to use CNNs on sentences. The sentence is represented by an $K \times N$ matrix, where N is the length of the sentence and K is the size of the word embedding that is used. A sliding window of dimensions $K \times M$ is then applied, where M is the number of words taken together in each convolution step. Note that the window size is of height K, as there is no sense of locality

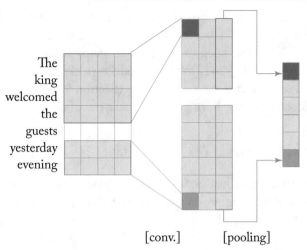

[conv.]   [pooling]

Figure 9.8: An example of CNN for encoding a sentence representation. The first layer is convolution, the second layer is max-pooling. There are two convolutions: one of size 4 and one of size 2. See detailed explanation in the text. Figure adapted from Narayan et al. (2018b).

among the different coordinates of the word embeddings (meaning, coordinates 1 and 2 in the embedding are not apriori related to each more than coordinates 1 and 3 are). As such, the entire word embedding is taken together when applying the sliding window.

The result of applying this convolution is a vector of dimension αM ($\alpha \leq 1$), depending on the stride size. It is often the case that many filters are applied on the sentence, each with a different sliding window, and then max-pooling or another type of pooling is applied on the results of all filters to get a fixed vector size. Similar to encoding with RNNs, this is an approach that can be used to reduce a variable-length sentence to a vector representing it with a fixed dimension. This fixed-dimension vector can now be readily used for a classification step.

Consider, for example, Figure 9.8. Two types of convolutions are described: the top one with a window size of four words and the bottom one with a window size of two words. Each word is represented by a word embedding of dimension 4. The windows slide over the sentence "The king welcomed the guests yesterday evening," and as such leads to 4 window applications for the window of size 4 and 6 window applications for the window size of 2. Note that one can also pad the sentence with beginning and end markers, in which case we would have 7 window applications for both windows (padding this way is often referred to as a "wide" convolution as opposed to a "narrow" convolution). The number of filters used for each convolution is 3, which is why we get a matrix of dimensions 4×3 for the upper convolution and a matrix of dimensions 6×3 for the bottom convolution. Finally, max-pooling is applied, taking the maximum across each row in each matrix, leading to a 6-dimensional vector representing the entire sentence. Note that this dimension of the vector is a function of the number of *filters* only, and not the length of the sentence. As such, we get fixed-dimension representations for varying-length sentences.

More recently, CNNs have been used for sequence-to-sequence modeling, such as machine translation (Gehring et al., 2017). These models—nicked `convseq2seq`, like `seq2seq` models that are based on recurrent neural networks (Section 9.4.3)—are also composed of an encoder and a decoder component, both of which make use of convolutions.

9.5   TUNING NEURAL NETWORKS

The backpropagation algorithm (Section 9.3.1) has been the mainstay for training neural networks and determining their weights, but it does not directly tackle issues such as choosing neural network size (the number of hidden layers and the number of neurons per layer), activation function types and other hyperparameters. In addition, backpropagation may lead to overfitting if used on its own. In this section, we describe how to regularize neural networks and fine tune their hyperparameters—and when relevant, describe connections to the Bayesian approach.

9.5.1   REGULARIZATION

Regularization is used as a way to prevent overfitting when estimating a model. Overfitting refers to the case in which the learning algorithm sets the weights of a model in such a way that it handles idiosyncrasies that appear in the training data, but do not necessarily represent the general rule. This leads to a significantly higher performance on the training data than on the held-out test data. Overfitting happens when the estimated model family is highly complex, and thus has the capacity to retain the idiosyncrasies mentioned above.

To avoid overfitting with model estimation, regularization is often used. With regularization, we add an additional term to the objective function (such as the log-likelihood) that we optimize during training, and this term is used as a penalty term for models deemed too complex. The most common regularization terms used with neural network training are the L_2 squared-norm of the weights in the neural network, or alternatively the L_1 norm (which leads to sparsity in the set of weights used—many weights are set to 0 during training). Both of these regularization terms have a Bayesian interpretation, as described in Section 4.2.1.

Another common way to perform regularization is dropout (Srivastava et al., 2014), in which certain neurons in the neural network are "dropped" during training. This means that their contribution to the activation and to the gradient computation is 0, which is achieved by dropping their connections to the rest of the network. Each unit in the hidden layer or in the input has a certain probability of being dropped at each phase in training (for example, in a batch of gradient optimization). This prevents network's dependence on a small number of inputs (or hidden neurons), or alternatively, co-dependence of neurons on each other to give the signal for predicting the output (Eisenstein, 2019).

Dropout has been interpreted in a Bayesian manner by Gal and Ghahramani (2016b). In their model, there is a Gaussian prior on the weights of a neural network. Furthermore, since inference is intractable, the authors use variational inference (Chapter 6) to find the posterior. The key idea they introduce is the form of the variational distribution, which is a neural network with a set of weights that are zeroed out with a certain probability. This is similar to the dropout approach mentioned in Section 9.4.4. The dropout formulation of Gal and Ghahramani makes a neural network equivalent to an approximation of deep Gaussian processes—an hierarchical model where Gaussian processes (see Section 7.5.1) are applied on each other (Damianou and Lawrence, 2013). Gal and Ghahramani (2016a) further extended their work to the use of CNNs (Section 9.4.4). The goal of the authors was to use the Bayesian approach on CNNs so that they also work on small amounts of data without overfitting. Gal and Ghahramani (2016a) tested their Bayesian neural networks on digit recognition datasets.

More recent work in the NLP community by Chirkova et al. (2018) sets a prior on the weights of an RNN. This prior is inversely proportional to the absolute value of the weights. Inference is then followed variationally, finding the approximate posterior. This prior is used to find a sparse set of parameters for the RNN.

9.5.2   HYPERPARAMETER TUNING

One of the main decisions that has to be made when building a neural model is its architecture (i.e., the network structure). Even with the architecture type being decided, there are still many decisions that must be made, such as determining the number of neurons per layer (in the case of a feed-forward network), the number of layers used, and the type of activation functions used (or neural units such as LSTMs vs. GRUs). Networks that are too large might overfit, while networks that are too small might not be able to generalize well from the data.

While there is recent research that shows it is possible to automatically learn or search for a well-performing neural network architecture (Liu et al., 2018, Real et al., 2018, Zoph and Le, 2017), most of these decisions are currently being made through the use of "trial and error:" a variety of values are tried, and then the final hyperparameters selected are those that perform the best on a validation set.[16] This process of optimizing the hyperparameters is crucial, in many cases, to obtain a neural network which behaves optimally.

Optimizing the hyperparameters using standard methods such as gradient descent is problematic. First, the performance or the proxy objective function such as log-likelihood is often not differentiable with respect to these hyperparameters. Even worse, we might not have an explicit functional or analytic form for the performance we would like to maximize as a function of the hyperparameters. This means that we must treat that performance function as a blackbox—given a specific set of hyperparameters, we can find the performance of the learned model. As

---

[16]This is less intensive than cross-validation, in which we repeat several experiments, at each time testing the model on one part of the training set that is left out.

an example, consider the BLEU metric in machine translation, which measures n-gram overlap between the output of a system and the correct target reference.

In recent years, several proposals have been made to develop "blackbox hyperparameter optimizers" that do not require gradient computations or an explicit form for the objective function they optimize. Derivative-free optimization (Rios and Sahinidis, 2013) is one example, and there are related ideas that date back to the 1950s (Chernoff, 1959). The black-box optimization algorithms usually take as an input a set of hyperparameters and the performance of a model with them, and return as an output the next hyperparameter to try out or, alternatively, the final decision on the hyperparameters to be used.

There is a Bayesian connection to hyperparameter tuning through the notion of *Bayesian optimization* (Močkus, 1975, 2012) that has recently been re-discovered in the machine learning community (Snoek et al., 2012). Say the performance function we are trying to maximize is $f(\alpha)$ where α is a set of hyperparameters such as neural network size. Bayesian optimization works by defining a prior over this function f (usually the prior is a Gaussian process; see more about Gaussian processes in Section 7.5.1). It then also defines an *acquisition function g*, a cheap-to-optimize proxy for f that chooses a point to evaluate using f given the previous points that were already evaluated. Bayesian optimization works by iterating between the optimization of the acquisition function, evaluating f at the point the acquisition function chooses and then updating the posterior over f with the new result the algorithm received.

The acquisition function must take into account the current state of beliefs about f in order to choose which point to evaluate next. Indeed, there are various types of acquisition functions, for example, those that choose a point to maximize expected improvement over the current distribution over f. In that case, we have:

$$g(\alpha' \mid \mathcal{D}) = E_{p(f'|\mathcal{D})}[\max\{0, f'(\alpha') - f(\alpha_{\max})\}],$$

where $\alpha_{\max}$ is the point for which f was evaluated to be the largest so far. An alternative to maximizing expected improvement is instead maximizing the *probability* of improvement through the acquisition function:

$$g(\alpha' \mid \mathcal{D}) = E_{p(f'|\mathcal{D})}[I(f'(\alpha') \geq f(\alpha_{\max}))].$$

This acquisition function is often less preferable than the expected improvement, as it ignores the size of the improvement and just focuses on maximizing the probability of *any* improvement.

The key idea is that the acquisition function has to balance between exploitation (in which it explores points that are likely to have a high value of f, and low variance according to the current maintained distribution over f) and exploration (in which it explores points that might have higher variance). A sketch of the Bayesian optimization algorithm is given in Algorithm 9.1. It can be seen from line 2 why this type of optimization is referred to as Bayesian. The algorithm takes as input the prior and the evaluations of f, and then finds the posterior over the optimized function. Following that, in lines 4–5, it chooses the next evaluation points for f.

Input: A function $f(\alpha)$ evaluated as a blackbox, a prior $p(f')$ over functions of the type of f, an acquistion function g.
Output: α^*, a proposed maximizer for f.

1: Set $n = 0, \mathcal{D} = \emptyset$
2: Set current posterior over f, $p(f' \mid \mathcal{D}) = p(f')$
3: **repeat**
4:     Set $\alpha_{n+1} = \arg\max_{\alpha'} g(\alpha' \mid \mathcal{D})$
5:     Let $y_{n+1} = f(\alpha_{n+1})$ (evaluate f)
6:     $\mathcal{D} \leftarrow \mathcal{D} \cup \{(\alpha_{n+1}, y_{n+1})\}$
7:     Update posterior $p(f' \mid \mathcal{D})$ based on new $\mathcal{D}$
8:     $n \leftarrow n + 1$
9: **until** stopping criterion met (such as $n > T$ for a fixed T)
10: **return** $\alpha^* = \alpha_n$

Algorithm 9.1: The Bayesian optimization algorithm.

9.6 GENERATIVE MODELING WITH NEURAL NETWORKS

Deep generative models make use of neural networks to learn probability distributions over a sample space without necessarily making any classification of the elements in that space, or at the very least, without including such classification labels during model training. Typical neural network models learn a conditional distribution in the form of $p(Z \mid X)$ where Z is an output random variable and X is an input random variable. Deep generative models, on the other hand, learn a distribution in the form $p(X)$, after being exposed to samples of X. This is especially useful when there is an interest in generating samples that are distributed with similar form to the training data.

While not Bayesian in the traditional sense of the word (as there is no placement of a prior distribution on the parameters of the neural network, or direct posterior inference), deep generative modeling shares some striking similarities with Bayesian learning, most prominently through the identification of a "posterior" distribution over a latent variable to help generate the inputs.

To this date, the two most popular approaches to modeling a distribution through deep generative models are variational autoencoders (VAEs; Kingma and Welling 2014) and generative adversarial networks (GANs; Goodfellow et al. 2014). The use of the term "generative" in these models usually refers to the use of a latent variable, often a continuous vector, which is used to generate an output of the model. While these two approaches to generative modeling have been developed independently, recently there has been exploration of the connections between them (Hu et al., 2018).

9.6.1 VARIATIONAL AUTOENCODERS

We begin this section with an intuition about VAEs, followed by their full derivation as variational approximation.

VAEs as Autoencoders

Autoencoders in general provide an approach to modeling an input distribution and extracting its salient features into a representation. These encoders work by passing a random variable Y through a "compression" layer to obtain a hidden representation z for each y. The hidden representation is then used to recover y in another step. The first step is referred to as "encoding," and the second step as "decoding." Note that we assume that samples from the random variable Y are observed, while Z is not observed.

Variational autoencoders draw on this basic approach of autoencoders by maintaining a probabilistic encoder, meaning that there is a distribution $q(Z \mid y)$ that probabilistically encodes every y into a z. When optimizing VAEs, this encoder is pushed to remain close to a prior distribution over Z (for example, a Gaussian with mean 0). The decoder, in turn, includes a distribution that takes the encoded z as input and tries to recover y. A key idea in VAEs is that both the encoders and decoders are represented using neural networks. More precisely, the encoder $q(Z \mid y)$ is often a Gaussian parametrized by, for example in NLP models, an RNN (that encodes a sentence y). The decoder, in turn, is a neural network (for example, again, an RNN) which is parametrized as a function of z.

The objective function we aim to minimize with VAEs would be:

$$\mathrm{KL}(q(Z \mid y)\|p(Z)) - E_{q(Z|y)}[\log p(y \mid Z)].$$

This objective demonstrates the intuition mentioned above. The first term is a KL-divergence term that maintains q closer to the prior $p(Z)$ (see Section A.1.2). The second term ensures that we can recover y well under the distribution of the possible latent representations that we get from the encoder.

In practice, VAE is implemented by specifying encoder and decoder networks. The encoder network which takes a y as input, together with a sample from a prior distribution $p(Z)$ provides a sample from the encoder $q(Z \mid y)$. Then the decoder network takes that sample as input and tries to recover the input y.

VAEs can also be set up in a "conditional" setting, in which there is an additional random variable X such that both the prior $p(Z \mid X)$ and the encoder $q(Z \mid Y, X)$ condition on it. In terms of the neural network architectures, this means that the instances from X, provided as part of the training set and the decoding process, are used as additional input to the encoder and decoder networks. For example, as mentioned below, VAEs in that form can be used for

Machine Translation—X would be the input sentence and Y would be the sentence in the target language.

Bowman et al. (2016) constructed a VAE model for sentences, where the latent representation aims at modeling the semantics of the sentence in a continuous manner. In contrast to recurrent language models (Mikolov et al., 2011), their model is aimed at creating a global representation of the sentence through the latent state Z. Both the encoder and decoder models are RNNs (with a single layer of LSTM cells). Bowman et al. experimented using their models with the problem of language modeling, where their model performed slightly worse than an RNN. They also tested their model on a missing-word imputation task, where their model significantly outperforms the RNN language model baseline.

The idea of using a global semantic space was later used for machine translation. Zhang et al. (2016) introduced a conditional VAE model (see section below), in which the latent random variable Z is used to represent a global semantic space. The posterior that is approximated in variational means is used for the semantic space variables that are conditioned both on the source and target sentences. During decoding, however, access to the sentence in the target language is eliminated, and instead a model that generates the target sentence is used. The model generates word y_j (jth word) in the target sentence conditioned on all previously generated words, z and x, and the source sentence. The authors use a Monte Carlo approximation to evaluate the objective function.

In the next section, we describe a full mathematical derivation of VAEs which draws on connections to Chapter 6. Our derivation is based on that of Doersch (2016).

VAEs through Variational Approximation

In Chapter 6 we thoroughly investigate variational inference in Bayesian NLP. The principle of maximizing a variational bound with respect to a posterior distribution can also be used to learn generative models that make use of neural networks. While the learned model is not necessarily Bayesian in the sense of having a prior over the model parameters, the learning objective has a strong relationship to variational inference and shares the common use of latent variables as those in Bayesian models.

The goal behind variational autoencoders is to learn a distribution over Y, an observed random variable. The distribution over Y is controlled by a latent variable that is not observed, and as such, in the neural network literature VAEs are referred to as learning in an unsupervised manner. The distribution $p(Y)$ that is learned using VAE can be sampled in order to generate samples that mimic and generalize the training data.

To this end, we consider a simple setup of latent-variable modeling which is familiar to us. We have a model $p(Y, Z \mid \theta)$ where Z is a latent variable and Y is an observed variable. Variational autoencoders were originally introduced in cases in which both Z and Y come from a vector sample space. This means that the sample space for $p(Y, Z \mid \theta)$ is a subset of $\mathbb{R}^d \times \mathbb{R}^k$, for integers d and k. The factorization of the distribution $p(Y, Z \mid \theta)$ is as usual $p(Y \mid Z, \theta) p(Z \mid \theta)$.

With variational autoencoders, the probability distribution $p(Y \mid Z = z, \theta)$ which is often used, and with which VAEs were introduced, is Gaussian, especially for applications such as Computer Vision. Still, we are not restricted to a Gaussian "decoder" distribution, and in NLP, as mentioned in the beginning of this section, this decoder distribution is often an LSTM RNN or another distribution over a discrete space such as the categorical distribution. When Y is a Gaussian, it holds that $Y \sim \text{Gaussian}(f(z, \theta), \sigma^2 I_{d \times d})$ where $I_{d \times d}$ is the identity matrix of dimension d and f is a deterministic function that defines the mean vector of the Gaussian distribution. Since the latent variable Z is masked through f before generating Y, it is not necessary to choose a complex distribution for it. As such, we often choose $Z \sim \text{Gaussian}(0, I_{k \times k})$.

The relationship to neural modeling begins with the choice of $f(z, \theta)$ which is defined through a neural network. The random variable Y is generated from a distribution that is parameterized by a set of parameters created using a neural network.

Learning of neural network function f and parameters θ is accomplished by maximizing the log-likelihood of the data. More specifically, we are given a set of i.i.d. training instances $y^{(1)}, \ldots, y^{(n)}$ and then aim to maximize the following objective with respect to θ and f (where f by itself is controlled by a set of neural network parameters):

$$\log p\left(y^{(1)}, \ldots, y^{(n)} \mid \theta, f\right) = \sum_{i=1}^{n} \log p\left(y^{(i)} \mid \theta, f\right)$$

$$= \sum_{i=1}^{n} \int_{z} p\left(y^{(i)} \mid z, \theta, f\right) p(z \mid \theta) dz.$$

Let $y = y^{(i)}$ for a specific i. To maximize the above we will use variational inference (see Section 6.1 for more detail). We define a variational distribution $q(z \mid y)$ (each training instance will have a corresponding variational distribution). Then, we aim to minimize the KL-divergence between $q(z \mid y)$ and $p(z \mid y, \theta, f)$. Using the definition of KL-divergence and using Bayes rule we get:

$$\text{KL}(q(Z \mid y), p(Z \mid y, \theta, f)) = E_{q(Z|y)}\left[\log q(z \mid y) - \log p(z \mid y, \theta, f)\right]$$

$$= E_{q(Z|y)}\left[\log q(z \mid y) - \log p(y \mid z, \theta, f) - \log p(z)\right]$$

$$+ \log p(y \mid \theta, f).$$

By rearranging the terms and again using the definition of KL-divergence again we get that:

$$\log p(y \mid \theta, f) - \text{KL}(q(Z \mid y), p(Z \mid y, \theta, f))$$

$$= E_{q(Z|y)}\left[\log p(y \mid z, \theta, f)\right] - \text{KL}(q(Z \mid y), p(Z \mid \theta)). \qquad (9.24)$$

The left term in the above equation is maximized (with respect to q) if $q(Z \mid y) = p(Z \mid y, \theta, f)$. In this case, q is the true posterior over the latent variables given a specific example.

For the Gaussian model at hand, it is typical to also choose $q(Z \mid y)$ as a Gaussian with mean value $\mu(y, \nu)$ and a diagonal covariance matrix $\Sigma(y, \nu)$. The mean value and covariance matrices are a deterministic function of y and some parameters ν; this function is also implemented through a neural network (e.g., ν could be used as parameters for such a network). In this case, the second term, $\text{KL}(q(Z \mid y), p(Z \mid \theta))$, in Equation 9.24 has a closed form (as a function of $\mu(y, \nu)$, $\Sigma(y, \nu)$) because it is a KL-divergence between two multivariate Gaussian distributions. See Doersch (2016).

To maximize the bound in Equation 9.24 we can use stochastic gradient descent (see Appendix A.3.1). For a given $y = y^{(i)}$, we can sample z from the current $q(Z \mid y, \mu(y, \nu), \Sigma(y, \nu))$ and update θ, f (through the first term in Equation 9.24) and θ and ν (through the second term). This requires taking the gradient of an objective function over a neural network for the first term, which can be done using backpropagation.

However, there is an issue with such a stochastic update. In principle, the first term in Equation 9.24, $E_{q(Z|y)} [\log p(y \mid z, \theta, f)]$, depends on $\mu(y, \nu)$ and $\Sigma(y, \nu)$, and as such, on ν. This dependence exists because $q(Z \mid y)$ is parameterized by ν. By sampling a single z from the current q and making a stochastic gradient update to the term in the expectation, we ignore this dependence and we do not make any update to $\mu(y, \nu)$ and $\Sigma(y, \nu)$ based on the first term.

To fix this problem, instead of sampling z from $q(Z \mid y)$, we sample ε from a Gaussian with mean-zero and an identity covariance matrix (where ε has the same dimension as z) and then substitute z in Equation 9.24 with $\mu(y, \nu) + \Sigma^{1/2}(y, \nu) \cdot \varepsilon$. Indeed, when using such formulation of z we get the same distribution as intended by $q(Z \mid y, \mu(y, \nu), \Sigma(y, \nu))$. This "reparameterization" trick (see also below) decouples the stochastic samples used in gradient approximation and the parameters for which we take the gradient. The need for this trick is also what makes VAEs less compelling for NLP, as discrete variables (as latent variables) cannot be as easily reparameterized as Gaussians (but see below).

The coining of the term *variational autoencoder* is inspired by the optimization process and by the variational bound that functions as an autoencoder, i.e., a mechanism that encodes an input (Y) through a latent representation (Z) that needs to recover the input (see Section 9.6.1). We first encode Y through variational distribution using the ν parameters and this creates a variational distribution $q(Z \mid Y)$. We then sample z and "decode" it back to Y through the θ parameters and the neural network f (the neural network output $f(z, \theta)$ gives the mean value of the decoded distribution over Y).

Learning of variational autoencoders can be viewed as an execution of stochastic gradient descent on an encoder-decoder neural network, where at each step, we sample a training instance by selecting $i \in [n]$ and then independently sample ε from a Gaussian with a mean 0 and an identity covariance matrix.

The final bound that we aim to optimize using stochastic gradient descent (with respect to the distribution over ε and the n training examples) is based on Equation 9.24 as follows:

$$\mathcal{L}\left(y^{(1)}, \ldots, y^{(n)} \mid \theta, f, v, \mu, \Sigma\right)$$

$$= \frac{1}{n} \sum_{i=1}^{n} \left(E_{\varepsilon}\left[\log p\left(y^{(i)} \mid Z = \mu(y^{(i)}, v) + \Sigma^{1/2}(y^{(i)}, v) \cdot \varepsilon, \theta, f\right)\right]\right.$$

$$\left. - \text{KL}(q(Z \mid y^{(i)}), p(Z \mid \theta)) \right).$$

VAEs provide a means for drawing samples for Y from the estimated neural network. This is done first by sampling z from a Gaussian$(0, I_{k \times k})$ and then decoding it by sampling y from Gaussian$(f(z, \theta), \sigma^2 I_{d \times d})$.[17] This simply follows the generative process described earlier. In doing so, with VAEs we learn a generative distribution over a sample space. However, it is also possible to construct VAE models that make predictions. Such VAEs are called *conditional* VAEs, and they assume the existence of another observed random variable X. Our goal in this case is to learn a conditional model $p(Y \mid X)$ which makes use of a latent variable Z: $p(Y \mid X) = \int_z p(Y \mid X, z) p(z \mid X) dz$. The main difference between this model and the model which does not include X is that in this case the neural network f is a function of z, θ and x. Most commonly, we have Y as a Gaussian with mean $f(z, x, \theta)$ and a diagonal covariance matrix with σ^2 on the diagonal.

The Reparameterization Trick

In this section, we include more details about the reparameterization "trick" mentioned previously. This trick is widely used with VAEs, or whenever we need to differentiate an objective function through a "stochastic node" in a neural network using the backpropagation algorithm (a stochastic node refers to a node in the neural network that is made up of a random variable, such as the latent variable Z with VAEs).[18]

Consider again that in order to maximize the variational bound with VAEs, it is necessary to be able to compute an expectation of the form $E_{q(z|\theta)}[f(z)]$ where $q(z \mid \theta)$ is a Gaussian with learned parameters θ (mean value and variance) and where f is a function of z. To do so, we instead compute the expectation with respect to a standard Gaussian ε (mean 0 and standard deviation 1) and then linearly transform ε by multiplying it by the learned variance and adding the mean to get a random variable equivalent to z (where a linear transformation on a Gaussian random variable remains a Gaussian random variable). More generally, $q(z \mid \theta)$ can be an arbitrary parameterized distribution for which we need to compute the expectation of $f(z)$ and its gradient.

---

[17]Alternatively, we may want to fully integrate out the latent variable Z to have a model over Y, but that is not always possible without a conjugacy of $p(Z)$ and $p(Y \mid Z)$.

[18]It is sometimes possible to integrate out a stochastic node as a hidden variable (for example, when it is a multinomial distribution over a small space), in which case the reparametrization trick is not necessary.

The reparameterization trick generally entails finding a distribution $q(\varepsilon)$ over a random variable ε such that $z = g(\varepsilon, \theta)$ (for a function g), and ε is independent of θ. (In the Gaussian case, g is a linear transformation using the variance and the mean value entailed by θ). Once we find such $q(\varepsilon)$, both the expectation $E_{q(z|\theta)}[f(z)]$ and the gradient of this expectation (with respect to θ) can be reparameterized as:

$$E_{q(z|\theta)}[f(z)] = E_{q(\varepsilon)}[f(g(\varepsilon, \theta))] \tag{9.25}$$

$$\nabla_\theta E_{q(z|\theta)}[f(z)] = E_{q(\varepsilon)}[\nabla_\theta f(g(\varepsilon, \theta))]. \tag{9.26}$$

The important outcome of this parameterization is that now the expectation and its gradient can be computed using samples *independently* of the distribution $q(z \mid \theta)$—we do not need to infer this distribution to calculate these quantities. For example, a set of independent samples $\varepsilon_1, \ldots, \varepsilon_n$ can be used to approximate Equation 9.25 as

$$E_{q(z|\theta)}[f(z)] \approx \frac{1}{n} \sum_{i=1}^{n} f(g(\varepsilon_i, \theta)). \tag{9.27}$$

In the case of z being a discrete random variable, a problem exists with this reparameterization, because there is no g that would be differentiable with respect to $\theta = (\theta_1, \ldots, \theta_K)$ over K events as necessary from Equation 9.26. This is where the Gumbel-softmax "trick" comes into play. Let $U_1, \ldots, U_K$ be a sequence of random variables drawn from a uniform distribution on the interval $[0, 1]$. It holds that if $G_k = -\log(-\log U_k)$ that if we define the random variable X as:

$$X = \arg\max_k \log \theta_k + G_k, \tag{9.28}$$

then X is distributed according to the categorical distribution (Appendix B.1) with parameters $(\theta_1, \ldots, \theta_K)$. The random variables G_k are said to have a *Gumbel* distribution. Note that this way we managed to reparameterize the categorical distribution with respect to θ. More specifically, if we wish $q(\cdot \mid \theta)$ to be a multinomial distribution, we can define $\varepsilon = (G_1, \ldots, G_K)$. The function $g(\varepsilon, \theta)$, in turn, outputs a one-hot vector of length K (i.e., a vector which is all zeros except for in one coordinate, where it is one) with 1 in the coordinate as specified in Equation 9.28. We then have a reparameterization, where expectations with respect to q can be calculated using samples from ε (as described in Equation 9.27).

However, there is still a remaining problem: the function g specified as above is not differentiable. This is where we relax the use of one-hot vectors to any vector in the probability simplex of dimension $K - 1$ (see also Chapter 2 regarding the probability simplex). We define $g \colon \mathbb{R}^K \to \mathbb{R}^K$ to be:

$$[g(\varepsilon, \theta)]_k = \frac{\exp\left((\log \theta_k + \varepsilon_k)/\tau\right)}{\sum_{j=1}^{K} \exp\left((\log \theta_j + \varepsilon_j)/\tau\right)},$$

where τ is a hyperparameter (the larger it is, the more peaked g is). Using this reparameterization trick followed by the application of the softmax distribution, we can use a latent-variable z

over the probability simplex, a better fit for discrete data. See Maddison et al. (2017) and also Section B.9.

9.6.2 GENERATIVE ADVERSARIAL NETWORKS

Generative Adversarial Networks (GANs; Goodfellow et al. 2014) are a type of neural network architecture designed to use discriminative modeling to create a generative model over a sample space. GANs are defined by a "generator" and a "discriminator." The generator generates inputs to the discriminator, which in turn tries to distinguish these inputs from examples from the training data. The objective function is built in such a way that the generator tries to maximize the error of the discriminator, and as such, attempts to create inputs that are most similar to the sample inputs, generalizing their distribution.

More specifically, GANs build their model on two neural networks, G (generator) and D (discriminator), where their internal structure remains underspecified. However, D needs to be a function from the space of Y, $\mathbb{R}^d$, to $[0, 1]$ (outputting a probability) and G needs to be a function from $\mathbb{R}^k$ to $\mathbb{R}^d$, mapping a vector z drawn from a "noise distribution" $p(Z)$ to the space of Y. Note that $p(Z)$ is fixed. This distribution is often assumed to be, for example, a multivariate Gaussian with the identity covariance and zero mean. If it is parameterized, one may need to use the reparameterization trick, as mentioned in Section 9.6.1.

The key idea behind GANs is that D identifies whether y is being drawn from the underlying distribution $p(Y)$. The generator, G, on the other hand, attempts to "fool" D by generating examples that D has difficulty discriminating from the true distribution. This idea is embodied in the following minimax objective that is used to train D and G:

$$\min_G \max_D \frac{1}{n} \sum_{i=1}^{n} \log D\left(y^{(i)}\right) + E_{p(Z)}\left[\log(1 - D(G(z)))\right].$$

The first term is just a reference to the data, and is there to tune D so that it indeed matches the distribution over the data. The second term represents the main idea behind the minimax objective. On the one hand, this term is maximized with respect to D, in an attempt to give low probability to elements that are generated by G. On the other hand, we also attempt to minimize this term, and thus "fool" D to identify examples generated by G as having high probability according to $p(Y)$.

We now specify a generative model over Y that is learned from the data by using G (once it is learned). The model over Y is specified using the following generative model to draw a y:

$$z \sim p(Z),$$
$$y = G(z).$$

In practice, D and G are parameterized through some parameters θ_D and θ_G, and in this manner the minimax objective is optimized with respect to these parameters. In line with neural network training, this objective can be optimized using optimization algorithms similar to those used in stochastic gradient descent.

While GANs in their vanilla form have been successfully applied to learn distributions over continuous domains (such as images and audio), their use in this form is more limited for NLP. GANs work better with observed data that is continuous, but not as well with discrete (observed) data, which are common in NLP. This is because it is a non-trivial task to build a generator (for which the gradients with respect to the parameters can be calculated) based on a noise distribution. Unlike with images, for example, where there is a spectrum of images according to a continuous measure of distance between them, it is less clear how to create such a spectrum for text and measure the distance between, say, a pair of sentences. Still, there has been some recent work in NLP that discusses GANs, for example, work by Caccia et al. (2018) and Tevet et al. (2018).

While GANs are intended to learn the distribution over the sample space represented by the given datapoints, they often just tend to memorize the training examples that they are trained with (known as "mode collapse"). In addition, because we also find a point estimate for a GAN and do not perform full posterior inference, we are unable to represent any multimodality over the parameter setting. In order to alleviate some of these problems, Saatci and Wilson (2017) introduced the idea of Bayesian GANs. In their formulation, there are priors that are placed on the parameters of the generator and the discriminator ($p(\theta_G \mid \alpha_G)$ and $p(\theta_D \mid \alpha_D)$). Inference is performed by iteratively sampling from the following posteriors:

$$p(\theta_G \mid z, \theta_D) \propto \left(\prod_{j=1}^{R} D\left(G(z^{(a_j)})\right) \right) p(\theta_G \mid \alpha_G),$$

$$p\left(\theta_D \mid z, y^{(1)}, \ldots, y^{(n)}, \theta_G\right) \propto \prod_{i=1}^{N} D\left(y^{(b_i)}\right) \times \prod_{j=1}^{R} \left(1 - D\left(G\left(z^{(a_j)}\right)\right)\right) \times p(\theta_D \mid \alpha_D),$$

where $z^{(1)}, \ldots, z^{(r)}$ are samples drawn from $p(Z)$ during each step of sampling. In addition, $\{a_j\}_{j=1}^{N}$ represents a subset of the samples from $p(Z)$ (used in a mini-batch) and $\{b_i\}_{i=1}^{R}$ represents a subset of the observed data $x^{(i)}$, $i \in [n]$ (also used in a mini-batch). Saatci and Wilson propose using a stochastic gradient Hamiltonian Monte Carlo (SGHMC; Chen et al. 2014) to sample from these posteriors.

The formulation of Goodfellow et al. (2014) for GANs is a specific case of Bayesian GANs in which we use uniform priors over the discriminators and generators. In addition, with Goodfellow et al.'s original formulation, we follow MAP estimation (see Section 4.2.1) rather than iterating between the posteriors over the generators and discriminators.

9.7 CONCLUSION

Representation learning and neural networks have become important tools in the NLP toolkit. They have replaced the need to manually construct "features" in linear models with automatic feature and representation construction. This requires *architecture engineering* of the neural network. It also marks a shift in NLP, which began with representing words, sentences, paragraphs and even whole documents as dense continuous vectors. The two most common neural network architectures used in NLP are recurrent and convolutional.

This chapter gives an overview of the main modeling neural network techniques prevalent in NLP, but covers just the tip of the iceberg. The use of neural networks in NLP is a moving target, and develops quite rapidly. For example, there is some evidence that models such as the "Transformer" model (Vaswani et al., 2017) or convolutional seq2seq models (Gehring et al., 2017) give high performance on certain NLP tasks, higher than that of recurrent seq2seq models. Their advantage is also computational, as their functions can be more easily parallelized on a GPU than recurrent neural network functions. The architectural details of these models and others are not covered in this chapter.

While neural networks have transformed much of NLP and have permeated most of the modeling currently done in the area (with this chapter covering a small part in this regard), it remains to be seen whether this research will be able to break a "barrier" that still exists in NLP: communicating and reasoning about natural language at more than just a shallow level, perhaps coming closer to human-level communication.

Reasoning at such a level requires a significant understanding of the world that is difficult to encode purely by looking at specific input-output pairs of a given problem as used in training a neural network model. Furthermore, neural networks have yet to overcome the problem of learning from smaller amounts of data. For example, with Machine Translation, it is claimed that for language pairs with small amounts of parallel data (low-resource setting), older statistical machine translation techniques outperform neural machine translation (Koehn and Knowles 2017; but see also Artetxe et al. 2018, Sennrich et al. 2016). Other important applications, such as complex question answering, summarization and dialog (for example, "chatbots") are also far from being solved. For example, many commercial dialog systems are still largely reliant on systems with manually crafted rules and scripts.

Bayesian learning can make a small, but significant contribution in that respect. Insights from latent-variable inference in the Bayesian setting (such as variational inference) have been used and can be further used to develop estimation and learning algorithms for neural networks. In addition, traditional Bayesian modeling requires construction of a generative model (for example, in the form of a graphical model), and therefore leads to more interpretable models. Neural networks, on the other hand, often yield "blackboxes," which make it difficult to understand how a specific neural network performs a task at hand. This is again a case where concepts from Bayesian learning, such as generation of interpretable latent structures, can help bring progress to the area of neural networks in NLP through understanding about neural model decisions.

This direction in understanding neural networks as an interpretable model, not necessarily in a Bayesian context, has spurred much current interest in the NLP community (Lei et al., 2016, Li et al., 2015, Linzen, 2018), including a recent series of workshops devoted to it.[19]

There is also a flipside to interpreting neural networks in a Bayesian context, in which representations originating in Bayesian modeling are used to augment the representations that neural networks obtain. For example, Mikolov and Zweig (2012), Ghosh et al. (2016), and Narayan et al. (2018a) used the latent Dirichlet allocation model (LDA; Chapter 2) in conjunction with neural networks to provide networks with additional contextual topical information.

For more information about the use of neural networks in NLP, see Goldberg (2017) and Eisenstein (2019).

---

[19]See https://blackboxnlp.github.io/.

9.8   EXERCISES

9.1.   Discuss: What are the desired properties of word embeddings and their relationship to each other in the embedding space? Does it depend on the problem at hand, and if so, how?

9.2.   Show that the XOR problem cannot be solved using a linear classifier. More specifically, show that if you are given a dataset with examples (x_1, x_2) and labels $y(x_1, x_2)$:

(x_1, x_2)	y
$(0, 0)$	0
$(0, 1)$	1
$(1, 0)$	1
$(1, 1)$	0

there are no weights w_1, w_2 and bias b such that

$$w_1 x_1 + w_2 x_2 + b \geq 0,$$

if and only if $y(x_1, x_2) = 1$. Derive a two-layered neural network for the same input with the step activation function such that the network perfectly classifies the XOR data above (you may choose the number of units for the middle layer).

9.3.   For the above neural network, change its activation function to the sigmoid function and derive the backpropagation update rules for it when using the log likelihood of the data as an objective function. The optimizer you need to create the update rules for is gradient descent (see Section A.3).

9.4.   Show that the log-likelihood function objective for the neural network above has multiple maxima.

9.5.   What update rules (for the log-likelihood objective function) do you get when following the backpropagation derivation recipe for the network in Figure 9.1? Will the update rules lead to convergence to the global maximum of the corresponding log-likelihood function?

9.6.   Calculate the derivative of each activation function in Table 9.1 and show that $\tanh(x) = 2\sigma(x) - 1$ where σ is the sigmoid function.

Closing Remarks (First Edition)

Bayesian NLP is a relatively new area in NLP, that has emerged in the early 2000s, and has only recently matured to its current state. Its future still remains to be seen. Dennis Gabor, a Nobel prize-winning physicist once said (in a paraphrase) "we cannot predict the future but we can invent it." This applies to Bayesian NLP too, I believe. There are a few key areas in which Bayesian NLP could be further strengthened.

- Applications for nonparametric models—Nonparametric modeling is one of the basic building blocks of Bayesian statistics, especially given the recent developments in Bayesian analysis that machine learning has gone through. Various nonparametric models have been suggested, some of them in a general form, and some in a more problem-specific form. Still, in Bayesian NLP, there is an immense focus on the Dirichlet process and its derivatives, with a few exceptions. Finding applications that can exploit nonparametric models to their fullest extent has the potential to make the NLP literature much richer in that respect.

- Construction of richer priors—The ability to use a prior distribution in Bayesian modeling stands at the core of such modeling. Priors can encapsulate knowledge and expert opinion about the problem at hand. This is especially true for language, where the potential for encoding prior linguistic knowledge is immense. Yet, the set of priors that have been used in NLP thus far is rather limited (mostly focusing on the Dirichlet distribution). Constructing and using new priors, for example, through prior elicitation of linguistic knowledge, has great potential.

  This means that we would have to step away from the traditional definition of conjugacy, as defined by Raiffa and Schlaifer (1961), who were concerned with the convenience of finding the posterior distribution with a specific prior and likelihood. Conjugacy has become interchangeable with "having a closed-form solution for the posterior" (though it is not its original definition), and perhaps it is time to think in terms of *computational conjugacy*—i.e., conjugacy between the prior and the likelihood that is computationally tractable, but does not necessarily lead to a simple mathematical formulation of the posterior. Computational conjugacy would mean that the posterior, as a blackbox perhaps, can be efficiently accessed for various tasks (where efficiency is measured in computational complexity terms), and that blackbox can be repeatedly updated with new data.

- Confluence with other machine learning techniques—In the recent years, neural networks have become an important tool in the NLP machine learning toolkit. Yet, very little work has been done in NLP to connect Bayesian learning with these neural networks, although previous work connecting the two exists in the machine learning literature. Bayesian learning can be used to control the complexity of the structure of a neural network, and it can also be used for placing a prior on the parameter weights.

- Scaling up Bayesian inference in NLP—In the past decade, the scale of text resources that NLP researchers have been working with has grown tremendously. One of the criticisms of Bayesian analysis in machine learning and NLP is that Bayesian inference does not scale (computationally) to large datasets in the "Big Data" age. Methods such as MCMC inference are slow to converge and process on a much smaller scale than we are now used to. Still, in the recent years, researchers in the Statistics and machine learning community have made progress in scalable Bayesian inference algorithms, for example, by creating stochastic versions of MCMC methods and variational inference methods. This knowledge has not yet transferred to the NLP community in full form, and in order to conduct inference with large datasets in a Bayesian context in NLP, this might be necessary. For a discussion of Bayesian inference in the Big Data age, see Jordan (2011) and Welling et al. (2014).

APPENDIX A

Basic Concepts

A.1 BASIC CONCEPTS IN INFORMATION THEORY

This section defines some basic concepts in information theory, such as entropy, cross entropy and KL divergence. For a full introduction to information theory, see Cover and Thomas (2012).

A.1.1 ENTROPY AND CROSS ENTROPY

The entropy of a discrete random variable X with distribution p and sample space Ω is defined as:

$$H(p) = -\sum_{x \in \Omega} p(X = x) \log p(X = x).$$

Entropy is always non-negative. If the entropy is 0, then the random variable is a constant value with probability 1. The larger the entropy is, the closer the uncertainty in the random variable, or in a sense, the random variable distribution is closer to a uniform distribution. (The convention is to use 0 for $0 \log 0$ terms, which are otherwise defined. The limit of $p \log p$ as $p \to 0$ is indeed 0.)

When $\log_2$ is used instead of $\log$, the entropy provides the expected number of bits required to encode the random variable as follows. Each value x is assigned with a code that consists of $\log_2 p(X = x)$ bits. The motivation behind this can be demonstrated through the notion of cross-entropy. The cross entropy $H(p, q)$ between two distributions for a given random variable is defined as:

$$H(p, q) = -\sum_x p(X = x) \log q(X = x).$$

When $\log_2$ is used, the cross entropy gives the expected number of bits used to encode random samples from p when using for each $x \in \Omega$ a code of length $\log_2 q(X = x)$. The cross entropy is minimized, $\min_q H(p, q)$ when $p = q$. In this case, $H(p, q) = H(p)$. Therefore, encoding random samples from p using a code that assigns each $x \in \Omega \log_2 p(X = x)$ bits is optimal in this sense.

When using the natural logarithm for calculating entropy, entropy is measured in "natbits." Entropies calculated with a different base for the logarithm change by a multiplicative factor, as $\log_a b = \dfrac{\log_c a}{\log_c b}$ for any $a, b, c > 0$.

The notion of entropy can be naturally extended to continuous random variables as well (as can be the notion of cross entropy). If θ is a random variable with density $p(\theta)$ taking values in $\mathbb{R}$, then the entropy $H(\theta)$ is defined as:

$$H(\theta) = \int_{-\infty}^{\infty} p(\theta) \log p(\theta) d\theta.$$

The entropy of a continuous random variable is also called "differential entropy." There are several differences between the entropy of discrete and continuous random variables: the entropy of a continuous random variable may be negative or diverge to infinity, and it also does not stay invariant under a change of variable, unlike discrete random variable entropy.

A.1.2   KULLBACK–LEIBLER DIVERGENCE

The Kullback–Leibler divergence (KL divergence) between two discrete distributions p and q is defined as:

$$
\begin{aligned}
\mathrm{KL}(p, q) &= \sum_x p(X = x) \log \left(\frac{p(X = x)}{q(X = x)} \right) \\
&= \sum_x p(X = x) \log p(X = x) - \sum_x p(X = x) \log q(X = x) \\
&= H(p, q) - H(p).
\end{aligned}
$$

KL divergence is a measure of dissimilarity between two distributions. The larger the KL divergence is, the more dissimilar p and q are. KL divergence is always non-negative, and equals zero only when $p = q$. KL divergence asymmetric in the general case, $\mathrm{KL}(p, q) \neq \mathrm{KL}(q, p)$.

Similarly to entropy, KL divergence can be generalized to the continuous case.

A.2   OTHER BASIC CONCEPTS

There are three concepts we mention in this book: Jensen's inequality, transformations of continuous random variables and the expectation-maximization algorithm—which we will review here.

A.2.1   JENSEN'S INEQUALITY

In the context of probability theory, Jensen's inequality states that if f is a convex function for a real-valued random variable X, then

$$f(E[X]) \leq E[f(X)].$$

As such, it immediately holds that for a concave function g, $g(E[X]) \geq E[g(X)]$ (i.e., the negation of a convex function is concave). Jensen's inequality is used to derive the evidence lower bound for variational inference (Chapter 6). The function g that is used is $g(x) = \log x$, with Jensen's inequality being applied on the marginal log-likelihood. See Section 6.1 for more details.

A.2.2   THE CHAIN RULE FOR DIFFERENTIATION

The chain rule is one of the most important principles used in machine learning and NLP to differentiate objective functions, such as the ones implied by variational inference or the back-propagation algorithm.

Let $f : \mathbb{R}^d \to \mathbb{R}$ be a differentiable function and let $g : \mathbb{R}^k \to \mathbb{R}^d$ be another differentiable function. The function f maps $x \in \mathbb{R}^d$ to $\mathbb{R}$, and as such, we can create the composition of the function $f(g(y))$ where $y \in \mathbb{R}^k$. We denote the composed function by h, i.e., $h(y) = f(g(y))$, where $h : \mathbb{R}^k \to \mathbb{R}$. With a change of variables, we can define the function $h(u) = f(u)$, where $u \in \mathbb{R}^d$ and $u_j = [g(y)]_j$ for $j \in \{1, \dots, d\}$.

The chain rule states that the derivative of h with respect to y_i can be expressed as:

$$\frac{\partial h}{\partial y_i} = \sum_{j=1}^{d} \frac{\partial h}{\partial u_j} \cdot \frac{\partial u_j}{\partial y_i}.$$

If we think of differentiation of h with respect to y_i as providing the "amount of change" in h when y_i is perturbed, then this amount of change can be computed as the sum of amounts of change in h with respect to each u_j multiplied by the amount of change in g (through the vector u) with respect to y_i.

A.2.3   TRANSFORMATION OF CONTINUOUS RANDOM VARIABLES

Sometimes the parametrization of a distribution is not appropriate for the application at hand. For example, in Section 4.2.2, we discuss the use of Laplace approximation for a posterior over a multinomial distribution. Since the posterior is defined over the probability simplex, but the Laplace approximation gives an approximate posterior that is defined over $\mathbb{R}^d$ for some d, it is perhaps better to first transform the probability simplex random variables so that they become unbounded, with each coordinate of the transformed multivariate random variable spanning $[-\infty, \infty]$. This can be done using the logit function.

The question that needs to be asked at this point is how to calculate the probability distribution of the newly transformed random variables, since this is required for following up with the Laplace approximation and to generally manipulate the random variables in the new space. This can be done using the Jacobian transformation.

The Jacobian transformation works as follows. Suppose we are given a PDF for a multivariate random variable in $\mathbb{R}^d$. This PDF is $f(\theta)$ for $\theta \in \Omega \subseteq \mathbb{R}^d$. In addition, suppose that we are given a function $r : \Omega \to \mathbb{R}^d$ such that r is differentiable and bijective. Let s be the inverse of r, i.e., $s(\mu) = r^{-1}(\mu)$. $\mu = r(\theta)$ defines a new multivariate random variable. Its density is going to be $g(\mu) = f(s(\mu))|\det(J(\mu)|$ where $J\colon f(\Omega) \to \mathbb{R}^d \times \mathbb{R}^d$ is defined as:

$$[J(\mu)]_{ij} = \frac{\partial s_i}{\partial \mu_j}(\mu),$$

where $s_i\colon \Omega \to \mathbb{R}$ defined as $s_i(\mu) = [s(\mu)]_i$ (the ith coordinate of s). J is also called "the Jacobian" (in this case of s).

   This transformation is also often used to compute integrals (whether in probability theory or outside of it), following a change of variables in the integral. It is often the case that following such a change, the integrals are easier to compute, or are reduced to well-known integrals that have analytic solutions.

A.2.4   THE EXPECTATION-MAXIMIZATION ALGORITHM

In Chapter 6 there is a thorough discussion of variational inference and the variational EM algorithm. This section completes it by giving some information about the expectation-maximization algorithm for estimating the parameters in a classic frequentist setting with incomplete data.

   The general scenario is as follows. We have a model $p(X, Z|\theta)$ where X is an observed random variable and Z is a latent random variable. We have n observations $x^{(1)}, \ldots, x^{(n)}$, sampled from $p(X|\theta^*) = \sum_z p(X, z|\theta^*)$, and our goal is to identify the true parameter θ^*. One way to do this is by trying to maximize the marginal log-likelihood $L(\theta)$ with respect to θ:

$$L(\theta) = \sum_{i=1}^{n} \log p\left(x^{(i)}|\theta\right) = \sum_{i=1}^{n} \log \left(\sum_z p\left(x^{(i)}, z|\theta\right)\right).$$

   Generally, this function is not convex, and has multiple global maxima. It is often also computationally difficult to find its global maximum. The EM algorithm is a coordinate ascent algorithm that iteratively creates a sequence of parameters $\theta_1, \theta_2, \ldots$ such that $L(\theta_i) \geq L(\theta_{i-1})$ and that eventually converges to a local maximum of $L(\theta)$.

   Note first that $L(\theta)$ can also be expressed in the following manner:

$$L(\theta) = \sum_{i=1}^{n} \log \left(E_{q_i(Z)}\left[\frac{p\left(x^{(i)}, z|\theta\right)}{q_i(z)}\right]\right),$$

for any set of fixed distributions $q_1(Z), \ldots, q_n(Z)$ over the latent variables with a support that subsumes the support of p for Z (to see this, just unfold the expectation under $q_i(Z)$, and consider that the term $q_i(z)$ in the numerator and the denominator will cancel). Jensen's inequality tells us we can define the following bound $B(\theta|q_1, \ldots, q_n) \leq L(\theta)$ for any θ and q_i as above:

$$B(\theta|q_1, \ldots, q_n) = \sum_{i=1}^{n} E_{q_i(Z)}\left[\log \left(\frac{p\left(x^{(i)}, z|\theta\right)}{q_i(z)}\right)\right].$$

It can be shown that for any θ, $B(\theta|q_1,\ldots,q_n) = L(\theta)$ when $q_i(Z) = p(Z|x^{(i)},\theta)$. The EM algorithm capitalizes on this observation, and iteratively maximizes the lower bound B by alternating between maximizing B with respect to θ and maximizing the bound with respect to q_i. Therefore, the EM algorithm works as follows.

- Initialize θ_1 with some value.

- Repeat until $B(\theta|q_1,\ldots,q_n)$ converges (or for a fixed number of iterations):
  - (E-Step:) Compute $q_i\left(Z|x^{(i)},\theta_1\right)$ for $i \in \{1,\ldots,n\}$ and identify the bound $B(\theta|q_1,\ldots,q_n)$.
  - (M-Step:) $\theta_{i+1} \leftarrow \arg\max_\theta B\left(\theta|q_1,\ldots,q_n\right)$.

Note that the EM algorithm is not the only option to maximize the lower bound $B\left(\theta|q_1,\ldots,q_n\right)$. Other optimization techniques can also be used, usually reaching a local maximum as well.

A.3 BASIC CONCEPTS IN OPTIMIZATION

In NLP and more generally, machine learning, there is often the need to optimize an objective function, whether it is finding its minimum or maximum. This is required, for example, when performing maximum likelihood estimation or training a neural network. While in some basic cases, such as the optimization of the log-likelihood of multinomial events, there is a closed-form solution, it is more often the case that there is no analytic solution for the optimization problem, and as such, an algorithm or a procedure that evaluates the objective function and its gradients is necessary.

Assume a real function that takes as an input a set $D = \{x^{(1)},\ldots,x^{(n)}\}$ and a set of parameters $\theta \in \mathbb{R}^d$ that maps the parameters to a real value, and that has the following structure:[1]

$$f(\theta \mid D) = \frac{1}{n} \sum_{i=1}^{n} \ell\left(\theta \mid x^{(i)}\right). \tag{A.1}$$

For example, D can be a set of training examples and ℓ can be the log-probability of $x^{(i)}$ under a model $p(\cdot \mid \theta)$. We also assume that ℓ is differentiable with respect to θ. Our goal is to identify

$$\theta^* = \arg\max_\theta f(\theta \mid D).$$

The most basic procedure is "gradient ascent" which operates by computing the gradient of ℓ with respect to θ and then using the following update rule:

$$\theta_{t+1} \leftarrow \theta_t + \mu \sum_{i=1}^{n} \nabla_\theta \ell\left(\theta_t \mid x^{(i)}\right). \tag{A.2}$$

---

[1]It is easy to focus this discussion to the optimization of a general differentiable function $f(\theta)$ with respect to θ, as is commonly described in the optimization literature.

that starts with a pre-initialized $\theta_0 \in \mathbb{R}^d$ and then creates a sequence $\theta_0, \theta_1, \ldots, \theta_t, \ldots$ of updated parameters. The key idea behind this update rule is to "take a step" with the current θ_t in the direction of the gradient, as the gradient gives the direction in which the function increases in value. When the goal is to minimize the function, the update rule changes to

$$\theta_{t+1} \leftarrow \theta_t - \mu \sum_{i=1}^{n} \nabla_\theta \ell \left(\theta_t \mid x^{(i)} \right),$$

this time, taking a step against the direction of the gradient. The value μ is a real number that is referred to as the "step size" or the "learning rate." It controls the magnitude of the step in the direction of the gradient. A small value may lead to a slow convergence on θ^*, while too large value may lead to alternating between points that could perhaps be close to θ^*, but "miss" it by some significant distance.

There are also second-order optimization methods that make use of the *Hessian* of the optimized function for faster convergence. (The Hessian of a real-value function $f : \mathbb{R}^d \to \mathbb{R}$ at point θ is the matrix $H \in \mathbb{R}^{d \times d}$ such that $H_{ij} = \dfrac{\partial^2 f}{\partial \theta_i \, \partial \theta_j}(\theta)$.) Second-order Newton's method uses an update rule that looks like:

$$\theta_{t+1} \leftarrow \theta_t + \mu H(\theta_t)^{-1} \nabla_\theta f(\theta_t).$$

This update is based on a second-order Taylor expansion of f around θ_t. Since calculating the inverse of the Hessian is expensive (as is even just calculating the Hessian itself, which is quadratic in d), methods that make use of an approximation of the Hessian are used. These are referred to as quasi-Newton methods.

A.3.1 STOCHASTIC GRADIENT DESCENT

As can be seen in Equation A.2, the update rule of gradient ascent requires the computation of the gradient of ℓ with respect to all $x^{(i)}$, along with summing these gradients together. This can be quite expensive if n is large, which is where stochastic gradient ascent (or descent) can be applied to optimize f.

Stochastic gradient descent (SGD) relies on the observation that one way to re-formulate the objective function in Equation A.1 is using the following expectation:

$$f(\theta \mid D) = E_{q(X)}[\ell(\theta \mid X)], \tag{A.3}$$

where $q(X)$ is a uniform distribution over the elements in D. As a result, the gradient of f can be (grossly) approximated using a single example as $\ell(\theta \mid x^{(i)})$ for a randomly (uniformly) sampled i from $\{1, \ldots, n\}$. Indeed, stochastic gradient descent works by repeatedly sampling uniformly an example $x^{(i)}$ from D and then making the update

$$\theta_{t+1} \leftarrow \theta_t + \mu \nabla_\theta \ell \left(\theta_t \mid x^{(i)} \right).$$

SGD can also be applied to batches of the data. In this case, a subset of D is sampled, and then the gradient is calculated with respect to $x^{(i)}$ in that sample. The expectation in Equation A.3 is approximated with the average of gradients from the sampled subset. This is often referred to as using "mini-batches" during the optimization process. This approach is widely used in practice when using SGD.

Since the gradient used with SGD is only approximate, the learning rate used is especially important. There has been much recent research that develops stochastic optimization algorithms with the motivation to determine the learning rate, sometimes adaptively. This means that each coordinate of θ may use a different learning rate that also changes between iterations. Two examples of such algorithms are AdaGrad (Duchi et al., 2011) and Adam (Kingma and Ba, 2014), used often with the optimization of neural network objective functions (Chapter 9). For a connection between SGD and posterior inference, in which SGD is shown to be equivalent to performing approximate posterior inference; see Mandt et al. (2016).

A.3.2 CONSTRAINED OPTIMIZATION

It is sometimes the case that we are interested in finding a maximum (or minimum) for an objective function in a specific domain, and not just generally in $\mathbb{R}^d$, as described until now. In this case, we are given some domain Θ and a function $f : \Theta \to \mathbb{R}^d$ and we are interested in determining:

$$\theta^* = \arg\max_{\theta \in \Theta} f(\theta).$$

For example, this is naturally the case with the optimization of objective functions when θ represents a collection of multinomial distributions, such as with PCFGs. In that case, Θ would correspond to a Cartesian product of probability simplexes. In other cases, Θ represents linear constraints on possible solutions of θ. The domain Θ gives us the set of *feasible* solutions.

There are various ways to optimize a function f under such constraints. When f is a linear function and Θ can be described as a set of linear constraints, we are in the realm of linear programming (Boyd and Vandenberghe, 2004). If θ is further constrained to consist of only integers or 0/1 values (as is the case for certain inference problems in NLP), then the problem of optimization falls under the category of *integer* linear programming (ILP). For an early use of ILP in NLP, see for example Roth and Yih (2005).

It is also often the case that algorithms such as gradient descent are used, but if a gradient step takes the current solution outside of Θ, we project that solution back into the domain of Θ, for example, by solving an easier optimization problem that minimizes the L_2 norm between the current *infeasible* solution and a point in Θ.

Finally, applying an invertible transformation g on Θ such that we are eventually left with an unconstrained problem in a new domain $g(\Theta)$ is also sometimes an option. Once we apply the transformation, we can operate with the usual optimization algorithms described up until now. Constrained optimization is beyond the scope of this book. To read more about it, see Boyd and Vandenberghe (2004).

APPENDIX B

Distribution Catalog

This appendix gives some basic information about the various distributions that are mentioned in this book.

B.1 THE MULTINOMIAL DISTRIBUTION

Parameters	$n, k \geq 1$ integer, $\theta_1, \ldots, \theta_k$ such that $\theta_i \geq 0$ and $\sum_{i=1}^{k} \theta_i = 1$
Sample space Ω	integer vectors $x = (x_1, \ldots, x_k)$ such that $\sum_{i=1}^{k} x_i = n$
PMF	$f(x) = \dfrac{n!}{\prod_{i=1}^{k} x_i!} \prod_{i=1}^{k} \theta_i^{x_i}$
Mean $E[X_i]$	$n\theta_i$
Variance Var (X_i)	$n\theta_i(1 - \theta_i)$
Covariance Cov(X_i, X_j)	$-n\theta_i\theta_j$ for $i \neq j$

Notes.

- The Dirichlet distribution is conjugate to the multinomial distribution.

- When $n = 1$, the distribution is a "categorical distribution" over binary vectors that sum to 1. With the categorical distribution, Ω can be any set of k objects. Sometimes the categorical distribution is referred to as a "multinomial distribution," since the categorical distribution is a specific case of the multinomial distribution when Ω are the binary vectors mentioned above.

- A distribution over a finite set $A = \{a_1, \ldots, a_d\}$ with a probability θ_i associated with each a_i may also often be referred to as a multinomial distribution.

B.2 THE DIRICHLET DISTRIBUTION

Parameters	integer $d \geq 2$, $\alpha_1, \ldots, \alpha_d$ positive values
Sample space Ω	$\theta \in \Omega \subset \mathbb{R}^d$ is such that $\theta_i \geq 0$ and $\sum_{i=1}^{d} \theta_i = 1$
PDF	$f(\theta) = \dfrac{1}{B(\alpha)} \times \left(\prod_{i=1}^{d} \theta_i^{\alpha_i-1} \right)$ where $B(\alpha)$ is the Beta function
Mode	$(\mu_1, \ldots, \mu_d)$ such that $\mu_i = \dfrac{\alpha_i - 1}{\sum_{i=1}^{d} \alpha_i - d}$ if $\alpha_i > 1$
Mean $E[\theta_i]$	$\dfrac{\alpha_i}{\sum_{i=1}^{d} \alpha_i}$
Mean $E[\log \theta_i]$	$\psi(\alpha_i) - \psi(\sum_{i=1}^{d} \alpha_i)$ where ψ is the digamma function
Variance Var (θ_i)	$\dfrac{\alpha_i (\alpha_* - \alpha_i)}{\alpha_*^2 (\alpha_* + 1)}$ where $\alpha_* = \sum_i \alpha_i$

Notes.

- $B(\alpha)$ is the Beta function, defined as:

$$B(\alpha) = \frac{\prod_{i=1}^{d} \Gamma(\alpha_i)}{\Gamma\left(\sum_{i=1}^{d} \alpha_i\right)},$$

  where $\Gamma(x)$ is the Gamma function (Weisstein, 2014).

- $\psi(x)$ is the digamma function, which is the first derivative of the log-Gamma function:

$$\psi(x) = \frac{d}{dx} \log \Gamma(x).$$

  It does not have an analytic form, and can be approximated using numerical recipes, or through series expansion approximation.[1] (Chapter 3).

- When $d = 2$, then the Dirichlet distribution can be viewed as defining a distribution over $[0, 1]$ (since $\theta_2 = 1 - \theta_1$). In that case, it is called the Beta distribution (see Section 2.2.1).

- The symmetric Dirichlet is a Dirichlet distribution in which the hyperparameters α_i are all the same.

- If $\alpha_i = 1$ for all $i \in \{1, \ldots, d\}$, the Dirichlet distribution becomes a uniform distribution over the probability simplex. (Its density is constant.)

[1] http://web.science.mq.edu.au/~mjohnson/code/digamma.c

B.3   THE POISSON DISTRIBUTION

Parameters	$\lambda > 0$, (called "rate")
Sample space Ω	Natural numbers including zero: $\{0, 1, 2, \ldots\}$
PMF	$f(n) = \dfrac{\lambda^n}{n!} \exp(-\lambda)$
Mode	$\lceil \lambda \rceil - 1$
Mean	λ
Variance	λ

Notes.

- A conjugate prior for λ is the Gamma distribution.

- If $X_1, \ldots, X_n$ are independent Poisson random variables with rates $\lambda_1, \ldots, \lambda_n$, then $p\left(X_1, \ldots, X_n \mid \sum_{i=1}^n X_i = K\right)$ is a multinomial distribution with parameters K and $\theta_i = \dfrac{\lambda_i}{\sum_{i=1}^n \lambda_i}$ (Section B.1).

B.4   THE GAMMA DISTRIBUTION

Parameters	$\alpha > 0$, shape $\theta > 0$ scale
Sample space Ω	$\Omega = \mathbb{R}^+$
PDF	$f(x) = \dfrac{1}{\Gamma(\alpha)\theta^\alpha} x^{\alpha-1} \exp(-x/\theta)$
Mean $E[X]$	$\alpha\theta$
Mode	$(\alpha - 1)\theta$ for $\alpha > 1$
Variance Var (X)	$\alpha\theta^2$
Entropy	$\alpha + \log\theta + \log(\Gamma(\alpha)) + (1 - \alpha)\psi(\alpha)$

Notes.

- Often used as a vague prior for hyperparameters in hierarchical Bayesian models.

- Another common parametrization for it is using two parameters, shape α and "rate" β where $\beta = \dfrac{1}{\theta}$.

- If $X_i \sim \text{Gamma}(\alpha_i, 1)$ for $\alpha_1, \ldots, \alpha_K$ are independently distributed, then $\left(\dfrac{X_1}{\sum_{i=1}^{K} X_i}, \ldots, \dfrac{X_K}{\sum_{i=1}^{K} X_i} \right)$ is distributed according to the Dirichlet distribution with parameters $(\alpha_1, \ldots, \alpha_K)$. See also Section 3.2.1.

B.5   THE MULTIVARIATE NORMAL DISTRIBUTION

Parameters	integer $d \geq 1$, $\mu \in \mathbb{R}^d$, $\sum \in \mathbb{R}^{d \times d}$, positive semidefinite
Sample space Ω	$\Omega = \mathbb{R}^d$
PDF	$f(\theta) = \dfrac{1}{(2\pi)^{d/2} \sqrt{\det(\Sigma)}} \exp\left(-\dfrac{1}{2} (\theta - \mu)^\top \Sigma^{-1} (\theta - \mu) \right)$
Mode	μ
Mean	μ
Variance and covariance	$\text{Cov}\,(\theta_i, \theta_j) = \Sigma_{ij}$
Entropy	$\dfrac{d}{2}(1 + \log(2\pi)) + \dfrac{1}{2}\log(\det(\Sigma))$

Notes.

- The PDF is symmetric around the mean.

- There is no closed form for the cummulative distribution function.

- The multivariate normal distribution is conjugate to itself, when considering the mean parameters.

- Often referred to as the multivariate Gaussian distribution, or just the Gaussian distribution, named after Carl Friedrich Gauss (1777-1855).

B.6   THE LAPLACE DISTRIBUTION

Parameters	$\mu \in \mathbb{R}, \ \lambda > 0$
Sample space Ω	$\Omega = \mathbb{R}$
PDF	$f(\theta) = \dfrac{1}{2\lambda} \exp\left(-\dfrac{|\theta - \mu|}{\lambda}\right)$
Mean $E[\theta]$	μ
Mode	μ
Variance Var (θ)	$2\lambda^2$
Entropy	$1 + \log(2\lambda)$

Notes.

- Can be used as a Bayesian interpretation for L_1 regularization (Section 4.2.1).

B.7   THE LOGISTIC NORMAL DISTRIBUTION

Parameters	integer $d \geq 2$, $\eta \in \mathbb{R}^{d-1}$, $\sum \in \mathbb{R}^{(d-1) \times (d-1)}$ positive semidefinite
Sample space Ω	$\theta \in \Omega \subset \mathbb{R}^d$ is such that $\theta_i \geq 0$ and $\sum_{i=1}^{d} \theta_i = 1$
PMF	See below
Mode (coordinate i)	$\dfrac{\exp(\eta'_i)}{1 + \sum_{i=1}^{d-1} \exp(\eta_i)}$ where $\eta'_i = \eta_i$ for $i \leq d - 1$ and $\eta'_d = 1$
Mean	No analytical solution
Variance	No analytical solution

Notes.

- The PDF is defined as:

$$f(\theta) = \frac{1}{\sqrt{(2\pi)^d \det(\Sigma)}} \times \left(\prod_{i=1}^{d} \theta_i\right)^{-1} \exp\left(-\frac{1}{2}(\log(\theta_{-d}/\theta_d) - \eta)^\top \Sigma^{-1} \log(\theta_{-d}/\theta_d) - \eta)\right).$$

The term $\log(\theta_{-d}/\theta_d) \in \mathbb{R}^{d-1}$ is defined as:

$$[\log(\theta_{-d}/\theta_d)]_i = \log(\theta_i/\theta_d) \ \forall i \in \{1, \ldots, d-1\}.$$

- A draw from the logistic normal distribution is equivalent to drawing a real-valued vector $\mu \in \mathbb{R}^{d-1}$ from the multivariate normal distribution (see below) with parameters (η, Σ) and then setting:

$$\theta_i = \frac{\exp(\mu_i)}{1 + \sum_{j=1}^{d-1} \exp(\mu_j)} \quad \forall i \in \{1, \ldots, d-1\},$$

$$\theta_d = \frac{1}{1 + \sum_{j=1}^{d-1} \exp(\mu_j)}.$$

B.8   THE INVERSE WISHART DISTRIBUTION

Parameters	$m, p \in \mathbb{N}, m > p - 1, \Psi \in \mathbb{R}^{p \times p}$ positive definite matrix
Sample space Ω	$T \in \Omega$ is an invertible positive definite matrix
PDF	$f(T) = \dfrac{\det(\Psi)^{m/2}}{\det(T)^{\frac{m+p+1}{2}} \, 2^{\frac{m+p}{2}} \, \Gamma_p(m/2)} \, \exp\left(-\dfrac{1}{2} \, \mathrm{tr}(\Psi T^{-1})\right)$
Mean $E[T]$	$\dfrac{\Psi}{m - p - 1}$
Mode	$\dfrac{\Psi}{m - p + 1}$
Variance Var (T_{ij})	$\dfrac{(m - p + 1)(\Psi_{ij})^2 + (m - p - 1)\Psi_{ii}\Psi_{jj}}{(m - p)(m - p - 1)^2(m - p - 3)}$

Notes.

- The function $\mathrm{tr}(A)$ for a matrix $A \in \mathbb{R}^{p \times p}$ is defined as the trace: the sum of all diagonal elements of A, $\sum_{i=1}^{p} A_{ii}$.

- If A is drawn from the Wishart distribution, then A^{-1} is drawn from the inverse Wishart distribution.

- The inverse Wishart is a conjugate prior for the covariance matrix parameter of a multivariate normal distribution.

B.9   THE GUMBEL DISTRIBUTION

Parameters	$\mu \in \mathbb{R}, \beta > 0$
Sample space Ω	$\Omega = \mathbb{R}$
PDF	$f(x) = \dfrac{1}{\beta} \exp\left(-\dfrac{x-\mu}{\beta} - \exp\left(-\dfrac{x-\mu}{\beta}\right)\right)$
Mode	μ
Mean	$\mu + \beta\gamma$, where $\gamma \approx 0.5772156649$ (Euler-Mascheroni constant)
Variance	$\dfrac{\pi^2}{6}\beta^2$
Entropy	$\log\beta + \gamma + 1$

Notes.

- If U is a uniform random variable on $[0, 1]$, then $G = \mu - \beta\log(-\log U)$ has a Gumbel distribution as above.

- For a sequence of K independent Gumbel random variables $G_1, \ldots, G_K$ with $\mu = 0$ and $\beta = 1$, and for $(\theta_1, \ldots, \theta_K)$ (denoting a categorical distribution), we may define the *concrete* distribution (Maddison et al., 2017) over the probability simplex of degree $K - 1$ with a random variable $X = (X_1, \ldots, X_K)$:

$$X_k = \frac{\exp\left((\log\theta_k + G_k)/\tau\right)}{\sum_{j=1}^{K} \exp\left((\log\theta_j + G_j)/\tau\right)},$$

where τ is a parameter of the distribution.

- In the same setting, the distribution of

$$Y = \arg\max_k \log\theta_k + G_k$$

is multinomial over $\{1, \ldots, K\}$ where the probability of event k is θ_k.

Bibliography

Abadi, M., Barham, P., Chen, J., Chen, Z., Davis, A., Dean, J., Devin, M., Ghemawat, S., Irving, G., Isard, M., et al. (2016). TensorFlow: A system for large-scale machine learning. In *Proc. of the 12th USENIX Conference on Operating Systems Design and Implementation (OSDI)*, vol. 16, pages 265–283. 217

Abney, S., McAllester, D., and Pereira, F. (1999). Relating probabilistic grammars and automata. In *Proc. of the 37th Annual Meeting of the Association for Computational Linguistics*, pages 542–549, College Park, MD. DOI: 10.3115/1034678.1034759. 182

Ahmed, A. and Xing, E. P. (2007). On tight approximate inference of the logistic normal topic admixture model. In *Proc. of the 11th International Conference on Artifical Intelligence and Statistics*. Omnipress. 88

Aitchison, J. (1986). *The Statistical Analysis of Compositional Data*. Chapman and Hall, London. DOI: 10.1007/978-94-009-4109-0. 59, 61, 63, 64, 65

Al-Rfou, R., Alain, G., Almahairi, A., Angermueller, C., Bahdanau, D., Ballas, N., Bastien, F., Bayer, J., Belikov, A., Belopolsky, A., et al. (2016). Theano: A python framework for fast computation of mathematical expressions. *ArXiv Preprint ArXiv:1605.02688*, 472:473. 217

Altun, Y., Hofmann, T., and Smola, A. J. (2004). Gaussian process classification for segmenting and annotating sequences. In *Proc. of the 21st International Conference on Machine Learning (ICML 2004)*, pages 25–32, New York, Max-Planck-Gesellschaft, ACM Press. DOI: 10.1145/1015330.1015433. 172

Andrieu, C., De Freitas, N., Doucet, A., and Jordan, M. I. (2003). An introduction to MCMC for machine learning. *Machine Learning*, 50(1-2), pages 5–43. 125

Artetxe, M., Labaka, G., Agirre, E., and Cho, K. (2018). Unsupervised neural machine translation. 254

Ash, R. B. and Doléans-Dade, C. A. (2000). *Probability and measure theory*. Access online via Elsevier. 2, 10

Bahdanau, D., Cho, K., and Bengio, Y. (2015). Neural machine translation by jointly learning to align and translate. In *Proc. of the 3rd International Conference on Learning Representations (ICLR)*. 237

Barkan, O. (2017). Bayesian neural word embedding. In *Proc. of the 31st Conference on Artificial Intelligence (AAAI)*, pages 3135–3143. 220, 221

Barnett, V. (1999). *Comparative Statistical Inference*. Wiley. DOI: 10.1002/9780470316955. xxvi

Beal, M. J., Ghahramani, Z., and Rasmussen, C. E. (2002). The infinite hidden Markov model. In *Machine Learning*, pages 29–245. MIT Press. 180

Bejan, C., Titsworth, M., Hickl, A., and Harabagiu, S. (2009). Nonparametric Bayesian models for unsupervised event coreference resolution. In Bengio, Y., Schuurmans, D., Lafferty, J., Williams, C., and Culotta, A., Eds., *Advances in Neural Information Processing Systems 22*, pages 73–81. Curran Associates, Inc. 27

Bengio, Y., Ducharme, R., Vincent, P., and Jauvin, C. (2003). A neural probabilistic language model. *Journal of Machine Learning Research*, 3(Feb):1137–1155. DOI: 10.1007/3-540-33486-6_6 216

Berger, J. O. (1985). *Statistical Decision Theory and Bayesian Analysis*. Springer. DOI: 10.1007/978-1-4757-4286-2. 41, 72, 89

Berger, A. L., Pietra, V. J. D., and Pietra, S. A. D. (1996). A maximum entropy approach to natural language processing. *Computational Linguistics*, 22(1), pages 39–71. 27

Bertsekas, D. P. and Tsitsiklis, J. N. (2002). *Introduction to Probability*, vol. 1. Athena Scientific Belmont, MA. 1

Bishop, C. M. (2006). *Pattern Recognition and Machine Learning*. Springer. 86, 141

Bisk, Y. and Hockenmaier, J. (2013). An HDP model for inducing combinatory categorial grammars. *Transactions of the Association for Computational Linguistics*, 1, pages 75–88. 210

Black, E., Abney, S., Flickenger, D., Gdaniec, C., Grishman, R., Harrison, P., Hindle, D., Ingria, R., Jelinek, F., Klavans, J., Liberman, M., Marcus, M., Roukos, S., Santorini, B., and Strzalkowski, T. (1991). A procedure for quantitatively comparing the syntactic coverage of English grammars. In *Proc. of DARPA Workshop on Speech and Natural Language*. DOI: 10.3115/112405.112467. 149

Blei, D. M., Ng, A. Y., and Jordan, M. I. (2003). Latent Dirichlet allocation. *Journal of Machine Learning Research*, 3, pages 993–1022. 27, 30, 31

Blei, D. M., Griffiths, T. L., and Jordan, M. I. (2010). The nested chinese restaurant process and Bayesian nonparametric inference of topic hierarchies. *Journal of the ACM (JACM)*, 57(2), page 7. DOI: 10.1145/1667053.1667056. 173

Blei, D. M. and Frazier, P. I. (2011). Distance dependent chinese restaurant processes. *Journal of Machine Learning Research*, 12, pages 2461–2488. 174

Blei, D. M. and Jordan, M. I. (2004). Variational methods for the Dirichlet process. In *Proc. of the 21st International Conference on Machine Learning*. DOI: 10.1145/1015330.1015439. 163, 196, 201

Blei, D. M. and Lafferty, J. D. (2006). Correlated topic models. In Weiss, Y., Schölkopf, B., and Platt, J., Eds., *Advances in Neural Information Processing Systems 18*, pages 147–154. MIT Press. 61, 62

Blunsom, P. and Cohn, T. (2010a). Inducing synchronous grammars with slice sampling. In *Human Language Technologies: The 2010 Annual Conference of the North American Chapter of the Association for Computational Linguistics*, pages 238–241, Los Angeles, CA. 27, 117, 118

Blunsom, P. and Cohn, T. (2010b). Unsupervised induction of tree substitution grammars for dependency parsing. In *Proc. of the 2010 Conference on Empirical Methods in Natural Language Processing*, pages 1204–1213, Cambridge, MA. Association for Computational Linguistics. 27

Blunsom, P., Cohn, T., Dyer, C., and Osborne, M. (2009a). A Gibbs sampler for phrasal synchronous grammar induction. In *Proc. of the Joint Conference of the 47th Annual Meeting of the ACL and the 4th International Joint Conference on Natural Language Processing of the AFNLP*, pages 782–790, Suntec, Singapore. Association for Computational Linguistics. DOI: 10.3115/1690219.1690256. 118, 205

Blunsom, P., Cohn, T., and Osborne, M. (2009b). Bayesian synchronous grammar induction. In Koller, D., Schuurmans, D., Bengio, Y., and Bottou, L., Eds., *Advances in Neural Information Processing Systems 21*, pages 161–168. Curran Associates, Inc. 205

Börschinger, B. and Johnson, M. (2014). Exploring the role of stress in Bayesian word segmentation using adaptor grammars. *Transactions of the Association for Computational Linguistics*, 2(1), pages 93–104. 29

Bouchard-côté, A., Petrov, S., and Klein, D. (2009). Randomized pruning: Efficiently calculating expectations in large dynamic programs. In Bengio, Y., Schuurmans, D., Lafferty, J., Williams, C., and Culotta, A., Eds., *Advances in Neural Information Processing Systems 22*, pages 144–152. Curran Associates, Inc. 118

Bowman, S. R., Vilnis, L., Vinyals, O., Dai, A. M., Jozefowicz, R., and Bengio, S. (2016). Generating sentences from a continuous space. *Proc. of the 20th SIGNLL Conference on Computational Natural Language Learning (CoNLL)*. DOI: 10.18653/v1/k16-1002 247

Boyd, S. and Vandenberghe, L. (2004). *Convex optimization.* Cambridge University Press. DOI: 10.1017/cbo9780511804441 265

Bražinskas, A., Havrylov, S., and Titov, I. (2017). Embedding words as distributions with a Bayesian skip-gram model. *ArXiv Preprint ArXiv:1711.11027.* 221

Bryant, M. and Sudderth, E. B. (2012). Truly nonparametric online variational inference for hierarchical Dirichlet processes. In Pereira, F., Burges, C., Bottou, L., and Weinberger, K., Eds., *Advances in Neural Information Processing Systems 25*, pages 2699–2707. Curran Associates, Inc. 167

Burstall, R. M. and Darlington, J. (1977). A transformation system for developing recursive programs. *Journal of the ACM*, 24(1), pages 44–67. DOI: 10.1145/321992.321996. 188

Caccia, M., Caccia, L., Fedus, W., Larochelle, H., Pineau, J., and Charlin, L. (2018). Language GANs falling short. *ArXiv Preprint ArXiv:1811.02549.* 253

Cappé, O. and Moulines, E. (2009). On-line expectation–maximization algorithm for latent data models. *Journal of the Royal Statistical Society: Series B (Statistical Methodology)*, 71(3), pages 593–613. DOI: 10.1111/j.1467-9868.2009.00698.x. 152

Carlin, B. P. and Louis, T. A. (2000). *Bayes and Empirical Bayes Methods for Data Analysis.* CRC Press. DOI: 10.1201/9781420057669. 52

Carpenter, B., Gelman, A., Hoffman, M., Lee, D., Goodrich, B., Betancourt, M., Brubaker, M. A., Guo, J., Li, P., and Riddell, A. (2015). Stan: a probabilistic programming language. *Journal of Statistical Software.* 141

Carter, S., Dymetman, M., and Bouchard, G. (2012). Exact sampling and decoding in high-order hidden Markov models. In *Proc. of the 2012 Joint Conference on Empirical Methods in Natural Language Processing and Computational Natural Language Learning*, pages 1125–1134, Jeju Island, Korea. Association for Computational Linguistics. 123

Casella, G. and Berger, R. L. (2002). *Statistical Inference.* Duxbury Pacific Grove, CA. DOI: 10.2307/2532634. 13

Casella, G. and George, E. I. (1992). Explaining the Gibbs sampler. *The American Statistician*, 46(3), pages 167–174. DOI: 10.2307/2685208. 132

Castano, A. and Casacuberta, F. (1997). A connectionist approach to machine translation. In *Proc. of the 5th European Conference on Speech Communication and Technology.* 236

Chang, J., Gerrish, S., Wang, C., Boyd-Graber, J. L., and Blei, D. M. (2009). Reading tea leaves: How humans interpret topic models. In Bengio, Y., Schuurmans, D., Lafferty, J., Williams, C., and Culotta, A., Eds., *Advances in Neural Information Processing Systems 22*, pages 288–296. Curran Associates, Inc. 36

Chen, H., Branavan, S., Barzilay, R., Karger, D. R., et al. (2009). Content modeling using latent permutations. *Journal of Artificial Intelligence Research*, 36(1), pages 129–163. 27

Chen, T., Fox, E., and Guestrin, C. (2014). Stochastic gradient Hamiltonian Monte Carlo. In *Proc. of the 31st International Conference on Machine Learning (ICML)*, pages 1683–1691. DOI: 10.24963/ijcai.2018/419 253

Chen, S. F. and Goodman, J. (1996). An empirical study of smoothing techniques for language modeling. In *Proc. of the 34th Annual Meeting of the Association of Computational Linguistics*, pages 310–318, Stroudsburg, PA. DOI: 10.3115/981863.981904. 82, 170

Chernoff, H. (1959). Sequential design of experiments. *The Annals of Mathematical Statistics*, 30(3):755–770. DOI: 10.1214/aoms/1177706205 244

Chi, Z. (1999). Statistical properties of probabilistic context-free grammars. *Computational Linguistics*, 25(1), pages 131–160. 183

Chinchor, N. (2001). Message understanding conference (MUC) 7, LDC2001T02, Linguistic Data Consortium. 92

Chinchor, N. and Sundheim, B. (2003). Message understanding conference (MUC) 6, LDC2003T13, Linguistic Data Consortium. 92

Chirkova, N., Lobacheva, E., and Vetrov, D. (2018). Bayesian compression for natural language processing. In *Proc. of the Conference on Empirical Methods in Natural Language Processing (EMNLP)*. DOI: 10.1162/coli_r_00310 243

Cho, K., Van Merriënboer, B., Gulcehre, C., Bahdanau, D., Bougares, F., Schwenk, H., and Bengio, Y. (2014). Learning phrase representations using RNN encoder-decoder for statistical machine translation. *Proc. of the Conference on Empirical Methods in Natural Language Processing (EMNLP)*. DOI: 10.3115/v1/d14-1179 235, 236

Cocke, J. and Schwartz, J. T. (1970). Programming languages and their compilers: Preliminary notes. Technical report, Courant Institute of Mathematical Sciences, New York University. 182

Cohen, S. B. (2017). Latent-variable PCFGs: Background and applications. In *Proc. of the 15th Meeting on the Mathematics of Language (MOL)*. DOI: 10.18653/v1/w17-3405 201

Cohen, S. B. and Collins, M. (2014). A provably correct learning algorithm for latent-variable PCFGs. In *Proc. of the 52nd Annual Meeting of the Association for Computational Linguistics (Volume 1: Long Papers)*, pages 1052–1061, Baltimore, MD. DOI: 10.3115/v1/p14-1099. 202

Cohen, S. B., Gimpel, K., and Smith, N. A. (2009). Logistic normal priors for unsupervised probabilistic grammar induction. In Koller, D., Schuurmans, D., Bengio, Y., and Bottou, L., Eds., *Advances in Neural Information Processing Systems 21*, pages 321–328. Curran Associates, Inc. 62, 149, 193

Cohen, S. B., Blei, D. M., and Smith, N. A. (2010). Variational inference for adaptor grammars. In *Human Language Technologies: The 2010 Annual Conference of the North American Chapter of the Association for Computational Linguistics*, pages 564–572, Los Angeles, CA. 196, 198

Cohen, S. B., Stratos, K., Collins, M., Foster, D. P., and Ungar, L. (2013). Experiments with spectral learning of latent-variable PCFGs. In *Proc. of the 2013 Conference of the North American Chapter of the Association for Computational Linguistics: Human Language Technologies*, pages 148–157, Atlanta, GA. 202

Cohen, S. B., Stratos, K., Collins, M., Foster, D. P., and Ungar, L. (2014). Spectral learning of latent-variable PCFGs: Algorithms and sample complexity. *Journal of Machine Learning Research*, 15, pages 2399–2449. 202

Cohen, S. B. and Johnson, M. (2013). The effect of non-tightness on Bayesian estimation of PCFGs. In *Proc. of the 51st Annual Meeting of the Association for Computational Linguistics (Volume 1: Long Papers)*, pages 1033–1041, Sofia, Bulgaria. 52, 124

Cohen, S. and Smith, N. A. (2009). Shared logistic normal distributions for soft parameter tying in unsupervised grammar induction. In *Proc. of Human Language Technologies: The 2009 Annual Conference of the North American Chapter of the Association for Computational Linguistics*, pages 74–82, Boulder, CO. DOI: 10.3115/1620754.1620766. 63

Cohen, S. and Smith, N. A. (2010a). Viterbi training for PCFGs: Hardness results and competitiveness of uniform initialization. In *Proc. of the 48th Annual Meeting of the Association for Computational Linguistics*, pages 1502–1511, Uppsala, Sweden. 139

Cohen, S. B. and Smith, N. A. (2010b). Covariance in unsupervised learning of probabilistic grammars. *Journal of Machine Learning Research*, 11, pages 3017–3051. 62, 64, 150

Cohn, T., Blunsom, P., and Goldwater, S. (2010). Inducing tree-substitution grammars. *The Journal of Machine Learning Research*, 11, pages 3053–3096. 210

Collobert, R., Bengio, S., and Mariéthoz, J. (2002). Torch: A modular machine learning software library. *Technical Report*, Idiap. 217

Collobert, R., Weston, J., Bottou, L., Karlen, M., Kavukcuoglu, K., and Kuksa, P. (2011). Natural language processing (almost) from scratch. *Journal of Machine Learning Research*, 12(Aug):2493–2537. 216

Cover, T. M. and Thomas, J. A. (2012). *Elements of Information Theory*. John Wiley & Sons. 259

Cox, R. T. (1946). Probability, frequency and reasonable expectation. *American Journal of Physics*, 14(1), pages 1–13. DOI: 10.1119/1.1990764. 66

Cybenko, G. (1989). Approximation by superpositions of a sigmoidal function. *Mathematics of Control, Signals and Systems*, 2(4):303–314. DOI: 10.1007/bf02551274 215

Damianou, A. and Lawrence, N. (2013). Deep Gaussian processes. In *Proc. of the 16th International Conference on Artificial Intelligence and Statistics (AISTATS)*, pages 207–215. 243

Daume, H. (2007). Fast search for Dirichlet process mixture models. In Meila, M. and Shen, X., Eds., *Proc. of the 11th International Conference on Artificial Intelligence and Statistics (AISTATS-07)*, vol. 2, pages 83–90. *Journal of Machine Learning Research—Proceedings Track*. 164

Daume III, H. (2007). Frustratingly easy domain adaptation. In *Proc. of the 45th Annual Meeting of the Association of Computational Linguistics*, pages 256–263, Prague, Czech Republic. 93

Daume III, H. (2009). Non-parametric Bayesian areal linguistics. In *Proc. of Human Language Technologies: The 2009 Annual Conference of the North American Chapter of the Association for Computational Linguistics*, pages 593–601, Boulder, CO. DOI: 10.3115/1620754.1620841. 27

Daume III, H. and Campbell, L. (2007). A Bayesian model for discovering typological implications. In *Proc. of the 45th Annual Meeting of the Association of Computational Linguistics*, pages 65–72, Prague, Czech Republic. 27

Dempster, A. P., Laird, N. M., and Rubin, D. B. (1977). Maximum likelihood from incomplete data via the EM algorithm. *Journal of the Royal Statistical Society, Series B*, 39(1), pages 1–38. 145

DeNero, J., Bouchard-Côté, A., and Klein, D. (2008). Sampling alignment structure under a Bayesian translation model. In *Proc. of the 2008 Conference on Empirical Methods in Natural Language Processing*, pages 314–323, Honolulu, HI. Association for Computational Linguistics. DOI: 10.3115/1613715.1613758. 111

Devlin, J., Chang, M.-W., Lee, K., and Toutanova, K. (2018). BERT: Pre-training of deep bidirectional transformers for language understanding. *ArXiv Preprint ArXiv:1810.04805*. 221

Doersch, C. (2016). Tutorial on variational autoencoders. *ArXiv Preprint ArXiv:1606.05908*. 247, 249

Doyle, G. and Levy, R. (2013). Combining multiple information types in Bayesian word segmentation. In *Proc. of the 2013 Conference of the North American Chapter of the Association for Computational Linguistics: Human Language Technologies*, pages 117–126, Atlanta, GA. 29

Dreyer, M. and Eisner, J. (2006). Better informed training of latent syntactic features. In *Proc. of the 2006 Conference on Empirical Methods in Natural Language Processing*, pages 317–326, Sydney, Australia. Association for Computational Linguistics. DOI: 10.3115/1610075.1610120. 202

Dreyer, M. and Eisner, J. (2011). Discovering morphological paradigms from plain text using a Dirichlet process mixture model. In *Proc. of the Conference on Empirical Methods in Natural Language Processing (EMNLP)*, pages 616–627, Edinburgh. Supplementary material (9 pages) also available. 27

Duchi, J., Hazan, E., and Singer, Y. (2011). Adaptive subgradient methods for online learning and stochastic optimization. *Journal of Machine Learning Research*, 12(Jul):2121–2159. 265

Dymetman, M., Bouchard, G., and Carter, S. (2012). Optimization and sampling for nlp from a unified viewpoint. In *Proc. of the 1st International Workshop on Optimization Techniques for Human Language Technology*, pages 79–94, Mumbai, India. The COLING 2012 Organizing Committee. 123

Earley, J. (1970). An efficient context-free parsing algorithm. *Communications of the ACM*, 13(2), pages 94–102. DOI: 10.1145/357980.358005. 188

Eisenstein, J. (2019). *Natural Language Processing*. MIT Press. 228, 242, 255

Eisenstein, J. and Barzilay, R. (2008). Bayesian unsupervised topic segmentation. In *Proc. of the 2008 Conference on Empirical Methods in Natural Language Processing*, pages 334–343, Honolulu, HI. Association for Computational Linguistics. DOI: 10.3115/1613715.1613760. 27

Eisenstein, J., Ahmed, A., and Xing, E. (2011). Sparse additive generative models of text. In Getoor, L., and Scheffer, T., Eds., *Proc. of the 28th International Conference on Machine Learning (ICML-11)*, pages 1041–1048, New York, NY, ACM. 68

Eisner, J. (2002). Transformational priors over grammars. In *Proc. of the ACL-02 Conference on Empirical Methods in Natural Language Processing*, vol. 10, pages 63–70. Association for Computational Linguistics. DOI: 10.3115/1118693.1118702. 73

Eisner, J., Goldlust, E., and Smith, N. A. (2005). Compiling comp ling: Weighted dynamic programming and the dyna language. In *Proc. of Human Language Technology Conference and Conference on Empirical Methods in Natural Language Processing*, pages 281–290, Vancouver, British Columbia, Canada. Association for Computational Linguistics. DOI: 10.3115/1220575.1220611. 186

Eisner, J. and Smith, N. A. (2005). Parsing with soft and hard constraints on dependency length. In *Proc. of the 9th International Workshop on Parsing Technology*, pages 30–41, Vancouver, British Columbia. Association for Computational Linguistics. DOI: 10.3115/1654494.1654498. 149

Eisner, J. (2016). Inside-outside and forward-backward algorithms are just backdrop (tutorial paper), In *Proc. of the Workshop on Structured Prediction for NLP*, pages 1–17. 228

Elman, J. L. (1990). Finding structure in time. *Cognitive Science*, 14(2):179–211. DOI: 10.1207/s15516709cog1402_1 230

Elman, J. L. (1991). Distributed representations, simple recurrent networks, and grammatical structure. *Machine Learning*, 7(2–3):195–225. DOI: 10.1007/bf00114844 214

Elsner, M., Goldwater, S., Feldman, N., and Wood, F. (2013). A joint learning model of word segmentation, lexical acquisition, and phonetic variability. In *Proc. of the 2013 Conference on Empirical Methods in Natural Language Processing*, pages 42–54, Seattle, WA. Association for Computational Linguistics. 29

Escobar, M. D. (1994). Estimating normal means with a Dirichlet process prior. *Journal of the American Statistical Association*, 89(425), pages 268–277. DOI: 10.2307/2291223. 163

Escobar, M. D. and West, M. (1995). Bayesian density estimation and inference using mixtures. *Journal of the American Statistical Association*, 90(430), pages 577–588. DOI: 10.1080/01621459.1995.10476550. 163

Feinberg, S. E. (2011). Bayesian models and methods in public policy and government settings. *Statistical Science*, 26(2), pages 212–226. DOI: 10.1214/10-sts331. 43

Ferguson, T. S. (1973). A Bayesian analysis of some nonparametric problems. *The Annals of Statistics*, 1(2), pages 209–230. DOI: 10.1214/aos/1176342360. 156

Finetti, B. d. (1980). Foresight; its logical laws, its subjective sources. In Kyberg, H.E. and Smokler, H.E., Eds., *Studies in Subjective Probability*, pages 99–158. 8

Finkel, J. R., Grenager, T., and Manning, C. D. (2007). The infinite tree. In *Proc. of the 45th Annual Meeting of the Association of Computational Linguistics*, pages 272–279, Prague, Czech Republic. 203

Finkel, J. R. and Manning, C. D. (2009). Hierarchical Bayesian domain adaptation. In *Proc. of Human Language Technologies: The 2009 Annual Conference of the North American Chapter of the Association for Computational Linguistics*, pages 602–610, Boulder, CO. DOI: 10.3115/1620754.1620842. 92

Firth, J. R. (1957). A synopsis of linguistic theory, 1930–1955. *Studies in Linguistic Analysis.* 218

Fortunato, M., Blundell, C., and Vinyals, O. (2017). Bayesian recurrent neural networks. *ArXiv Preprint ArXiv:1704.02798.* 232

Frank, S., Keller, F., and Goldwater, S. (2013). Exploring the utility of joint morphological and syntactic learning from child-directed speech. In *Proc. of the 2013 Conference on Empirical Methods in Natural Language Processing*, pages 30–41, Seattle, WA. Association for Computational Linguistics. 29

Frank, S., Feldman, N. H., and Goldwater, S. (2014). Weak semantic context helps phonetic learning in a model of infant language acquisition. In *Proc. of the 52nd Annual Meeting of the Association for Computational Linguistics (Volume 1: Long Papers)*, pages 1073–1083, Baltimore, MD. DOI: 10.3115/v1/p14-1101. 29

Fullwood, M. and O'Donnell, T. (2013). Learning non-concatenative morphology. In *Proc. of the 4th Annual Workshop on Cognitive Modeling and Computational Linguistics (CMCL)*, pages 21–27, Sofia, Bulgaria. Association for Computational Linguistics. 29

Funahashi, K.-I. (1989). On the approximate realization of continuous mappings by neural networks. *Neural Networks*, 2(3):183–192. DOI: 10.1016/0893-6080(89)90003-8 215

Gal, Y. and Ghahramani, Z. (2016a). Bayesian convolutional neural networks with Bernoulli approximate variational inference. In *Proc. of the 4th International Conference on Learning Representations (ICLR) Workshop Track.* 243

Gal, Y. and Ghahramani, Z. (2016b). Dropout as a Bayesian approximation: Representing model uncertainty in deep learning. In *Proc. of the 33rd International Conference on Machine Learning (ICML)*, pages 1050–1059. 243

Gal, Y. and Ghahramani, Z. (2016c). A theoretically grounded application of dropout in recurrent neural networks. In Lee, D. D., Sugiyama, M., Luxburg, U. V., Guyon, I., and Garnett, R., Eds., *Advances in Neural Information Processing Systems 29*, pages 1019–1027, Curran Associates, Inc. 232

Gao, J. and Johnson, M. (2008). A comparison of Bayesian estimators for unsupervised Hidden Markov Model POS taggers. In *Proc. of the 2008 Conference on Empirical Methods in Natural Language Processing*, pages 344–352, Honolulu, HI. Association for Computational Linguistics. DOI: 10.3115/1613715.1613761. 101, 128

Gasthaus, J. and Teh, Y. W. (2010). Improvements to the sequence memoizer. In Lafferty, J., Williams, C., Shawe-Taylor, J., Zemel, R., and Culotta, A., Eds., *Advances in Neural Information Processing Systems 23*, pages 685–693. Curran Associates, Inc. 175

Gehring, J., Auli, M., Grangier, D., Yarats, and Dauphin, Y. N. (2017). Convolutional sequence to sequence learning. In *Proc. of the 34th International Conference on Machine Learning (ICML)*, vol. 70, pages 1243–1252, Sydney, Australia. 242, 254

Gelman, A., Carlin, J. B., Stern, H. B., and Rubin, D. B. (2003). *Bayesian Data Analysis*, 2nd ed., Chapman and Hall/CRC Texts in Statistical Science. 88, 93

Gelman, A. and Shalizi, C. R. (2013). Philosophy and the practice of Bayesian statistics. *British Journal of Mathematical and Statistical Psychology*, 66(1), pages 8–38. DOI: 10.1111/j.2044-8317.2011.02037.x. 22

Geman, S. and Geman, D. (1984). Stochastic relaxation, Gibbs distributions, and the Bayesian restoration of images. *IEEE Transactions on Pattern Analysis and Machine Intelligence*, 6(6), pages 721–741. DOI: 10.1109/tpami.1984.4767596. 101, 111

Geweke, J. (1992). Evaluating the accuracy of sampling-based approaches to the calculation of posterior moments. *Bayesian Statistics*, 4, pages 169–193. 120

Ghosh, S., Vinyals, O., Strope, B., Roy, S., Dean, T., and Heck, L. (2016). Contextual LSTM (CLSTM) models for large scale NLP tasks. *ArXiv Preprint ArXiv:1602.06291*. 255

Gimpel, K. and Smith, N. A. (2012). Concavity and initialization for unsupervised dependency parsing. In *Proc. of the 2012 Conference of the North American Chapter of the Association for Computational Linguistics: Human Language Technologies*, pages 577–581, Montréal, Canada. 149

Glorot, X. and Bengio, Y. (2010). Understanding the difficulty of training deep feedforward neural networks. In *Proc. of the 30th International Conference on Artificial Intelligence and Statistics (AISTATS)*, pages 249–256. 228

Goldberg, Y. (2017). *Neural Network Methods for Natural Language Processing*. Morgan & Claypool Publishers. DOI: 10.2200/s00762ed1v01y201703hlt037 255

Goldwater, S., Griffiths, T. L., and Johnson, M. (2006). Contextual dependencies in unsupervised word segmentation. In *Proc. of the 21st International Conference on Computational Linguistics and 44th Annual Meeting of the Association for Computational Linguistics*, pages 673–680, Sydney, Australia. DOI: 10.3115/1220175.1220260. 29

Goldwater, S., Griffiths, T., and Johnson, M. (2009). A Bayesian framework for word segmentation: Exploring the effects of context. *Cognition*, 112(1), pages 21–54. DOI: 10.1016/j.cognition.2009.03.008. 29

Goldwater, S. and Griffiths, T. (2007). A fully Bayesian approach to unsupervised part-of-speech tagging. In *Proc. of the 45th Annual Meeting of the Association of Computational Linguistics*, pages 744–751, Prague, Czech Republic. 26, 56, 66

Goller, C. and Kuchler, A. (1996). Learning task-dependent distributed representations by backpropagation through structure. In *Proc. of IEEE International Conference on Neural Networks*, vol. 1, pages 347–352. DOI: 10.1109/icnn.1996.548916 231

Goodfellow, I., Pouget-Abadie, J., Mirza, M., Xu, B., Warde-Farley, D., Ozair, S., Courville, A., and Bengio, Y. (2014). Generative adversarial nets. In *Advances in Neural Information Processing Systems 27*, pages 2672–2680. 245, 252, 253

Goodfellow, I., Bengio, Y., Courville, A., and Bengio, Y. (2016). *Deep Learning*. MIT Press, Cambridge. DOI: 10.1038/nature14539 214

Goodman, J. (1996). Parsing algorithms and metrics. In *Proc. of the 34th Annual Meeting of the Association for Computational Linguistics*, pages 177–183, Santa Cruz, CA. DOI: 10.3115/981863.981887. 90

Graves, A. (2011). Practical variational inference for neural networks. In Shawe-Taylor, J., Zemel, R. S., Bartlett, P. L., Pereira, F., and Weinberger, K. Q., Eds., *Advances in Neural Information Processing Systems 24*, pages 2348–2356, Curran Associates, Inc. 229, 232

Graves, A. (2012). Supervised sequence labelling. In *Supervised Sequence Labelling with Recurrent Neural Networks*, pages 5–13, Springer. DOI: 10.1007/978-3-642-24797-2_2 235

Griffiths, T. (2002). Gibbs sampling in the generative model of Latent Dirichlet Allocation. Technical report, Stanford University. 107

Griffiths, T. L., Kemp, C., and Tenenbaum, J. B. (2008). Bayesian models of cognition. In Sun, R., Ed., *Cambridge Handbook of Computational Cognitive Modeling*, pages 59–100. Cambridge University Press, Cambridge. 29

Griffiths, T. L., Chater, N., Kemp, C., Perfors, A., and Tenenbaum, J. B. (2010). Probabilistic models of cognition: exploring representations and inductive biases. *Trends in Cognitive Sciences*, 14(8), pages 357–364. DOI: 10.1016/j.tics.2010.05.004. 29

Griffiths, T. and Ghahramani, Z. (2005). Infinite latent feature models and the Indian buffet process. *Gatsby Computational Neuroscience Unit, Technical Report*, 1. 172

Gu, J., Lu, Z., Li, H., and Li, V. O. (2016). Incorporating copying mechanism in sequence-to-sequence learning. pages 1631–1640. DOI: 10.18653/v1/p16-1154 238

Haghighi, A. and Klein, D. (2007). Unsupervised coreference resolution in a nonparametric Bayesian model. In *Proc. 45th Annual Meeting of the ACL*, pages 848–855, Prague, Czech Republic. Association for Computational Linguistics. 27

Harris, Z. S. (1954). Distributional structure. *Word*, 10(2–3):146–162. DOI: 10.1080/00437956.1954.11659520 217

Harris, C. L. (1992). Connectionism and cognitive linguistics. In *Connectionist Natural Language Processing*, pages 1–27, Springer. DOI: 10.1007/978-94-011-2624-3_1 214

Hastings, W. K. (1970). Monte Carlo sampling methods using Markov chains and their applications. *Biometrika*, 57(1), pages 97–109. DOI: 10.2307/2334940. 114

Henderson, J. (2003). Inducing history representations for broad coverage statistical parsing. In *Human Language Technologies: The 2003 Annual Conference of the North American Chapter of the Association for Computational Linguistics*. DOI: 10.3115/1073445.1073459 216

Henderson, J. and Lane, P. (1998). A connectionist architecture for learning to parse. In *Proc. of the 17th International Conference on Computational Linguistics (Volume 1: Long Papers)*, pages 531–537, Association for Computational Linguistics. DOI: 10.3115/980451.980934 216

Hochreiter, S. and Schmidhuber, J. (1997). Long short-term memory. *Neural Computation*, 9(8):1735–1780. DOI: 10.1162/neco.1997.9.8.1735 233

Hoffman, M., Bach, F. R., and Blei, D. M. (2010). Online learning for latent Dirichlet allocation. In Lafferty, J., Williams, C., Shawe-Taylor, J., Zemel, R., and Culotta, A., Eds., *Advances in Neural Information Processing Systems 23*, pages 856–864. Curran Associates, Inc. 152

Hofmann, T. (1999a). Probabilistic latent semantic analysis. In *Proc. of Uncertainty in Artificial Intelligence*, pages 289–296. 57, 216

Hofmann, T. (1999b). Probabilistic latent semantic indexing. In *Proc. of the 22nd Annual International ACM SIGIR Conference on Research and Development in Information Retrieval, SIGIR'99*, pages 50–57, New York. DOI: 10.1145/312624.312649. 31

Hornik, K., Stinchcombe, M., and White, H. (1989). Multilayer feedforward networks are universal approximators. *Neural Networks*, 2(5):359–366. DOI: 10.1016/0893-6080(89)90020-8 215

Hovy, E., Marcus, M., Palmer, M., Ramshaw, L., and Weischedel, R. (2006). Ontonotes: The 90% solution. In *Proc. of the Human Language Technology Conference of the NAACL, Companion Volume: Short Papers*, pages 57–60, New York. Association for Computational Linguistics. 92

Hu, Z., Yang, Z., Salakhutdinov, R., and Xing, E. P. (2018). On unifying deep generative models. 246

Huang, Y., Zhang, M., and Tan, C. L. (2011). Nonparametric Bayesian machine transliteration with synchronous adaptor grammars. In *Proc. of the 49th Annual Meeting of the Association for Computational Linguistics: Human Language Technologies*, pages 534–539, Portland, OR. 205

Huang, Y., Zhang, M., and Tan, C.-L. (2012). Improved combinatory categorial grammar induction with boundary words and Bayesian inference. In *Proc. of COLING 2012*, pages 1257–1274, Mumbai, India. The COLING 2012 Organizing Committee. 210

Huang, Z., Xu, W., and Yu, K. (2015). Bidirectional LSTM-CRF models for sequence tagging. *ArXiv Preprint ArXiv:1508.01991*. 238

Jaynes, E. T. (2003). *Probability Theory: The Logic of Science*. Cambridge University Press. DOI: 10.1017/cbo9780511790423. xxvi, 22, 66

Jeffreys, H. (1961). *Theory of Probability*. Oxford University. DOI: 10.1063/1.3050814. 68, 82

Jelinek, F. and Mercer, R. L. (1980). Interpolated estimation of Markov source parameters from sparse data. In *Proc. of Workshop on Pattern Recognition in Practice*, Amsterdam, The Netherlands. 82

Jiang, T., Wang, L., and Zhang, K. (1995). Alignment of trees—an alternative to tree edit. *Theoretical Computer Science*, 143(1), pages 137–148. DOI: 10.1016/0304-3975(95)80029-9. 208

Johnson, M. (2007a). Transforming projective bilexical dependency grammars into efficiently-parsable CFGs with unfold-fold. In *Proc. of the 45th Annual Meeting of the Association of Computational Linguistics*, pages 168–175, Prague, Czech Republic. 188

Johnson, M. (2007b). Why doesn't EM find good HMM POS-taggers? In *Proc. of the 2007 Joint Conference on Empirical Methods in Natural Language Processing and Computational Natural Language Learning (EMNLP-CoNLL)*, pages 296–305, Prague, Czech Republic. Association for Computational Linguistics. 146

Johnson, M. (2008). Using adaptor grammars to identify synergies in the unsupervised acquisition of linguistic structure. In *Proc. of ACL-08: HLT*, pages 398–406, Columbus, OH. Association for Computational Linguistics. 29

Johnson, M., Griffiths, T., and Goldwater, S. (2007a). Bayesian inference for PCFGs via Markov chain Monte Carlo. In *Human Language Technologies 2007: The Conference of the North American Chapter of the Association for Computational Linguistics; Proceedings of the Main Conference*, pages 139–146, Rochester, NY. 26, 190

Johnson, M., Griffiths, T. L., and Goldwater, S. (2007b). Adaptor grammars: A framework for specifying compositional nonparametric Bayesian models. In Schölkopf, B., Platt, J., and Hoffman, T., Eds., *Advances in Neural Information Processing Systems 19*, pages 641–648. MIT Press. 27, 128, 194, 198

Johnson, M., Demuth, K., Jones, B., and Black, M. J. (2010). Synergies in learning words and their referents. In Lafferty, J., Williams, C., Shawe-Taylor, J., Zemel, R., and Culotta, A., Eds., *Advances in Neural Information Processing Systems 23*, pages 1018–1026. Curran Associates, Inc. 29

Johnson, M., Christophe, A., Dupoux, E., and Demuth, K. (2014). Modelling function words improves unsupervised word segmentation. In *Proc. of the 52nd Annual Meeting of the Association for Computational Linguistics (Volume 1: Long Papers)*, pages 282–292, Baltimore, MD. DOI: 10.3115/v1/p14-1027. 29

Johnson, M. and Goldwater, S. (2009). Improving nonparameteric Bayesian inference: experiments on unsupervised word segmentation with adaptor grammars. In *Proc. of Human Language Technologies: The 2009 Annual Conference of the North American Chapter of the Association for Computational Linguistics*, pages 317–325, Boulder, CO. DOI: 10.3115/1620754.1620800. 117

Jones, B., Johnson, M., and Goldwater, S. (2012). Semantic parsing with Bayesian tree transducers. In *Proc. of the 50th Annual Meeting of the Association for Computational Linguistics (Volume 1: Long Papers)*, pages 488–496, Jeju Island, Korea. 210

Jordan, M. I. (2011). Message from the president: The era of big data. *International Society for Bayesian Analysis (ISBA) Bulletin*, 18(2), pages 1–3. 258

Joshi, M., Das, D., Gimpel, K., and Smith, N. A. (2010). Movie reviews and revenues: An experiment in text regression. In *Human Language Technologies: The 2010 Annual Conference of the North American Chapter of the Association for Computational Linguistics*, pages 293–296, Los Angeles, CA. 40

Joshi, A. K. and Schabes, Y. (1997). Tree-adjoining grammars. In *Handbook of Formal Languages*, pages 69–123. Springer. DOI: 10.1007/978-3-642-59126-6_2. 210

Kalchbrenner, N. and Blunsom, P. (2013). Recurrent continuous translation models. In *Proc. of the Conference on Empirical Methods in Natural Language Processing (EMNLP)*, pages 1700–1709. 236

Kalchbrenner, N., Grefenstette, E., and Blunsom, P. (2014). A convolutional neural network for modelling sentences. In *Proc. of the 52nd Annual Meeting of the Association for Computational Linguistics (Volume 1: Long Papers)*, vol. 1, pages 655–665. DOI: 10.3115/v1/p14-1062 240

Kallmeyer, L. and Maier, W. (2010). Data-driven parsing with probabilistic linear context-free rewriting systems. In *Proc. of the 23rd International Conference on Computational Linguistics (Coling 2010)*, pages 537–545, Beijing, China. Coling 2010 Organizing Committee. DOI: 10.1162/coli_a_00136. 177

Kasami, T. (1965). An efficient recognition and syntax-analysis algorithm for context-free languages. Technical Report AFCRL-65-758, Air Force Cambridge Research Lab. 182

Katz, S. M. (1987). Estimation of probabilities from sparse data for the language model component of a speech recognizer. In *IEEE Transactions on Acoustics, Speech and Signal Processing*, pages 400–401. DOI: 10.1109/tassp.1987.1165125. 82

Kingma, D. P. and Ba, J. (2014). Adam: A method for stochastic optimization. *ArXiv Preprint ArXiv:1412.6980.* 265

Kingma, D. P. and Welling, M. (2014). Auto-encoding variational Bayes. In *Proc. of the 2nd International Conference on Learning Representations (ICLR).* 245

Klein, G., Kim, Y., Deng, Y., Senellart, J., and Rush, A. M. (2017). OpenNMT: Open-source toolkit for neural machine translation. In *Proc. of the System Demonstrations of the 55th Annual Meeting of the Association for Computational Linguistics*, pages 67–72. DOI: 10.18653/v1/p17-4012 239

Klein, D. and Manning, C. (2004). Corpus-based induction of syntactic structure: Models of dependency and constituency. In *Proc. of the 42nd Meeting of the Association for Computational Linguistics (ACL'04), Main Volume*, pages 478–485, Barcelona, Spain. DOI: 10.3115/1218955.1219016. 62, 149, 208

Kneser, R. and Ney, H. (1995). Improved backing-off for m-gram language modeling. In *Proc. of the IEEE International Conference on Acoustics, Speech and Signal Processing*, vol. I, pages 181–184, Detroit, MI. IEEE Inc. DOI: 10.1109/icassp.1995.479394. 82, 170

Koehn, P. and Knowles, R. (2017). Six challenges for neural machine translation. In *Proc. of the 1st Workshop on Neural Machine Translation*, pages 28–39, Association for Computational Linguistics. DOI: 10.18653/v1/w17-3204 254

Koller, D. and Friedman, N. (2009). *Probabilistic Graphical Models: Principles and Techniques.* MIT Press. 19, 151

Krizhevsky, A., Sutskever, I., and Hinton, G. E. (2012). ImageNet classification with deep convolutional neural networks. In *Advances in Neural Information Processing Systems 25*, pages 1097–1105. DOI: 10.1145/3065386 240

Kübler, S., McDonald, R., and Nivre, J. (2009). *Dependency Parsing.* Synthesis Lectures on Human Language Technologies. Morgan & Claypool. DOI: 10.2200/s00169ed1v01y200901hlt002. 203

Kucukelbir, A., Tran, D., Ranganath, R., Gelman, A., and Blei, D. M. (2016). Automatic differentiation variational inference. *arXiv preprint arXiv:1603.00788.* 141

Kulis, B. and Jordan, M. I. (2011). Revisiting k-means: New algorithms via Bayesian nonparametrics. *arXiv preprint arXiv:1111.0352.* 155

Kumar, S. and Byrne, W. (2004). Minimum bayes-risk decoding for statistical machine translation. In Susan Dumais, D. M. and Roukos, S., Eds., *HLT-NAACL 2004: Main Proceedings*, pages 169–176, Boston, MA. Association for Computational Linguistics. 90

Kwiatkowski, T., Goldwater, S., Zettlemoyer, L., and Steedman, M. (2012a). A probabilistic model of syntactic and semantic acquisition from child-directed utterances and their meanings. In *Proc. of the 13th Conference of the European Chapter of the Association for Computational Linguistics*, pages 234–244, Avignon, France. 152

Kwiatkowski, T., Goldwater, S., Zettlemoyer, L., and Steedman, M. (2012b). A probabilistic model of syntactic and semantic acquisition from child-directed utterances and their meanings. In *Proc. of the 13th Conference of the European Chapter of the Association for Computational Linguistics*, pages 234–244, Avignon, France. 210

Le, Q. and Mikolov, T. (2014). Distributed representations of sentences and documents. In *Proc. of the 31st International Conference on Machine Learning (ICML)*, pages 1188–1196. 222

LeCun, Y., Boser, B., Denker, J. S., Henderson, D., Howard, R. E., Hubbard, W., and Jackel, L. D. (1989). Backpropagation applied to handwritten zip code recognition. *Neural Computation*, 1(4):541–551. DOI: 10.1162/neco.1989.1.4.541 214

Lei, T., Barzilay, R., and Jaakkola, T. (2016). Rationalizing neural predictions. In *Proc. of the Conference on Empirical Methods in Natural Language Processing (EMNLP).* DOI: 10.18653/v1/d16-1011 255

Levenberg, A., Dyer, C., and Blunsom, P. (2012). A Bayesian model for learning scfgs with discontiguous rules. In *Proc. of the 2012 Joint Conference on Empirical Methods in Natural Language Processing and Computational Natural Language Learning*, pages 223–232, Jeju Island, Korea. Association for Computational Linguistics. 111, 205

Levy, R. P., Reali, F., and Griffiths, T. L. (2009). Modeling the effects of memory on human online sentence processing with particle filters. In Koller, D., Schuurmans, D., Bengio, Y., and Bottou, L., Eds., *Advances in Neural Information Processing Systems 21*, pages 937–944. Curran Associates, Inc. 129

Li, J., Chen, X., Hovy, E., and Jurafsky, D. (2015). Visualizing and understanding neural models in NLP. *ArXiv Preprint ArXiv:1506.01066.* DOI: 10.18653/v1/n16-1082 255

Liang, P., Petrov, S., Jordan, M., and Klein, D. (2007). The infinite PCFG using hierarchical Dirichlet processes. In *Proc. of the 2007 Joint Conference on Empirical Methods in Natural Language Processing and Computational Natural Language Learning (EMNLP-CoNLL)*, pages 688–697, Prague, Czech Republic. Association for Computational Linguistics. 200

Liang, P. and Klein, D. (2009). Online EM for unsupervised models. In *Proc. of Human Language Technologies: The 2009 Annual Conference of the North American Chapter of the Association for Computational Linguistics*, pages 611–619, Boulder, CO. DOI: 10.3115/1620754.1620843. 152

Lidstone, G. J. (1920). Note on the general case of the Bayes-Laplace formula for the inductive or posteriori probabilities. *Transactions of the Faculty of Actuaries*, 8(182). 82

Lin, C.-C., Wang, Y.-C., and Tsai, R. T.-H. (2009). Modeling the relationship among linguistic typological features with hierarchical Dirichlet process. In *Proc. of the 23rd Pacific Asia Conference on Language, Information and Computation*, pages 741–747, Hong Kong. City University of Hong Kong. 27

Lindsey, R., Headden, W., and Stipicevic, M. (2012). A phrase-discovering topic model using hierarchical Pitman-Yor processes. In *Proc. of the 2012 Joint Conference on Empirical Methods in Natural Language Processing and Computational Natural Language Learning*, pages 214–222, Jeju Island, Korea. Association for Computational Linguistics. 117

Linzen, T. (2018). What can linguistics and deep learning contribute to each other? *ArXiv Preprint ArXiv:1809.04179*. DOI: 10.1353/lan.2019.0001 255

Liu, H., Simonyan, K., and Yang, Y. (2018). Darts: Differentiable architecture search. *ArXiv Preprint ArXiv:1806.09055*. 243

Luong, T., Pham, H., and Manning, C. D. (2015). Effective approaches to attention-based neural machine translation. In *Proc. of the Conference on Empirical Methods in Natural Language Processing (EMNLP)*, pages 1412–1421. DOI: 10.18653/v1/d15-1166 238

Maas, A. L., Hannun, A. Y., and Ng, A. Y. (2013). Rectifier nonlinearities improve neural network acoustic models. In *Proc. of the 30th International Conference on Machine Learning (ICML)*, page 3. 224

MacKay, D. J. (1992). A practical Bayesian framework for backpropagation networks. *Neural Computation*, 4(3):448–472. DOI: 10.1162/neco.1992.4.3.448 228

Maddison, C. J., Mnih, A., and Teh, Y. W. (2017). The concrete distribution: A continuous relaxation of discrete random variables. In *Proc. of the 5th International Conference on Learning Representations (ICLR)*. 252, 273

Mandt, S., Hoffman, M., and Blei, D. (2016). A variational analysis of stochastic gradient algorithms. In *Proc. of 33rd International Conference on Machine Learning (ICML)*, pages 354–363. 265

Marcus, M. P., Santorini, B., and Marcinkiewicz, M. A. (1993). Building a large annotated corpus of English: The Penn treebank. *Computational Linguistics*, 19(2), pages 313–330. 181

Matsuzaki, T., Miyao, Y., and Tsujii, J. (2005). Probabilistic CFG with latent annotations. In *Proc. of the 43rd Annual Meeting of the Association for Computational Linguistics (ACL'05)*, pages 75–82, Ann Arbor, MI. DOI: 10.3115/1219840.1219850. 201, 211

McCulloch, W. S. and Pitts, W. (1943). A logical calculus of the ideas immanent in nervous activity. *The Bulletin of Mathematical Biophysics*, 5(4):115–133. DOI: 10.1007/bf02478259 214

McGrayne, S. B. (2011). *The Theory that Would not Die: How Bayes' Rule Cracked the Enigma Code, Hunted Down Russian Submarines, and Emerged Triumphant from Two Centuries of Controversy*. Yale University Press. xxvi

Metropolis, N., Rosenbluth, A. W., Rosenbluth, M. N., Teller, A. H., and Teller, E. (1953). Equation of state calculations by fast computing machines. *Journal of Chemical Physics*, 21, pages 1087–1092. DOI: 10.1063/1.1699114. 114

Mikolov, T., Kombrink, S., Burget, L., Černocky, J., and Khudanpur, S. (2011). Extensions of recurrent neural network language model. In *Proc. of the IEEE International Conference on Acoustics, Speech and Signal Processing (ICASSP)*, pages 5528–5531. DOI: 10.1109/icassp.2011.5947611 247

Mikolov, T., Chen, K., Corrado, G., and Dean, J. (2013a). Efficient estimation of word representations in vector space. *ArXiv Preprint ArXiv:1301.3781.* 218, 219, 220

Mikolov, T., Sutskever, I., Chen, K., Corrado, G. S., and Dean, J. (2013b). Distributed representations of words and phrases and their compositionality. In Burges, C. J. C., Bottou, L., Welling, M., Ghahramani, Z., and Weinberger, K. Q., Eds., *Advances in Neural Information Processing Systems 26*, pages 3111–3119, Curran Associates, Inc. 219

Mikolov, T. and Zweig, G. (2012). Context dependent recurrent neural network language model. *SLT*, 12(234–239):8. DOI: 10.1109/slt.2012.6424228 255

Mimno, D., Wallach, H., and McCallum, A. (2008). Gibbs sampling for logistic normal topic models with graph-based priors. In *NIPS Workshop on Analyzing Graphs*. 61

Mimno, D., Wallach, H., Talley, E., Leenders, M., and McCallum, A. (2011). Optimizing semantic coherence in topic models. In *Proc. of the 2011 Conference on Empirical Methods in Natural Language Processing*, pages 262–272, Edinburgh, Scotland, UK. Association for Computational Linguistics. 36

Minka, T. (1999). The Dirichlet-tree distribution. Technical report, Justsystem Pittsburgh Research Center. 55

Minka, T. (2000). Bayesian linear regression. Technical report, Massachusetts Institute of Technology. 41

Minsky, M. and Papert, S. (1969). Perceptrons. DOI: 10.7551/mitpress/11301.001.0001 214

Mitchell, J. and Lapata, M. (2008). Vector-based models of semantic composition, pages 236–244. 216

Močkus, J. (1975). On Bayesian methods for seeking the extremum. In *Proc. of the IFIP Technical Conference on Optimization Techniques*, pages 400–404, Springer. DOI: 10.1007/978-3-662-38527-2_55 244

Močkus, J. (2012). *Bayesian Approach to Global Optimization: Theory and Applications*, vol. 37, Springer Science & Business Media. DOI: 10.2307/2008419 244

Murphy, K. P. (2012). *Machine Learning: A Probabilistic Perspective*. MIT Press. 17, 222

Nakazawa, T. and Kurohashi, S. (2012). Alignment by bilingual generation and monolingual derivation. In *Proc. of COLING 2012*, pages 1963–1978, Mumbai, India. 111

Narayan, S., Cohen, S. B., and Lapata, M. (2018a). Don't give me the details, just the summary! Topic-aware convolutional neural networks for extreme summarization. In *Proc. of the Conference on Empirical Methods in Natural Language Processing (EMNLP)*, pages 1797–1807. 255

Narayan, S., Cohen, S. B., and Lapata, M. (2018b). Ranking sentences for extractive summarization with reinforcement learning. In *Proc. of the Conference of the North American Chapter of the Association for Computational Linguistics: Human Language Technologies*, pages 1747–1759. DOI: 10.18653/v1/n18-1158 241

Neal, R. M. (2000). Markov chain sampling methods for Dirichlet process mixture models. *Journal of Computational and Graphical Statistics*, 9(2), pages 249–265. DOI: 10.2307/1390653. 161, 163

Neal, R. M. (2003). Slice sampling. *Annals of Statistics*, 31, pages 705–767. DOI: 10.1214/aos/1056562461. 115

Neal, R. M. (2012). *Bayesian Learning for Neural Networks*, vol. 118, Springer Science & Business Media. DOI: 10.1007/978-1-4612-0745-0 229

Neal, R. M. and Hinton, G. E. (1998). A view of the EM algorithm that justifies incremental, sparse, and other variants. In *Learning in Graphical Models*, pages 355–368. Springer. DOI: 10.1007/978-94-011-5014-9_12. 152

Neco, R. P. and Forcada, M. L. (1997). Asynchronous translations with recurrent neural nets. In *Proc. of the International Conference on Neural Networks*, vol. 4, pages 2535–2540, IEEE. DOI: 10.1109/icnn.1997.614693 214, 236

Neiswanger, W., Wang, C., and Xing, E. P. (2014). Asymptotically exact, embarrassingly parallel MCMC. In *Proc. of the 30th Conference on Uncertainty in Artificial Intelligence, UAI*, pages 623–632, Quebec City, Quebec, Canada. AUAI Press. 112

Neubig, G., Watanabe, T., Sumita, E., Mori, S., and Kawahara, T. (2011). An unsupervised model for joint phrase alignment and extraction. In *Proc. of the 49th Annual Meeting of the Association for Computational Linguistics: Human Language Technologies*, pages 632–641, Portland, OR. 205

Neubig, G., Dyer, C., Goldberg, Y., Matthews, A., Ammar, W., Anastasopoulos, A., Ballesteros, M., Chiang, D., Clothiaux, D., Cohn, T., et al. (2017). DyNet: The dynamic neural network toolkit. *ArXiv Preprint ArXiv:1701.03980.* 217

Newman, D., Asuncion, A., Smyth, P., and Welling, M. (2009). Distributed algorithms for topic models. *Journal of Machine Learning Research*, 10, pages 1801–1828. 112

Newman, D., Lau, J. H., Grieser, K., and Baldwin, T. (2010). Automatic evaluation of topic coherence. In *Human Language Technologies: The 2010 Annual Conference of the North American Chapter of the Association for Computational Linguistics*, pages 100–108, Los Angeles, CA. 36

Noji, H., Mochihashi, D., and Miyao, Y. (2013). Improvements to the Bayesian topic n-gram models. In *Proc. of the 2013 Conference on Empirical Methods in Natural Language Processing*, pages 1180–1190, Seattle, WA. Association for Computational Linguistics. 170

O'Neill, B. (2009). Exchangeability, correlation, and Bayes' effect. *International Statistical Review*, 77(2), pages 241–250. DOI: 10.1111/j.1751-5823.2008.00059.x. 9

Och, F. J. and Ney, H. (2003). A systematic comparison of various statistical alignment models. *Computational Linguistics*, 29(1), pages 19–51. DOI: 10.1162/089120103321337421. 206, 209

Omohundro, S. M. (1992). *Best-first Model Merging for Dynamic Learning and Recognition*. International Computer Science Institute. 211

Pajak, B., Bicknell, K., and Levy, R. (2013). A model of generalization in distributional learning of phonetic categories. In Demberg, V. and Levy, R., Eds., *Proc. of the 4th Workshop on Cognitive Modeling and Computational Linguistics*, pages 11–20, Sofia, Bulgaria. Association for Computational Linguistics. 29

Pascanu, R., Mikolov, T., and Bengio, Y. (2013). On the difficulty of training recurrent neural networks. In *Proc. of the 30th International Conference on Machine Learning (ICML)*, pages 1310–1318. 230, 232

Pearl, J. (1988). *Probabilistic Reasoning in Intelligent Systems: Networks of Plausible Inference*. Morgan Kaufmann, San Mateo, CA. 18

Perfors, A., Tenenbaum, J. B., Griffiths, T. L., and Xu, F. (2011). A tutorial introduction to Bayesian models of cognitive development. *Cognition*, 120(3), pages 302–321. DOI: 10.1016/j.cognition.2010.11.015. 29

Peters, M., Neumann, M., Iyyer, M., Gardner, M., Clark, C., Lee, K., and Zettlemoyer, L. (2018). Deep contextualized word representations. In *Proc. of the Conference of the North American Chapter of the Association for Computational Linguistics: Human Language Technologies, (Volume 1: Long Papers)*, vol. 1, pages 2227–2237. DOI: 10.18653/v1/n18-1202 221

Petrov, S., Barrett, L., Thibaux, R., and Klein, D. (2006). Learning accurate, compact, and interpretable tree annotation. In *Proc. of the 21st International Conference on Computational Linguistics and 44th Annual Meeting of the Association for Computational Linguistics*, pages 433–440, Sydney, Australia. DOI: 10.3115/1220175.1220230. 202, 211

Pitman, J. and Yor, M. (1997). The two-parameter Poisson-Dirichlet distribution derived from a stable subordinator. *The Annals of Probability*, 25(2), pages 855–900. DOI: 10.1214/aop/1024404422. 168

Pollack, J. B. (1990). Recursive distributed representations. *Artificial Intelligence*, 46(1–2):77–105. DOI: 10.1016/0004-3702(90)90005-k 231

Post, M. and Gildea, D. (2009). Bayesian learning of a tree substitution grammar. In *Proc. of the ACL-IJCNLP 2009 Conference Short Papers*, pages 45–48, Suntec, Singapore. Association for Computational Linguistics. DOI: 10.3115/1667583.1667599. 211

Post, M. and Gildea, D. (2013). Bayesian tree substitution grammars as a usage-based approach. *Language and Speech*, 56, pages 291–308. DOI: 10.1177/0023830913484901. 211

Preoțiuc-Pietro, D. and Cohn, T. (2013). A temporal model of text periodicities using gaussian processes. In *Proc. of the 2013 Conference on Empirical Methods in Natural Language Processing*, pages 977–988, Seattle, WA. Association for Computational Linguistics. 172

Prescher, D. (2005). Head-driven PCFGs with latent-head statistics. In *Proc. of the 9th International Workshop on Parsing Technology*, pages 115–124, Vancouver, British Columbia. Association for Computational Linguistics. DOI: 10.3115/1654494.1654506. 201, 211

Rabiner, L. R. (1989). A tutorial on hidden Markov models and selected applications in speech recognition. *Proc. of the IEEE*, 77(2), pages 257–286. DOI: 10.1109/5.18626. 179

Raftery, A. E. and Lewis, S. M. (1992). Practical Markov chain Monte Carlo: Comment: One long run with diagnostics: Implementation strategies for Markov chain Monte Carlo. *Statistical Science*, 7(4), pages 493–497. 121

Raiffa, H. and Schlaifer, R. (1961). *Applied Statistical Decision Theory*. Wiley-Interscience. 52, 257

Rasmussen, C. E. and Williams, C. K. I. (2006). *Gaussian Processes for Machine Learning*. MIT Press. DOI: 10.1007/978-3-540-28650-9_4. 172

Ravi, S. and Knight, K. (2011). Deciphering foreign language. In *Proc. of the 49th Annual Meeting of the Association for Computational Linguistics: Human Language Technologies*, pages 12–21, Portland, OR. 111

Real, E., Aggarwal, A., Huang, Y., and Le, Q. V. (2018). Regularized evolution for image classifier architecture search. *ArXiv Preprint ArXiv:1802.01548*. 243

Rios, L. M. and Sahinidis, N. V. (2013). Derivative-free optimization: A review of algorithms and comparison of software implementations. *Journal of Global Optimization*, 56(3):1247–1293. DOI: 10.1007/s10898-012-9951-y 244

Robert, C. P. and Casella, G. (2005). *Monte Carlo Statistical Methods*. Springer. DOI: 10.1007/978-1-4757-3071-5. 119, 121, 122, 123, 128

Rosenblatt, F. (1958). The perceptron: A probabilistic model for information storage and organization in the brain. *Psychological Review*, 65(6):386. DOI: 10.1037/h0042519 214

Rosenfeld, R. (2000). Two decades of statistical language modeling: Where do we go from here? *Proc. of the IEEE*, 88(8), pages 1270–1278. DOI: 10.1109/5.880083. 170

Roth, D. and Yih, W.-t. (2005). Integer linear programming inference for conditional random fields. In *Proc. of the 22nd International Conference on Machine Learning (ICML)*, pages 736–743, ACM. DOI: 10.1145/1102351.1102444 265

Rozenberg, G. and Ehrig, H. (1999). *Handbook of Graph Grammars and Computing by Graph Transformation*, vol. 1. World Scientific, Singapore. DOI: 10.1142/9789812384720. 177

Rumelhart, D. E., Hinton, G. E., Williams, R. J., et al. (1988). Learning representations by back-propagating errors. *Cognitive Modeling*, 5(3):1. DOI: 10.1038/323533a0 214

Saatci, Y. and Wilson, A. G. (2017). Bayesian GAN. In *Advances in Neural Information Processing Systems 30*, pages 3622–3631. 253

Sankaran, B., Haffari, G., and Sarkar, A. (2011). Bayesian extraction of minimal scfg rules for hierarchical phrase-based translation. In *Proc. of the 6th Workshop on Statistical Machine Translation*, pages 533–541, Edinburgh, Scotland. Association for Computational Linguistics. 205

Sato, M.-A. and Ishii, S. (2000). On-line EM algorithm for the normalized Gaussian network. *Neural Computation*, 12(2), pages 407–432. DOI: 10.1162/089976600300015853. 152

Saxe, A. M., McClelland, J. L., and Ganguli, S. (2013). Exact solutions to the nonlinear dynamics of learning in deep linear neural networks. *arXiv preprint arXiv:1312.6120*. 228

Sennrich, R., Haddow, B., and Birch, A. (2016). Improving neural machine translation models with monolingual data. In *Proc. of the 54nd Annual Meeting of the Association for Computational Linguistics (Volume 1: Long Papers)*. DOI: 10.18653/v1/p16-1009 254

Sennrich, R., Firat, O., Cho, K., Birch, A., Haddow, B., Hitschler, J., Junczys-Dowmunt, M., Läubli, S., Miceli Barone, A. V., Mokry, J., and Nadejde, M. (2017). Nematus: A toolkit for neural machine translation. In *Proc. of the Software Demonstrations of the 15th Conference of the European Chapter of the Association for Computational Linguistics*, pages 65–68, Valencia, Spain. DOI: 10.18653/v1/e17-3017 239

Sethuraman, J. (1994). A constructive definition of Dirichlet priors. *Statistica Sinica*, 4, pages 639–650. 157

Shareghi, E., Haffari, G., Cohn, T., and Nicholson, A. (2015). Structured prediction of sequences and trees using infinite contexts. In *Machine Learning and Knowledge Discovery in Databases*, pages 373–389. Springer. DOI: 10.1007/978-3-319-23525-7_23. 175

Shareghi, E., Li, Y., Zhu, Y., Reichart, R., and Korhonen, A. (2019). Bayesian learning for neural dependency parsing. *Proc. of the Annual Conference of the North American Chapter of the Association for Computational Linguistics (NAACL)*. 229

Shindo, H., Miyao, Y., Fujino, A., and Nagata, M. (2012). Bayesian symbol-refined tree substitution grammars for syntactic parsing. In *Proc. of the 50th Annual Meeting of the Association for Computational Linguistics (Volume 1: Long Papers)*, pages 440–448, Jeju Island, Korea. 27, 211

Sirts, K., Eisenstein, J., Elsner, M., and Goldwater, S. (2014). Pos induction with distributional and morphological information using a distance-dependent Chinese restaurant process. In *Proc. of the 52nd Annual Meeting of the Association for Computational Linguistics (Volume 2: Short Papers)*, pages 265–271, Baltimore, MD. DOI: 10.3115/v1/p14-2044. 174

Smith, N. A. (2011). *Linguistic Structure Prediction*. Synthesis Lectures on Human Language Technologies. Morgan & Claypool. DOI: 10.2200/s00361ed1v01y201105hlt013. 186

Snoek, J., Larochelle, H., and Adams, R. P. (2012). Practical Bayesian optimization of machine learning algorithms. In *Advances in Neural Information Processing Systems 25*, pages 2951–2959. 244

Snyder, B. and Barzilay, R. (2008). Unsupervised multilingual learning for morphological segmentation. In *Proc. of ACL-08: HLT*, pages 737–745, Columbus, OH. Association for Computational Linguistics. 27

Snyder, B., Naseem, T., Eisenstein, J., and Barzilay, R. (2008). Unsupervised multilingual learning for POS tagging. In *Proc. of the 2008 Conference on Empirical Methods in Natural*

Language Processing, pages 1041–1050, Honolulu, HI. Association for Computational Linguistics. DOI: 10.3115/1613715.1613851. 27, 206

Snyder, B., Naseem, T., and Barzilay, R. (2009a). Unsupervised multilingual grammar induction. In *Proc. of the Joint Conference of the 47th Annual Meeting of the ACL and the 4th International Joint Conference on Natural Language Processing of the AFNLP*, pages 73–81, Suntec, Singapore. Association for Computational Linguistics. DOI: 10.3115/1687878.1687890. 208

Snyder, B., Naseem, T., Eisenstein, J., and Barzilay, R. (2009b). Adding more languages improves unsupervised multilingual part-of-speech tagging: a Bayesian non-parametric approach. In *Proc. of Human Language Technologies: The 2009 Annual Conference of the North American Chapter of the Association for Computational Linguistics*, pages 83–91, Boulder, CO. DOI: 10.3115/1620754.1620767. 208

Spitkovsky, V. I., Alshawi, H., and Jurafsky, D. (2010). From baby steps to leapfrog: How "less is more" in unsupervised dependency parsing. In *Human Language Technologies: The 2010 Annual Conference of the North American Chapter of the Association for Computational Linguistics*, pages 751–759, Los Angeles, CA. 149

Srivastava, N., Hinton, G., Krizhevsky, A., Sutskever, I., and Salakhutdinov, R. (2014). Dropout: A simple way to prevent neural networks from overfitting. *Journal of Machine Learning Research*, 15(1):1929–1958. 242

Steedman, M. (2000). *The Syntactic Process*, vol. 35. MIT Press. 210

Steedman, M. and Baldridge, J. (2011). Combinatory categorial grammar. In Borsley, R. and Borjars, K. Eds. *Non-Transformational Syntax Oxford*, pages 181–224. 177

Steyvers, M. and Griffiths, T. (2007). Probabilistic topic models. *Handbook of Latent Semantic Analysis*, 427(7), pages 424–440. DOI: 10.4324/9780203936399.ch21. 34

Stolcke, A. (2002). SRILM-an extensible language modeling toolkit. In *Proc. International Conference on Spoken Language Processing*, pages 901–904, Denver, CO. International Speech Communication Association (ISCA). 81

Stolcke, A. and Omohundro, S. (1994). Inducing probabilistic grammars by Bayesian model merging. In *Grammatical Inference and Applications*, pages 106–118. Springer. DOI: 10.1007/3-540-58473-0_141. 73, 211

Sutskever, I., Vinyals, O., and Le, Q. V. (2014). Sequence to sequence learning with neural networks. In Ghahramani, Z., Welling, M., Cortes, C., Lawrence, N. D., and Weinberger, K. Q., Eds., *Advances in Neural Information Processing Systems 27*, pages 3104–3112, Curran Associates, Inc. 236, 237

Synnaeve, G., Dautriche, I., Börschinger, B., Johnson, M., and Dupoux, E. (2014). Unsupervised word segmentation in context. In *Proc. of COLING 2014, the 25th International Conference on Computational Linguistics: Technical Papers*, pages 2326–2334, Dublin, Ireland. Dublin City University and Association for Computational Linguistics. 29

Teh, Y. W. (2006a). A Bayesian interpretation of interpolated Kneser-Ney. Technical report. 170

Teh, Y. W. (2006b). A hierarchical Bayesian language model based on Pitman-Yor processes. In *Proc. of the 21st International Conference on Computational Linguistics and 44th Annual Meeting of the Association for Computational Linguistics*, pages 985–992, Sydney, Australia. DOI: 10.3115/1220175.1220299. 169, 180, 181

Teh, Y. W., Jordan, M. I., Beal, M. J., and Blei, D. M. (2006). Hierarchical Dirichlet processes. *Journal of the American Statistical Association*, 101(476), pages 1566–1581. DOI: 10.1198/016214506000000302. 166

Teh, Y. W., Kurihara, K., and Welling, M. (2008). Collapsed variational inference for hdp. In Platt, J., Koller, D., Singer, Y., and Roweis, S., Eds., *Advances in Neural Information Processing Systems 20*, pages 1481–1488. Curran Associates, Inc. 167

Teh, Y. W., Thiery, A. H., and Vollmer, S. J. (2016). Consistency and fluctuations for stochastic gradient langevin dynamics. *The Journal of Machine Learning Research*, 17(1):193–225. 229

Tenenbaum, J. B., Kemp, C., Griffiths, T. L., and Goodman, N. D. (2011). How to grow a mind: Statistics, structure, and abstraction. *Science*, 331(6022), pages 1279–1285. DOI: 10.1126/science.1192788. 29

Tesnière, L. (1959). *Élément de Syntaxe Structurale*. Klincksieck. 202

Tesnière, L., Osborne, T. J., and Kahane, S. (2015). *Elements of Structural Syntax*. John Benjamins Publishing Company. DOI: 10.1075/z.185. 202

Tevet, G., Habib, G., Shwartz, V., and Berant, J. (2018). Evaluating text gans as language models. *ArXiv Preprint ArXiv:1810.12686*. 253

Titov, I. and Henderson, J. (2010). A latent variable model for generative dependency parsing. In *Trends in Parsing Technology*, pages 35–55, Springer. DOI: 10.3115/1621410.1621428 216

Titov, I. and Klementiev, A. (2012). A Bayesian approach to unsupervised semantic role induction. In *Proc. of the 13th Conference of the European Chapter of the Association for Computational Linguistics*, pages 12–22, Avignon, France. 174

Tjong Kim Sang, E. F. and De Meulder, F. (2003). Introduction to the CoNLL-2003 shared task: Language-independent named entity recognition. In Daelemans, W. and Osborne, M., Eds., *Proc. of the 7th Conference on Natural Language Learning at HLT-NAACL 2003*, pages 142–147. DOI: 10.3115/1119176. 92

Toutanova, K. and Johnson, M. (2008). A Bayesian LDA-based model for semi-supervised part-of-speech tagging. In Platt, J., Koller, D., Singer, Y., and Roweis, S., Eds., *Advances in Neural Information Processing Systems 20*, pages 1521–1528. Curran Associates, Inc. 57

Tromble, R., Kumar, S., Och, F., and Macherey, W. (2008). Lattice Minimum Bayes-Risk decoding for statistical machine translation. In *Proc. of the 2008 Conference on Empirical Methods in Natural Language Processing*, pages 620–629, Honolulu, HI. Association for Computational Linguistics. DOI: 10.3115/1613715.1613792. 90

Turian, J., Ratinov, L., and Bengio, Y. (2010). Word representations: A simple and general method for semi-supervised learning. In *Proc. of the 48th Annual Meeting of the Association for Computational Linguistics*, pages 384–394. 215

Turney, P. D. and Pantel, P. (2010). From frequency to meaning: Vector space models of semantics. *Journal of Artificial Intelligence Research*, 37:141–188. DOI: 10.1613/jair.2934 216

Upton, G. and Cook, I. (2014). *A Dictionary of Statistics*, 3rd ed., Oxford University Press. DOI: 10.1093/acref/9780199679188.001.0001. 121

Van Gael, J., Saatci, Y., Teh, Y. W., and Ghahramani, Z. (2008). Beam sampling for the infinite hidden Markov model. In *Proc. of the 25th International Conference on Machine Learning*, pages 1088–1095. ACM Press. DOI: 10.1145/1390156.1390293. 118, 181

Vaswani, A., Shazeer, N., Parmar, N., Uszkoreit, J., Jones, L., Gomez, A. N., Kaiser, Ł., and Polosukhin, I. (2017). Attention is all you need. In *Advances in Neural Information Processing Systems 30*, pages 5998–6008. 254

Vijay-Shanker, K., Weir, D. J., and Joshi, A. K. (1987). Characterizing structural descriptions produced by various grammatical formalisms. In *Proc. of the 25th Annual Meeting of the Association for Computational Linguistics*, pages 104–111, Stanford, CA. DOI: 10.3115/981175.981190. 177

Vilnis, L. and McCallum, A. (2015). Word representations via Gaussian embedding. In *Proc. of the 3rd International Conference on Learning Representations (ICLR)*. 221

Wainwright, M. and Jordan, M. (2008). Graphical models, exponential families, and variational inference. *Foundations and Trends in Machine Learning*, 1(1–2), pages 1–305. DOI: 10.1561/2200000001. 139

Wallach, H. M. (2006). Topic modeling: beyond bag-of-words. In *Proc. of the 23rd International Conference on Machine Learning*, pages 977–984, Pittsburgh, PA. ACM Press. DOI: 10.1145/1143844.1143967. 170

Wallach, H., Sutton, C., and McCallum, A. (2008). Bayesian modeling of dependency trees using hierarchical Pitman-Yor priors. In *ICML Workshop on Prior Knowledge for Text and Language Processing*, pages 15–20, Helsinki, Finland. ACM. 169

Wang, C., Paisley, J. W., and Blei, D. M. (2011). Online variational inference for the hierarchical Dirichlet process. In *International Conference on Artificial Intelligence and Statistics*, pages 752–760. 152, 167

Weir, D. (1988). *Characterizing Mildly Context-Sensitive Grammar Formalisms*. Ph.D. thesis, Department of Computer and Information Science, University of Pennsylvania. Available as Technical Report MS-CIS-88-74. 210

Weisstein, E. W. (2014). Gamma function. from MathWorld–a Wolfram web resource. `http://mathworld.wolfram.com/GammaFunction.html`, Last visited on 11/11/2014. 268

Welling, M., Teh, Y. W., Andrieu, C., Kominiarczuk, J., Meeds, T., Shahbaba, B., and Vollmer, S. (2014). Bayesian inference with big data: a snapshot from a workshop. *International Society for Bayesian Analysis (ISBA) Bulletin*, 21(4), pages 8–11. 258

Welling, M. and Teh, Y. W. (2011). Bayesian learning via stochastic gradient Langevin dynamics. In *Proc. of the 28th International Conference on Machine Learning (ICML)*, pages 681–688. 229

Werbos, P. J. (1990). Backpropagation through time: What it does and how to do it. *Proc. of the IEEE*, 78(10):1550–1560. DOI: 10.1109/5.58337 231

Williams, P., Sennrich, R., Koehn, P., and Post, M. (2016). *Syntax-based Statistical Machine Translation*. Synthesis Lectures on Human Language Technologies. Morgan & Claypool. 205

Wood, F., Archambeau, C., Gasthaus, J., James, L., and Teh, Y. W. (2009). A stochastic memoizer for sequence data. In *Proc. of the 26th Annual International Conference on Machine Learning*, pages 1129–1136. ACM. DOI: 10.1145/1553374.1553518. 175

Wu, D. (1997). Stochastic inversion transduction grammars and bilingual parsing of parallel corpora. *Computational Linguistics*, 23(3), pages 377–403. 205

Yamamoto, M. and Sadamitsu, K. (2005). Dirichlet mixtures in text modeling. Technical Report CS-TR-05-1, University of Tsukuba. 51

Yamangil, E. and Shieber, S. M. (2010). Bayesian synchronous tree-substitution grammar induction and its application to sentence compression. In *Proc. of the 48th Annual Meeting of the Association for Computational Linguistics*, pages 937–947, Uppsala, Sweden. 205

Yamangil, E. and Shieber, S. M. (2013). Nonparametric Bayesian inference and efficient parsing for tree-adjoining grammars. In *Proc. of the 51st Annual Meeting of the Association for Computational Linguistics (Volume 2: Short Papers)*, pages 597–603, Sofia, Bulgaria. 210

Yang, R. and Berger, J. O. (1998). A Catalog of Noninformative Priors. 68

Yang, Y. and Eisenstein, J. (2013). A log-linear model for unsupervised text normalization. In *Proc. of the 2013 Conference on Empirical Methods in Natural Language Processing*, pages 61–72, Seattle, WA. Association for Computational Linguistics. 129

Younger, D. H. (1967). Recognition and parsing of context-free languages in time n^3. *Information and Control*, 10(2). DOI: 10.1016/s0019-9958(67)80007-x. 182

Zhai, K. and Boyd-Graber, J. L. (2013). Online latent Dirichlet allocation with infinite vocabulary. In Dasgupta, S. and Mcallester, D., Eds., *Proc. of the 30th International Conference on Machine Learning (ICML-13)*, vol. 28(1), pages 561–569. JMLR Workshop and Conference Proceedings. 30

Zhai, K., Boyd-Graber, J., and Cohen, S. (2014). Online adaptor grammars with hybrid inference. *Transactions of the Association for Computational Linguistics*, 2, pages 465–476. 200

Zhang, H., Quirk, C., Moore, R. C., and Gildea, D. (2008). Bayesian learning of noncompositional phrases with synchronous parsing. In *Proc. of ACL-08: HLT*, pages 97–105, Columbus, OH. Association for Computational Linguistics. 205

Zhang, B., Xiong, D., Su, J., Duan, H., and Zhang, M. (2016). Variational neural machine translation. In *Proc. of the Conference on Empirical Methods in Natural Language Processing (EMNLP)*. DOI: 10.18653/v1/d16-1050 247

Zipf, G. K. (1932). *Selective Studies and the Principle of Relative Frequency in Language*. Harvard University Press. DOI: 10.4159/harvard.9780674434929. 171

Zoph, B. and Le, Q. V. (2017). Neural architecture search with reinforcement learning. In *Proc. of the 5th International Conference on Learning Representations (ICLR)*. 243

Author's Biography

SHAY COHEN

Shay Cohen is a Lecturer at the Institute for Language, Cognition and Computation at the School of Informatics at the University of Edinburgh. He received his Ph.D. in Language Technologies from Carnegie Mellon University (2011), his M.Sc. in Computer Science from Tel-Aviv University (2004) and his B.Sc. in Mathematics and Computer Science from Tel-Aviv University (2000). He was awarded a Computing Innovation Fellowship for his postdoctoral studies at Columbia University (2011–2013) and a Chancellor's Fellowship in Edinburgh (2013–2018). His research interests are in natural language processing and machine learning, with a focus on problems in structured prediction, such as syntactic and semantic parsing.

Index

Printed in the United States
by Baker & Taylor Publisher Services